FOOD AND THE CITY IN EUROPE SINCE 1800

Dedicated to the memory of John Burnett (1925–2006), social historian and founder member of ICREFH

Books are to be returned on or before
the last date below.

WITHDRAWN

Food and the City in Europe since 1800

Edited by
PETER J. ATKINS
Durham University, UK
PETER LUMMEL
Freilichtmuseum Domäne Dahlem, Germany
DEREK J. ODDY
University of Westminster, UK

ASHGATE

Published by
Ashgate Publishing Limited
Gower House
Croft Road
Aldershot
Hampshire GU11 3HR
England

Ashgate Publishing Company
Suite 420
101 Cherry Street
Burlington, VT 05401-4405
USA

Ashgate website: http://www.ashgate.com

British Library Cataloguing in Publication Data
International Commission for Research into European Food
    History. Symposium (2005 : Berlin, Germany)
    Food and the city in Europe since 1800
    1. Food supply - Europe - History - 19th century -
    Congresses 2. Food supply - Europe - History - 20th century
    - Congresses 3. Food - Quality - Europe - History - 19th
    century - Congresses 4. Food - Quality - Europe - History -
    20th century - Congresses
    I. Title II. Atkins, P. J. (Peter J.) III. Lummel, Peter
    IV. Oddy, Derek J.
    363.8'094'09034

Library of Congress Cataloging-in-Publication Data
Food and the City in Europe since 1800 / edited by Peter J. Atkins, Peter Lummel, and Derek J. Oddy.
        p. cm.
    Includes bibliographical references and index.
    ISBN 978-0-7546-4989-2 (alk. paper)
    1. Food habits--Europe, Western--History. 2. Food supply--Europe, Western--History. 3. Food--Political aspects--Europe, Western. 4. Urbanization--Europe--History. 5. Europe, Western--History. 6. Europe, Western--Social conditions. I. Atkins, P. J. (Peter J.) II. Lummel, Peter. III. Oddy, Derek J.

    GT2853.E8F67 2007
    394.1'2094--dc22

                                                                2006103480

ISBN 13: 978-0-7546-4989-2

Printed and bound in Great Britain by Antony Rowe Ltd, Chippenham, Wiltshire.

Contents

List of Figures

List of Tables

List of Contributors

Virginie Amilien, SIFO, National Institute for Consumption Research, PB 4682 Nydalen, 0405 Oslo 1, Norway. Email: Virginie.Amilien@sifo.no

Peter J. Atkins, Department of Geography, Durham University, Durham DH1 3LE, UK. Email: p.j.atkins@durham.ac.uk

Alain Drouard, Centre Roland Mousnier, UMR 8596 du CNRS, Université de Paris – Sorbonne (Paris IV). Mail: 16, rue Parrot, 75012 Paris, France. Email: adrouard01@noos.fr

Martin Franc, Masaryk Institute, Archives of the Academy of Sciences of Czech Republic. Gabcikova 2362/10, 182 00 Praha 8, Czech Republic. Email: francmartin@seznam.cz

Jukka Gronow, Department of Sociology, Uppsala University, PO Box 624, SE- 751 26 Uppsala, Sweden. Jukka.Gronow@soc.uu.se

Adel P. den Hartog, Formerly Wageningen University, Division of Human Nutrition, The Netherlands. Mail: Langhoven 28, 6721 SK, Bennekom. Email: apdenhartog@planet.nl

Vera Hierholzer, Landesmuseum für Technik und Arbeit in Mannheim, Museumsstr. 1, 68165 Mannheim, Germany. Email: vera.hierholzer@web.de

Peter Lummel, Freilichtmuseum Domäne Dahlem, Königin-Luise-Str. 49, 14195 Berlin, Germany. Email: lummel@domaene-dahlem.de

Derek J. Oddy, University of Westminster, 309 Regent Street, London W1R 8AL, UK. Email: ProfDJOddy@aol.com

Anneke H. van Otterloo, Department of Sociology and Anthropology, University of Amsterdam, Oudezijds Achterburgwal 185, 1012 DK Amsterdam, The Netherlands. Email: A.H.vanOtterloo@uva.nl

Panikos Panayi, School of English Performance and Historical Studies, Faculty of Humanities, De Montfort University, The Gateway, Leicester LE1 9BH, UK. Email: ppanayi@dmu.ac.uk

Roser Nicolau-Nos and Josep Pujol-Andreu, Facultata de Ciències Económiques i Emrepsarials, D. Economia i Història Econòmica, Edifici B- Campus de Bellaterra (Cerdanyola del Vallès), Barcelona, Spain 08193. Emails: Roser.nicolau@gmail.com; Josep.pujol.andreu@uab.es

Jürgen Schmidt, Wissenschaftszentrum Berlin für Sozialforschung, Reichpietschufer 50, D-10785 Berlin, Germany, jschmidt@wz-berlin.de

Peter Scholliers, Vrije Universiteit Brussel (VUB), Vakgroep Geschiedenis, Pleinlaan 2, 1050 Brussel, Belgium. Email: pscholli@vub.ac.be

Alessandro Stanziani, IDHE-Cachan, CNRS, 61 avenue Président Wilson, 94235 Cachan, France. Email: stanzian@idhe.ens-cachan.fr

Isabelle Téchoueyres, Laboratoire d'Analyses des Problèmes Sociaux et de l'Action Collective (LAPSAC) EA 495, Université Victor Segalen Bordeaux 2, Bordeaux, France. Email: i.techoueyres@orange.fr

Hans Jürgen Teuteberg, Westfälische Wilhelms-Universität Münster, Historisches Seminar, Domplatz 20–22, 48143 Münster, Germany. Email: Teuteber@uni-muenster.de

Ulrike Thoms, Institut für Geschichte der Medizin, Zentrum für Human- und Gesundheitswissenschaften, Humboldt Universität / Freie Universität Berlin, Klingsorstr.119,12203 Berlin, Germany. Email: ulrike.thoms@charite.de

Corinna Treitel, Department of History, Campus Box 1062, Washington University in St. Louis, 1 Brookings Drive, St. Louis, MO 63130-4899, USA. Email: ctreitel@artsci.wustl.edu

Preface

The International Commission for Research into European Food History (ICREFH) was founded in 1989 with the aim of studying the history of food and nutrition since the late eighteenth century. Every two years the ICREFH organizes a symposium and publishes a book based on a selection of peer-reviewed papers. The 2005 ICREFH symposium took place at the 'Domäne Dahlem', an open-air museum located in the outskirts of Berlin and in the grounds of a former estate property. The Domäne Dahlem is a museum dedicated to the history of agriculture and food in Berlin and the region of Brandenburg and, as such, it was the perfect place to discuss the interrelationship between food and the growth of cities from the eighteenth century onwards.

Although our topic was 'Food and the City', the scholarship on display in Berlin was very different from what one might find at a congress of urban historians. We had contributions with an historical dimension from practitioners of geography, nutrition, cultural studies, anthropology, ethnology, sociology, museology, contemporary history, social and cultural history and economic history. This interdisciplinary and international flavour is a crucial ingredient in the deliberations of ICREFH, which are an innovative fusion of perspectives from the social sciences and humanities. In Berlin, there was an interesting range of research questions, and of methodological approaches, leading to lively and productive discussions during each session. ICREFH adds value to the historical themes it discusses at its biennial symposia, as witnessed by the excellence of its resulting publications.

The second unique feature of ICREFH is its organization. The Commission limits the number of participants at its symposia. This means that the lecture sessions can be held in relatively small rooms in a relaxed and collegial atmosphere. Colleagues who attend an ICREFH meeting for the first time often comment on how much more productive our proceedings are than a session at a large conference. All of the papers are available well in advance, and delegates are asked to read them so that they are informed about all of the sub-themes. The lecturers are asked to keep their presentations short, with the bulk of the time devoted to discussion. Again, this maximizes the opportunity for fruitful debate. The published book arising from the symposium is then a selection of the most appropriate papers, which are modified with the benefit of inputs made by colleagues in the discussion periods.

ICREFH Symposia

The Current State of European Food History Research (Münster, 1989)
The Origins and Development of Food Policies in Europe (London, 1991)

Food Technology, Science and Marketing (Wageningen, 1993)
Food and Material Culture (Vevey, 1995)
Order and Disorder: The Health Implication of Eating and Drinking (Aberdeen, 1997)
The Landscape of Food: Town, Countryside and Food Relationships (Tampere, 1999)
Eating and Drinking Out in Europe since the late Eighteenth Century (Alden Biesen, 2001).
The Diffusion of Food Culture: Cookery and Food Education during the last 200 years (Prague, 2003)
Food and the City in Europe since the Late Eighteenth Century: Urban Life, Innovation and Regulation (Berlin, 2005)
From Under-Nutrition to Obesity: Changes in Food Consumption in Twentieth-Century Europe (Oslo, 2007)

ICREFH Publications

ICREFH I – Teuteberg, H.J. (ed.), *European Food History: A Research Overview*, Leicester, 1992.
ICREFH II – Burnett, J. and Oddy, D.J. (eds), *The Origins and Development of Food Policies in Europe*, London, 1994.
ICREFH III – Hartog, A.P. den (ed.), *Food Technology, Science and Marketing: European Diet in the Twentieth Century*, East Linton, 1995.
ICREFH IV – Schärer, M.R. and Fenton, A. (eds), *Food and Material Culture,* East Linton, 1998.
ICREFH V – Fenton, A. (ed.), *Order and Disorder: The Health Implications of Eating and Drinking in the Nineteenth and Twentieth Centuries*, East Linton, 2000.
ICREFH VI – Hietala, M. and Vahtikari, T. (eds), *The Landscape of Food: The Food Relationship of Town and Country in Modern Times*, Helsinki, 2003.
ICREFH VII – Jacobs, M. and Scholliers, P. (eds), *Eating Out in Europe: Picnics, Gourmet Dining and Snacks Since the Late Eighteenth Century*, Oxford, 2003.
ICREFH VIII – Oddy, D.J. and Petráňová, L. (eds), *The Diffusion of Food Culture in Europe from the Late Eighteenth Century to the Present Day*, Prague, 2005.

Acknowledgements

ICREFH is especially grateful to the organizers of this symposium for their generous hospitality and to the Freilichtmuseum Domäne Dahlem, Berlin for allowing us to use their facilities. We also wish to thank the Fritz Thyssen Foundation, Cologne, for their sponsorship as well as the German Federation of Food Law and Food Science, Bonn, and the friends of the Domäne Dahlem, Berlin.

Chapter 1

Food and the City

Peter J. Atkins and Derek J. Oddy

This book is about food in the city in all its manifestations from the production, processing, marketing and consumption of food to the impact of urbanization upon diets and food systems. The International Commission for Research into European Food History (ICREFH) has given thought to cities and towns before, but has never concentrated on the larger urban aggregations, often with multiple centres, that grew up in Europe in the late nineteenth century, and which were characterized by Patrick Geddes (1854–1932) – the Scottish biologist – as 'conurbations'.[1] By 1900, Europe contained several large urban agglomerations, notably London, Paris, Berlin, followed in size by Moscow and Vienna.[2] Their size meant that the supply and distribution of foodstuffs was complex, creating problems that required the state, the municipal institutions, and also the town-dwellers themselves, to make numerous adaptations. After collection and long-distance transportation to such markets, food might be stale on arrival, in which case wholesalers and retailers alike sought to delay the deterioration of perishable items. The Symposium considered especially those large and important European cities which, in differing national contexts, developed outstanding economic and political importance and a cultural charisma as centres of innovations and changes. It also analysed the 'metropolitan effect' that was felt in smaller countries, focused on cities such as Barcelona and Brussels, as the stages in the food chain between farm gate and consumers' kitchens grew, and in Prague where post-World War II Czechoslovakia struggled to meet the regime's showcase requirements.

No summary historical treatment of these developments exists in a comparative European perspective, taking account of all interests along the chain from the producer to the consumer. Yet food history has been a constituent part of modernization and food has shaped European urban life just as cities have influenced the systems of supply and the shifting currents of consumption. The resulting social and cultural transformation of urban society created a dynamic for changes in food consumption that had never been known before. As cities expanded, the lower social classes had to offset the higher cost of living against their limited incomes, while urban elites formulated new wants. The interplay of these factors led to new urban consumption patterns in Europe. A modern urban lifestyle came into being in European cities and

---

1   See Welter, 2002.

2   Urban-industrial areas such as the Ruhr or industrial areas of northern England were not considered by the Symposium. Sutcliffe, 1984, includes essays on the growth of the principal European cities.

the Berlin philosopher and sociologist Georg Simmel in his essay *The Metropolis and Mental Life* provided a basic vocabulary to discuss these changes.[3]

There are many ways of testing assertions about the impact of cities. In the present volume we have chosen a framework of four themes (A. Feeding the Multitude; B. Food Regulation; C. Food Innovations – the Product Perspective; D. Eating Fashions – the Consumer Perspective), each of which is addressed by four or five papers. All of the authors were participants in ICREFH's Berlin Symposium in September 2005 and come from ten countries and a number of different disciplines. The Symposium resided, appropriately, in Harnack House, named after Adolf Harnack, President of the *Kaiser-Wilhelm-Gesellschaft* (*KWG*), which, from its opening in 1929 was a discussion forum symbolizing German scientific excellence and international networks. The open-air and food museum, Domäne Dahlem, was the second venue. This has its own 800 years old agricultural history and it contributed to feeding Berlin until the time of the Cold war and, as such, it was the perfect place to discuss the interrelationship between food and the growth of cities.

Our focus is upon Europe in the last 200 years but we note that at the present the Food and Agriculture Organization of the United Nations and other development organizations are investing a great deal in studying similar structures and processes in present-day third-world cities. A sense of how fundamental the link with food remains in the process of urbanization can be gained from FAO's 'Feeding the Cities' programme. On a global scale they argue that:

> One of the main challenges … will be to achieve an efficient distribution of nutritional and inexpensive foodstuffs to urban inhabitants. Failure to meet this challenge could lead to a repeat of the widespread political unrest and rising social instability already well-documented in cities throughout the world when sharp rises in food prices have been precipitated by the need to cut food subsidies…Creation and expansion of markets has often lagged behind the growth in urban populations and merchandise flows….[4]

A discussion of historical problems of feeding cities in Europe seems to be particularly relevant against the contemporary background of rapid urban growth in developing countries, leading to food and housing shortages as well as severe social problems. In the mid-twentieth century ten per cent of human beings lived in towns and cities but this proportion has now passed half. Worldwide a million people move into cities daily.[5]

Many historians have contributed understandings of the relationship between urban growth and the raw materials that feed it. The work of Campbell *et al.*, and

---

3   Originally published in 1903, translated in 1950. See also the objectives and principles of the Georg Simmel Centre for Metropolitan Studies (GSZ) in Berlin: < http://www.gsz.hu-berlin.de/php/index.php?style=0&size > (accessed 29 November 2006).

4   FAO, 1999, 1. There is now a large literature in this area, with helpful commentaries on websites entitled 'Food for the Cities', and 'Food into Cities'. The emphasis is upon improving urban food supply systems in the developing world, especially in Africa. See: < http://www.fao.org/fcit/doc.asp >; < http://www.eldis.org/static/DOC8851.htm > (accessed 29 November 2006).

5   Burdett, 2006.

Galloway on medieval London is notable, as is the classic work of Fisher on early modern London.[6] For Paris, Kaplan and Abbad have published detailed studies of provisioning under the Ancien Régime and there are many other European studies.[7]

Despite the sophistication of their food-supply systems, very large European cities of the late nineteenth and early twentieth centuries did not escape food crises. Expansionary policies of aggrandisement, for instance colonialism, were costly in manpower and communications, and caused Europe's rulers to be concerned about food supply. In particular, policymakers were unimpressed by the physique of the urban males of military age they saw around them; and lamented their undernourishment or 'irrational nutrition'. Although famines were essentially a rural experience linked to harvest failure, no metropolitan centre in Europe could avoid food crises in the twentieth century. Varying in intensity, food shortages ranged from queues at shops and food rationing to periods of near starvation during the times when European cities were at the centre of two world wars. Europe's last peacetime famine was in Russia in 1891/2 but armed conflict and totalitarian politics caused major disruptions to urban food supplies up to the middle of the twentieth century.[8] Even Germany, which had done so much to create the science of nutrition, failed to utilize it rationally in World War I.

Although food habits might be used to generate nationalism, as in Norway, no political regime successfully incorporated nutritional science into food policy or planning, as the examples from Soviet Russia and Czechoslovakia discussed in section C indicate. Indeed, famine in the USSR in the 1930s was due to collectivization of agriculture rather than crop failure, while in Czechoslovakia under post-World War II communism, planning the socialist diet failed due to supply limitations. Modern examples of urban food habits, such as fast-food consumption, or the increase in body weights leading towards obesity, fall outside the scope of this book. For this, have a look on previous ICREFH symposia, such as ICREFH VII, which dealt with eating out in Europe and noted in some detail the dramatic changes in urban food habits in the second-half of the twentieth century, particularly in the 1980s and 1990s.[9]

A. Feeding the Multitude

The burgeoning urban markets of the nineteenth and twentieth centuries presented food producers with new opportunities. An issue here is scale and intensity because one would expect a different functional response at the lower end of the urban hierarchy from that in the largest of cities, so recognizing regional difference is an important element in ICREFH's deliberations, as is the identification of temporal disjuncture in the pace of change between cities and between nations. As conurbations and urban-industrial fields developed in the late nineteenth and early twentieth centuries, it was often integrated hierarchies of marketing potential that mattered more rather

6   Fisher, 1935; Galloway and Murphy, 1991; Campbell *et al.*, 1993.
7   Kaplan, 1984; Clark and Lepetit, 1996; Abad, 2002.
8   Robbins, 1974.
9   Jacobs and Scholliers, 2003.

than single settlements and their consumers. The theme of feeding cities is of course familiar in food history but there is room in the literature for two developments.

First, we are in need of the type of overview paper written here by Hans Jürgen Teuteberg. He sets the scene in general terms for the rest of this book with the German-speaking part of middle Europe in mind, and his overview explains how the web of modern production, processing, and retailing systems gradually replaced the traditional guild restrictions on commerce. It is interesting to note that urban food systems here evolved structurally at a rather different pace to, say, the United Kingdom. Although German scientists and food technologists were in the forefront of nutritional theory and manufacturing processes, the food retailing environment seems to have been constrained in its development before the mid-nineteenth century and was therefore slow to modernize.

Peter Atkins suggests that one answer to the question of regional disparities may be to engage with the comparative history of superficially similar metropolises, such as London and Paris, in order to tease out the factors that were in common and the divergent paths that followed. The mid-nineteenth century was a hinge point in the urban experience of both countries, with powerful forces bearing upon their ability to make available sufficient food of a reasonable quality in their capital cities. Some variations of context are revealed on both the supply and demand sides, with the result that these two world cities went into the second half of the nineteenth century with subtly different strategies for 'feeding modernity'.

The contribution by Corinna Treitel reviews the career and ideas of the German physiologist, Max Rubner. Although less well-known than Liebig and Voit, he nevertheless contributed to the late nineteenth and early twentieth century debate about the diet of the urban working class. Professor Treitel argues that Rubner had a lasting impact upon consumers' understanding of their diet, for instance through the standard value of the calorie. Building on the work of Liebig and Voit, he saw nutrition as a social question and suggested that the foodways of the urban working class were dangerously irrational, to the point of mass chronic undernutrition. However, Rubner could not persuade the Imperial German government to reduce the high protein allowance, conventionally regarded as essential for adult males, in favour of more emphasis on the energy available from cereals. In consequence, during World War I, all of the combatant nations maintained high-energy, high-protein rations for their armed services and looked to their civilians to limit their food consumption.[10] It has been claimed that Britain's Corn Production Act, 1917, by encouraging cereal production from grasslands and permanent pasture, achieved a change in nutrition policy that Germany failed to make: shortages and food queues in London in the winter of 1917–18 did not lead to the collapse of morale that occurred in Berlin and other German and Austrian cities.[11]

Second, there is a need for more research on the links between food supply and the changing diets of urban dwellers. This addresses the issue of prime cause: the respective weight in food habits between food culture, on the one hand, as filtered

---

10 For Italy, see Dentoni, 1994 and 2003.

11 Signs of malnutrition appeared amongst children in German towns as early as 1915. See Eltzbacher, cited in Corinna Treitel's chapter.

through demand and influenced by consumers' relative priorities in expenditure, and, on the other hand, the profile of goods presented in the market, as an expression of the relative competitiveness of commodity *filières*, determined by organizational factors and regional agro-ecology. Both are implicated simultaneously, along with other influences such as food politics and international trade, but the balance in each city is different. Roser Nicolau-Nos and Josep Pujol-Andreu, by looking at the inter-relationship between urbanization and dietary change in Barcelona raise issues about the standard of living that have broader implications for the economic history of Spain. While the changes that they reveal are broadly in line with European trends at this time, consumer income was not the driving force that might have been expected in the early twentieth century.

European history also yields many examples of the fragility of urban food systems in the face of wars, civil disruption, terrorism and natural hazards. Jürgen Schmidt provides one case study in his paper on the food supply problems of post-war Berlin. He writes about what happens 'when networked urbanism goes wrong'.[12] The topic is rarely tackled in food history but this approach to the food shortages in post-war Berlin is relevant to many cities in the aftermath of a civil emergency, such as an earthquake or fire, or the disruption caused by epidemic disease. Important elements here are the responses of the regulatory authorities and also of the general public, along with the moral dilemmas of emergency conditions.

Readers may wish to consult previous ICREFH volumes for further commentary on 'feeding the multitude'.[13] In particular, ICREFH VI, on the food relationship of town and country, is helpful on urban meat and vegetable supplies (papers by Koolmees, Teuteberg, den Hartog and Godina-Golija), and on the 'urban-rural interface' (papers by Burnett, Oddy, de Knecht-van Eekelen, and Atkins).[14]

B. Food Regulation

One of the recent strengths of food history has been a concern with state policy and regulation. There has been a recognition, particularly within the literature on the emergence of agreed norms on quality, of a need to look at the implementation of standards.[15] In this section we are interested in the inspection and laboratory analysis undertaken by the local state and by private individuals in four European countries.

First, Peter Scholliers uncovers the early history of the response by the Brussels city authorities to the problem of food adulteration. This was a very common problem around Europe and it seems that Brussels was one of the first cities to establish a laboratory in the hope that organic chemistry might provide a solution. Derek Oddy then looks at the equivalent system of expertise in London, starting at a somewhat later date. The central argument of his paper is that investigations were hampered by a struggle between local authority analysts and chemists employed by the government, for scientific and regulatory ascendancy. The strength of this

---

12 Graham and Marvin, 2001.
13 See list in Preface.
14 Hietala and Vahtikari, 2003.
15 See French and Phillips.

historical approach is that it recognizes the importance of debate and networked influence in policy-making and implementation.

Alessandro Stanziani also deals with a municipal laboratory in the late nineteenth century, this time in Paris. He puts the need for counter-measures against falsification into a context of economic theory and shows, rather like in London, that institutional struggle and controversy were never far away. The key to this paper is that both legislation and regulation were compromises between mutually-incompatible interests: between consumers and the food industry and among the various parties in the food chain.

Finally, Vera Hierholzer looks at the early years of the united Germany and finds that citizens' self-help associations were important in developing ideas about the quality of food and drink. Although short-lived, they acted as a surrogate local state in establishing analytical laboratories and prosecuting traders who sold adulterated food, until their facilities were eventually absorbed by local authorities.

Since the end of the nineteenth century the main focus of consumers moved more and more from the quantitative guarantee of a food supply to the qualitative question of food safety. With urbanization, the growing separation from producers led consumers to experience deeply-felt emotional uncertainties. At the same time, numerous innovations by the farming and food-processing industries and retailers created a more regular and a more varied supply of foodstuffs, which will be the topic of chapter 2.

C. Food Innovations – the Product Perspective

European cities have been powerful engines of innovation and change in food habits and in the development of new products. This section investigates three aspects of these phenomena, product innovation, retail systems and the entry of foreign foods into metropolitan markets. Food products have received attention before in ICREFH symposia, for instance, in ICREFH IV, which was an exploration of food and material culture.[16] The emphasis in Berlin, however, was less on the physical form of food and its associated technology than on the role of large European cities in the innovation process.

First, Adel den Hartog looks at tinned sweetened condensed skim milk, which was manufactured in the Netherlands in the late nineteenth century as a by-product of the dairy industry and then exported to poor consumers in urban Britain. He shows that new is not always good, in the sense of being healthy. The account of the introduction of condensed skim milk is one of commercial rivalry and nutritional misunderstanding. The tins were profitable for the Dutch dairy industry to produce and cheap and convenient for consumers. However, when fed to babies as a substitute for breast milk, skim milk is unfortunately lacking in vitamins A and D and, in the absence of complementary feeding, led to malnutrition. Considerable commercial friction was generated by this trade, with British farming interests trying to prevent imports that appeared to threaten their markets. At the political level,

---

16 Schärer and Fenton, 1998.

there was also activity, with calls for tariff barriers. The paper shows that there were misunderstandings on both sides of the debate, not least on the Dutch side, where the milk processors were in denial about the lack of vitamin content of their product. As a result, there was malnutrition among infants in working-class families in large industrial cities in Britain.

Second, Jukka Gronow deals with the emergence of Soviet food culture in first-class restaurants and gastronomic food shops in the 1930s. Consumerism at this time might be associated with shortages but a full account of communist food retailing must also take into account its surprising attachment to luxuries. The paper charts the rise of the chain stores, *Gastronom* and *Bakaleya*, which were supposedly showcases of socialist abundance and prosperity; the reality was that they served only a privileged minority, as did the small number of 'first-class' restaurants. The point here, rather like that in Martin Franc's paper which follows, is that socialist food planning in reality was very far from the innovative and egalitarian ideals it espoused. Martin Franc deals with food retailing in Prague under the communist regime, but his argument could equally well apply to the inefficiencies of supermarket location planning in west European 'advanced' economies which has created 'food deserts' in many poor inner-city neighbourhoods.[17] Communist Czechoslovakia was not in physical ruins like Berlin but all food items that people may have wished to buy, beyond the basics, were in short supply, an urban problem beyond the solutions available to dysfunctional bureaucracies. Again the paper is of greater significance than a history of Prague because it reminds us that our complacent familiarity with free market and mixed food economies under conditions of surplus is only part of the European story. An interesting conclusion is that socialist policies about shop hierarchies were quite varied in their attempts to match supply with demand but were linked to shifting ideologies of town planning.

Peter Lummel analyses product innovation in the second half of the twentieth century by using trade journals to trace the introduction of self-service, particularly the scaling-up of outlets to supermarkets in Germany, which were a child of big cities such as Berlin. Not only was 'everything under one roof' but a wider variety of food lines was carried, and new technologies were employed such as refrigeration, cook-chill, and advanced packaging. There were also significant shifts in the relationship between retailers and modern urban consumers as well as between retailers and their suppliers, which caused a ripple effect of change throughout the food chain. This story might be told, with variations, in every European city since World War II.

Thirdly, to end this section, two contributors discuss the acceptance of foreign influence in major cities. Anneke van Otterloo investigates the coming of 'exotic' food to Amsterdam and its progress to become deeply embedded in the local economy and culture. The city's geographical position and the colonial heritage of the Netherlands encouraged this broadening of the diet, but Amsterdam's cosmopolitan culture has also been a facilitating factor. Panikos Panayi's chapter deals with another global city, London. He also narrates a history of immigrant impact, over the longer period since 1850. This shows that immigrants have played a major role in the evolution

---

17 Wrigley, 2002.

of the dietary patterns of Londoners, from street sellers or high-class chefs in the Victorian period to take-away restaurants more recently.

D. Eating Fashions – the Consumer Perspective

Our eating habits are influenced by intellectual fashions and cultural change, although it is notoriously difficult to measure any specific impact. Only one chapter in this final section has any institutional context or any association with metropolitan society: the other three reflect how ideas about food find expression in dietary fashions. Generally, these chapters are based on the rejection of the values of urban society.

Ulrike Thom's study of German scientists shows how they accepted bourgeois standards of eating as a demonstration of their new-found status and importance in metropolitan society. Initially, scientists valued asceticism, indicating that their working and celebratory meals were of lower priority than scientific discussions and social networking. These values gave way eventually to more visually impressive fare as scientists came to realize that their meals were an important means of communicating the status of their profession to the general public.

The remaining chapters discuss consumers outside the main stream of urban-industrial life. Alain Drouard takes a wider view of dietary reform at the end of the nineteenth century. He draws upon case studies of the United Kingdom, Germany, France and Switzerland, and concludes that, although the diagnosis of the failings of contemporary diets was quite similar, the solutions were not. The degeneracy and decline that was universally attributed to modernity could be cured, according to campaigners as varied as Bircher Benner, Carton and Steiner, through the adoption of dietary restrictions (vegetarian or vegan), new foods (muesli), a new philosophical outlook (theosophy, anthroposophy), or a new attitude to the body (exercise, nudism). Although cities were seen as problematic concentrations of dietary and social shortcomings, at the same time they were intellectual catalysts – the breeding ground of social movements – where campaigners developed their ideas and found the most fertile ground for recruiting followers.

Virginie Amilien finds that Norwegian food habits, right down to the present day, have been influenced by a debate that took place in the romantic period of nationalism in the nineteenth century on what could be said to be authentic national dishes. In Norway, the struggle for independence, first from Denmark and then Sweden, has left an indelible imprint upon consumers' notions of the good diet. Because the former ruling elites were foreigners associated with cities, nationalists sought truly Norwegian foods and recipes in the countryside. Only relatively recently has this simple dietary been embellished through the popularity of cookery books and exotic ingredients.

In France, the role and influence of direct selling in a regional primary city, Bordeaux, from the 1960s to the present day is explored by Isabelle Téchoueyres. She describes the changing fortunes of different types of marketing experience, emphasizing the recent rise of open-air retailing, associated with *produits de terroir* and farmers' markets, and she also recreates a sense of what it is like to be a consumer there. Finally, the editors hope that this selection of papers from the ninth ICREFH symposium in Berlin will offer readers a coherent and structured view of changes in food marketing and regulation, eating habits and nutrition in Europe's largest cities during the nineteenth and twentieth centuries. It begins, appropriately, with an overview of changes in German-speaking Europe by ICREFH's Founding President and organizer of the first symposium in Münster, in 1989, Professor Hans Jürgen Teuteberg.

References

Abad, R. *Le Grand Marché: l'Approvisionnement Alimentaire de Paris sous l'Ancien Régime*, Paris, 2002.

Burnett, J. and Oddy, D.J. (eds), ICREFH II, London, 1994.

Burdett, R. *Feeling the Urban Age*, Paper for the Urban Age Summit, Berlin, November 2006, <http://www.urban-age.net/0_downloads/Berlin_Ricky_Burdett_2006-Feeling_the_Urban_Age.pdf> (accessed 29 November 2006).

Campbell, B.M.S., Galloway, J.A., Keene, D. and Murphy, M. *A Medieval Capital and its Grain Supply: Agrarian Production and Distribution in the London Region c. 1300*, London, 1993.

Clark, P. and Lepetit, B. (eds), *Capital Cities and their Hinterlands in Early Modern Europe*, Aldershot, 1996.

Dentoni, M.C. 'Black Bread and Social Peace: Italy's Dietary Politics during the First World War', in ICREFH II, 1994, 13–14.

Dentoni, M.C. 'Refrigeration and the Italian Meat Crisis during the First World War', in ICREFH VI, 2003, 157–170.

Fisher, F.J. 'The Development of the London Food Market, 1540–1640', *Economic History Review* 5, 1935, 46–64.

Food and Agriculture Organization, *Feeding the Cities*, Paper Submitted to the 101st Inter-Parliamentary Conference, Brussels, 1999, <http://www.fao.org/ag/ags/agsm/sada/DOCS/PDF/AC2099E.PDF> (accessed 29 November 2006).

French M. and Phillips, J. *Cheated not Poisoned? Food Regulation in the United Kingdom, 1875–1938*, Manchester, 2000.

Galloway, J.A. and Murphy, M. 'Feeding the City: Medieval London and its Agrarian Hinterland', *London Journal* 16, 1991, 3–14.

Graham, S. and Marvin, S. *Splintering Urbanism: Networked Infrastructures, Technological Mobilities and the Urban Condition*, London, 2001.

Hietala, M. and Vahtikari, T. (eds), ICREFH VI, Tampere, 2003.

Jacobs, M. and Scholliers, P. (eds), ICREFH VII, Oxford, 2003.

Kaplan, S. *Provisioning Paris: Merchants and Millers in the Grain and Flour Trade during the Eighteenth Century*, Ithaca, 1984.

Robbins, R.G. *Famine in Russia 1891–92*, New York, 1974.

Schärer, M.R. and Fenton, A., *Food and Material Culture*, East Linton, 1998.

Simmel, G. 'The Metropolis and Mental Life', 1903, reprinted in Weinstein, D. (ed.), *The Sociology of Georg Simmel*, New York, 1950, 409–424.

Sutcliffe, A. (ed.) *Metropolis 1890–1940*, London, 1984.

Welter, V. *Biopolis – Patrick Geddes and the City of Life*, Cambridge, MA, 2002.

Wrigley, N. 'Food Deserts in British Cities: Policy Context and Research Priorities', *Urban Studies* 39, 2002, 2029–40.

Part A
Feeding the Multitude

Chapter 2

Urbanization and Nutrition: Historical Research Reconsidered

Hans Jürgen Teuteberg

During the nineteenth century the increase of population accelerated, along with the transition to both industrialization and urbanization. These three waves of structural change created the foundation of our modern prosperous society, with high average living standards in many European countries, but they also posed new social questions. What do we understand by the term 'urbanization'? It is a multidimensional phenomenon with a progressive character and our historical perspective depends upon our methodological approach and the region and period of investigation. This means that we comprehend not only different forms but also various grades of urban change. In essence, urbanization is:

(1) The social upheaval of a change in centre of gravity of the population from agrarian to urban, together with a large general population growth.
(2) A shift from an agrarian economy to one based on industry and the service sector.
(3) A new social structure exhibiting at the same time both regional and social mobility.
(4) The diffusion of a modern urban mentality to the whole society and culture.

Historical scholarship has taken as objects of research the individual urban inhabitants, the formation of social groups and classes as well as of institutions, the city as an historical unit, and the town as a subsystem of society. We must also differentiate here between external and internal functions, in other words the history of one specific city structure as a small world of its own and the development of the whole town in larger urban systems and the need therefore for different instruments of research.

Nutrition should be in the first rank of research themes on urbanization, firstly because most households had to spend most of their income on eating and drinking. The change was fundamental, from being a frugal rural subsistence producer, threatened often by bad harvests, catastrophes and famines, to a modern urban consumer, who could select from a variety of foodstuffs and articulate new demands but who also became dependent upon monetary exchange, anonymous market mechanisms and fast changing, fashion-conscious lifestyles. Looking back, we now realize that economically determined requirements have been transformed by urbanization into choice-led, free socio-cultural demand.

Studies of this radical change in our food supplies in the context of urbanization, for a long time only fragmentary, have become more focused in the last decade in several European countries. The present chapter seeks to sketch in brief the main results of this work, with an emphasis on the German-speaking areas of central Europe in the nineteenth century, during the explosion of city growth. Now it seems incontrovertible that this involved fundamental changes in human life that we can compare with other contemporary 'revolutions', such as the division of capital and labour or the separation of work and residence. A discussion of the principal connections between food and the city in the transitional period from the eighteenth century onwards helps to throw light on the upheaval of modernity.

Outline of Pre-industrial Urban Food Provision

The influences of urbanization on our daily fare can be explained best by first reminding ourselves of the pre-industrial food situation. At that time the majority of the population were still living mainly from their own-produced agrarian products and the underdeveloped transport system meant that the possibilities for trade were limited. In the countryside pedlars carried small manufactured items or luxuries like tobacco, spices, coffee and sugar to small circles of well-known customers. Everywhere there were also corn and cattle dealers, many of whom were Jews, because it was strictly forbidden by the Christian guilds of the bakers and butchers for their members to practice these professions. Dealers carried corn from the peasants to the town granaries or arranged deals to slaughter animals. Another forerunner of the modern provision dealer was the hawker. This small peasant or his wife frequented urban weekly markets with milk, butter, cheese, eggs and poultry or fish, greens and fruits.

Beside the butcher and the baker, one of the main providers of urban food was the small shopkeeper (*krämer* in German). He was bound to a local guild, which prescribed what commodities could be offered and at what price, and also influenced the place and size of his shop or stall in the weekly market. Until the period of full liberal trade, shopkeepers belonging to a guild could only sell goods not produced in their town. Only the few great merchant families who were engaged in long-distance trade were discharged from such regulations. At this early stage, when nearly 80 per cent of the population lived in the countryside, the daily lives of peasants were not touched to any great extent by the urban markets.

Looking at the main foodstuff – cereals – during the decades around 1800 at the threshold of modern urbanization, we can adduce the following general insights:

(1) Supply, in quantity as well as quality, continued to be determined by harvests in the immediate vicinity.
(2) Town supplies of corn, flour and bread were affected by sudden price peaks and also price differentials between the numerous small regional markets.
(3) Interventions by city authorities and kings only mitigated food crises, but did not stop them.
(4) During the periods of price inflation, export trade was prohibited and houses

were searched for hidden stocks. Surplus grain had to be sold at a fixed price, and speculative hoards were confiscated.

(5) In the times of need, grain from urban and military stores was distributed to the poor at low prices. Only the continuation of own food production by some townspeople restricted this need.

(6) But, in spite of many punishments against shady dealing, the adulteration of flour and use of dishonest weights were common.

Driving Forces of Change in Urban Food Provision

With the introduction of liberal 'free trade' in Germany in 1810 by a Prussian tax edict, the traditional separation between rural and urban economies was juridically abolished, along with all the privileges of the guilds of handicrafts and retailers. Five decades of reform encouraged an increase in the number of urban shopkeepers selling food and 'colonial products'. The landless youngest sons of peasants and journeymen in declining handicraft trades rushed now to this newly flourishing sector, which was tied to rapid urban population growth.

The profession of provision-dealer was particularly attractive because there was no need for specialist knowledge and the start-up capital investment was small. Further, this trade could be carried on together with farm work or selling beer. Urban butchers and bakers resisted this development but in the long run the 'victory of free trade' could not be denied. The traditional shopkeepers, with their mixed goods, were hard pressed at first, since the new retail shops also offered industrially produced foodstuffs, which were more durable. The modern, specialized provision-dealers eventually monopolized the sale of food in cities, with the exception of bread and meat, and the traditional shopkeepers turned to non-food items.

In the last third of the nineteenth century it became evident that weekly markets and yearly fairs, along with pedlars and hawkers, were together no longer capable of satisfying the needs of the swelling 'gigantic cities'. The steep growth in demand was partly due to mass migration from the countryside, in which most families ceased own food production, and now, through their money wages, became dependent on urban market systems. In addition, the increasing real wages of the working classes were used by them for an improvement of their diets during the late nineteenth century. All other consumption wants, like better housing, clothing and hygiene took second place to the 'stomach question'. The increased consumption of many commodities, which can be seen in the per-head statistics after 1850, was facilitated by increases in the price of pork, sugar, bread, potatoes and beer being slower than the increase of wages. After a certain time, as Ernst Engel's law predicted, in a period of steadily raising incomes, the proportion spent on food tended to drop. The fast and continuously growing demand for food from the markets corresponded also with increasing agrarian productivity, linked to mechanization, the creation of allotments, and the use of chemical fertilizers. The modernization of the transport and communication systems also meant that, for the first time in history, not only expensive tropical luxuries, but also plain, daily foodstuffs like cereals and frozen meat were carried with the help of telegraphy, railways and steam ships from other continents and were so cheap that they could successfully compete with domestic products. New national commodity exchanges promoted uniform prices, so that the formerly common practices of hoarding and speculative sales declined. The price movements of cereals, which in some places in the eighteenth century fluctuated in the ratio of 1:7 in any one year, now eased to 1:2. Increasing competition, assisted by international free trade treaties from the 1860s, condemned small dealers to decreasing profit margins, which could often only be compensated for by increased turnover.

The large expansion of the food products on sale in German cities towards the end of the nineteenth century was partly due to the enterprise of the emerging food industry, partly to new processing and manufacturing processes, and partly to the greater range of raw materials due to foreign imports. The advent of mass sales meant that the large producers in agriculture and industry could no longer communicate directly with the consumer and therefore advertising became more and more important as a new bridge of communication.

Variations of Purchasing Customs

Increased purchasing power and the new necessity to buy food each day changed former purchasing habits. Although allotment gardens continued, even in large cities, it was the norm for urban families around 1900 to buy the bulk of their food in shops and no longer primarily at the weekly market. Wages were paid weekly and storage space was limited, so housewives bought only small amounts, usually from shops in their immediate neighbourhood. For a time the old custom continued of chalking up credit on a slate or writing it down in an account book. But after 1900 this 'bad habit' was criticized and the suppliers of small shopkeepers insisted on shorter payment times.

Because of the fast increasing competition, urban food retailers began looking for new methods of attracting customers, such as making special offers. Around 1900 specialist shops began, which, alongside corner shop provision dealers, butchers and bakers, sought their own market segment. Rather than foods of handicraft origin, they offered specifically chosen food articles and luxuries of different qualities and price classes, such as tobacco, coffee, wine and spirits or delicacies. Those that were most successful established multiple-stores under a uniform name or trade mark. Sales of this highly graded food often made enough profit to enable a location in the central retail district, where the highest turnover could be achieved. There was one other shop type, where all possible foodstuffs were found under one roof. This concept succeeded first with the special food sections of large department stores in the late nineteenth century, and may be seen as the forerunner of the modern supermarket.

The Role of the Emerging Food Industry

The food industry, which had been growing steadily since the late eighteenth century, owed much of its early impetus to the creation of the nutrition sciences, which for the first time pointed out that foods are chemical compounds that fuel the various functions of the human body. New technologies of the preservation of foodstuffs became possible, which relieved some of the pressure of seasonal shortages. Progress in mechanical engineering, the employment of new motive power, and new medical insights, all assisted the integration of food into the process of industrialization. The rationalization of agriculture, improved means of preparation and cooking in the kitchen, increased opportunities of eating out in public institutions and restaurants, and rising demand for better tasting meals and the better packaging of food, again encouraged this trend of industrial processing. Large flour mills, breweries and sugar factories worked by steam, and factories for the manufacture of chicory (the most popular coffee substitute), chocolate, biscuits and margarine multiplied. There were enterprises processing sausages, fish, fruit and vegetables, and, last but not least, dairies producing butter and milk. The combined contribution of these food innovations has been significantly to change the daily fare in middle Europe since the nineteenth century.

The press of urbanization (see Table 2.1) was such that in the space of a few decades the established division of labour between country and town, which stretched back to the Middle Ages, was essentially dissolved. The former restrictions on sales, the imposition of market rules and numerous different taxes and tolls were all swept away within the course of just one generation. The industrial mass production that was often closely associated with urban growth was first located with respect to raw materials, energy and transport connections. At the same time there was the first phase of the urbanization of the countryside, later named 'rurbanization', which became a dominating pattern in the twentieth century, and 'dual economies' emerged in which industrial workers were part-time, food-producing small-holders. Self-sufficiency became less of a goal, with produce from peasants close to cities going increasingly to urban markets with the assistance of agricultural cooperatives.

New Regulation through the Construction of Market Halls

Urban population growth created new tasks for local authorities. In theory, balance in the old weekly markets should have been easy to achieve: if demand exceeded supply then market prices and the number of market sellers would rise, and vice versa. This was helped by the abolition of taxes on bread and meat, so that prices were easier to monitor in relation to supply. But until the 1860s the provision of fresh foodstuffs was variable according to seasons and the regional harvest, and farmers selling at weekly markets had little knowledge of their real production costs or of general price structures. Their sales took place still 'in good faith' and through personal acquaintances. This meant a frame of local habits rather than rational calculations. Though there was always hard bargaining, optimal pricing was difficult to achieve.

In cities with more than 100,000 inhabitants, more and more markets were established after 1860. In Berlin in 1885, for instance, there were already 20 weekly markets, the largest one having 1,300 stalls. By then the privileged places for local butchers and bakers had all disappeared. Around this time, additional market

Table 2.1 **Population growth of the most important German and British cities in the age of urbanization 1800–1910, in thousands**

Germany	1800	1850	1880	1900	1910
Berlin	172	419	1,122	1,889	3,730
Hamburg	130	132	290	706	932
Munich	30	110	230	500	595
Leipzig	40	63	149	456	588
Dresden	60	97	221	396	547
Cologne	50	97	145	373	516
Breslau	60	114	273	423	512
Frankfort /M	48	65	137	289	415
Dusseldorf	10	27	95	214	358
Elberfeld –B.	25	84	190	299	339
Nuremberg	30	54	100	261	333
Charlottenburg	—	—	30	189	305
Hanover	18	29	123	236	302
Essen	4	9	57	119	295
Chemnitz	14	32	95	207	287
Stuttgart	18	48	117	177	286
Magdeburg	36	72	98	230	280
Bremen	40	55	112	163	247
Koenigsberg	60	76	141	184	246
Neu-Köln	—	—	19	36	237
Stettin	24	49	92	211	236
Duisburg	—	—	41	93	229
Dortmund	—	—	67	143	214
Kiel	7	15	44	108	211
Mannheim	—	—	53	141	193
England/Wales/ Scotland/Ireland					
London	959	2,363	3,830	4,537	4,523
Liverpool	82	397	624	685	747
Manchester	77	336	462	544	714
Birmingham	71	243	437	522	526
Sheffield	46	135	285	381	455
Leeds	53	172	309	429	496
Bristol	61	154	255	329	357
West Ham	—	19	129	267	289
Bradford	13	140	240	280	289
Kingston	30	88	166	240	278
Newcastle	33	88	145	215	267
Nottingham	29	99	187	240	260
Stoke-on-Trent	—	—	—	215	235
Salford	18	85	176	221	231
Portsmouth	33	72	128	188	231

Leicester	17	63	137	212	227
Cardiff	2	20	83	164	182
Glasgow	77	329	511	762	785
Edinburgh	85	162	228	317	720
Belfast	40	87	208	349	385
Dublin	—	—	250	291	304

Source: W. Woytinsky, *Die Welt in Zahlen*, vol. 1 Berlin 1925, 123–33. The German figures relate to urban administrative areas, and in 1910 to Berlin and its suburbs.

halls were built by local authorities, with about twenty new ones by the turn of the century. The advantages were that the market could take place at any time without disturbing the traffic and the continuously rented stands facilitated business and market surveys. The covered hall also offered protection against weather and pollution, and it could also easily be cleaned and lit. Many of these market halls had modern transport connections, so that it was much easier to deliver and store food in bulk. Distant farmers had only to bring their produce to a nearby railway station and it would be forwarded to a central market hall, where a wholesale-dealer would sell it on commission. The producers, salesmen and customers now for the first time had reliable information about wholesale prices, which were published daily or weekly and given to interested authorities, newspapers, trade magazines and economic associations.

Refrigeration technology, in addition to reducing the spoilage of foods in transit, and thereby increasing average distance over which perishable foodstuffs could be carried, also in a sense helped market stabilization. Sometimes the option to export such goods served as a safety valve to defend home producers against the price peaks and troughs that were the result of fluctuations in supply. Bad harvests, cattle plagues and natural catastrophes were additional hazards for urban food provision; however, they affected only the movement of prices and did not lead to the total breakdown of an urban food economy as they had threatened to do right up to the middle of the nineteenth century.

The development of wholesalers independent from the market halls, especially dealing in fresh fish and fruits, and the rise of mail-order houses for delicacies, luxuries and preserved meat, also contributed to the enrichment of the urban food scene. New urban lifestyles, for instance commuting to work from suburbs, and different roles for women, have led to new experiences of shopping and eating. For the urban household, depending now on money wages, it became important to go shopping regularly for small portions of food and competition among the numerous small food retailers prevented high prices.

The Small 'Corner Grocer's Shop' and 'Flying' Street Hawkers

The normal urban grocer's shop around 1900 was a family business, just as it had been in the time of the guilds. While the man sought supplies from the peasant or wholesale dealer, his wife had to sell during his absence. But still before World War I the number of small cellar shops began to decrease and well-off retailers took over the shops of their competitors or went into partnership with a wholesale dealer. With the growth of the cities, itinerant street-dealers also began to multiply. They bought left-overs from the market hall, especially perishables such as fresh fruits, vegetables or fish. These street hawkers offered their goods in baskets or carts at crowded street crossings and railway stations or in those urban quarters which had few small shop-keepers. Since they had no fees to pay for a market stand or rent for a shop, they could offer their goods at a discount and often managed a good turnover in a short time. Their business was tolerated by the town authorities, because they kept prices low for certain basic foodstuffs.

In summary, we can state that the market halls, like the slaughter houses which had been established as communal undertakings and produce exchanges, successfully prevented cartels, silent price arrangements and monopolies. Uniform official food control became possible, and a private wholesale food trade came into being, so that urban food provisioning was lifted to a higher level. Consumers were freed from the previously monotonous simple fare taken only from the close vicinity and they could now match quality, quantity and diversity of meals to their incomes. A by-product of all this was the erosion of pre-industrial regional food differences.

Development of the Research Literature

After this brief, and surely still imperfect, review of the complex relations between food and urbanization, We will finally discuss the progress of the contemporary research literature. As before, we will take into consideration only developments in German-speaking countries in central Europe, from about 1800 to the outbreak of the First World War.

Already during the eighteenth century the production and technological processing of the main foodstuffs had been explored sporadically, as articles in encyclopaedias of the day indicate. One hundred years later, especially after 1865, for the first time larger enquiries on food consumption at home were organized. Thousands of household budgets were collected, with information on quantities and the cost of foods that families had bought. These made possible the comparison of data on annual consumption per head analysis by age, sex, profession, residence and income. More valuable were the results of enquiries and debates published in several volumes by the *Verein für Socialpolitik* [Association for Social Policy] between 1888 and 1915. The influences on food purchases were discussed in terms of wages and prices among the towns and regions in Germany, as well as in other European countries, and forecasts made for the future of living standards.

The municipal politician Hugo Lindemann suggested that supplying the urban masses daily with fresh food was one of the most urgent tasks of a modern communal administration, and urban statistics played an important role in evaluating progress. For instance, between 1909 and 1912 detailed information was collected in the newly erected municipal facilities (primarily market halls and slaughter houses), but these data have never been carefully evaluated by historians. Among other large studies, there were monographs on variations in the bakery and butcher's trades, as well as on the inspection of food. In 1911 a dissertation was written on the development of the whole modern food provision of Berlin. In the First World War, with its official concern about food supplies, there was a further wave of investigations in this direction.

After the collapse of the imperial monarchies in Germany and Austria in 1918, several summaries of knowledge up to that point were published as articles in concise dictionaries, contributions to conferences, and scientific journals. Much of the new research focused on macro-economic trends in the national supply of agrarian goods, but the tradition of micro-level studies continued in 1927/28 and in 1937 when budgets were taken of 2,000 private households. In 1962/63 this approach was picked up once again in random samples about the relationship between income and consumption in West Germany.

At first, in the nineteenth and early twentieth centuries, cultural historians were mainly interested in the food habits that they assumed had remained fixed in towns from the Middle Ages until 1800. Folklorists by comparison looked only at rural food customs; therefore neither addressed our topic of food and urbanization. Consumption histories published during the 1920s argue that there was better information about the meal habits of the 'old Germans' from the sixteenth to the eighteenth centuries than on food in the nineteenth century. Geographers and botanists also tried to give a concise overview of the world history of food, but failed totally because of research gaps. The few popular books on food history were filled with historical notes but no proper sources and were mixed with legends. Hitler's Third Reich brought no further progress here because, for ideological reasons, priority was given to explorations on 'rustic nationhood'.

In the years immediately after World War II, publications by historians, folklorists and popular freelance writers ignored the problem of food in the modern city and left it to the political, economic and social sciences. Also, there was less interest in history, with the exception of the economist Wilhelm Abel from Göttingen University, who during the 1930s investigated the history of urban food prices in connection with cycles of hunger in pre-industrial Europe. He now made suggestions for further explorations in food history after 1850. But his colleague at the Department of Economics, Erich Egner, who was a founder of modern consumption theory and of the new discipline of home economics in Germany, was unable to take this lead much further.

Modern food history has remained a disregarded stepchild by medical history and historical sociology. Even economic and social history, which was established in the 1960s as an autonomous university discipline, did not take much notice of the development of general consumption, although in Britain a vehement debate took place about the standard of living during the period of industrialization. The change of the food system under the influence of industrialization and urbanization became a central object of historical research and a long controversy began between the 'optimists' and the 'pessimists'. How backward German research was in this debate was demonstrated in the *Handbook of German Economic and Social History* published in 1976. Here the history of private consumption received little attention, based on theoretical debate or antiquated monographs with narrow limits in time and space. Their statements were not sophisticated and partly contradicted the new British research.

The 'Workshop of Modern Social History', founded by the Heidelberg historian Werner Conze under the influence of the French Annales School, organized two large conferences on the problem of living standards in the nineteenth century. In his introduction to one of these, the Swiss historian Rudolf Braun commented that there was minimal agreement on what should be the aim of such investigations, but participating historians at least provided an agenda for further research on consumption in the past. Since the subject of food and industrialization had hitherto only touched on macro-economic and theoretical aspects or on limited case studies, in 1974 the folklorist Günter Wiegelmann and the present author presented new research on this topic as an encouragement to fill this gap in knowledge. In more than 40 reviews their book was called 'a pioneering study'.

Since the 1980s hundreds of explorations of the dramatic changes in culinary culture during the last two hundred years have been published. But still today multi-disciplinary research about the relations between food and city is needed, especially more local, regional and specific international comparisons. The specific topic of food and urbanization, which has become of significance in studies of development in poor countries, urgently needs further research.

References

Andritzky, M. (ed.), *Oikos. Von der Feuerstelle zur Mikrowelle: Haushalt und Wohnen im Wandel* [From Fireplace to Microwave: Household and Dwelling in Change] Giessen, 1992.

Borscheid, P. and Wischermann, C. (eds), *Bilderwelt des Alltags. Werbung in der Konsumgesellschaft des 19. und 20. Jahrhunderts. Festschrift für Hans Jürgen Teuteberg* [Daily Life in the World of Illustrations. Advertising in the Consumer Society], Stuttgart, 1995.

Ellerbrock, K.-P. *Geschichte der Deutschen Nahrungs- und Genußmittelindustrie 1750–1914* [History of German Food and Luxury Industries] Stuttgart, 1993.

Grüne, J. *Anfänge Staatlicher Lebensmittelüberwachung in Deutschland: Der 'Vater der Lebensmittelchemie' Joseph König 1843–1930* [Beginnings of State Food Control in Germany], Stuttgart, 1996.

Hänger, P. *Das Fleisch und der Metzger. Fleischkonsum und Metzgerhandwerk in Basel seit der Mitte des 19. Jahrhunderts* [Meat Consumption and Butcher's Handicrafts in Basle from the Middle of the Nineteenth Century], Zürich, 2000.

Hengartner, T. and Merki, C.M. (eds), *Genußmittel. Ein Kulturgeschichtliches Handbuch* [Luxuries. An Historical and Cultural Handbook], 2nd ed., Frankfurt a.M. and Leipzig, 2001.

König, W. *Geschichte der Konsumgesellschaft* [History of Consumer Society], Stuttgart, 2000.

Köllmann, W. *Bevölkerung in der Industriellen Revolution* [Population in the Industrial Revolution], Göttingen, 1974.

Lesniczak, P. *Alte Landschaftsküchen im Sog der Modernisierung. Studien zur Ernährungsgeographie Deutschlands zwischen 1860 und 1930* [Old Regional Kitchens in the Pull of Modernization], Stuttgart, 2003.

Matzerath, H. *Urbanisierung Preußens 1815–1914* [Urbanization in Prussia], Stuttgart, 1985.

May, H. and Schilz, A. (eds), *Gasthäuser: Geschichte und Kultur* [Inns: History and Culture], Petersberg, 2004.

Pohl, H. (ed.), *Kommunale Unternehmen. Geschichte und Gegenwart* [Municipal Firms – History and Present] Wiesbaden, 1987.

Reinhard, W. *Lebensformen Europas. Eine Historische Kulturanthropologie* [Ways of Life in Europe], München, 2004.

Reulecke, J. (ed.), *Die Deutsche Stadt im Industriezeitalter* [The German Town in the Industrial Age] Wuppertal, 1978.

Sandgruber, R. *Die Anfänge der Konsumgesellschaft: Konsumgüterverbrauch, Lebensstandard und Alltagskultur in Österreich im 18. und 19. Jahrhundert* [The Beginnings of the Consumer Society], München, 1982.

Tanner, J. *Fabrikmahlzeit, Ernährungswirtschaft, Industriearbeit und Volksernährung in der Schweiz 1890–1950* [Nutrition Economy and Popular Feeding in Switzerland], Zürich, 1999.

Spiekermann, U. *Basis des Konsums. Entstehung und Entwicklung des Modernen Kleinhandels in Deutschland 1850–1914* [Origins and Development of the Modern Retail Trade in Germany], München, 1999.

Teuteberg, H.J. (ed.), *Urbanisierung im 19. und 20. Jahrhundert. Historische und geographischer Aspekte* [Urbanization in the Nineteenth and Twentieth Centuries], Köln, 1983.

Teuteberg, H.J. (ed.), *Durchbruch zum Massenkonsum. Lebensmittelmärkte und Lebensmittelqualität im Städtewachstum des Industriezeitalters* [Break-through to Mass Consumption. Food Markets and Food Quality During Urban Growth in the Industrial Age], Stuttgart, 1987.

Teuteberg, H.J. (ed.), *Revolution am Esstisch. Neue Studien zur Nahrungskultur des 19./20. Jahrhunderts* [Revolution at the Dining Table. New Studies on Food Culture of the Nineteenth and Twentieth Century], Stuttgart, 2004.

Teuteberg, H.J. and Wiegelmann, G. *Nahrungsgewohnheiten in der Industrialisierung* [Food Habits during Industrialization], 2nd ed., Münster, 2005.

Chapter 3

'A Tale of Two Cities': A Comparison of Food Supply in London and Paris in the 1850s

Peter J. Atkins

Introduction

London and Paris were the two largest centres of consumption in mid-nineteenth century Europe. London was the capital of an ever-extending global Empire and financial hub of the United Kingdom's industrial revolution. A rapidly growing city in the first half of the nineteenth century (2.4 million in 1851), she relied upon her food wholesalers, retailers and transport managers to keep her metabolism in a state of positive balance. For a considerable period of time London's demand had been a stimulation to increasingly specialized food producers all over the nation, and beyond, but the introduction of steam-powered railways and ships added the possibility of moving perishable items such as fish and meat quickly over longer distances without loss of quality, and her nodal accessibility in the new transport network yielded a greater volume and variety of foodstuffs than available in other cities of equivalent status. Paris was smaller (1.2 million) and drew the bulk of her provisions from a shorter radius but the growth of the French railway system, focused on the capital city, opened up supplies beyond the Île de France.[1]

Interestingly, it was in the 1850s, at the point when the railways were facilitating the import of a greater variety of raw materials, that writing about urban food supplies entered a new phase. In Britain there were a number of well-known attempts to quantify food production and consumption, as part of a self-conscious drive to take stock of national economic progress.[2] Then in 1856, coincidentally in both cities in the same year, there were detailed books published on the specifics of food supply. George Dodd's *The Food of London* was innovative but it makes frequent reference to the problems of quantifying individual commodities consumed in that city. Armand Husson, in his *Les Consommations de Paris*, had no such difficulty: he wrote a path-breaking volume that is a treasure trove of information for the food

---

1   Clark and Lepetit suggest that Paris was a city intermediate between two extremes: on the one hand cities such as London and Lisbon, which had broad hinterlands and a positive spread effect, and, on the other hand, cities such as Naples, which were parasitic and somewhat negative in their impact.

2   Porter, 1851; McCulloch, 1849, 1854.

historian.[3] He was fortunate to have access to the official *octroi* records and he also drew upon other sources, such as key informants in the police department and the market authorities. The bureaucratic inclinations of the Second Empire worked to his advantage, and Husson seems to have exploited his own position as a state official to extract data.[4] In fact his book has the feel of a semi-official publication and would no doubt have been gratefully received by city authorities constantly worried about food shortages and their potential for sparking food riots. One of the most impressive aspects of Husson's work is his critical reflection on the quality and completeness of his information.

The purpose of this chapter is to provide an outline comparison of London and Paris in the middle of the nineteenth century, an outline that will emphasize the supply side of what Andrew Wynter called the urban 'commissariat'.[5] The argument is illustrated with original data from the 1850s.

Sites of Production: The Tyranny of Nature?

Out-of-season products have been a feature of diets in London and Paris for centuries. In the 1850s both cities had flourishing markets for early horticultural products for wealthy tables – at a cost, of course, always at a cost for the conquest of nature.

For Paris, we can identify three phases in the season. First, there was a substantial industry of *primeur* fruits and vegetables growing around the city, and even within the city walls. The growers, generally known as *maraîchers*, developed one of the most productive horticultural systems ever seen.[6] This reached its peak in the 1850s and 1860s and survived intact until the early part of the twentieth century.[7] Between three and six fruit, salad and vegetable crops were taken annually from each plot, made possible by a build up of fertility in the soil and the control of temperature. The 1,800 or so market gardens were highly labour-intensive, employing 9,000 gardeners on 1,400 ha of land, much of it within the city walls. Applications of manure ranged from 300–1,000 tonnes per ha on holdings that, on average, were 25 per cent covered in glass (84 per cent frames and the remainder under 2.2 million bell-shaped cloches), both implying a significant investment of capital.[8] Further wind and frost protection was provided by two metre high windbreaks (mostly walls) and straw mats. In some cases there were greenhouses heated with stoves or steam boilers and using the principle of the thermosiphon to pipe warm water close to the

---

3   Porter, 1847, 588 had earlier complained, for London, that 'it is impossible to estimate, with anything approaching to exactness, the consumption of the metropolis'.

4   He was Directeur de l'Assistance Publique, which included running hospitals.

5   [Wynter] 1854.

6   Courtois, 1858; Stanhill, 1977.

7   In the early twentieth century urban transport switched from horse power to the internal combustion engine and the market gardeners lost their cheap and plentiful supply of manure.

8   Start up costs for a market garden were Fr28,400 in 1869, with working costs of Fr16,810. These figures had increased by 1900 to Fr60,000 and Fr30,000 respectively. Ponce, 1869; Phlipponneau, 1956.

roots of their most precious plants. The return was up to 100 tonnes of produce per hectare, by comparison with 74 tonnes on the most intensive English equivalent market gardens.[9]

In the greenhouses, pineapples, grapes, peaches, cherries, raspberries and figs were raised, with peri-urban locations such as Montreuil, Meudon and Versailles particularly famous for the appearance and tastiness of their produce. In the frames and cloches, strawberries and asparagus were 'forced', along with a wide range of other vegetable and salad crops. In order to reap the maximum premium on what were called 'high early products', the *maraîchers* forced those species that were susceptible to modifications in their season and that were in demand in the luxury market. Thus, strawberries were available by 15 February, grapes by 25 March. Green asparagus started in October and continued as an early product until the end of March, white asparagus from November to early April, and French beans from 10 February to 30 March.

Success was not guaranteed. In the second edition of Husson's book, he notes that the forced culture of peas had recently been abandoned by *primeurists*, along with cucumbers, cauliflowers, lettuce, chicory, carrots and radishes. They seem to have been ruthless in their assessment of profitability and, of course, these crops could always be substituted with others. There was less flexibility in medium-term investments such as fruit trees, and so such crops were discarded by peri-urban horticulture, which became as adaptable as it could possibly be.

Second in the season, there were consignments by railway from the south of France, where climatic factors gave growers a comparative advantage. Husson's book came at a crucial time in the transport revolution in parts of rural France and he recounts the influence this had in encouraging greater consumption, increasing the variety of produce marketed in Paris, and, also, in its spatial impact of restructuring the portfolio of consignments of fruit and vegetables.

The season's third phase was dominated by the non-*primeur* crops of the market gardeners beyond the suburbs but still within 10 km of Paris, operating sometimes without much investment in frames, cloches or manure.[10] The open field growing season was of course shorter and ripening times later than the south of France, but these growers were nevertheless able to drive their competitors out of the market during the height of the season in northern France. This was because of their relatively low transport costs and lower likelihood of spoilage in transit, but also on quality grounds. Thus Perpignan peaches, although tender and good-looking, unfortunately had adherent cores and were not equal in smoothness of texture to those of Montreuil.

Producers around London never adopted on a large scale the most intensive methods of what came to be called 'French gardening'. Nevertheless, Malcolm Thick has shown that high output market gardening has a long history near the city.[11] He describes the use of large glass bell cloches as early as the late seventeenth century

---

9   Kropotkin, 1899.

10   The two principal districts were at the confluence of the Seine and the Marne, to the south, and in the north from Bobigny to Saint Denis.

11   Thick, 1998.

and focused particularly on the Neat House gardens in Pimlico, where micro-climate modification by glass allowed the production of out-of-season melons and asparagus. The main factor was the addition of large quantities of horse and cow manure from the streets, stables and cow-houses of central London. This dung was used cleverly in creating specially constructed hotbeds that heated the soil for delicate crops. The Neat House gardens were built over in the 1830s but other commercial horticulture continued within easy range of the centre of London, with added accessibility provided by the railways and an improved road system.

The major growers of fruits and vegetables around both Paris and London sent their produce to the wholesale markets. The systems at Les Halles and Covent Garden were similar. Both had a limited number of tenants with large businesses sourcing supplies from near and far. In Paris, Husson's data indicate that business was divided roughly equally between, on the one hand, commission agents who made private deals through established channels to wholesalers, and, on the other hand, auctions (*à la criée*).[12] In both cases the sales were made on behalf of growers, and the agents did not at any stage own the goods. Much had to be taken on trust and a great deal depended on the skills and contact networks of the agents, as well as on the vagaries of the weather and day-to-day fluctuations in prices.

Both London and Paris also had minor specialist food wholesale markets. In Paris, the market of the Mail, near the Île St Louis on the Quai de l'Hotel de Ville, supplied low grade fruit to itinerant retailers and to manufacturers of jams and preserves. This amounted to about five per cent of the total, against 57 per cent passing through Les Halles, 18 per cent received by commission agents outside Les Halles, eight per cent taken from growers by wholesale merchants, and 13 per cent that was pitched at the *quartier* street markets in various parts of the city.[13]

Milk was another commodity that was initially produced close to both cities. In Paris it was never liable to the *octroi* and Husson therefore had to rely upon various surveys and estimates in his description. The impact of the railways from the outset was widespread in the Île de France, mediated by contractors touring the countryside offering guaranteed returns, buying up all of the milk coming from a farmer's cattle sheds, and forwarding it to the nearest station. Paris became dependent earlier than London upon such milk brought by rail, replacing an initial enthusiasm for using rapid road transport. The radius of regular supply quickly stretched to over 100 km, especially northward on the lines to Amiens and Rouen.[14]

In his 1875 edition, Husson notes that milk consumption had fallen in the previous twenty years from 103 to 60 litres per capita. There are two possible reasons for this.[15] First, Haussmann's annexation of the suburbs in 1860 doubled the city's

---

12 Most fruit (and beans and potatoes) was sold by commission agents but more vegetables, especially bulk lots of cabbage and watercress went to auction.

13 Husson, 1856, 1875.

14 Eventually the milkshed stretched to the specialist dairying areas of Normandy, the pays d'Auge and le Bessin. This was facilitated by the development of special railway wagons. Jenkins, 1879.

15 There is a third possible explanation, that the estimates are inaccurate. This is more likely for the 1856 figure because further information became available after that date.

area and increased its population by 400,000, but these new citizens were relatively poor and their dietary profile would undoubtedly have affected the average for the metropolitan area as a whole. Since milk had a high income elasticity of demand, it would not be at all surprising if its consumption per capita for the city as a whole therefore immediately fell. Second, the technical limitations of moving milk by rail were substantial and may well have made it difficult to source sufficient supply. In common with Britain, there was a lack of proper cooling facilities, along with inadequate rolling stock and inconvenient timetabling.[16] Either way, it seems that there was a need for an increase in supply from near at hand and in Paris the number of stall-fed cows in the city grew, with 6,850 still kept by 490 cow-keepers as late as 1887.[17] This was the opposite trend to London, where regulation with a sanitary intent increased the costs of city milk producers and eventually forced them out of business. The London milk trade solved the problem of supply by drawing on consignments from ever-distant railway stations, helped by the use from the 1880s of chemical preservatives to prevent the visible deterioration of the milk in transit.[18]

With regard to meat, the regulation of beef, mutton and veal butchers in Paris undoubtedly had an impact upon the retail environment and probably on consumption. The abolition of registration and price controls in 1858 led to a tripling in the number of butchers shops from 501 in 1856 to 1,805 in 1875, with a further 417 operating in street markets. By comparison, the pork butchers (*charcutiers*), who had not been restricted in the same way, increased more in line with the expansion of population, from 422 to 654.

The red meat butchers drew their supplies from wholesale markets, rather like their colleagues in London, but before 1858 they were expected to slaughter their purchases themselves, and the concept of a dead meat market was yet to develop in the same way as at Smithfield, Newgate and Leadenhall. One fascinating difference between the cities lay in the extraordinary nature of the supply of hams to Paris. This was facilitated by the institution of the ham fair, held for three days every year at Easter, when ham dealers came from all over the country and sold up to 300,000 kg in this short period.[19]

Feeding Modernity: London and Paris in the 1850s

Although Paris in the 1850s was somewhat smaller than London, to Walter Benjamin she was nevertheless 'the capital of the nineteenth century', and to David Harvey the 'capital of modernity'.[20] This was because the coup d'état of 1851 was an important historical threshold. Not only did it lead to the Second Empire and elevate Napoleon III to absolute power, but also the 1850s and 1860s saw the release of a creative energy that restructured large portions of the central city on modernist lines of rational order. The planning genius behind this make-over was Georges-Eugène Haussmann, Prefect

---

16 Atkins, 1978.
17 Gaubeaux, 1887.
18 Atkins, 1991.
19 Husson, 1856, 1875.
20 Benjamin, 1970; Harvey, 2003.

from 1853 to 1870. In addition to designing the new boulevards and sewers, for which he is renowned, he also turned his mind to the food supply of the city. Existing facilities had long been considered inadequate and a start had even been made on a new central market. Both Napoleon and Haussmann disliked the design of this building and considered it to be insufficiently emblematic of their brave new world. The architect, Victor Baltard, was instructed to demolish it and to start again under the supervision of Haussmann himself. The result was a series of six pavilions built between 1854 and 1857, with four more 1866–68, housing a substantial portion of the city's wholesale trades in meat, fish, fruit and vegetables and creating the world's largest covered food market. At 84,000 square metres, it had ten times the space available than before and was supplied with water and gas lamps to facilitate night working.[21]

The redevelopment of Les Halles did not depend upon consensus or goodwill. First, to contemporary eyes the sheer scale of the market buildings and their path-breaking architecture made them as uncomfortable in the townscape as the Centre Pompidou has been more recently in a neighbouring *arrondissement*. Second, the demolition of some slum properties was not an accidental side effect, but rather an attempt to fulfill one of Haussmann's gentrifying objectives.[22] In a sense, therefore, it was political. It was also ideological in that both Les Halles and, later, La Villette, the vast slaughterhouse and meat market opened in 1867, neatly meshed with Haussmann's new ideas of urban order and represented 'a new perception of the operation of urban space'.[23]

The significance of Les Halles is perhaps best captured in contemporary novels, notably Emile Zola's *Le Ventre de Paris*.[24] William Berg argues that Zola's are 'visual' novels that are closely related to painterly techniques and to later filmic styles in the evocation of storylines.[25] Thus in *Le Ventre de Paris*, literally 'the belly of Paris', he uses Les Halles as a 'set', and the description is somewhat like a still life, with both superficial and deeper meanings.[26] The market represents the fat of the land, the luxurious excess of the bourgeois lifestyle, juxtaposed with its urban context, one of the poorest parts of the city, and Zola stresses the phantasmagoria of the market as a gas-lit Aladdin's cave of exotic wonders: sights, smells, sounds. It represents at the same time the stuff of life and the rapid onset of decay in delicate foods; it therefore encompasses both *nourriture* and *pourriture*.

Although London was clearly different in political terms, with no experiment equivalent to the national socialist style of Napoleon and no overarching city planning to match the vision of Haussmann, nevertheless modernity was making its mark. It is not coincidental, for instance, that the mid-century saw general dissatisfaction with the state of the wholesale food markets. A good example is the 'new' Smithfield meat market, which opened in 1861, not long after the slaughtering function had been transferred (1855) to the new Metropolitan cattle market in Islington. According to

---

21 Chemla, 1994.
22 Johnson, 2004.
23 Chemla, 1994, 39.
24 Originally published in 1873, translated in 1996.
25 Berg, 1992.
26 Tunstall, 2004.

Patrick Joyce, this relegation of animal death to the suburbs was a part of a need to make it invisible and anonymous in an age that was increasingly squeamish about the industrialization of blood-letting.[27]

There were major differences between London and Paris. First, the bold planning that has characterized French urban politics, right down to the present day, delivered in Les Halles and La Villette the world's two largest food markets. By comparison, London's wholesaling functions were both more specialized and dispersed. In addition to Smithfield, there were markets devoted to fish, fruit and vegetables, potatoes, poultry, wheat and tea, along with some for mixed goods. In addition, there were a number of commodities that did not pass through markets at all, notably various grocery provisions, eggs and milk.

Second, in Paris there were still restrictions on butchers and bakers as providers of the basic foodstuffs, particularly with regard to controlling prices and therefore defusing potential civil unrest.[28] The city had a long history of popular uprisings and the authorities were nervous that food riots about high prices might have wider political consequences. According to Husson (1856), there were only 600 authorized bakers and their prices were fixed each fortnight according to the price of flour.[29] In 1854 there was even a decree obliging all bakers to deposit flour equivalent to 90 days production in the municipal stores. Eventually, in 1863, licensing and price controls were replaced by a tax on flour and the bakery trade quickly adapted to a market reality much more like that of London. The similar regulation of butchers was abolished in 1858, so the Second Empire was a period of fundamental change in the state's involvement in metropolitan food supplies.

On the Streets

'Oh, herring red, thou art good with 'tatoes or with bread'.[30]

A nineteenth-century *flâneur* of foodscapes would have exercised all available senses. His sense of taste would have been somewhat challenged by the basic foods available to most of the urban population but, as Rebecca Spang has shown, in Paris at least, modern gastronomic culture was taking shape through the invention of the restaurant.[31] Our *flâneur* would certainly have smelled the numerous pig-styes close to the centre of London, seen tens of thousands of cattle driven to market through the streets, and perhaps have slipped in the blood that oozed from the many small slaughterhouses. In a performative sense he might also have experienced the surround-sound street theatre of open markets and the shrill cries of itinerant costermongers and milkmaids.[32]

---

27 Joyce, 2003.

28 The equivalent Assize of Bread had been abolished for prices in London in 1709 and for standard weights in 1822.

29 Husson, 1856.

30 Wright, 1867.

31 Spang, 2000.

32 Mayhew, 1851.

Table 3.1   The street sellers of food in London, 1851

Food item	Sellers	Value (£)	Food item	Sellers	Value (£)
Wet fish		1,177,000	Pickled whelks	150	5,000
Dry fish		127,000	Lemonade, sherbet	700	4,900
Shell fish	11,000	156,650	Pea soup	150	4,050
Fruit and nuts		332,400	Pies	50	3,000
Dry fruit		1,000	Cakes and tarts	150	2,350
Vegetables		292,200	Ham sandwiches	60	1,800
Game		80,000	Water	60	780
Coffee and tea	300	31,200	Cheap cakes	30	450
Hot eels	240	19,448	Curds and whey	100	412
Poultry		14,800	Milk	28	344
Ginger beer	900	14,660	Rice milk	75	320
Baked potatoes	200	14,000	Hot cross buns	500	300
Watercress	500	13,949	Boiled meat and currant puddings	6	270
Meat	150	12,450	Plum duff	6	250
Fried fish	300	11,400	Hot green peas	4	250
Sweets	200	10,000	Elder wine	50	200
Bread	25	9,000	Cough drops	6	130
Gingerbread nuts	150	6,630	Peppermint water	4	125
Muffins and crumpets	500	6,000	Ice creams	20	42
Sheep's trotters	300	6,000	Total	16,918	2,360,760

Source: Mayhew, 1851.

Notes: 1. Does not include doorstep delivery 2. Many of these trades were temporary or seasonal, e.g. hot cross buns for Easter; muffins and crumpets, baked potatoes, cough drops, elder wine, and rice milk all in winter; ginger beer, lemonade, ice cream, curds and whey all in summer. 3. Mayhew counted 3,000 sellers of 'eatables and drinkables', 4-5,000 in winter.

In London, retailing of basic foodstuffs seems to have been more of a street phenomenon than in its rival city.[33] Journalist Henry Mayhew was the master of describing the charivari of street life and particularly the many characters who were involved. According to the information he collected in 1849 and 1850, there were 3,900 food stalls in 37 street markets, and a further 7,800 itinerants, mainly

---

33 Some care is required here. Husson makes little mention of costermongers but they certainly existed. The famous 'cries of London', a centuries-old genre of painting and print-making depicting street vendors, had in fact been copied from a Parisian idea in the early sixteenth century. Shesgreen, 2002. See also p. 91 of this volume.

selling fish, fruit and vegetables. Most of these 'costermongers' bought their wares in bulk early in the morning at the wholesale markets and then worked the most profitable pitches around central London. Their numbers had increased even faster than the general population of the city, no doubt in response to the problems of many immigrants in finding anything other than casual work. Over 70 per cent of wet fish was sold in this way, especially cheaper species such as herrings (100,000 tonnes p.a.),[34] and other food groups were similarly channelled: watercress (46 per cent), game (45 per cent), vegetables (33 per cent), dried and salted fish (26 per cent), poultry (25 per cent), and shell fish (23 per cent). With fruit and vegetables, the chief line was imported potatoes, dwarfing all other products by an order of magnitude, and also cabbage, onions, potatoes, turnips, apples, pears, and gooseberries, all home-grown. Bread and meat were not conveniently sold from barrows in all weathers and so continued to be the monopoly of fixed shops and their delivery boys. In addition to these raw commodities, Mayhew's street sellers also sold processed food and drink for the refreshment of passing customers. There were piemen, sellers of ham sandwiches and cakes and, depending on the season, of hot or cold drinks and snacks (Table 3.1).

Because of Mayhew's reputation as a journalist of the gothic poverty on London's streets, the serious intent of his work has often been undervalued. However, according to Eileen Yeo, his systematic, empirical social investigations bear comparison with later field workers such as Charles Booth and Seebohm Rowntree.[35] He worked in a team of collaborators and collected data through interviews of key informants and the use of questionnaires.[36] Some of his data, for instance wholesale market sales, can be at least partially corroborated from independent sources, and the information on street sellers of food is both detailed and suitably nuanced with comments on overlapping sales of individual products and on the casual and seasonal nature of such occupations. There are obvious faults, for instance occasional errors in the column and row sums of his statistical tables, but overall the Mayhew surveys are valuable raw material for a study of London's foodscape in the mid-nineteenth century.

By comparison, in Paris the street had a shifting significance from the 1850s. As the urban texture was opened out by Haussmann, revealing vistas that had never existed before, so the streetscape was reassessed by everyone. Cafés quickly multiplied on the brightly lit new boulevards and English writers visiting Paris often commented on a decrease in bourgeois domesticity in favour of public sociability in cafés.[37] The balance between private and public space was therefore very different from London. There was also a much denser population in Paris, up to five times more per building, which generated greater spending power per hectare in the city centre and favoured the multiplication of fixed shops rather than street markets.

---

34 There was trade for fixed-shop fishmongers but only 477 were listed in the *Post Office London Directory* for 1860.

35 Yeo, 1971, 55.

36 Yeo, 1971, 61-4.

37 Haine, 1996; Marcus, 1999. By 1909 there were 30,000 cafés in Paris but only 5,900 in London, a city twice the size.

Table 3.2   A detailed comparison of the consumption of fruit and vegetables (kg per capita per annum)

	London, 1851	Paris, 1856	Paris, 1869-73
Vegetables			
Potatoes	212.7	22.6	24.7
Cabbage	34.5	17.8	22.7
Turnip	20.5	3.4	15.0
Onions	16.3	2.6	5.5
Cauliflowers	13.6	2.1	23.0
Carrots	3.5	17.8	21.3
Green peas	1.7	3.5	9.4
Watercress	0.0	0.5	1.8
Salads	0.9	5.2	13.6
Rhubarb	0.8	0.0	0.0
Cucumbers	0.8	0.1	0.6
Green haricots	0.6	2.9	2.8
Beans	0.5	0.2	0.1
Red radish	0.4	0.4	0.4
Celery	0.3	1.3	1.4
Spring onions	0.2	0.1	0.1
Marrow	0.1	0.0	0.0
Asparagus	0.1	4.9	4.9
Leeks	0.0	10.9	12.4
White haricots, in pod	0.0	2.6	5.1
Pumpkins	0.0	2.3	0.9
Artichokes	0.0	2.1	2.6
Chicory	0.0	1.9	2.8
Parsnips	0.0	1.1	5.3
White haricots, shelled	0.0	0.8	0.2
Melons	0.0	0.7	4.1
Beetroot	0.0	0.6	1.5
Mushrooms	0.0	0.4	0.6
Black radish	0.0	0.4	0.5
Spinach	0.0	0.3	0.6
Tomatoes	0.0	0.3	0.5
Gherkins	0.0	0.2	0.3
Brussels sprouts	0.0	0.1	0.7
Cardoons	0.0	0.8	0.1
Shallots	0.0	0.0	0.1
Rape	0.0	0.0	0.0
Aubergines	0.0	0.0	0.1
Long pepper	0.0	0.0	0.0

	London, 1851	Paris, 1856	Paris, 1869-73
Burnet	⎫	0.0	0.0
Chervil		0.2	0.2
Chives		0.0	0.0
Garlic		0.5	0.7
Purslane	⎬ 0.1	0.1	0.0
Parsley		0.1	0.2
Salsify		0.2	0.2
Sorrel		6.6	8.4
Tarragon		0.0	0.0
Thyme	⎭	0.0	0.0
Fruit			
Raisins	8.3	0.0	0.9
Apples	7.8	97.5	9.2
Pears	4.0	130.4	5.5
Oranges	4.4	0.0	1.5
Currants and gooseberries	3.8	7.5	0.7
Plums	2.4	102.3	2.3
Lemons	0.7	0.0	0.3
Figs	0.5	2.8	0.5
Cherries	0.5	12.4	5.4
Prunes	0.3	0.0	0.7
Strawberries	0.3	8.1	2.7
Grapes	0.3	4.0	3.0
Fresh pineapple	0.0	0.0	0.0
Mulberries	0.0	0.0	0.0
Raspberries	0.0	1.2	0.4
Apricots	0.0	3.6	0.8
Medlars and service berries	0.0	0.1	0.0
Peaches	0.0	0.1	0.4
Olives	0.0	0.0	0.1
Dates	0.0	0.0	0.0
Pistolles	0.0	0.0	0.0
Nuts			
Other nuts	3.3	0.6	0.6
Almonds	0.3	0.0	0.2
Chestnuts and sweet chestnuts	0.3	0.6	2.7
Coconuts	0.2	0.0	0.0

			Hazel nuts	0.1	0.0	0.1
Herbs						
Bay leaves	?	0.1	0.2			

Sources: Mayhew, 1851; Wynter, 1854; Dodd, 1856; Husson, 1856, 1875.

Table 3.3   Comparison of consumption in main food groups (kg per capita per annum unless otherwise stated)

	London, 1850s	Paris, early/ mid 1850s	Paris, late 1860s/ early 1870s
Bread	148.8[1]; 118.0[2]	180.2	157.8
Red meat, offal		62.6	63.8
Pigmeat		10.3	12.2
Poultry and game	95.7[9]; 22.0[3]; 136.0[4]; 81.6[10]	9.8	12.7
Horse meat		0.0	0.7
Fish	62.6[5]; 90.9[6]	12.8	14.6
Butter	4.9; 7.7[1]; 5.2[3]	9.7	7.7
Cheese	6.1[5]; 7.7[1]	4.8	5.0
Eggs	?	8.3	7.8
Pastries	?	4.8	2.8
Paté, rice, starch	?	3.8	3.6
Sugar	?	7.1	8.0
Confectionery	?	0.6	0.7
Jam and raisiné	?	0.9	0.8
Ice cream	?	0.5	0.5
Honey	?	0.2	0.3
Coffee	?	2.8	3.2
Chicory	?	0.3	0.3
Chocolate	?	0.9	1.5
Tea	?	0.0	0.0
Early season fruits	?	0.0	0.0
Seasonal fruits	19.9[7]	225.3	31.8
Oranges, lemons	3.3[7]	2.0	1.8
Fresh pineapple	?	0.0	0.0
Dried fruits	8.2[7]	3.8	2.3
Tinned pineapple	?	0.0	0.0
Olives	?	0.1	0.1
Early season vegetables		0.0	0.0
Seasonal vegetables		127.2	204.4
Dried vegetables	64.0[1]; 150.2[7]	8.2	8.1
Pickled, tinned, bottled veg		1.6	1.6
Truffles	?	0.0	0.2
Salt	?	5.7	7.0
Mustard	?	0.2	0.3
Pepper, spices, vanilla	?	0.1	0.8
Wine (litres)	15.2[5]	113.3	210.8

Beer (litres)	167.9[5]; 139.7[1]	13.3	12.9
Cider (litres)	?	2.5	1.8
Spirits (litres)	25.7[5]	12.1	9.0
Milk (litres)	95.4[1]; 39.7-42.2[8]	103.8	60.3
Liqueurs (litres)	?	1.2	2.2
Candied fruits in brandy (litres)	?	0.3	0.2
Syrup (litres)	?	0.6	0.6
Oil (litres)	?	1.9	2.6
Vinegar (litres)	?	1.9	2.3

Sources: Paris estimates all from Husson, 1856, 1875. For London: 1. Porter, 1852; 2. McCulloch, 1849; 3. McCulloch, 1854; 4. Mayhew, 1849; 5. Mogg, 1844; 6. Mayhew, 1851; 7. Atkins, 1985; 8. Atkins, 1977; 9. Dodd, 1856; 10. Poole, 1852.

Conclusion

In such a short paper it is difficult to do justice to the complexities of the food supply systems in London and Paris. Nevertheless, a number of interesting points have been identified that require further comparative analysis.

First, the political imperatives and planning imaginations in the two cities were different. While London continued with its well-established laissez-faire attitude, exemplified by a lack of the collection of official statistics, Paris under the Second Empire was in the grip of a top-down authoritarian mentality that provided new marketing facilities, the lifting of controls on butchers and bakers, and an official interest in the minutiae of food provision.

Second, while the transport revolution seems to have affected both cities by the 1850s, there were important differences. The Parisian diet continued to rely upon fruits, vegetables and milk produced within the city limits to a greater degree and for much longer than was the case for London. This was partly due to indirect encouragement by the city authorities and partly to technicalities of production, which for a number of reasons were more intensive in Paris.

Third, retailing systems were different in the 1850s. One might understandably be tempted by a stage model that indicates earlier innovation in shop retailing in Paris, as instanced by the arcades in the early nineteenth century and later by department stores, but the reality is that there were other factors. For instance, in London a vast influx of migrants was responsible for an army of desperate people seeking casual employment on the streets of the city, and, since there was no equivalent to Haussmann's revanchist campaign to 'cleanse' the city centre of the poor, street vendors were able to establish a niche in the food economy similar in importance to the street vendors found nowadays in third world cities.

Finally, the evidence suggests dietary differences between the two cities. There is insufficient household budget data to comment on the food consumption of individuals, or even of particular social groups, but Tables 3.2 and 3.3 do provide indicative city-level comparative data. Thus, the London diet was more reliant upon heavy vegetables (potatoes, cabbage, onions) for its calories, and Paris on bread. The Parisian consumer had a much broader spectrum of fruits and vegetables to choose from but less fish. The availability of meats, dairy produce and alcohol seems to have been similar in the two cities, although, as expected, there was a clear difference in the preference for wine or for beer.

References

Atkins, P.J. 'The Growth of London's Railway Milk Trade, c. 1845–1914', *Journal of Transport History* new series 4, 1978, 208–226.

Atkins, P.J. 'The Production and Marketing of Fruit and Vegetables 1850–1950', in Oddy, D.J. and Miller, D. (eds), *Diet and Health in Modern Britain*, London, 1985, 102–33.

Atkins, P.J. 'The Charmed Circle: von Thünen and Agriculture around Nineteenth Century London', *Geography* 72, 1987, 129–39.

Atkins, P.J. 'Sophistication Detected: or, The Adulteration of the Milk Supply, 1850–1914', *Social History* 16, 1991, 317–39.

Atkins, P.J. 'Is it Urban? The Relationship between Food Production and Urban Space in Britain, 1800–1950', in ICREFH VI, 2003, 133–44.

Benjamin, W. 'Paris, Capital of the 19th century', in Idem., *Reflections*, New York, 1978.

Clark, P. and Lepetit, B. (eds), *Capital Cities and their Hinterlands in Early Modern Europe*, Aldershot, 1996.

Coffignon, A. *L'Estomac de Paris* [The Stomach of Paris][Paris, 1889].

Courtois, G. *Manuel Pratique de Culture Maraîchère* [Practical Manual of Market Gardening], Paris, 1858.

Gaubeaux, A. *Nouveau Rapport sur les Vacheries du Département de la Seine* [New Report on the Cow-keepers of the Department of the Seine], Paris, 1887.

Haine, W.S. *The World of the Paris Café: Sociability among the French Working Class, 1789–1914*, Baltimore, 1996.

Harvey, D. *Paris, Capital of Modernity*, New York, 2003.

Jenkins, H.M. 'Report on the Dairy farming of North-West France', *Journal of the Royal Agricultural Society of England* series 2, 15, 1879, 278–322.

Johnson, S.P. 'Cleansing Les Halles: Discourses of Health and Disease in Zola's Le Ventre de Paris', *Romance Quarterly* 51, 2004, 226–40.

Kropotkin, P. *Fields, Factories and Workshops Tomorrow*, London, 1912.

McCulloch, J.R. *A Dictionary, Geographical, Statistical, and Historical*, 2 vols, London, 1849.

McCulloch, J.R. *A Descriptive and Statistical Account of the British Empire*, 2 vols, London, 1854.

Marcus, S. *Apartment Stories: City and Home in Nineteenth Century Paris*, Berkeley, 1999.

Mayhew, H. 'Letter I', *Morning Chronicle* October 19th, 1849.

Mayhew, H. *London Labour and the London Poor*, 2 vols, London, 1851.

Mogg, E. *Mogg's New Picture of London and Visitor's Guide to its Sights*, London, 1844.

Phlipponneau, M. *La Vie Rurale de la Banlieue Parisienne* [The Rural Life of the Paris Suburbs], Paris, 1956.

Ponce, I. *La Culture Maraîchère, Pratique des Environs de Paris*, Paris [Market Gardening], 1869.

Poole, B. *Statistics of British Commerce*, London, 1852.

Porter, G.R. *The Progress of the Nation in its Social and Economic Relations since the Beginning of the Nineteenth Century*, London, 1847 and 1851 eds.

Shesgreen, S. *Images of the Outcast: The Urban Poor in the Cries of London*, Manchester, 2002.

Spang, R. *The Invention of the Restaurant: Paris and the Modern Gastronomic Culture*, Cambridge, MA, 2000.

Stanhill, G. 'An Urban Agro-ecosystem: The Example of Nineteenth Century Paris', *Agro-Ecosystems* 3, 1977, 269–284.

Thick, M. *The Neat House Gardens: Early Market Gardening around London*, Totnes, 1998.

Thompson, V.E. 'Telling "Spatial Stories": Urban Space and Bourgeois Identity in Early Nineteenth-Century Paris', *Journal of Modern History* 75, 2003, 523–56.

Tunstall, K.E. 'Crânement Beau Tout de Même: Still Life and Le Ventre de Paris', *French Studies* 58, 2004, 177–87.

Wright, T. *Some Habits and Customs of the Working Classes*, London, 1867.

[Wynter, A.] 'The London Commissariat', *Quarterly Review* 95, 190, 1854, 271–308.

Yeo, E. 'Mayhew as a Social Investigator', in Thompson, E.P. & Yeo, E. (eds) *The Unknown Mayhew*, London, 1971, 51–95.

Zola, E. *The Belly of Paris*, Los Angeles, 1996.

Chapter 4

Urbanization and Dietary Change in Mediterranean Europe: Barcelona, 1870–1935[1]

Roser Nicolau-Nos and Josep Pujol-Andreu

Introduction

The relationships between income, food and health have been the subject of considerable controversy for more than a century. Recent detailed research means that we now know more than ever before about two aspects of these relationships: first, that they have not always been the same over time, and, second, that there have been changes in the various factors conditioning the transformation of income into food and of food into health.[2] Such factors include: scientific and technological knowledge, along with access to that knowledge; social living conditions; and the institutional context.[3] In this paper, we will focus our attention on the transformation of income into food. As a case study we will take the city of Barcelona and analyse the changes that occurred in the consumption of livestock food products between 1870 and 1935.

Barcelona is of interest because in this period it was developing into a major economic centre in Mediterranean Europe. Its economy was rooted in industry and commerce, and it was particularly dynamic in generating and assimilating new scientific and technological knowledge. Throughout the period, the consumption of animal protein was closely related in the public mind with health and bodily strength. Its growth has been thought to be the result of increasing income per head income generated by the industrialization process, but we will attempt to show that changes in income are only a partial explanation of the nutritional changes in Barcelona. Other factors include the development and diffusion of scientific and technical knowledge; and the new working, living and social conditions generated by urban life. The population's demographic structure and income distribution will not be considered in the present paper.

---

1   Research financed by DGICYT: SEJ2004-00799, 'Food, Mortality and Standard of Living in Spain (19th and 20th Centuries)'.

2   Preston, 1975; McKeown, 1976; Mokyr, 2003.

3   For more detail, see also ICREFH II on food policies, ICREFH III on food and technology, ICREFH IV on material culture, ICREFH V on food and health, and ICREFH VI on food, towns and countryside.

The Consumption of Animal Protein in Barcelona

Researchers studying dietary trends are well aware of the difficulty in estimating change, even when estimates are based on aggregate data. Because we usually do not have information on consumption, it is necessary to use imprecise sources. This is not a problem at the national level, provided that suitable production and foreign-trade statistics are available. However, local estimates of apparent consumption cannot be calculated for most foods. Other indicators must therefore be used, for example family budgets or the food rations supplied to certain groups – the sick, soldiers, schoolchildren or prisoners.

These problems are also present in our case study. Although Barcelona City Council backed several initiatives from the nineteenth century onwards to estimate the city's food consumption, these initiatives did not always achieve the results

Table 4.1   Approximate consumption of animal foods and proteins in Barcelona, 1870–1933

Products	units	Overall consumption (in thousands)				
		1870	1881	1900	1914	1933
Meat	kg	8,778	11,674	24,347	30,938	38,671
fresh meat	kg	*6,062*	*8,101*	*17,590*	*23,122*	*27,793*
heads, entrails, feet	kg	*910*	*1,359*	*3,444*	*4,466*	*3,808*
fowls, rabbits	kg	*1,686*	*2,066*	*3,000*	*3,000*	*6,000*
other	kg	*120*	*148*	*313*	*350*	*1,170*
Fish	kg	5,195	5,050	9,900	11,600	30,050
fresh	kg	*175*		*4,300*	*6,000*	*22,000*
salted	kg	*3,200*	*2,600*	*1,300*		
dried (cod)	kg	*1,820*	*2,450*	*4,300*	*5,600*	*8,050*
Milk	l			7,000	37,000	80,000
Eggs	no			53,000	82,000	181,000
		Consumption per person per year				
Meat	kg	30.0	32.4	46.5	52.1	39.4
Fish	kg	40.0	29.5	18.4	19.1	29.4
Milk	l			13.0	60.9	78.2
Eggs	no			98.7	135.1	176.9
		Consumption of protein per person per year				
Meat	kg	4.9	5.2	7.2	8.1	6.2
Fish	kg	10.0	7.4	4.6	4.8	7.3
Milk	kg			0.4	2.1	2.7
Eggs	kg			1.0	1.4	1.9
TOTAL	kg			13.2	16.4	18.1

Source: Nicolau-Nos and Pujol-Andreu, 2004, 110, 113, 117.

that they were seeking. They were basically guided by two objectives: to tax food consumption and to prevent conflicts that could be caused by price rises and food adulteration. But the Council's interest in determining the city's food consumption was one thing, and its capacity for achieving it was quite another. As a result, we will not only use the foods that entered Barcelona daily collected by the council officers, but also various reports on the activities of the city's abattoirs, more scattered information on the city's food imports and exports, and various estimates of food consumption by the Veterinary Body. We will also use other estimates from family budgets and the food expenditure of various institutions. In all of these sources, the main estimates we will provide are based on the food supply available in the market. We have no information on food that did not pass through the market or of wastage in the market. Our estimates are shown in Table 4.1.

From this table, we would initially highlight two points. First, the consumption of animal protein was low at the end of the nineteenth century. Indeed, without considering the unevenness of its distribution, such consumption stood at only 12–14 kg per inhabitant per year until 1900. Second, note the later increase in that consumption, especially between 1900 and 1914, and the considerable changes in its composition. Unpacking this latter point in more detail, we can see: (a) the growing importance of meat products between 1870 and 1914 to the detriment of fish consumption, and the reversal of these tendencies in the 1920s and 30s; (b) the expansion of milk and egg consumption between 1900 and 1933, especially before the First World War; and, (c) an increase in the consumption of other meat products – largely poultry and rabbit – after the war.

There were other significant changes. Until 1881, most fresh meat consumption in Barcelona still came from adult beasts, especially rams, slaughtered in the city's abattoirs. That year, 18,000 bullocks and cows, and almost 206,000 rams were slaughtered, together with 12,000 calves and 15,000 lambs. Almost 19,000 pigs and 23,000 goats were slaughtered too. In 1933 the supply was very different. 15,000 bullocks and cows and 55,000 rams were slaughtered, together with 122,000 calves, more than 600,000 lambs and 95,000 pigs, and almost 80,000 kids. This means that up to 1881 meat from young animals hardly accounts for more than 15 per cent of the total meat consumed within the city, rising to almost 50 per cent by around 1933. In addition, the relative importance of pork consumption increased from about 25 to 35 per cent, and meat from bullocks, cows and rams fell from more than 50 per cent to less than 20 per cent. Fish consumption in the city underwent another important change. While at the end of the nineteenth century, fish was principally consumed dried or salted – particularly cod – this situation changed with the new century, especially after the First World War. So, while until the 1880s the annual consumption of fresh fish did not exceed 200 or 300 tonnes, in the 1930s its consumption easily exceeded 20,000 tonnes, making up about 75 per cent of total fish consumption.[4]

In summary, these observations highlight two important aspects of the food changes undergone in Barcelona from the 1880s. First, consumption of animal protein increased after the agrarian crisis at the end of the nineteenth century, particularly

---

4   Figuerola, 1849, 220–47; *Anuario Estadístico de la Ciudad de Barcelona 1902–1923*; *Butlleti Mensual d'Estadistica de la Generalitat de Catalunya 1933–1936*.

so up until 1914. Second, this process was accompanied by three changes in the composition of consumption: (a) the growing consumption of fresh meat from young animals – calves, lambs, kids – and, to a lesser extent, pork, poultry and rabbit; (b) the progressive replacement of dried or salted fish by fresh fish, and the growing consumption of such fish instead of meat in the 1920s and 1930s; (c) the notable expansion in milk and egg consumption. Expansion in the consumption of the first of these foods occurred later, but was also very marked between the end of the nineteenth century and 1914. How can we explain these changes?

Technical Change, Urban Living Conditions and Protein Consumption

One of the main factors generally used to explain the evolution of food consumption is income.[5] Moreover, it is usually argued that increases in income tend to generate increases in the consumption of those goods whose income elasticity is high. In our context, this would be meat, poultry, milk or fresh fish.[6] The information available for Barcelona initially seems to confirm this argument.

Between the 1880s and the 1930s, the city's economic growth was very important, and population increased from around 400,000 in 1885, to around 620,000 during World War I, and settled at around 1,000,000 in the 1930s. At the same time, workers wages increased 1870–1895 by 60 per cent in spending power with respect to bread. They then deteriorated slightly in the closing years of the century, and between 1900 and 1914 they remained at about 50 per cent above the levels that had existed up to 1871. After the war wages increased again, reaching a point in the 1920s and 1930s between 45 per cent and 55 per cent above the 1914 levels.[7] Finally, a study carried out in 1933 on family budgets found that families with incomes of less than 500 *pesetas* a month, the largest group in the city, still spent over 65 per cent of their income on food. This same group devoted 50–55 per cent of its total food expenditure to animal foods.[8]

These studies seem to confirm that families' income growth in Barcelona up to the 1930s produced an increase in the consumption of animal protein, but in our opinion income increases do not convincingly explain the changes in animal food consumption. They do not provide a full explanation of the new consumption patterns of animal foods that developed over time and we will argue that other factors should be taken into account.

Problems of Supply in Animal-Protein Consumption in Barcelona during the Nineteenth Century

There are several reasons why Barcelona diets were lacking in animal protein before the early twentieth century. First, feeding the city depended, for most products, on

---

5   See, for instance, Grigg, 1992, 68–70.

6   Gómez Mendoza and Simpson, 1988, 77–8.

7   Garrabou, Pujol-Andreu and Colomé, 1991, 46; Maluquer de Motes and Llonch, 2005, 1222–4.

8   Butlletí de l'Institut d'Investigacions Econòmiques, 1933, 225–33.

imports from other Spanish regions or from abroad, because the Catalan agrarian sector specialized in vineyards, olives, and fruit trees.[9] There was a scarcity of fodder resources over large areas of Catalonia that discouraged livestock production. Second, the range of food available for consumption was small because preservation techniques were still very limited. Third, there were poor communications between Catalonia and the cattle breeding areas (Cantabrian and Atlantic regions), so few live cattle could be imported, although some sheep were brought by sea from Valencia. Anyway the availability of young cattle and sheep was limited because it was more profitable for farmers to keep adult animals for ploughing or wool production. Finally, pigs were bred in Catalonia on scattered rural farms and there were considerable problems with their long-distance trade. It is not surprising, therefore, that the few pigs reaching Barcelona arrived by sea, particularly from Palma de Majorca.

However, these are not the only circumstances that conditioned meat consumption. Mutton was very fatty, and this characteristic was highly appreciated, particularly in the preparation of stocks and stews. A renowned book on nutrition also emphasized that mutton was tastier and more tender than beef, as well as being equally digestible and healthy. It also indicated that meat from young animals was suitable for anyone with digestive problems in spite of having a low nutritional value.[10]

Overall, meat consumption from mature animals could be justified by state-of-the-art knowledge on nutrition, and it was better suited to the city's conditions of supply. But such meat was generally a by-product of farming and was therefore a supply that could not easily be adapted to rising demand. Cows and bullocks were only transformed into meat when they were no longer useful for ploughing, and rams were merely the surplus males from sheep flocks, castrated for fattening. Given such supply problems, it is not surprising that dried and salted fish became so important in Barcelona. Under the technological conditions of the time, fresh fish deteriorated quickly and its consumption could cause serious illness. In contrast, dried or salted fish was preserved much longer and, since it could be obtained from remote areas, the supply was more stable and secure.[11]

The low milk consumption in the city until 1900 can also be understood when we consider supply conditions. Production was limited in Catalonia due to the fodder shortage mentioned above, low milk yields of local cattle breeds, and a very short shelf life in hot weather.[12] As a result, although the nutritional value of this food was partially known, consumption was limited to milk that could be produced in Barcelona and its immediate environs, and then mainly as a medicine for the sick. Supplies were limited even for infants, who tended to be fed on mothers' milk or through the services of a wet nurse.[13]

9   Garrabou and Pujol-Andreu, 1987, 60–77.
10 Agreda, 1877, 169–76.
11 Cussó and Garrabou, 2003–4, 69–72.
12 Pujol-Andreu, 2002, 193–4, 208–9.
13 Segalà, 1899.

Figure 4.1 **Relative prices of beef and pork compared to mutton, expressed as kilos of meat from rams per kilo of meat from bullocks, calves and pigs**

Source: Nicolau-Nos and Pujol-Andreu, 2004, 122

Economic Transformation and Dietary Changes at the End of the Nineteenth and Beginning of the Twentieth Centuries

Two important changes in the city's supply conditions are observable from the closing years of the nineteenth century. First, railway connections were made between Barcelona and the northern part of the peninsula and inland regions. Second, Spanish agriculture underwent an important restructuring after the sectoral crisis at the end of the century, and cattle and pig farming grew. This expansion was possible for two reasons. First, the import of improved English, French, Swiss and Dutch breeds for meat or milk production improved the national herd's genetic profile. Second, the supply of feed and fodder also increased, as a result of: (a) the spread of more intensive crop rotation and new means of production (seeds, fertilizers, ploughs, harvesters and threshing machines); (b) an expansion of the area under irrigation;

and, (c) the intensification of internal trade in agricultural products.[14] So, while higher income levels increased demand for meat, changes on the supply side also facilitated the changes we have observed in consumption patterns. The evolution of relative prices points in the same direction (Figure 4.1). Over the final decades of the nineteenth century and the opening years of the twentieth, mutton became more expensive compared to beef and pork and this can only be explained by the changes indicated earlier.

We also believe that there was another factor conditioning meat consumption after 1890. This was the growing preference of consumers and wholesalers for young cattle, for different reasons. In 1921, the City Council officers suggested that consumers were showing a preference for small cattle as the cuts were smaller, therefore more suitable for an individual main course.

A look at other sources of animal protein is instructive. In the case of eggs, relative prices tended to fall compared to meat, and this probably favoured their consumption. While the terms of trade between pork and eggs was 1 kg to 1.2 dozen between 1881 and 1885, from 1895 to 1899 it stood at 1:1.6 and between 1909 and 1913 it was at 1:1.7. As regards mutton, the terms of trade were, respectively, 1:1.2, 1:1.5 and 1:1.8. The same could be said with respect to milk. Between 1898 and 1920, its current price was very stable while the prices of other foods increased, and as a result, its real price decreased by 14 per cent. However, other factors also stimulated the consumption in both cases. Eggs keep for longer than meat and fresh fish and enable a wide range of quick dishes to be made. Since the turn of the century, progress made in the science of microbiology and the discovery of the micro-nutrients needed for a balanced diet –vitamins and minerals – changed the popular concept of fresh milk and demand for it grew and took on a new significance. Activities conducted by doctors and various public institutions were strategic in that growth.[15] Other factors favouring it were: the spread of new kinds of baby bottles using sterilized milk, and the growing consumption of coffee and cocoa.[16]

Finally, although access to fresh fish improved with technological changes in the fishing sector and in the commercialization processes, its price with respect to meat, eggs and milk was still high and improvements in income were therefore used for the consumption of the latter products rather than fish.

New Food Patterns in the 1920s and 1930s

Changes observed after World War I are complex. The continuing increase in animal protein consumption is not surprising. In that period, wages increased strongly, outstripping general price inflation. As a result, between 1911/1913 and 1931/1935, real wages grew around 50 to 60 per cent. However, it is also understandable, for at least two reasons, why the expansion in the animal food consumption slowed down by comparison with the previous period. It had already increased considerably up to 1914, and, except for mutton, price increases for those products were particularly

---

14 Pujol-Andreu et al., 2001.

15 Murcott, 1999, 315–27 ; Institut Municipal de la Salut, 1991, 31–74, 171–92.

16 Institut Municipal de la Salut, 1991, 174 ; Martí Escayol, 2004, 148–59.

Table 4.2   Evolution of the consumption per person per year of animal foods and protein, 1914–1930s

		1914	1933	1914–1933 (%)
Fresh meat		38.2	27.2	-28.8
Poultry and other meat	kg	4.9	6.0	22.4
Fish	kg	19.1	29.4	53.9
Eggs	u	135.1	176.9	30.9
Milk	l	60.9	78.2	28.4
Cured meats and others	kg	1.9	3.3	73.7
Total animal protein	kg	16.3	18.0	10.4

Source: Nicolau-Nos and Pujol-Andreu, 2004, 125.

strong. In that period, beef and pork retail prices increased 70 per cent, and eggs, cod and milk increased respectively, 125 per cent, 100 per cent and 80 per cent. On the other hand, mutton, bread, rice and potato retail prices, increased less, between 50 per cent and 65 per cent.

The strong showing of beef and pork prices was due, according to a study by the City Council, to a combination of factors. There were new problems facing the cattle-breeding sector in keeping pace with demand; railway freight rates increased after the War; and of the presence of too many intermediaries in the meat trade caused inefficiencies.[17] Other research has highlighted the dependence of the cattle-breeding sector on imported feed, which was subject to a high customs duty.[18]

With fresh fish, the prices of low quality varieties – sardines, herrings – tended to move in the low inflation band whilst the opposite was true of white fish – hake, monkfish. A recent study on prices in Barcelona in the twentieth century indicates that the price of top-quality beef doubled between 1909/1912 and 1932/1933, whereas the price of hake from the north increased by 88 per cent, and sardines by 45 per cent.[19] Another study of the Spanish fishing sector during the first third of the twentieth century also indicates that the relative prices for fresh fish tended to fall, because of the technological improvements in fishing operations.[20] In summary, we can see why fresh fish consumption – especially of low quality fish – increased strongly after the war, at the expense of meat and even cod.

Other changes in the consumption animal foods after the First World War are less easy to explain in terms of income and prices (Table 4.2). For instance, milk, and eggs registered the highest price increases, and so did their consumption, although not as rapidly as in the previous period. As regards mutton, an opposite relationship between prices and consumption can be seen. Its price increased less than that of

17 Algarra, 1912, 75.
18 Rossell i Vilar, 1921, 49–53.
19 Ajuntament de Barcelona, 2002.
20 Giráldez, 1996, 147–86.

other meat and animal products, but its consumption dropped. In conclusion, animal food consumption after the war was related to other factors.

As we have argued, living conditions and a better knowledge of nutrition changed consumer preferences, increasing the consumption of eggs and milk. A contemporary analyst highlighted the considerable influence of medical recommendations on the growing consumption of these foods.[21] With respect to the lower consumption of mutton we have to remember that the scarcity both of time and fuel in the cities must have made stew-based culinary practices difficult, and, anyway, the nutritional value of such dishes and the advisability of their consumption were being called into doubt.[22] In our opinion, both points help provide a fuller explanation of the replacement of mutton by beef and pork, or even by fresh fish and eggs·

Conclusions

Our research confirms that dietary change in Barcelona was broadly in line with other European cities during industrialization, being characterized by the growing consumption of meat products, fresh fish and a wide range of milk and poultry products.[23] However, there were wrinkles. Between the 1880s and 1930s, the consumption of animal protein in Barcelona did increase but this was particularly marked in the period before the war, and with time there were substantial changes in its composition. Specifically, while the consumption of mutton declined, the consumption of beef and pork increased. Furthermore, meat from young beasts replaced that of adult animals, and the consumption of milk, egg and fresh fish became increasingly important. In addition, milk and egg consumption increased, above all, in the period before 1914, whereas that of fresh fish did so in the twenties and thirties.

We have also tried to show that such changes were not only the result of income increases, but also due to other factors. This does not mean that we should over-emphasize the problems of interpretation. The complexity of working with several variables should not hinder historical explanations.[24] In our opinion, the relationship between diet and income is most important in the short term, when differences in consumption are compared to income distribution. However, this relationship is less clear in the long term when technological, scientific and social conditions vary. For this reason, income elasticity for a particular product at a particular time cannot be used to explain changes in consumption patterns, because this measurement assumes that the other factors affecting demand remain constant. In Barcelona, for example, demand for mutton must have had a high-income elasticity in the nineteenth century, but a very low one in the 1930s. Fresh milk was not really a food, *sensu stricto*, before 1880; yet it ended up becoming a basic food. Initially, beef from adult animals was considered more nutritious than that from young animals, but the latter eventually surpassed the former.

---

21 Raventós, 1923, 30–1.
22 Raventós, 1923, 31.
23 Teuteberg, 1992.
24 Fogel, 1988; Diamond, 1997, chapter 13.

In summary, although income and nutritional patterns are related, when analysing changes we should not lose sight of the fact that the relationships between these variables tend to vary for different reasons, for example because of technological change in the production and commercialization processes, or as a result of new preference structures attributable to the developing and expanding urban centres and scientific advancement regarding nutritional awareness. In our view, when we consider these factors, we can best explain three aspects of the changes we have seen in the Barcelona diet between the end of the nineteenth century and the 1930s. These are: (a) the reduction in consumption of mutton, together with the expansion in consumption of beef and pork; (b) the progressive replacement of older animals by younger beasts in meat consumption; and (c) the expansion at different rates in the consumption of milk, eggs and fresh fish.

References

Agreda, F.J. *Falsificación de Alimentos y Bebidas* [Adulteration of Food and Drink], Barcelona, 1877.

Algarra, J. *La Formación del Precio de las Carnes en el Mercado de Barcelona* [Meat Price Formation in the Barcelona Market], Barcelona, 1912.

Ajuntament de Barcelona, *Cent Anys d'Estadística Municipal* [A Hundred Years of Municipal Statistics], Barcelona, 2002.

Butlletí de l'Institut d'Investigacions Econòmiques, Barcelona, 1931–7.

Cussó, X. and Garrabou, R. 'La Transició Nutricional a la Catalunya Contemporània: Una Primera Aproximació' [The Nutrition Transition in Contemporary Catalonia], *Recerques* 47–8, 2003–4, 51–80.

Diamond, J. *Guns, Germs and Steel: The Fates of Human Societies*, London, 1997.

Figuerola, L. *Estadística de Barcelona en 1849* [Barcelona Statistics in 1849], Barcelona, 1849.

Fogel, R.W. 'Nutrition and the Decline in Mortality since 1700: Some Additional Preliminary Findings', in Brandstrom, A. and Tedebra, L. (eds) *Society, Health, and Population during the Demographic Transition*, Stockholm, 1988, 369–83.

Garrabou, R. and Pujol-Andreu, J. 'El Canvi Agrari a la Catalunya del Segle XIX' [Agricultural Change in Nineteenth-Century Catalonia], *Recerques* 19, 1987, 35–83.

Garrabou, R., Pujol-Andreu, J. and Colomé, J. 'Salaris, Ús i Explotació de la Força de Treball Agrícola (Catalunya, 1818–1936)' [Wages, Use and Operation of the Agricultural Labour Force], *Recerques* 24, 1991, 23–52.

Giráldez, J., *Crecimiento y Transformación del Sector Pesquero Gallego, 1880–1936* [Growth and Transformation of the Galician Fishing Sector], Madrid, 1996.

Gómez Mendoza, A. and Simpson, J. 'El Consumo de Carne en Madrid durante el Primer Tercio del Siglo XX' [Consumption of Meat in the First Third of the Twentieth Century], *Moneda y Crédito* 186, 1988, 57–91.

Grigg, D. *The Transformation of Agriculture in the West*, Oxford, 1992.

Institut Municipal de la Salut, *Cent Anys de Salut Pública a Barcelona* [A Hundred Years of Public Health in Barcelona], Barcelona, 1991.

Maluquer de Motes J. and Llonch M. 'Trabajo y Relaciones Laborales' [Work and Labour Relations], in Carreras A. and Tafunell X. (eds), *Estadísticas Históricas de España. Siglos XIX–XX* [Spanish Historical Statistics], Madrid, 2005, 1155–1245.

Martí Escayol, M.A. *El Plaer de la Xocolata. La Història i la Cultura de la Xocolata a Catalunya* [The History and Culture of Chocolate in Catalonia], Valls, 2004.

McKeown, T. *The Modern Rise of Population*, London, 1976.

Mokyr, J. *The Gifts of Athena: Historical Origins of the Knowledge Economy.* Princeton, 2003.

Murcott, A. 'Scarcity in Abundance: Food and Non-Food', *Social Research* 66, 1999, 305–39.

Nicolau-Nos, R. and Pujol-Andreu, J. 'Urbanización y Consumo: La Ingesta de Proteínas Animales en Barcelona durante los Siglos XIX y XX' [Animal Protein Intake in Barcelona in the Nineteenth and Twentieth Centuries], *Investigaciones de Historia Económica* 3, 2004, 101–134.

Preston, S.H. 'The Changing Relation between Mortality and Level of Economic Development', *Population Studies* 20, 1975, 231–248.

Pujol-Andreu, J. 'Especialización Ganadera, Industrias Agroalimentarias y Costes de Transacción: Cataluña, 1880–1926' [Cattle Specialization, Agricultural Industry and Transactions Costs: Catalonia, 1880–1926], *Historia Agraria* 27, 2002, 192–219.

Pujol-Andreu, J. Gónzalez de Molina, M., Fernández Prieto, L., Gallego, D. and Garrabou, R., *El Pozo de Todos los Males: Sobre el Atraso de la Agricultura Española contemporánea* [On Constraints in Contemporary Spanish Agriculture], Barcelona, 2001.

Raventós, J. *L'Alimentació Humana* [Human Nutrition], Barcelona, 1923.

Rosenberg, N. *Exploring the Black Box: Technology, Economics, and History*, Cambridge, 1994.

Rossell I. Vilar. P.M. *El Problema de les Carns* [The Problem of Meat], Barcelona, 1921.

Segalà, M. *Lactancia Mercenaria de Barcelona* [Wet Nursing in Barcelona], Barcelona, 1899.

Teuteberg, H.J. (ed), *ICREFH I*, Leicester, 1992.

Chapter 5

Food Science/Food Politics: Max Rubner and 'Rational Nutrition' in Fin-de-Siècle Berlin

Corinna Treitel

Few of us have ever heard of the German physiologist Max Rubner (1854–1932), yet all of us eat, work, exercise, diet, and die in the bioenergetic world that he did so much to create. As a scientist, Rubner demonstrated experimentally in the 1880s and 1890s that the first law of thermodynamics governed living organisms. He also established calorific 'standard values' for basic foodstuffs that grounded nutritional planning throughout the twentieth century.[1] As a political actor, moreover, Rubner helped make the Calorie [kilocalorie in modern usage] central to the nutritional activities and calculations of social policy institutions that structure the modern world, including the welfare state.[2] It was Rubner's major achievement, in short, to establish food as the thermodynamic fulcrum on which the health of the individual and the collective alike rested.

But if Max Rubner helped create the calorific world in which we live, what of the world that created Max Rubner? This essay answers that question by exploring Rubner's activities as an urban progressive on the eve of the First World War.[3] These were the years in which he first articulated his project of 'rational nutrition' and began to put his scientific capital to work to change the way the German state managed the nutritional needs of the masses, particularly the urban poor. Indeed, Rubner's rational nutrition project was a scientific answer to an essentially political question then being asked in every industrialized country of the world: what was to be done about the revolutionary potential of the urban poor? By giving this question a nutritional answer, Rubner helped turn food into a meeting ground of science and the urban public sphere.

People's Nutrition Questions

The intertwining of modern nutrition science with political and economic questions has a long, complex, and under-researched history. Closely linked with the German

---

1   For a mixed diet Rubner used energy conversion factors as follows: 1 g protein = 4.1 kcals; 1 g fat = 9.3 kcals; 1 g carbohydrate = 4.1 kcals. See Rubner, 1902.

2   Leibfried, 1992.

3   Wildt, 1979; Fick, 1932; Rothschuh, 1970.

chemist Justus von Liebig (1803–1873), Liebig's student Carl Voit (1831–1908), and Voit's student Max Rubner, modern nutrition science took a chemical approach to diet by separating food into its component parts (protein, fats, carbohydrates, minerals, and water). Advocates argued that food should be eaten because it was nutritious rather than because it was traditional, tasted good, or looked appetizing. By the late nineteenth century, the new nutrition science regularly informed calls for political and economic reform. In 1895, for instance, the American chemist Wilbur O. Atwater (1844–1907), Voit's student and Rubner's close colleague, published an important series of studies for the United States Department of Agriculture in which he warned that unless Americans improved their diet, particularly the diet of the urban poor, national economic and moral decline would follow.[4]

In Germany, too, the new nutrition science quickly came to inform debate over the so-called 'social question' of what to do with the urban poor. Germany's educated middle classes (*Bildungsbürgertum*), including its scientists, feared that if they failed to find ways to integrate the industrial proletariat into the state, labour unrest and political revolution would follow. Given that food riots and widespread hunger had helped spark the revolutions of 1848 and that urban labour unrest often focused on issues of food price and supply, the political meanings of nutrition were not hard to discern.[5] This same bourgeois group, moreover, saw direct links between nutrition and questions of national efficiency and competitiveness. How much protein did industrial workers need to maintain maximum productivity? How much did soldiers require to achieve peak performance? In the event of a pan-European war, a possibility discussed with dread in the years before 1914, what were the absolutely minimal nutritional requirements below which civilian, industrial, and military populations could no longer function? By asking and answering such questions, leading scientists and doctors of the day, including Max Rubner, helped make nutrition central to issues of national identity and survival.[6]

From the late 1870s to the mid–1940s, the German debate over nutrition and the social question coalesced around the key concept of *Volksernährung,* or the 'people's nutrition'.[7] An important theme in this debate, in turn, concerned the question of how much and what kind of protein the human body required. Voit had framed this part of the debate between 1876 and 1881, when he set the daily protein minimum for an average working adult at 118 grams and threw his support behind Liebig's 'meat makes meat' thesis (i.e., that animal protein was a necessary nutrient for human health).[8] Very quickly, Voit's claims about protein and meat became the basis for numerous policy studies framed around the concept of *Volksernährung.* In 1880, for example, C. A. Meinert published a manual on popular nutrition entitled

---

4   Levenstein, 1988.

5   Gailus, 1994.

6   For nutrition science, see Kamminga and Cunningham, 1995. For mechanical conceptions of the human body, see Rabinbach, 1990.

7   Interest in *Volksernährung* exploded during the First World War as the Allied blockade pushed millions of Germans towards starvation. See, for instance, Eltzbacher, 1914, which contained an essay by Max Rubner; Winckel, 1915; Rubner, 1916a; 1916b; and *Abhandlungen zur Volksernährung* 1915– .

8   Voit, 1876, 1881.

The Army and People's Nutrition that drew heavily on Voit's work.[9] Both Rubner and Atwater initially supported Voit's protein recommendation as a daily minimum and Voit's standards also became the basis in 1902 for *On Changes in the People's Nutrition* by Alfred Grotjahn (1869–1931). Grotjahn, a socialist who later became one of Germany's leading eugenicists, focused on the links between household budgets and dietary patterns among urban working-class families, concluding that household budgets were so constrained as to produce chronic undernourishment among working families.[10]

Provoked in part by Grotjahn's 1902 study, whose social hygienic approach he strenuously opposed, Max Rubner began to weigh in on what he called the people's nutrition questions or *Volksernährungsfragen*.[11] Influenced by the experimental work of R.H. Chittenden (1856-1943), who recommended the reduction of protein requirements for a 70 kg man to 60 g per day, Rubner became convinced that it was possible to get by on much less protein than Voit had recommended.[12] How had urban living changed traditional eating patterns? What were the nutritional consequences of this shift? How and why should the state respond to these changes? How might physiologists contribute to the state's response? In answering these questions, Rubner acknowledged that much had already been done. In Germany, social legislation had established workplace safety rules, shorter work hours, and protections for working women and children, all of which had helped reduce mortality.[13] Specific measures such as workers' restaurants had emerged, moreover, to feed the hungry.[14] But, although the masses no longer starved, Rubner worried that neither had they yet learned to eat scientifically. Indeed, from a nutritional point of view, their diet was dangerously irrational and could do long-term damage to the health and wealth of the nation. To meet this danger, physiologists and economists should collaborate in the new century on a project of rational nutrition. This, in a nutshell, was the proposal Rubner developed between 1908 and 1913 in a series of high profile speeches and publications.[15]

Focused on the industrial labourers then migrating to large cities like Hamburg and Berlin, the project of rational nutrition was primarily an urban project that combined pessimism about the costs of industrial progress with optimism about the power of science, especially physiology, to minimize these costs. Rubner's pessimism manifested itself in his mantra that urbanization had done more harm

---

9   Meinert, 1880.

10   Grotjahn, 1902.

11   Rubner, 1908, 37-41, 69, estimated a worker's protein requirements ranged between 30 g and 118 g per day.

12   Chittenden, 1907, 272.

13   Rubner, 1913a, 385.

14   Rubner, 1908, 45.

15   Rubner gave two major lectures on the 'people's nutrition question' at the 14th International Congress for Hygiene and Demography (Berlin, September 1907). He published these the next year (Rubner 1908). In a plenary lecture delivered at the 15th International Congress on Hygiene and Demography (Washington, D.C., September 1912), he returned to this topic and his remarks were published both in English and, in expanded form, in German. See Rubner, 1913a, and Rubner, 1913b.

than good to the human body. Any hygienist touring the great European cities could verify that, although city folk were living longer, their bodily efficiency (*körperliche Kraft und Leistungsfähigkeit*) was diminishing. Indeed, this was as true of the urban bourgeoisie as of the working classes. The sedentary life- and work-style of the bourgeoisie had caused their muscular capacity (*muskuläre Leistung*) to plummet; were it not for sports, many would not know what to do with their muscles at all. For industrial workers mired in poverty, in contrast, the drop in bodily efficiency had a quite different set of causes. Although some fault lay with the increasing use of machinery and shortening of the working week, both of which decreased the demands put on workers' bodies, the main problem was chronic undernourishment, or what Rubner called 'the struggle for daily bread'.[16]

Confident in the unique ability of physiologists to illuminate this aspect of the social question, Rubner blamed the chronic undernourishment of urban industrial workers on what he called irrational nutrition and traced this to the ways that urban living tended to change diet for the worse. To make his point, Rubner imagined the hypothetical case of a peasant who moved to the city and took a less physically taxing job than he had had in the countryside. Having lightened his work load, the new urban dweller found that he could also lighten his diet. One option was to stick to his traditional low-meat diet, but eat less of it. Whereas in the countryside he ate 3,080g of potatoes per day, for a total intake of 54 g protein and 3,800 kcals [15,900 kj], in the city he reduced his potato intake to 2,400 g per day, for a total intake of 42 g protein and 2,400 kcals [10,042 kj]. By reducing a diet that had worked perfectly well in the countryside, the man came perilously close to dropping below the minimum levels of protein and energy needed to keep his body in good working order. Indeed, if his country diet had centred not on potatoes but rather on other traditional staples such as rice, bread, or cereals, a reduced diet dropped him into a state of undernourishment. But there was also a second option. Rather than reducing it, a new urban dweller might choose to change the composition of his diet by giving up his habitual vegetable foods to eat more meat. Meat was an excellent source of protein, but because it was expensive, and growing more expensive by the day, a typical worker could not buy enough meat to meet his protein and energy needs and still pay for his other living expenses.[17] Whichever option he chose, in short, the result was clear: the peasant-turned-industrial-labourer was in constant danger of ingesting either too little protein or too few kilocalories or both and thus ate a diet that was, from a nutritional point of view, irrational.

Rubner's analysis of nutritional irrationality was an iconoclastic reading of the changes that urbanization had brought to traditional food ways. Contemporary observers and historians alike have emphasized that the diet of urban workers had actually improved over the second half of the nineteenth century, when periodic bouts of famine, which had been a problem as recently as the 1840s, receded into memory. An older diet of legumes, rye bread, and potatoes gave way to a modern diet centred on meat, wheat bread, sugar, vegetables and fruits, and milk products like cheese. A variety of factors accounted for this 'nutritional revolution'. First, by

---

16 Rubner, 1913b, 3, 53–4, and 57–8.
17 Rubner, 1908, 116-7.

1900 or so, German workers had experienced a real rise in their standard of living, which meant that more of their household budget was available to purchase food. With more money in their pockets, German workers were also able to take advantage of the expanding urban food market, another important factor in the nutritional revolution. Cheap and readily available in small pieces that could be bought on a daily basis, precooked sausages and other kinds of ready-to-eat meats became particularly popular. The drop in sugar prices enabled workers to sweeten their diet and, although fresh green vegetables and fruits remained out of reach, most began to incorporate dried or preserved vegetables and fruits into their daily meals. The diet of urban workers may not have been 'balanced' according to our own standards, but the problem of chronic malnourishment had been definitively overcome.[18]

Rubner recognized these gains and did not deny their value, but insisted nonetheless that this nutritional revolution also had a dark side. Workers had access to a wider variety and greater abundance of foods, it was true, but they did not yet know how to make good use of what the city offered in order to eat a truly economical and adequately nourishing diet. Indeed, Rubner argued, there was a great deal of evidence that workers were doing just the contrary.[19] Eagerly adopting the urban 'cult of meat', for instance, they gobbled up all manner of sausages and meat-filled sandwiches from the many kiosks and vending machines now dotting the metropolitan landscape. Meat was a perfectly good food, Rubner acknowledged, but it became nutritionally irrational when its cost overwhelmed the tight budget of the working-class family.[20] To make matters worse, increased meat consumption also meant that city folk were eating ever more fat, either because they could only afford cheaper, fattier cuts of meat or because their meat-filled sandwiches came thickly spread with butter and margarine. Fat was expensive as well as satiating, which meant that workers who ate too much of it could end up in a state of undernourishment.[21] Urban alcohol consumption showed a similar pattern: as beer consumption increased, protein and caloric intake decreased. All of this led Rubner to bemoan the vicious circle in which the urban poor were locked. Yielding to the temptations of the city, they ate more meat and drank more alcohol, and in the process unknowingly robbed their bodies of protein and energy and thus decreased their physical health and bodily efficiency.[22]

What, then, did 'rational' mean in Rubner's rational nutrition project? It meant the merging of physiological and economic calculations about Marks, energy needs, and grams of protein, fat, and carbohydrate. In answer to the social question of what to do with the urban poor, it replied that modern states like Germany had the resources with which both to tame the unruly masses and achieve political greatness, if only energy intakes and financial resources were allocated and utilized properly.

---

18 Teuteberg in Conze and Engelhardt, 1981, 57–73.
19 Teuteberg, ICREFH IX. See also ICREFH VII, especially the essays by Hans Jürgen Teuteberg and Ulrike Thoms.
20 Rubner, 1908, 31–2, 46, and 129; Rubner, 1913b, 91–6.
21 Rubner, 1913b, 96–100.
22 Rubner, 1908, 118–24.

The Politics of Urban Diets

As an attempt to manage the health of populations scientifically, the rational nutrition project belongs to the history of biopolitics. Examined more closely as such, moreover, the rational nutrition project offers a useful corrective to the overemphasis scholars have put on the authoritarian tendencies of biopolitical practices in the twentieth century. Rubner's story also suggests ways in which European food historians might use biopolitics as a concept for linking their research to other branches of European history.

Understood as a set of ideas, institutions, and practices devoted to regulating health, welfare, and reproduction, biopolitics has been a central part of twentieth-century modernity. Targeted at collectivities (for instance nations), biopolitical practices have included public health campaigns to discourage smoking, social welfare programmes to promote higher (or lower) rates of reproduction among different social groups, industrial hygiene studies to optimize the working capacity of the human body, and racial hygienic or eugenic policies, including murder of the 'genetically unfit', to safeguard a group's hereditary material. All of these biopolitical practices aim to create a more powerful society by boosting efficiency through careful regulation of bodily health.

Following the lead of Michel Foucault, scholars have consistently linked biopolitics to the coercive aspect of twentieth-century states.[23] 'Social control', indeed, has been the overarching theme of scholarly work on biopolitics, nowhere more emphasized than in German history, where studies of Nazi eugenics and racial hygiene continue to pile up.[24] But do biopolitical practices always and only point to the authoritarian power of modern states? Here, the Rubner story can provide a useful corrective, for, although the rational nutrition project aimed at improving the diet of the urban poor through expert knowledge and state action, Rubner was in fact quite pessimistic about the power of the state to control or even change mass habits. When we attend closely to Rubner's words, moreover, his political leanings emerge less as authoritarian than as somewhere between socialist and laissez-faire liberal. Typically dismissed as a 'conservative' in the scholarly literature, Rubner might be better labelled a 'progressive': not in our left-leaning social democratic sense of the term, but in the early twentieth-century sense of bourgeois reformism.[25]

Max Rubner's progressivism manifests itself in at least three ways. First, he spoke the language of social modernity, a language that was simultaneously biological and economic in its emphasis on efficiency and performance.[26] In other words, if a rational diet could boost, a poor diet could wreak havoc with the performance of the individual and national body alike. Undernourished children, to take an important example that Rubner often used, would grow into physiologically malfunctioning workers and soldiers, whose care would sap national resources and diminish national

---

23 For the classic statement on biopolitics, see Foucault, 1980, 133–59.

24 For a useful review and critique of this literature, see Dickinson, 2004. For a classic statement on the coercive aspects of German medical science, see Labisch, 1985.

25 Eley and Retallack, 2003; Bruch, 1985.

26 Sarasin and Tanner, 1998; Aronson, 1982.

wealth and strength.[27] By comparison with public expenditure on sanitation, a small input of state finances to support, say, school lunch programmes would prevent the 'overdrawn account' and ground national productivity for years to come. In this sense, then, Rubner's rational nutrition project was an exercise in resource allocation, whether of energy (and protein) in the physiological budget of the body or of Marks in the financial budget of the wage-earning urban household. Nor, it is worth noting, was Rubner's message about efficiency simply an expression of German nationalism. When he gave the plenary lecture at the Fifteenth International Congress on Demography and Hygiene, held in Washington DC in September 1912, for instance, he urged all modern states to address the irrational nutritional habits of the urban proletariat.[28]

These remarks about the state point, then, to a second aspect of Rubner's progressivism: his criticism of laissez-faire liberalism and his call for the state to take social action. Why had nothing yet been done to address the dramatic changes in urban eating patterns? For Rubner, the answer lay with the ideology of free choice (*die bürgerlichen Freiheiten*) according to which individuals simply 'chose' to eat new foods upon migration to the city and were tacitly applauded for doing so. Left unattended, Rubner warned, this would have serious nutritional consequences. The service that nutrition science could now perform for the state, then, was to make this national malady visible and lay out guidelines for promoting the nation's physical welfare. Rubner also took direct aim at politicians who ignored the people's nutrition because they thought it impossible to guarantee the minimal income level needed to purchase nutritious foods. This, Rubner stated bluntly, was a layman's approach founded on ignorance; indeed, he warned, ignoring the problem would not make it go away. As urbanization proceeded, the nutritional problems of the masses would grow in tandem. 'The study of public nutrition', he concluded in 1908, 'is an extraordinarily important task; to promote this task is in the interest of the state'.[29]

Having admonished the state to pay attention, Rubner then proceeded to offer remedies. Overall, the priority must be to base social policy (*Sozialpolitik*) on a solid scientific foundation combining research from economics and physiology. While economists would attend to the system of food production and the analysis of how food costs related to the income levels of various social groups, physiologists like Rubner would study how the body converted food into energy, investigate ways of preserving food, explore how diets varied with social groups, and analyse popular eating habits to discern their significance for both health and nutrition.[30] Economists and physiologists would work together to study the nutritional aspects of urban poverty or, as Rubner put it, how best to 'feed those of little means' (*die Minderbemittelten*).[31]

---

27 Rubner, 1908, 48 and 137–40.
28 Rubner, 1913b, 24–8 and 133.
29 Rubner, 1908, 47 and 141.
30 Rubner, 1913b, 4.
31 Rubner, 1908, 51.

What Rubner had in mind was a wide range of programmes and institutions that would create and apply scientific knowledge directly to the problem of the people's nutrition. Rubner urged the state to:

- create a central Food Office (*Nahrungsamt*) to study mass nutrition systematically;
- establish workers' restaurants in the cities to provide low-cost nutritious meals, and / or move factories to the countryside, where food was cheaper and of better quality;
- promote housing reform by making rents cheaper (so that more of the household budget could go to purchase food) and redesign apartments to contain small kitchens (so that families could eat cheap and nutritious meals at home, rather than squandering money on unwholesome food purchased on the street);
- educate school-age children, especially girls (as future housewives), about the basic principles of hygiene and nutrition;
- set up school lunch programmes to deal with the problem of childhood undernutrition.[32]

What Rubner did *not* recommend was as significant as what he did and reflected the third aspect of his bourgeois progressivism: the assumption that the best way to head off social conflict was not through political or socio-economic change but by changing the environment and behaviour of urban workers themselves. He was sceptical that lowering meat prices or raising wages were sufficient or even necessary measures to solve undernutrition. Like most fin-de-siècle progressives, instead, Rubner emphasized that with rational management undertaken by the state in concert with scientific experts like himself, national efficiency could be maximized and social conflict minimized. Implicitly rejecting both the free-market faith of nineteenth-century liberalism and the Marxist claim that only by overthrowing capitalism would the war between capital and labour end, Rubner promised that rational nutrition would have a political payoff as well. 'A well nourished population', he observed simply, 'is easily governed'.[33] In a period of escalating conflict between workers and owners and against the backdrop of the 1912 election that made the Social Democratic Party the single largest party in the German *Reichstag*, it is impossible to view Rubner's rational nutrition project, couched so carefully in economic and biological terms, as anything but also a deeply political one.

But if Rubner's biopolitics were 'progressive' in the fin-de-siècle sense of the term, is it still not possible to discern an authoritarian intent embedded within this progressivism? Here, Rubner's hard-nosed realism about the practical limits of his project argues against such a conclusion.

For one thing, Rubner was deeply sceptical about the quest for 'norms'. He criticized previous approaches to the people's nutrition question for trying to define how much food was enough food by establishing what a 'normal diet' (*Normalkost*) was. This method failed to recognize that people varied in size, age, living condition,

32 Rubner, 1913b, 7, 71, 90, and 118–127; Rubner 1908, 88–90.
33 Rubner, 1908, 103–106 and 137.

and type of employment, and that what the masses ate was intimately related to local products and traditions. Rubner scoffed at the idea that there was any unitary *Normalkost* to be discovered. For similar reasons, he rejected simple answers to the other great 'normalizing' question of the fin de siècle: what was the minimum amount of protein required to sustain life? Not only did nutrition scientists not know the answer to this question yet, Rubner doubted that there would ever be an accurate answer good for all times and places. Although in theory the same chemical principles applied to the individual and the masses, in practice varied life- and work-styles meant that menus and quantities had to be adjusted to fit local needs and habits.[34]

Just as Rubner's appreciation for the complexity and importance of environmental factors made it impossible for him to embrace the quest for universal norms, he also shunned utopian thinking. Consistently, for example, Rubner expressed pessimism about the ability of his rational nutrition project to effect any rapid change in popular eating habits.[35] He also always distinguished between 'ideals' and practical realities. As he wrote on the eve of the First World War:

> The ideal of the people's nutrition must be to offer each person sufficient food and to organize earning opportunities so as to make it possible to keep the body normal and healthy. It is not my task to determine what social provisions must be made, but surely it would be utopian to want to find a social order that would be able to offer all people this end. In life one never accomplishes ideals because the conditions of life are never ideal.[36]

Rubner's pragmatism was sorely tested during the early days of the war, when his repeated warnings to the government about the necessity to plan for the nutritional needs of the nation went unheeded. During the war he joined other scientists in recommending a minimum of 127 g of protein per day for men in Germany's armed forces, rising to 165 g for men doing hard physical work. This high-protein, high-energy policy has been regarded as one possible cause of Germany's defeat in World War I. Whether or not Rubner and other German scientists should be criticized for their relative ineffectiveness in guiding food policy during the war has yet to be settled, though the charge has been levelled against them repeatedly since 1918.[37] What is certain, however, is that all wartime programmes for the rational nutrition of nations, whether German or other, expanded on what Rubner had learned and spoken about so tirelessly with regard to the pre-war nutritional errors and needs of the urban masses.

This, then, brings us back to biopolitics and our topic 'food and the city'. As a scientific response to the social question of what to do with the urban poor, the rational nutrition project was an important example of fin-de-siècle progressive biopolitics. In numerous lectures and publications bristling with calculations about the allocation of nutritional and financial resources in Germany's cities, Rubner

---

34 Rubner, 1908, 47 and 54–7; Rubner, 1913b, 60.
35 See, for example, Rubner, 1908, 56–7.
36 Rubner, 1913b, 23.
37 For example, see Teich in Kamminga and Cunningham, 1995, 229.

couched his analysis in the language of social modernity. Built on the cooperation of physiologists and economists, knowledge of rational nutrition, he promised, would create a more stable, powerful, and productive society. But, despite the grandness of his vision, Rubner did not offer a totalizing vision: he aimed to manage social problems, not eliminate them. By using the Rubner case as a model of how the city helped turn food into a biopolitical object, finally, European food historians might find new ways to link their research area to the larger agenda of European social and cultural history.

References

Aronson, N. 'Nutrition as a Social Problem: A Case Study of Entrepreneurial Strategy in Science', *Social Problems* 29, 1982, 474–87.

Abhandlungen zur Volksernährung [Papers on Human Nutrition], Berlin, Zentral Einkaufsgesellschaft m.b.H., 1915–.

Bruch, R. von (ed.), *Weder Kommunismus noch Kapitalismus: Bürgerliche Sozialreform in Deutschland vom Vormärz bis zur Ära Adenauer* [Neither Communism nor Capitalism: Bourgeois Social Reform in Germany from the Vormärz to the Adenauer Era], Munich, 1985.

Chittenden, R.H. *The nutrition of man*, Cambridge MA, 1907.

Conze, W. and Engelhardt, U. (eds), *Arbeiterexistenz im 19 Jahrhundert: Lebensstandard und Lebensgestaltung deutscher Arbeiter und Handwerker* [Workers' Lives in the Nineteenth Century], Stuttgart, 1981.

Dickinson, E.R. 'Biopolitics, Fascism, Democracy: Some Reflections on our Discourse about Modernity', *Central European History* 37, 2004, 1–48.

Eley, G. and Retallack, J. (eds), *Wilhelminism and its Legacies: German Modernities, Imperialism, and the Meanings of Reform, 1890–1930*, New York, 2003.

Eltzbacher, P. (ed.), *Die deutsche Volksernährung und der englische-Aushungerungsplan: eine Denkschrift* [The German People's Nutrition], Braunschweig, 1914.

Fick, R. 'Gedächtnisrede', *Sitzungsberichte der Preussischen Akademie der Wissenschaften* [Minutes of the Meeting of the Prussian Academy of Sciences], 1932, cxxviii–cxlvi.

Foucault, M. *The History of Sexuality, Volume 1: An Introduction*, New York, 1980.

Gailus, M. 'Food Riots in Germany in the Late 1840s', *Past and Present* 145, 1994, 157–93.

Grotjahn, A. 'Über Wandlungen in der Volksernährung' [On Changes in the People's Nutrition], in Schmoller, G. (ed.), *Staats- und Socialwissenschaftliche Forschungen* [State and Social Science Research], vol. 20, Leipzig, 1902.

Kamminga, H. and Cunningham, A. (eds), *The Science and Culture of Nutrition 1840–1940*, Amsterdam, 1995.

Labisch, A. 'Doctors, Workers and the Scientific Cosmology of the Industrial World: the Social Construction of "Health" and the "Homo Hygienicus"', *Journal of Contemporary History* 20, 1985, 599–615.

Leibfried, S. 'Nutritional Minima and the State: On the Institutionalization of Professional Knowledge in National Social Policy in the US and Germany', *Zentrum für Sozialpolitik-Arbeitspapier Nr. 10/92*, Bremen, 1992.

Levenstein, H. *Revolution at the Table: The Transformation of the American Diet*, New York, 1988.

Meinert, C.A. *Armee- und Volksernährung: Ein Versuch Professor C. von Voit's Ernährungstheorie für die Praxis zu Verwerthen* [Military and Civilian Nutrition], Berlin, 1880.

Rabinbach, A. *The Human Motor: Energy, Fatigue, and the Origins of Modernity*, Berkeley, 1990.

Rothschuh, K.E. 'Rubner, Max', in Gillespie, C. (ed.), *Dictionary of Scientific Biography* vol. XI, New York, 1970, 585–6.

Rubner, M. *Gesetze des Energieverbrauchs bei der Ernährung* [Laws of Energy Consumption in Nutrition], Leipzig, 1902.

Rubner, M. *Volksernährungsfragen* [Questions of Public Nutrition], Leipzig, 1908.

Rubner, M. 'The nutrition of the people', *Transactions of the Fifteenth International Congress on Hygiene and Demography* 1, Washington, DC, 1913. [1913a]

Rubner, M. *Wandlungen in der Volksernährung* [Transformations of Public Nutrition], Leipzig, 1913. [1913b]

Rubner, M. *Deutschlands Volksernährung im Kriege* [German Public Nutrition in Wartime], Leipzig, 1916. [1916a]

Rubner, M. *Volksernährung, Massenspeisung* [Public Nutrition, Mass Food Supply], Berlin, 1916. [1916b]

Sarasin, P. and Tanner, J. (eds), *Physiologie und Industrielle Gesellschaft: Studien zur Verwissenschaftlichung des Körpers im 19 und 20 Jahrhundert* [Physiology and Industrial Society], Frankfurt, 1998.

Teich, M. 'Science and Food during the Great War: Britain and Germany', in Kamminga and Cunningham, 1995, 213–34.

Teuteberg, H.J. 'Urbanization and Nutrition: Historical Research Reconsidered', chapter 2 in this volume.

Voit, C. 'Ueber die Kost in Öffentlichen Anstalten' [On the Food in Public Institutions], *Zeitschrift für Biologie* 12, 1876, 1–59.

Voit, C. 'Physiologie des Allgemeines Stoffwechsels und der Ernährung' [General Physiology of Metabolism and Nutrition], in Hermann, L. (ed.), *Handbuch der Physiologie* [Manual of Physiology] 6, Leipzig, 1881.

Wildt, S. 'Bemerkungen zu Max Rubners Tätigkeit als Ordinarius f. Hygiene an der Berliner Universität (1891-1908)' [Max Rubner's Activity as a Professor of Hygiene at Berlin University], *Wissenschaftliche Zeitschrift der Humboldt Universität zu Berlin, Mathematisch-Naturwissenschaftliche Reihe* 28, 1979, 301–7.

Winckel, M. *Krieg und Volksernährung* [War and Public Nutrition], Munich, 1915.

Chapter 6

How to Feed Three Million Inhabitants: Berlin in the First Years after the Second World War, 1945–1948

Jürgen Schmidt

Introduction

In the immediate post-war period the provision of food to German cities was tied into a network of connections laden with tension. First, paternalistic, municipal (or government) interventions were confronted with liberal-market economic approaches; second there were different forms of civil-societal involvement of the consumers themselves, and a strong affinity for regulation by the municipal authorities that made the consumers into objects of governmental activity. Third, guaranteeing supplies to the population remained linked to an aspect of power: the administration and the authorities saw themselves, on the one hand, honour-bound to supply the population in order to legitimate their rule; and, on the other hand, it was necessary to support market-economic forces. By contrast, consumers expected from the state and the community – in the spirit of a 'moral economy' – that their provisions should be secured at reasonable prices. As a whole, the complex interconnections between the state, the private sphere and the economy becomes clear in the food provision of cities.[1]

These problem areas remained in times of crisis. But they were overshadowed by one basic question that overarched everything else: 'how could the population be provided with sufficient and affordable foodstuffs?' This is the leading question of this essay too. A decision of general principles became apparent in the crises of the twentieth century. In times of national emergency, separate markets and limited trade routes the state and community authorities took over the direction and management functions. Entrepreneurial and economic decision-making processes had to adjust or subordinate themselves to governmental regulations. Although the power to decide on a course of action was only forcefully asserted in the First World War,[2] during the National Socialist rule the government intervened to direct and regulate consumption in the years preceding the war. In the agricultural sector, freedom of trade and the

---

1   Horowitz, Pilcher and Watts, 2005; for Berlin, see Lummel, 2001.
2   Cf. Wehler's 2003 summary, 57f. For more detail about food supply in World War I Berlin, see Davis, 2000; see also ICREFH II, 1994, especially the articles in Part 1, 7–53, and the article of M. Essmyr about food politics in Sweden during the World Wars.

market economy were annulled by three imperial laws (*Reichsgesetze*) in 1933. The *Reichsnährstand* 'took over the whole direction of production and sales, of retail prices and trade margins'.[3]

Under this rigid system of direction, combined with the ruthless plundering of the occupied areas, the government was able to maintain the supply of the population in Germany and Berlin – with a slow decline – well into the last year of the war. Those are the basic conditions, preconditions and past history under which the provisioning of Berlin between 1945 and 1949 must be viewed.

Agricultural Production and Municipal Self-Sufficiency

The supply structure of a large city like Berlin with more than four million inhabitants before 1939 brought with it many difficulties, even in times of peace and prosperity. But within an organization of people used to working with each other, and with established trade traditions, connections and channels, these were problems that were mastered in the modern large cities in the late nineteenth and early twentieth century. The self-provision of a city with agricultural products produced within its borders played only a very limited role in this supply system.

There was a worldwide nutritional crisis in the years directly following the war, and in 1946 'the entire food production in Europe only amounted to 36 per cent of the year 1938/39 while the index of agricultural production of wheat in the world in 1945 had sunk to a level of 69.3 per cent compared to 1934/38'.[4] As a result, the Allied occupation forces requested that the Berlin city authorities drastically increase their own production.

The degree to which Berlin was dependent on imports into the city can be shown clearly through the vegetables distributed. Only 20.7 per cent produced were within the city from September to December 1946, but even this would not have been achieved without subsidies. The provision of potatoes and grains was much less favourable. The delivery quota for the harvest of 1947 of around 15,000 tons of potatoes did not supply Berlin's needs for even one month.[5] In order to achieve higher degrees of self-provision, the city authority moved heaven and earth to allow city property to be used for agricultural use. The Allies formulated the key principles for this – in the Potsdam Accord. The abstract formulations in the Potsdam Accord were made concrete for Berlin in the 'Fallow-Land Ordinance' of October 15, 1945. There were no limits to production at the local level: sheep and goats grazed in the *Charlottenburger Schlosspark,* beet grew in the *Olivaer Platz,* parsley on the bicycle racetrack in *Weißensee,* and the interior area of the trotting race course in *Mariendorf*

---

3   Berghoff, in Gosewinkel, 2005; for the agrarian economy, see Corni and Gies, 1997; Wehler 2003, 701f.

4   Erker, 1990, 52.

5   Report from the *Magistrat*, main nutrition office, to the British Military Government, February 11, 1947, *Landesarchiv Berlin* (LAB), C-Rep. 101, Nr. 587. Between 1945 and 1947 the city needed an average of 40,000 to 45,000 tons of potatoes, 29,300 tons of breadgrains, 4,500 tons of other cereals, 4,400 tons of meat, 2,300 tons of sugar, 1,800 tons of salt, 1,400 tons of fat, 415 tons of surrogate-coffee per month, and 182,000 litres of milk per day.

was divided up and allocated to those interested in growing their own vegetables. In the spring of 1946 the educational film 'the resident of Berlin and his Fallow-Land Action' played in the cinemas. Despite all of the inventiveness and news of successes that grew up around the fallow-land action, we should not overlook the rather unsatisfactory results. Furthermore, the practical and administrative realization of the provisions of the fallow-land action started too slowly from the point of view of the Allies.

The results of agriculture in the city were thus ambivalent. As a whole, around 1,700 hectares were brought into cultivation in the course of the fallow-land action up to 1947 and the city was then able to provide almost half of its vegetables itself. By 1947 – also thanks to the fallow-land action – around 391,000 garden owners were growing vegetables for themselves without being required to hand them over to the government. But in regard to basic foodstuffs, such as potatoes and bread grains, both municipal agriculture and self-provisioning of households only played a subordinate role. These efforts in the 'asphalt province' – as the city councillor for nutrition, Gustav Klimpel, characterized Berlin – could not be more than an additional morsel in empty stomachs.[6]

The city was thus dependent on its surrounding countryside, had become a supplicant of the agricultural areas. The food that was allowed for in the supply plans of the Allies had to be acquired and contractually secured in tough negotiations because the administrative authorities in the production areas were primarily concerned with the provision of their own population. The farmers and residents of the delivery areas saw themselves subject in to part massive pressure to fulfil their delivery obligations and disadvantaged in comparison to the urban population. In the *Magistrat* meeting on November 26, 1945 Karl Maron referred drastically to the fact 'that the nutritional level in the country is considerably lower than in Berlin. There are ill feelings among the farmers out there against Berlin because Berlin eats up everything'.[7]

As the municipal self-provision was subject to narrow limits and agriculture in the supply areas could only produce around a thousand calories daily per capita, an important role in the provision for the city fell to the Allies.[8] The first years after the war cannot only be described as a time of occupation, but rather as an 'interaction between the victors and the conquered'.[9] The Soviet troops, who had the sole sovereignty in the entire city from May until the beginning of July, brought thousand of tons of food from troop supplies into the city, thereby securing survival on the meagre basis of rationing.[10] The Americans gave up the restrictive policy of food imports. Food reached Germany relatively quickly, above all at the instigation of Lucius D. Clay. It was a substantial component of the basic provision of the

---

6   Meeting of the *Magistrat* committee 'Agriculture and Gardening' on Sept. 26, 1945, LAB, B-Rep. 10 B, Acc. 1888, Nr. 528.

7   31. *Magistrat* meeting on November 26, 1945, in Hanauske, 1995, 647.

8   Trittel, 1999, 119.

9   Kleßmann, 2005, 5.

10 Keiderling, 1986, 54.

population of Germany and Berlin.[11] In 1947 the city commandant Howley fixed the value of the 400,000 tons of food that came from the USA to Berlin between July 15, 1945 and the middle of May 1947 at $84 million.[12]

Under the conditions of the post-war period 'feeding the multitude' meant above all the administration of hunger. There was a huge administrative apparatus behind the provision of the population, which employed, according to the account of Josef Orlopp, 'around 5,000 persons full-time in 1946'.[13] The main nutrition office (official name: Magistrate Department for Nutrition) was, among other things, responsible for the general administration of 'Agriculture, Gardening and the Office of Animal Husbandry', the supply of different foodstuffs, monitoring the stocks, statistics, invoicing and auditing, as well as transport. The leadership of the main nutrition office was characterized by a lack of personnel continuity in the first year after the end of the war. Parallel to this discontinuity, the administration ran by no means in well-ordered paths at the beginning. In view of the countless responsibilities and different levels that had to be coordinated – between the Allies, the main nutrition office, the district offices, wholesale distributors and retail stores – this was not surprising. In addition, they were faced with the fact that there was a different situation in each district. While wholesale distributors were permitted to operate again relatively early in *Wilmersdorf*, *Prenzlauer Berg* went its own way and eliminated the wholesale distributors entirely for the time being.[14] It took time until the many parts of the administrative structure, from the city councillor to the head of the rationing card office, had stabilized themselves and contributed decisively to distributing the scarce foodstuffs relatively fairly to the population.

The three-tier agricultural production (municipal self-provision, supplies from the agrarian areas, Allied relief shipments), as well as the many parts of the administrative system, formed the base conditions on which the economy, the consumers and the legitimation of the representatives of government were dependent.

Governmental Regulation of Production: The Role of the Food-Processing Industry in the Provision of the City

The food-processing industry suffered as a result of a production crisis in the agrarian sector. Companies like the meat product factory, *Hanka*, could have easily expanded their production directly after the end of the war, but there was a lack of raw materials for the factories.[15] The Berlin slaughterhouse, on the other hand, was only partially operational due to serious war damage. In addition, there were conflicts between the slaughterhouse director and the large-scale butchers about the

---

11 Rohrbach, 1955, 251.

12 *Der Tagesspiegel*, May 23, 1947.

13 Orlopp, 1947, 7.

14 Report of the nutrition office, *Prenzlauer Berg*, May 2, 1945–January 31, 1946, LAB, C-Rep. 134/8, Nr. 1.

15 Meat products factory *R. Hanka*, writing to the borough mayor of *Weißensee*, June 2, 1945, *Heimatarchiv Weißensee*.

organization of the slaughterhouse, which lasted until the spring of 1946 and led to 'considerable disturbances in carrying out the process of slaughtering'.[16]

The fact that craft, small business, and decentralized structures still strongly characterized the food industry was a certain advantage for the provision of the city.[17] As the large industrial factories were severely limited through destruction of their premises, a basic provision could be maintained for the time being by the small businesses. Josef Orlopp determined for the period directly after the war:

> the bread factories were at a standstill. In this time of emergency the bakery trade earned a glorious chapter in the history of Berlin. The bakeries worked day and night with the help of antifascists to at least be able to give the residents of Berlin bread.[18]

Despite all the hymns of praise – the bakers had to deal with extremely tangible problems. The baking quotas set by the Soviets immediately after the end of the war could only be met with difficulty by the bakers.[19] With a quota of 150 per cent for rye flour – that is from one kilogram of flour 1.5 kilogram of bread must be baked – and 140 per cent for wheat flour, they had to use high-quality flour, which, however, could not be delivered in sufficient quantities. Either the results of baking remained under the quotas or the bread contained a high water content and thus spoiled more easily. The debate about the lowering of the baking quotas ran through all committees and authorities. The baking quota remained unchanged, however.

Under the conditions of rationing they not only determined how the bakers should bake, but also what they would bake. The apportionment of rolls was thus always a good topic for a newspaper article and was even used as a weapon in the East-West conflict.[20] The struggle over baking cakes was more than just a marginal note in the history of the provisioning of Berlin.[21] It was an expression of the will to fight for individual freedoms under the strict regulations of control that would secure a better source of income for the producers and give the consumers a little diversion from the daily monotony – perhaps also a bit of regained normality.

In the interests of consumers, the main nutrition office endeavoured to ensure the quality of the allocated foodstuffs. All products were subject to the food quality laws, many of which had been in force for decades; but additional quality criteria appeared necessary under these exceptional conditions, in order to reassure consumers.[22]

---

16 *75 Jahre Vieh- und Schlachthof Berlin*, 1956.

17 Lenger, 1988, 174–6.

18 Orlopp, 1947, 5. According to a letter to Lord Mayor Werner on August 7, 1945 there were 2,344 middle-sized bakeries and 68 bread factories operating (LAB, C-Rep. 101, and Nr. 559).

19 Protocol of the conference of the borough mayors, June 20, 1945, LAB, F-Rep. 280, Nr. 3829; memorandum, No. 70 of a meeting in the Soviet *Kommandantura*, August 13, 1945, LAB, C-Rep. 113, Nr. 1, fol. 88–93.

20 Cf. *Berliner Zeitung*, March 19, 1947; *Der Tagesspiegel*, February 24, 1948.

21 Circular of the borough office *Wedding*, nutrition office, February 5, 1948, LAB, B-Rep. 203, Acc. 919, Nr. 5109.

22 Fifth meeting of the committee for food industry, January 25, 1946, LAB, B-Rep. 10B, Acc. 1888, Nr. 736; 9th meeting of the committee for food industry, February 26, 1946, ibid.

With the end of the rationing system after 1949, new problems emerged for the food-processing industry. First, producers from the Western zones pressed into the Berlin market, second, the East German factories began to offer less expensive bread and other foodstuffs and, third, with the free sale of their products, the bread factories acted in the grey area between the black market and the free economy. Added to this came the fact that the buying habits of the consumers changed rapidly and products like canned meat became difficult to sell. The call for subsidies in agriculture and in the food-processing industry thus became increasingly loud.

Consumers' Initiatives and Self-Organization by Civil Society?

The three million inhabitants of Berlin in the post-war period did not simply allow themselves to be fed as a submissive multitude.[23] The consumers developed individual strategies of action; they acted as subjects and did not allow themselves to be degraded to the status of objects.[24] Theoretically, three possibilities presented themselves: first, they could secure their individual share of the food outside of government allocations; second, they could attempt to force an improvement in the provision through protests; and third, there was the possibility of strengthening their position by organizing consumer interests in the regulated market. In practice, only the first strategy was viable: the organization of consumer interests did not prove to be very successful under the conditions of occupation and production shortages.[25]

In contrast to the cities in the Ruhr area, protests failed to materialize in Berlin. On the one hand, it was easier for the residents of West Berlin to accept the western Allies, as they were seen as protection against the Soviets; on the other hand protests also failed to materialize because Berlin was better provided for than other large cities.[26]

The individual supplementary provision beyond the regulating state and regulated market remained as the variant with the most chance of success. Many possibilities presented themselves here. Both legal and illegal methods were open to consumers. On the one hand, vegetables from the woods and the fields as well as the garden plots offered a bit of variety.[27] At any rate, around 12 per cent of the population of Berlin

23 The number of inhabitants increased from about 2.9 millions in July 1945 to 3.3 millions in June 1948.

24 For the relation between civil society and consumption, see Trentmann, 2001.

25 Protocol of the conference of the district mayors on September 28, 1945, LAB, F-Rep. 280, Nr. 3837; Kluge, 2001, 234.

26 This last argument held true only to a limited extent for the French sector as they had the most problems with provisioning among the western sectors (see Führe, 2001). The *Berliner Zeitung* gave an overview about the foodstuffs delivered between January 1 and January 20, 1948. In accordance with this data, Berlin inhabitants received one kilogram more bread per capita than did the inhabitants of Leipzig and Dortmund, two kilograms more than did inhabitants of Bielefeld and Hanover and nearly four kilograms more than did inhabitants of Freiburg; *Berliner Zeitung*, January 23, 1948 (because of the different rationing systems it is difficult to compare the figures). See in general Gries, 1991.

27 Added to this came further possibilities for supplemental provision, like school lunches, factory lunches or aid packages, which were dependent on the allocation practices of

grew food in their garden in 1947. On the other hand, there were the dark channels of the black market and the tedious foraging trips into the countryside.

The black market transactions were of particular importance in two respects. On the one hand, they fulfilled a central function in the organization of additional food. According to estimates in 1948, between one-fifth and one-third of the products – based on the entire agricultural production – went into the black market. This meant that in the western zones, 150 calories per person daily were available from these sources on the black market.[28] How realistic these figures are is uncertain. According to a survey in the American and British sectors of Berlin for example, 53 per cent of those questioned said that they could procure additional food. Only 15 per cent of them bought this food on the black market, though.[29] Although we can assume that the first figures are too high and the second clearly too low, we should not lose sight of the fact that the black market, with its exorbitant prices, was in fact only an option for procuring food for part of the population of the city. Those whose homes had been destroyed and the many refugees remained almost entirely excluded from this market due to the lack of objects to exchange.

That is why, on the other hand, the black market was morally a highly loaded 'institution' that burdened and split urban society. With the 'morality of a thousand calories', those who could afford it justified their black market transactions, attempted to get things that were missing for exorbitant prices or in exchange for other highly desired goods. Consumers grew to know market mechanisms in this distorted form.[30] The parties and politicians repeatedly appealed to the people to stay away from the black market transactions, as the black marketeers were said to be the only winners in these dealings.[31] But, while the large-scale black marketeer was built up into an image of an enemy, the personal involvement of individuals in this market mechanism was trivialized and repressed.[32] Hunger confused feelings of morality and justice. Hunger-related criminality became a mass phenomenon in which the moral borders could not be drawn clearly. In his sermon on New Year's Eve 1946, Cardinal Frings in Cologne suspended the seventh commandment 'thou shalt not steal!' when there was no other way to secure one's life: 'we are living in times where the individual in need should be allowed to take what he cannot get in any other way, through work or by pleading.'[33] This offence went into the vernacular of the post-war era as *Fringsen*.

The black market was fed by many different sources.[34] First, goods came from the depots of the Allies and members of the occupying powers took part in black market

---

the government offices or assistance organizations, though. After the introduction of school lunches without rationing coupons, for which the Allies provided additional food, around 90 per cent of the school children in all of the districts took part in the school lunch programme.

28 Stüber, 1984, 608. These were very rough estimates.

29 Merritt and Merritt, 1970, 96ff.

30 See in detail Erker, 1990, 135ff.

31 12th meeting of the city council assembly (*Stadtverordnetenversammlung*) on January 23, 1947, 4–8; 31st meeting on May 29, 1947, *Protokolle 1946-1948*, 52–68.

32 See the poem by Erich Kästner, *Der Schieber*, 1947, quoted in Müller, 1993, 122.

33 Quoted in Boelcke, 1986, 175.

34 See Boelcke, 1986, 138.

transactions – either in small, private dealings or large-scale criminal activities.[35] Food came, second, from undelivered farmers' consignments to the market. Third, numerous material assets from private owners were brought on to the black market or surplus produce was offered.[36] Fourth, much of the food that was offered on the black market came from burglaries carried out by organized bands. Although the buyers on the black market came at least indirectly in contact with these criminal doings – that no longer had anything to do with *Fringsen* – they ignored them with the 'morality of a thousand calories'.

Hoarding, a common tactic of procuring additional food, was illegal but generally not prosecuted.[37] But this form of survival technique was a double-edged sword. Just when someone had spent a lot of time and effort to travel to a farm in the country as far from Berlin as possible, and where there was the least competition possible, such supplies were often confiscated at police checkpoints when returning to the city.[38] In her study that resulted from direct observation, Hilde Thurnwald came to the conclusion that the 'expenditure of time and energy' on hoarding 'was disproportionately great'.[39] Nevertheless hoarding remained widespread in the post-war years and the state government of Mecklenburg was still warning against foraging trips there in the autumn of 1948.[40]

'Feeding the multitude' thus found supplements in addition to the official allocation practice in the individual strategies of the consumers themselves for dealing with the scarcity. This behaviour proved to be extremely ambivalent. On the one hand, the consumers got to know the market economy with all its chances, risks and drawbacks and saw that they could not depend on the state and the administration alone and that initiative and involvement paid off. On the other hand, the practices were aimed at selfish interest and not the common good. They were widely practised, but remained individual, isolated actions that were not directed at organizing or 'socializing' consumers. These actions can thus not be characterized as civil-societal involvement, as this behaviour ran contrary to normative core elements of the concept of civil society.[41]

---

35 Weekly report of the criminal investigation department, October 27–November 3, 1945, LAB, C-Rep. 303/9, vol. 241, fol. 88.

36 Diary of F. v. Göll, LAB, E-Rep. 200–43, Acc. 3221, Nr. 90 (Diary entry from June 24, 1946).

37 Gries, 1991, 107f.; *Berliner Zeitung*, October 27, 1946. The fact that allowing or prosecuting hoarding was also dependent on political considerations was shown by Gries, ibid., 108. See also the references regarding to measures against hoarding, *Bundesarchiv Berlin*, SAPMO-DDR, DY 30/IV 2/7, Nr. 269.

38 *Berliner Zeitung*, March 9, 1947; *Der Tagesspiegel*, June 11, 1947.

39 Thurnwald, 1948, 50.

40 Press release, September 9, 1948, LAB, C-Rep. Nr. 132.

41 Schmidt, 2004; Gosewinkel et. al., 2005.

Concluding Remarks

'Feeding the multitude' was brought about by the interplay between agricultural production, administrative action, private economic initiative, private commitment and Allied help. An alternative to the regulated system for providing Berlin (and the country) was not in sight. Rationing and regulation of the market was also to the fore in the victor countries. In Great Britain the trend toward regulation was even increased after the end of the Second World War.[42] Crisis management that was based on deregulation and liberalization was not a priority. As it became apparent that the provision crisis was contained, more and more observers called for breaking out of the rigid provision system. The spread and in part toleration of 'grey' half-legal markets in post-war Berlin are an indication of this development. On the other hand, a subvention mentality became lastingly entrenched through the rationing system, which was further strengthened by the isolated situation of Berlin.

In addition, the relationship to the western occupying forces attained a new quality in the East-West conflict and after the blockade. They were seen as guarantees of a progressive increase in prosperity and democratic, liberal conditions. The solving of the problem of how to feed millions of people in a city under the conditions of a blockade led to an approval for a western form of democracy and liberalism.

Although the provisioning of Berlin was mostly successful, except for the far-reaching experience of the hunger winter of 1946/47,[43] hunger remained as an experience in the collective consciousness. This privation was compensated for in the 1950s and 1960s, when there was not a 'wave of gluttony' but rather the development of a culturally and socially differentiated consumer behaviour. As a whole, the two poles of the 'hunger years' and the 'economic miracle' became founding myths of the Federal Republic of Germany.[44]

References

Berghoff, H. 'Methoden der Verbrauchslenkung im Nationalsozialismus' [Methods of Consumption Control under National Socialism], in Gosewinkel, D. (ed.), *Wirtschaftskontrolle und Recht in der nationalsozialistischen Diktatur* [Economic Control and Law under the National Socialist Regime], Frankfurt am Main, 2005, 281–316.

Boelcke W.A. *Der Schwarzmarkt 1945–1948* [The Black Market], Braunschweig, 1986.

---

42 Zweiniger-Bargielowska, 2003.

43 In his diary Franz von Göll gives a precise description of the development of the provision of food in Berlin. He wrote, for example, on January 1, 1948: 'the situation for the provision of food is still serious, but not as catastrophic as it was some time ago. In the meantime, there have been perceptible improvements, but rations are still insufficient' (LAB, E-Rep. 200–43, Acc. 3221, Nr. 90).

44 Wildt, 1994; Gries, 2005, 16–17.

Corni, G. and Gies, H. *Brot – Butter – Kanonen. Die Ernährungswirtschaft in Deutschland unter der Diktatur Hitlers* [Bread – Butter – Cannons], Berlin, 1997.

Davis, B.J. *Home Fires Burning: Food, Politics, and Every Day Life in World War I Berlin*, Chapel Hill, NC, 2000.

Erker, P. *Ernährungskrise und Nachkriegsgesellschaft. Bauern und Arbeiterschaft in Bayern 1943–1953* [Nutrition Crisis and Postwar Society], Stuttgart, 1990.

Führe, D. *Die Französische Besatzungspolitik in Berlin von 1945 bis 1949: Déprussianisation und Décentralisation* [French Occupation Policy in Berlin 1945–1949], Berlin, 2001.

Gosewinkel, D., Rucht, D., Daele, W. van den and Kocka, J. (eds) *Zivilgesellschaft: National und Transnational* [Civil Society], Berlin, 2005.

Gries, R. *Die Rationen-Gesellschaft. Versorgungskampf und Vergleichsmentalität: Leipzig, München und Köln nach dem Kriege* [The Rationed Society], Münster 1991.

Gries, R. 'Mythen des Anfangs' [Myths of the Beginning], *Aus Politik und Zeitgeschichte*, 18-19/2005, 12–18.

Hanauske, D. (ed.), *Die Sitzungsprotokolle des Magistrats der Stadt Berlin 1945/1946, I: 1945* [Minutes of the Meeting of Municipal Authorities of the City of Berlin], Berlin, 1995; *II: 1946*, Berlin, 1999.

Horowitz, R., Pilcher, J.M. and Watts, S. 'Meat for the Multitude: Culture in Paris, New York City, and Mexico City over the Long Nineteenth Century', *American Historical Review* 109, 2005, 1055–1083.

Keiderling, G. *Berlin 1945–1986. Geschichte der Hauptstadt der DDR* [Berlin 1945–1986. History of the Capital of the GDR], Berlin, 1986.

Kleßmann, C. 'Konturen einer integrierten Nachkriegsgeschichte' [Outline of an Integrated Postwar History], *Aus Politik und Zeitgeschichte* 18–19, 2005, 3–11.

Kluge, U. 'Die Krisen der Lebensmittelversorgung 1916–1923 und 1945–1950' [Crises in the Food Supply], in Zimmermann, C. (ed.), *Dorf und Stadt. Ihre Beziehungen vom Mittelalter bis zur Gegenwart* [Village and Town], Frankfurt am Main, 2001, 209–239.

Lenger, F. *Sozialgeschichte der deutschen Handwerker seit 1800* [Social History of German Craftsmen since 1800], Frankfurt am Main, 1988.

Lummel, P. 'Sauber, schnell und kundennah. Die Entstehung der Lebensmittelindustrie und des modernen Kleinhandels in Berlin' [The Development of the Food Industry and of Modern Retail Trade in Berlin], in Museumsverbund des Landes Brandenburg e. V. (eds), *Ortstermine. Stationen Brandenburg-Preußens auf dem Weg in die moderne Welt* [Stages of Brandenburg-Prussia on its Way to the Modern World], Berlin, 2001.

Der Magistrat berichtet... Aus der Arbeit des Jahres 1948, Ernährung von Stadtrat Paul Fuellsack [Municipal Authority Report ... From the Work of 1948, Nutrition], Berlin, 1948, 82–95.

Merritt, A. and Merritt, R.L. (eds), *Public Opinion in Occupied Germany: The OMGUS Surveys, 1945–1949*, Urbana, 1970.

Müller, F. *Die Verwaltung des Hungers 1945–1948. Eine Dokumentation der Arbeit des Regional Food Office* [The Administration of Hunger 1945–1948], Kiel, 1993.

Orlopp, J. *Im Kampf gegen den Hunger* [The Fight against Hunger], Berlin, 1947.

Protokolle der Stadtverordnetenversammlung von Groß-Berlin 1946/1948 [Minutes of the Council of Greater Berlin], Berlin 1946–1948.

Rohrbach, J. *Im Schatten des Hungers. Dokumentarisches zur Ernährungspolitik und Ernährungswirtschaft in den Jahren 1945–1949* [In the Shadow of Hunger], Schlange-Schoeningen, H. (ed.), Hamburg, 1955.

Schmidt, J. *Zivilgesellschaft und nichtbürgerliche Trägerschichten. Das Beispiel der frühen deutschen Arbeiterbewegung (ca. 1830–1880)* [Civil Society and Non-Middle Class Actors], WZB Discussion Paper, Berlin, 2004.

Stüber, G. *Der Kampf gegen den Hunger 1945–1950. Die Ernährungslage in der Britischen Zone Deutschlands, insbesondere in Schleswig-Holstein und Hamburg* [The Fight against Hunger 1945–1950], Neumünster, 1984.

Thurnwald, H. *Gegenwartsprobleme Berliner Familien. Eine soziologische Untersuchung an 498 Familien* [Present Problems of Berlin Families], Berlin, 1948.

Trentmann, F. 'Bread, Milk and Democracy: Consumption and Citizenship in Twentieth-Century Britain', in Daunton, M. and Hilton, M. (eds), *The Politics of Consumption: Material Culture and Citizenship in Europe and America*, Oxford 2001, 129–163.

Trittel, G.J. 'Ernährung' [Nutrition], in Benz, W. (ed.), *Deutschland unter Alliierter Besatzung 1945–1949. Ein Handbuch* [Germany Under the Allies 1945–1949], Berlin, 1999, 117–123.

Wehler, H-U. *Deutsche Gesellschaftsgeschichte, vol. 4: Vom Beginn des Ersten Weltkriegs bis zur Gründung der beiden deutschen Staaten 1914–1949* [A History of German Society], München, 2003.

Wildt, M. *Am Beginn der 'Konsumgesellschaft'. Mangelerfahrung, Lebenshaltung, Wohlstandshoffnung in Westdeutschland in den fünfziger Jahren* [At the Beginning of the Consumer Society], Hamburg, 1994.

Zweininger-Bargielowska, I. *Austerity in Britain: Rationing, Controls, and Consumption, 1939–1955*, Oxford, 2003.

Part B
Food Regulation

Chapter 7

Food Fraud and the Big City: Brussels' Responses to Food Anxieties in the Nineteenth Century

Peter Scholliers

With the words, 'Gentlemen, the *Collège* believes that it is essential that a chemist is attached to the administration of the town of Brussels, to repress as much as possible of the adulteration that occurs in foodstuffs',[1] the Mayor of Brussels in April 1856 proposed the establishment of a laboratory for food analysis. His proposal was accepted, and a municipal laboratory was set up, which still functions today. As far as I can tell, this is one of the first municipal laboratories in Europe.[2] I will consider its history (accomplishments, status, and problems) up to 1914, questioning its role in matters of food safety, product quality and fair trade. Until recently, such research would have chiefly focused on health matters related to food falsification that appeared through the violation of (nationwide) laws or (municipal) regulations.[3] Such violation occurred very regularly, and historians labelled the nineteenth century as the golden age of food falsification.[4] This focus is relevant and connects to present-day concerns about food safety. However, recent literature has commented that nineteenth-century food control was also about correct price and competition, protectionism, producers' interests, product classification, quality norms, and relations between the state and private interests.[5] It also stresses the fact that norms (of trade, quality or classification) and codification were the outcome of power relations, and therefore were adaptable to different times and places. My narration of the Brussels food control system oscillates between concerns about health, trade, and social monitoring, emphasizing the social dimension. The leading part, however, is played by the city of Brussels, as I intend to question its role as an innovator and model in the field of food control. Hence, the emphasis of this chapter will be on this city's discourses and practices (and not on those of manufacturers, lobby groups or consumers).

---

1   *Bulletin Communal*, 1856, I, 294.
2   See chapters 8 and 9 by Stanziani and Oddy in this volume.
3   See for example Hietala, 1994, and Teuteberg, 1994.
4   Darquenne, 1986, 39; Ferrières, 2002, 370.
5   French and Phillips, 2000, 1–10; Bruegel and Stanziani, 2004, 7–16. Law, 2003, focuses entirely on the market.

Capital Problems

The city of Brussels, with only 66,000 inhabitants around 1800, acquired political weight when it became a part-time capital of the United Kingdom of the Netherlands in 1815, and a full-time capital with Belgium's independence in 1830. Along with its thriving political role, Brussels regained industrial, financial, cultural and social importance. The city had a complex population pattern, with a growing (petty) bourgeois component. Moreover, the capital cherished a liberal reputation that attracted many Belgians and foreigners of diverse rank. Its cosmopolitan ambition can be detected through the frequent organization of international meetings and world exhibitions.[6] The population of the city grew rapidly, reaching 124,000 in 1846 and 177,000 in 1910, i.e. a dramatic growth rate up to 1850. With fast expanding industrial and residential suburbs (which kept their own administrative status), the conurbation's population grew from 211,000 around 1850 to 756,000 in 1910. Brussels evolved into a significant city, which the local leading circles loved to promote and underline.[7] The following view that Dr Eugène Janssens, chief registrar, expressed in 1871 should be understood within this context: 'Can we allow to hang over Brussels a reputation of unhealthiness that it has acquired? That seems impossible to me'.[8] It was inconceivable that the Belgian capital could have a bad reputation.

Janssens' anxiety referred to the fact that Brussels' many narrow streets with their small houses were inadequate for accommodating the growing mass of inhabitants. In the first half of the century, this had resulted in doubled rents, a sharper social-spatial segregation, flight of the richer people to newly developed suburbs, and a deterioration of housing conditions for the poorer classes.[9] The overcrowding in particular districts had immediate implications for health conditions. As in many other European cities, Brussels found itself invaded with filth. This gave way to repeated epidemics that swept throughout all districts (e.g. cholera in 1831, 1848, 1854, 1859 and, again, 1866), with particularly high losses in the poorer quarters. Janssens declared in 1871 that the Brussels' average death rate (27 per thousand) was above that of London or Paris, which to him implied that Brussels should expand its sanitary efforts.[10] In the same year, the idea of a *Bureau d'hygiène* was launched in the Brussels city council, and in May 1874 this bureau was founded to co-ordinate all efforts against 'insalubrity'.[11]

In previous decades, local physicians, administrators, journalists and politicians discussed problems that had become much more pressing than in the eighteenth century, such as water supply and drainage, stench, housing conditions, slaughterhouses, public urinals, or cemeteries. This concern was part of a broader anxiety that addressed also somewhat more covert problems, such as alcohol

---

6   Scholliers, 2001, 506–9.

7   Since the 1830s, the capital was represented as 'une grande ville', 'une ville très importante' or 'une ville de première ordre'.

8   Janssens, 1871, 2.

9   Van den Eeckhout, 1990, 71–2, 85, 99.

10   Janssens, 1871, 10.

11   Martin, 1890, 1.

misuse, child labour, asylums, prostitution, or personal hygiene.[12] To discuss and advise on such matters, the *Conseil central de salubrité publique de Bruxelles* was established in 1836,[13] followed by the *Commission centrale des comités locaux de salubrité de l'agglomération bruxelloise* (1863). At the national level, the *Académie royale de médecine* (1841) and the *Conseil supérieur d'hygiène* (1849), with many representatives from Brussels, advised the government on health matters. Also, international meetings, that brought together the most eminent hygienists from Europe, were organized in Brussels from 1850.

A mixture of morality, anxiety, and commercial virtue emerged from the debates within these organizations. Partly because of this discourse, some legislation was enacted, the existing crude statistics elaborated, and minor interventions made in the city's infrastructure in the 1830s and 1840s. After 1850, these people became more influential and significant action was taken, such as large-scale clearance works (without, however, building new working-class dwellings), the construction of modern sewer systems, and major vaccination campaigns. Actual sanitary problems probably did not differ in Brussels from other European cities. Yet, the Brussels leading circles wished to act according to the status of a capital, i.e. as the prime mover in the battle against *insalubrité*, and to emulate achievements in metropolises like London and Paris.

Innocent and Dangerous Food Frauds

The hygienists and their predecessors had included food fraud in their many interests since the 1800s. This, of course, was not new: corporations and communes in the *Ancien Régime* had also decreed food regulations.[14] With the annexation of the Southern Netherlands to France in 1794, these regulations were abolished, but new laws for repressing food fraud came into being. A clear definition of fraud, however, was lacking.[15] Laws in 1810, 1829 and 1836 refined and enlarged the 1790s legislation by specifying the notion of addition of dangerous or poisoned products, by penalising both the production *and* sale of falsified goods, by allowing chemists to assist police officers, or by letting policemen investigate all places at all times. So, theoretically this set of laws guaranteed a fierce struggle against food fraud.

In practice, the main concern then was food scares and fair trade, and not so much health or the (pure) quality of the product. This is illustrated by the fact that the addition of field beans (*féverole*) to flour was regarded as an infraction but not as a danger, and hence it was generally dealt with in a mild way. The yearly report of the Mayor of Brussels to his council in 1855, demonstrated this: 'Although dangerous frauds were not discovered, we nevertheless noted that a great quantity of wholewheat flour was mixed with field beans. Many warnings were given'.[16] So, warnings were given and no fines imposed, and this report explicitly mentioned

---

12 All this is well documented in Bruneel, 1998, 21–6, and Velle, 1998, 130–5.
13 Referring to the Paris example, La Berge, 1992, 147.
14 Ferrières, 2002, 88–92.
15 Kestens, 1990, 58.
16 Bulletin Communal, 1855, II, 149.

that no *dangerous* frauds had been detected. This (theoretical) divide between *safe* and *dangerous* frauds, and the concern about fair trade, appears in several events reported in the Brussels *Conseil de salubrité publique*. In 1840, for example, bread was suspected of containing copper sulphate (used to mask spoiled flour), and this was confirmed in analysis by the *Commission d'analyse chimique*, created by the *Conseil* in 1838. The report noted that there was indeed copper sulphate in the bread, but 'in such a small quantity that it could not be said to be bread that was dangerous or harmful to health'.[17] Neither the *Conseil de salubrité* nor the *Commission d'analyse chimique* questioned the origin of the sulphate, nor the quality of the (possibly spoiled) bread.

Another episode in the same year reveals the complex issues at stake.[18] A Mr. Kopzcynski, a pharmacist, analysed samples of bread. He did not find sulphate but rather the addition of spurred rye, which would explain the many gastric-intestinal illnesses of the day. His investigation was commented upon in a newspaper and in a leaflet, which caused some anxiety in the city. The *Conseil de salubrité* saw it as its duty to check Kopzcynski's findings, to 'reassure the public', and eventually, 'to remove concerns produced by the publication of erroneous assertions, and to defend the interests of the bakers, wrongfully accused'. Mention of the old fear of rumours with regard to bread supply and quality,[19] the belief that official action may mitigate the public's food fears, and the fact that the *Conseil* (an authoritative body) should eventually defend the bakers of Brussels, show that health was not the prime motivation in setting up the *Commission d'analyse chimique*. It is, however, difficult to make a clear division between fair trade and health, in that contemporary concerns about fair trade included a social dimension in two ways. Good health of the worker was evoked as a tool that would provide him with a decent income; and fair trade assured the worker the possibility of purchasing decent food, which guaranteed his good health. In short, fair trade implied good health.

The adroitness of people who adulterated food made control difficult. Dishonest traders applied the scientific progress of the day, as was stressed in the journal *La Santé* of December 1854: 'adulteration grows as chemistry progresses'.[20] Moreover, not only bread was implicated but more diverse food products became the target of fraudulent traders. This contributed to the general perception of increasing food fraud in the 1850s, leading to the passing of a new nationwide bill in March 1856. The *exposé des motifs* mentioned the reasons for submitting this bill to Parliament: increasing fraud was due to the fast development of (food) industry, scientific progress, the sharp price increases of 1853 and 1855, and profiteering by dishonest tradesmen. Neither health nor pure quality was mentioned.[21] Fraud was better defined than before, and punishment was severe. The innovation of the 1856 bill was clearly revealed in a meeting of the Brussels city council. It was said that,

---

17 Annales Conseil salubrité, 1841, xxvi.

18 'Compte-rendu pendant l'année 1840', *Annales Conseil salubrité* 1845, vi–vii.

19 Kaplan, 1996, 495–497.

20 'Sophistication des Denrées Alimentaires' [Adulteration of Foodstuffs], *La Santé* 1854, 134.

21 Kestens, 1990, 67.

under the old legislation, adulteration of foodstuffs was punishable only in so far as one the substances used was harmful to health. Today, Gentlemen, all types of fraud, all unspecified mixtures, even from inoffensive matter, fall under the application of the law.[22]

A straightforward and even naïve concern about honest trade prevailed, implying that when a trader informed the public (orally would suffice) about the composition of goods on sale, he did not commit fraud if he mixed rye with wheat.[23]

It is unclear what was meant by 'public' in the discourses about safe food.[24] Because of the importance of bread in the daily consumption of all social classes, I assume that 'public' referred to a very large group of consumers. But other food items (meat, vinegar, beer, milk, sugar) became part of this discourse, and such products were less consumed by the poorer social classes (which contemporaries repeatedly stressed).[25] From about 1850 to 1880 the poorer classes would do with 'fruits, vegetables, fish, eggs, etc. which the poor get cheaply only because they are starting to deteriorate, which means they are rejected by the comfortably off'.[26] Would food control have considered food of the poor who were viewed as people who hardly minded what they were eating? I therefore suggest that a shift in the significance of 'public' occurred around 1850 with effects up to the 1880s. Then, more people could afford a better diet, and the discourse again implied a very wide group (see below).

In Search of Purity

Since 1838 the works and findings of the *Commission pour l'analyse chimique* had led to a discussion about honest trade, the need to reassure the general public about food scares, and the lack of efficacy of the current laws. This public was alarmed by the increasing frequency of food frauds. At least, this is what may be read in the *Bulletin communal* and the *Annales du Conseil de salubrité publique* during the 1840s and early 1850s, which were periods of extremely sharply fluctuating food prices. The *Annales*, for example, wrote that 'Hardly a day goes by that residents do not bring bread to be analysed by one of the pharmacists'.[27] Some years later, the *Bulletin* wrote, 'The Medical Commission made various bread analyses in 1848, either at the

---

22 *Bulletin Communal*, séance du 10 mai, 1856, 314.

23 Kestens, 1990, 68.

24 This problem of the public, or the users, is central to chapter 9 by Stanziani in this volume.

25 The small quantities of meat, fish or milk that working-class families consumed, were chiefly of the lowest price and poorest quality (e.g., *Mémoire*, 1846, 264). In this respect I agree with Bruegel and Stanziani, 2004, 10, when they claim that norms about food fraud classify luxury and common food, but I disagree when they claim that meat would be a common item, without making a clear social distinction that includes quantity and especially quality of meats.

26 Dieudonné, 1841, 194.

27 'Compte Rendu Pendant l'Année 1840' [Proceedings in the year 1840], *Annales Conseil salubrité* 1845, vi.

request of private individuals, or on instructions from the *Collège*.[28] These citations suggest that bread was the main concern; that not only the *Commission médicale* (i.e. the *Conseil de salubrité*) but also pharmacists were asked to perform food analyses; and that citizens as well as the municipality took the initiative in the analysis of foodstuffs.

In April 1856, the Mayor, Charles de Brouckère, saluted the great efforts of the *Commission médicale locale*, but he deplored the long period between the analysis of a product and the submission of a report. He concluded,

> In a large city like Brussels, the public's food is so important ... that it is essential that we have someone available to the chief of police and the mayor, to obtain instantaneously, either analyses or conclusions from the facts at hand.[29]

The mayor did not deem it necessary to argue the case. A brief discussion followed his equally brief proposal. No-one doubted the increase of food frauds or the need to have better control. One councillor underlined the fact that more foods than just bread were involved, another insisted on organizing recurrent controls, and a third feared that the chemist would become the target of corruption. The proposal was sent to the *Section de police*, which advised hiring a chemist for eighteen months, after which a final decision would be taken. This proposal was accepted unanimously. During the debate, one councillor commented that not only the poor classes were the victims of food frauds, but also the rich: fraud had become a general problem. In the discussion no mention was made of lobby groups (in contrast to what happened when the Paris laboratory was set up in 1878).[30]

After eighteen months, the results of the laboratory were considered satisfactory, and a chemist was appointed permanently to a full-time job. In the 1870s, a second chemist was engaged, in the 1880s three people worked full-time, and in the 1890s there were four. Moreover, after 1893 two doctors operated part-time in the *laboratoire de bactériologie*. In addition to the laboratory, in 1883, two policemen were added to the *Bureau d'hygiène*, which improved its efficiency.[31] The laboratory did not immediately cause the end of the food analyses by the *Commission médicale* (that continued up to the 1870s).

During the first decades of the laboratory's existence, the mayor was pleased with the results. In 1867 for example, he concluded that,

> the foodstuffs sold in Brussels are generally of a good quality. The monitoring service which has functioned for a few years in the Town Hall [i.e the laboratory] and the efforts of the Medical Commission were responsible for this happy result.[32]

---

28 'Rapport sur la Ville de Bruxelles', *Bulletin Communal* 1849, 214.

29 *Bulletin Communal*, séance du 26 avril, 1856, 293.

30 Stanziani, 2005, 333.

31 'Thanks to the system currently in use, a greater number of falsifiers were reached, at the same time as a lesser sum spent on the purchase of food substances', *Bulletin Communal* 1885, II, 412.

32 'Rapport sur la Ville de Bruxelles', *Bulletin Communal* 1867, II, 141.

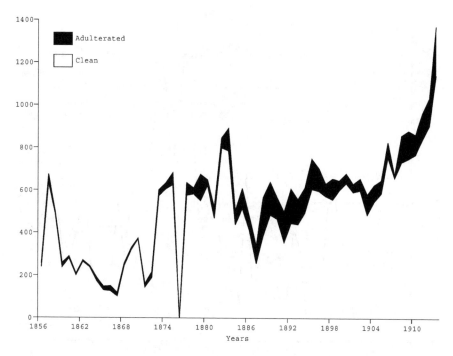

Figure 7.1   Number of tests performed by the Brussels laboratory, showing clean and adulterated foods, 1856–1913

Source: *Bulletin Communal*.
Note: No data for 1876.

Again, in 1873, the laboratory was praised. Bergé, the city's chemist and professor with the *Université Libre de Bruxelles*, emphasized optimistically that there were less food frauds in Brussels than previously, and that 'In large cities such as Brussels... frauds are not able to spread. It is desirable for this monitoring to be organized nationwide'.[33] Such claims were echoed in the city council and often found their way into the newspapers.[34] A final sign of the satisfaction with the *laboratoire* may be found in the report that Bergé wrote for the Antwerp world exhibition of 1885. He claimed that the laboratory performed 1,500 tests per year, and concluded dryly, 'The creation of the municipal laboratory of the city of Paris was on August 1, 1878 and its reorganization was on March 1, 1880; the creation of the laboratory of the city of Brussels goes back to 1864, with its reorganization being in 1871' (note the incorrect date for Brussels).[35]

With some satisfaction, the Mayor noted in 1885 that 'At their request, we have provided information on the progress of this service to several provincial towns and

33 *Bulletin Communal*, séance de 17 mars, 1873, 101.

34 Such was testified in the *Rapport Annuel* dans la séance du 9 janvier 1879, Commission Centrale (1877–1880), 4.

35 In this respect, see Stanziani, 2005, 65.

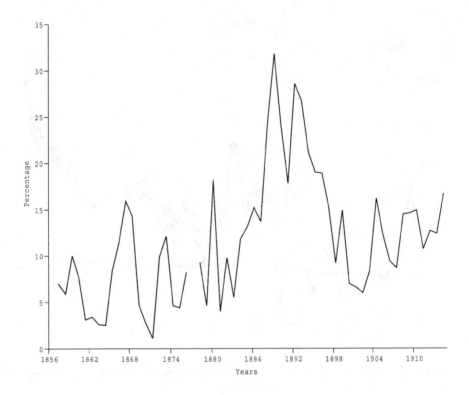

Figure 7.2　Adulterated samples as percentage of total analyses, Brussels, 1856–1913

Source: *Bulletin Communal*.

certain communes in the Brussels conurbation',[36] which again underlines the model function of the capital in this field. And, indeed, municipal laboratories were set up in Antwerp (1875) and Ghent (1887).[37] However, the same report announced a complete reorganization of the laboratory because, although it was working well, it could be improved. What went wrong? Figure 7.1 shows the number of 'clean' and adulterated foods in the total of food products analysed, as listed in the Mayor's annual report to the city council between 1856 and 1913.[38] First, a fall in the total number of examinations occurred (from 900 in 1883, to 500 in 1884, and a low of 340 in 1887). Second, the number of frauds doubled between 1880 and 1885 (clearly shown in Figure 7.2). The latter may be seen either as a sign of an efficient laboratory or as a sign of escalating dishonesty. Because of the Mayor's satisfaction with the performance of the laboratory, I am inclined to accept the second explanation.

36　'Rapport sur la Ville de Bruxelles', *Bulletin Communal* 1885, II, 412.

37　Kestens, 1990, 79–80.

38　The Brussels laboratory would only consider foods that were traded or sold within the limits of the city of Brussels (and not in the neighbouring *communes*).

The following tends to confirm this. In the reports of the 1880s the general public was solicited to assist the work of the Mayor and the *police sanitaire*. In 1886, it read, perhaps too dramatically, 'The Administration counts on the cooperation of all inhabitants to help to repress adulteration, which is very often the cause of serious illnesses and fatal accidents'.[39] This call was repeated in other years too, when it was strongly emphasized that tests were free for the public.[40] From 1884 onwards, the annual reports divided between the tests that were initiated by the city and those of the public (*particuliers*), thus stressing the importance of the role of the latter. The call upon the public was successful: in the 1880s, 13 per cent of the analyses were done on request by the public. This share diminished to eight per cent in the 1890s, and only five per cent in the 1900s and 1910s, by which time the call had disappeared. Why was the public invited to play an active role in the food control in the 1880s and 1890s? One reason might have been to give them the idea of being in control, and another aim was to soothe food anxieties.

This leads me back to the issue of the 'public': one should question whether these *particuliers* were traders, medical doctors, consumers (which ones?) or a mix of different groups.[41] If consumers (or their organizations) took the initiative, this may reveal increasing consumer alertness, but if traders took samples to the laboratory, commercial interests were probably involved. The sort of foodstuffs that were analysed in the 1880s and later does not lead us to assume that the *average* consumer took food to the laboratory. If flour and bread had made up the largest part of the analyses (e.g. 79 per cent in 1859), gradually more and more of other foodstuffs were examined. Up to the early 1880s, the city administration piloted the analyses, which resulted in specific campaigns (for example chicory in 1870, which that year accounted for 30 per cent of the total tests, the same share as for bread). In 1885, when 15 per cent of the tests were requested by the public, 505 tests were performed on some thirty different foodstuffs, ranging from alcohol (15 per cent), sugar (nine per cent), milk (eight per cent) and chicory (seven per cent), to sweets (six per cent), and salt (five per cent). But pasta, tea, butter and chocolate were analysed too, while bread accounted for only five per cent of the total. The *particuliers* brought wine, flour, butter and marmalade to the laboratory. A working-class housewife might have brought flour or butter to the laboratory, but surely not wine or marmalade (and chocolate, tea or sweets).[42]

Food Modernization

This call upon the public does not explain the huge fluctuations in the total number of tests or the increasing registration of frauds between 1884 and 1894, but, as I argued

---

39 'Rapport sur la ville de Bruxelles', *Bulletin Communal* 1886, II, 288.

40 'Rapport sur la ville de Bruxelles', *Bulletin Communal* 1890, II, 344. In this respect Brussels differed from Paris, where in 1886 a tariff list was applied. See Stanziani, 2005, 334–335, and chapter 9 in this volume.

41 Paquy, 2004, 52.

42 In Paris, very often producers or traders presented food products to the laboratory, which often led to criticising it severely. Stanziani, 2005, 337, and chapter 9.

earlier, they are another sign of new, more complex problems. In this period, more and more people warned against a new wave of *refined* frauds, which was seen as a real and permanent social danger. In the *Académie de médecine* in 1886, for example, a member proposed the creation of a *cordon sanitaire* using scientific advancement once and for all to get rid of the pernicious effects of food frauds.[43] A few years later, the Mayor's annual report to the council testified to the fact that the analyses were becoming increasingly complex and delicate, because falsifications were done with the help of chemists. Moreover, when frauds were discovered, chemists went to court to plead in favour of the industry or retailer,[44] thus clearly questioning the legal interpretation of 'fraud'. In 1907, the report noted,

> The research field extends each year and there continues to be an active struggle between the official laboratory and the laboratories of unscrupulous manufacturers advised and defended by agents who use scientific knowledge in their service.[45]

In his overview of public sanitation in Belgium, H. Kuborn stressed that adulteration was escalating, because of the growing international competition in food and drink. He considered beer as a good example: due to foreign imports, Belgian brewers first claimed protective taxes, then they turned to new technology but, meanwhile, they saw opportunities via addition of harmful or harmless substances.[46] Other new problems were linked to unsafe wrapping paper, colouring agents, and deceitful labelling.

Scientific knowledge was increasingly being used to *alter* the composition of foodstuffs, which was generally seen as wrong.[47] Hence, the 1906 annual report to the Brussels council stressed the fact that not only *traditional* frauds (e.g. mixing harmless rye or sand with wheat) should be controlled, but also and especially the *modifications* and the (chemical) colouring of the food, preserving technologies, as well as plain cheating. The following example illustrates the complexity. A patent was taken out for a tablet (based on grape peel) that in a mixture with water and alcohol gave a drink that looked and tasted like wine. The inventor had received a first prize for this. As long as the mixture was not sold as 'wine' there was no problem, but of course dishonest wine traders made use of the cheap tablets to raise their profits.[48] Similarly, vinegar, fruit juices, butter and many other foodstuffs were treated with several chemical additives. So, the question of the *nature* of a modified product was raised.

To deal with the growing problems, a new national law was passed in August 1890, leading to the establishment of a national bureau of food control. One of the main motives was the fact that so few laboratories for food analyses existed in the country. Next to the Brussels one, only Antwerp and Ghent operated, as well as some

---

43 Bonnewyn, 1886, 2.
44 'Rapport sur la Ville de Bruxelles', *Bulletin Communal* 1906, II, 421.
45 'Rapport sur la Ville de Bruxelles', *Bulletin Communal* 1907, II, 497.
46 Kuborn, 1897, 82.
47 As in England. French and Phillips, 2000, 30.
48 Kestens, 1990, 86.

laboratories in universities and smaller towns.[49] From 1890 the state recognised or founded seven laboratories that performed very well right from the start.[50] The solution, thus, was to be found in more, qualified, and state-controlled laboratories.

The Brussels laboratory proceeded with renewed enthusiasm (Figure 7.1): there was an increase in analyses in the early 1890s and a strong expansion after 1905. The range of analysed foodstuffs attained forty and more, with common food (bread, milk, flour, or sugar), refined foods (wine, chocolate, pasta or tea) and luxury foods (liquors, sweets, or condiments). In 1913, milk made up 40 per cent of the total analyses, with cans of vegetables, fish and meat (seven per cent), butter (seven per cent), pasta (four per cent) and sweets (four per cent) coming next. Bread and flour accounted for only three per cent. This attention to manufactured and dairy foods may be seen as an indication of the more complex food pattern of *all* classes.

The tables published in the yearly report to the city council mirrored the complexity of the analyses. Next to the two traditional categories (*sans fraude ni matière toxique*, and *avec fraude, matières toxiques ou suspectes*), a third category was applied from 1908 onward: *avec remarques défavorables*. It was as if there was no certainty whether a product was falsified or not. In the late 1890s, the number of samples shown to be adulterated had fallen vis-à-vis the 1880s, with a low around 1900 (Figure 7.2). Then, the share of falsified goods fluctuated between eight and sixteen per cent. In 1913, 83 per cent of the analyses were 'clean', 12 per cent were falsified, and the remaining five per cent were uncertain.[51]

Despite the ongoing efforts in terms of organization, financial means, and personnel since the 1850s, many people felt that the battle against food fraud was impossible to win. The 'enemy' (*les commerçants et industriels peu scrupuleux*) was strong, well supported, and extremely clever. Around 1900, falsifications could be discovered readily, but modifications were a different matter. Pessimism ruled when the chairman of the concluding session of the 1913 *Congrès international pour la lutte contre l'altération et la falsification des denrées alimentaires*, admitted that 'The current organization of anti-adulteration service is inadequate in our country, and it needs modifying'.[52] That chairman was the head of the Brussels laboratory, J. Wauters.

Did the Brussels Food Control System Succeed in Securing Healthy Food and Honest Trade, and Did it Ease Food Anxieties?

This chapter has emphasized the discourses and practices of the Brussels government, but through these, the public, the manufacturers, the traders, and the state have also

---

49 'Exposé des motifs. Loi relative à la falsification des denrées alimentaires' [Motives revealed: law relating to the adulteration of foodstuffs], Pasinomie, Brussels, 1890, 267.

50 Kuborn, 1897, 88.

51 'Rapport sur la ville de Bruxelles', *Bulletin Communal* 1914, II, 848. In England and Wales in the 1900s, 9 per cent of controlled foods were adulterated. French and Phillips, 2000, 53; also Oddy, chapter 8.

52 *Congrès International* 1914, 215. Compare to the reforms in Helsinki around the same period. See Hietala, 1994, 121.

appeared. Throughout the nineteenth century the administration used new tactics and means of organization to cope with food fraud. By so doing, it got a stronger grip upon matters of food health, trade and quality norms, and it certainly changed the old relations between the public and the private sphere with regard to food.

What 'fraud' actually meant, however, was varied: the policy, products, and targeted public changed. Up to about 1850 a difference was made between *dangerous* and *safe* frauds. Both were prohibited, but harmless frauds, in terms of health, were hardly punished. Because bread was the main concern of the Brussels food control in that period, I can link this conclusion to the city's concern about working-class food anxieties, both in quantitative and qualitative terms. So, health did matter but, through the reassuring messages about safe bread, social monitoring of the mass of consumers prevailed.

The 1856 bill codified the changing meaning of fraud, by including 'safe frauds', and during two decades, the combination of this bill with municipal action (the laboratory and its reputation) pleased the Brussels council. Regularly, the Mayor declared that many analyses had been carried out, and that, in general, food was safe. Not once did the city council mention food scares or scandals. Around 1880, however, fraud acquired a new meaning. *Plain* adulteration, i.e. adding (un)safe ingredients to a product, gave way to *complex* alterations of food via additions or modifications. I will suggest two new developments. First, health matters were still important, but between 1850 and 1890 they were less oriented toward working-class anxieties, and more toward concerns of the middle and upper classes. Second and connected to the first point, issues of honest trade seemed to gain weight.

Because of the progress of industry and science, the Brussels laboratory and city council had to admit ceaselessly that combating frauds was not an easy matter. Yet, in the hygienist discourse, in discussions in Parliament, in numerous brochures, and in initiatives in other cities and countries, the Brussels food control system was referred to as a genuine example. A capital could not do less.

References

Annales du Conseil Central de Salubrité Publique de Bruxelles [Annals of the Brussels Central Council of Public Health], Brussels, 1841–7.

Bonnewyn, H. 'Discours Orononcé à l'Académie Royale de Médecine de Belgique, dans la Discussion sur la Répression de la Falsification des Denrées Alimentaires' [Speech Made to the Belgian Royal Academy of Medicine, in the Debate about the Elimination of Food Adulteration], *Bulletin de l'Académie Royale de Médecine* 13, 3e série, 8 (1886), 2–7.

Bruegel, M. and Stanziani, A. 'Pour une Histoire de la "Sécurité Alimentaire"' [Towards a History of Food Safety], *Revue d'Histoire Moderne et Contemporaine* 51, 2004, 7–16.

Bruneel, C. 'Ziekte en Sociale Geneeskunde: De Erfenis van de Verlichting' [Sickness and Social Medicine], in De Maeyer, J. et al. (eds), *Er is Leven voor de Dood. Tweehonderd Jaar Gezondheidszorg in Vlaanderen* [Two Hundred Years of Health Care in Flanders], Kapellen, 1998, 17–31.

Bulletin Communal. Ville de Bruxelles, Brussels, 1846–1913.

Commission Centrale des Comités de Salubrité de l'Agglomération Bruxelloise [Central Commission of Health Committees of the City of Brussels], *Compte Rendu des Séances* [Proceedings], Brussels, 1877–1880.

Congrès International pour la Lutte contre l'Altération et la Falsification des Denrées Alimentaires (Gand, Août 1913)[International Congress on the Struggle against the Adulteration of Foodstuffs], *Rapport et Comptes Rendus des Séances*, [Report and Proceedings] Brussels, 1914.

Darquenne, R. 'A propos des Falsifications Alimentaires' [On Food Adulteration], *Annales de la Société Belge d'Histoire des Hôpitaux et de la Santé Publique* [Annals of the Belgian Society for the History of Hospitals and Public Health] 22, 1986, 29–68.

Dieudonné, Dr. 'Rapport sur l'Hygiène de l'Ouvrier' [Report on the Hygiene of Working People], *Annales du Conseil Central de Salubrité Publique de Bruxelles* Annals of the Brussels Central Council of Public Health, Brussels, 1841, 177–95.

Ferrières, M. *Histoire des Peurs Alimentaires. Du Moyen Âge à l'Aube du XXe Siècle* [History of Food Scares], Paris, 2002.

French, M. and Phillips, J. *Cheated not Poisoned? Food Regulation in the United Kingdom 1875–1938*, Manchester, 2000.

Hietala, M. 'Hygiene and the Control of Food in Finnish Towns at the Turn of the Century: A Case Study from Helsinki', in ICREFH II, 113–129.

Janssens, E. *Considérations Statistiques sur la Salubrité Comparée de la Ville de Bruxelles* [Statistical Considerations on the Comparative Healthiness of the City of Brussels], Brussels, 1871.

Kaplan, S. *Le Meilleur Pain du Monde. Les Boulangers de Paris au XVIIIe Siècle* [The Bakers of Paris in the Eighteenth Century], Paris, 1996.

Kestens, C. *Voeding en Recht. Historische en Juridische Inleiding op het Voedingsrecht. Naar Aanleiding van Honderd Jaar Rijkseetwareninspectie in België* [The Results of Two Hundred Years of Food Inspection in Belgium], Brugge, 1990.

Kuborn H. *Aperçu Historique sur l'Hygiène Publique en Belgique depuis 1830* [Historical Observations on the Public Health of Belgium since 1830], Brussels, 1897.

La Berge, A. *Mission and Method. The Early Nineteenth-Century French Public Health Movement*, Cambridge, 1992.

Law, M. 'The Origins of State Pure Food Regulation', *Journal of Economic History* 63, 2003, 1103–1130.

Martin, A.J. 'Le Bureau d'Hygiène de Bruxelles (1874–1890)' [The Brussels Bureau of Hygiene], *Revue d'Hygiène et de Police Sanitaire* [Review of Hygiene and of Sanitary Police] 12, 5, 1890, 1–22.

'Mémoire sur la Condition des Classes Ouvrières et sur le Travail des Enfants [Report on the Condition of the Working Classes and on Work by Children', in *Annales du Conseil Central de Salubrité Publique de Bruxelles*, 1846, 181–277.

Paquy, L. 'Santé Publique, Répression des Fraudes et Action Municipale à la Fin du XIXe Siècle: Le Laboratoire Grenoblois d'Analyses Alimentaires [Public Health,

Repression of Frauds and Municipal Action at the End of the Nineteenth Century: The Grenoble Laboratory of Food Analyses]', *Revue d'Histoire Moderne et Contemporaine* 51, 3, 2004, 44–65.

La Santé. Journal d'Hygiène Publique et Privée. Salubrité Publique et Police Sanitaire [Health. Newspaper of Public and Private Health. Public Health and Medical Police Force], Brussels, 1849–1859.

Scholliers, P. 'An Essay on the History of the Internationalization and Representation of Brussels, 1800–2000', in Witte E. and Mares, A. (eds), *19 Times Brussels* (Series Brussels Themes 7), Brussels, 2001, 497–514.

Stanziani, A. *Histoire de la Qualité Alimentaire (XIXe–XXe siècles)* [History of Food Quality)], Paris, 2005.

Teuteberg, H.J. 'Food Adulteration and the Beginnings of Uniform Food Legislation in Late-Nineteenth Century Germany', in ICREFH II, 1994, 146–160.

Van den Eeckhout, P. 'Brussels', in Daunton, M. (ed.), *Housing the Workers, 1850–1914: A Comparative Perspective*, Leicester, 1990, 67–106.

Velle, K. 'De Overheid en de Zorg voor de Volksgezondheid' [The Government and the Care of Public Health], in De Maeyer, J. et al. (eds), *Er is Leven voor de Dood. Tweehonderd Jaar Gezondheidszorg in Vlaanderen* [Two Hundred Years of Health Care in Flanders], Kapellen, 1998, 130–50.

Chapter 8

Food Quality in London and the Rise of the Public Analyst, 1870–1939

Derek J. Oddy

The London Food Market

In the nineteenth and early twentieth centuries, London was the biggest urban centre in Europe. Its population grew from nearly four million in 1871 to 7.26 million on the eve of the First World War. From 1931 onwards it contained more than eight million people and covered more than 700 square miles (1,800 km²) in area. It was the prime example of a conurbation which absorbed many nearby small communities as it spread.[1] London had no central retail food market or market hall where people might buy food. Its three great wholesale markets, Smithfield (meat), Billingsgate (fish) and Covent Garden (fruit and vegetables) were longstanding suppliers of London's retailers, though they functioned increasingly as national markets as the nineteenth century progressed.[2] Local retail food markets, some of which had functioned for two centuries or more, were cleared away as their site-values rose.[3] They were replaced by public buildings, railway stations, roads and commercial premises, leaving Londoners in central districts to buy food from street markets and street traders, such as costermongers, who were not covered by the food legislation. This weakened local authority controls over the retailing of food and increased the possibility that it might be contaminated or adulterated.

The Question of Adulteration

It was widely suspected, particularly amongst the middle classes who relied on servants to make purchases, that much of London's food was adulterated.[4] Some sensational writings about adulteration occurred until a sustained campaign developed

---

1   The word 'conurbation' is attributed to Patrick Geddes, biologist and pioneer town planner. The London County Council administered the central and inner areas of London from 1889 until 1965.

2   Schmiechen and Carls, 1999, xi–xii.

3   Tames, 2003, 73–8. The purpose-built but unsuccessful Columbia market opened in the late 1860s and closed in 1885.

4   For details of food adulteration in the nineteenth century, see Burnett, 1989, chs 5 and 10 and, for the legislative process, Paulus, 1974.

during the 1850s, inspired by Dr Thomas Wakley, editor of *The Lancet*.[5] He engaged Dr Arthur Hassall, to investigate all major items of food and drink and write reports for publication.[6] These reports attracted much attention, becoming known as *The Lancet*'s 'Sanitary Commission'.[7] A parliamentary inquiry followed, with a Select Committee of the House of Commons taking evidence.[8] Newspaper accounts of adulteration provoked parliamentary action, though the resulting Adulteration of Foods Act, 1860, was permissive rather than mandatory legislation. It permitted local authorities to appoint public analysts to examine food samples when private citizens complained. In London, the separate local authorities were the City of London's Commissioners of Sewers and, at the very local level, the Parish Vestries and District Boards of Works; there was no single post of public analyst for the whole of London. Nevertheless, it was in the metropolis that most of the early appointments of public analyst were made.[9] *The Lancet* continued to press for reform throughout the 1860s, reinforced from 1871 by the Anti-Adulteration Association. The ensuing Adulteration of Food, Drink and Drugs Act, 1872, made the addition of any undeclared substances an offence punishable by a fine, but even the later Sale of Food and Drugs Act, 1875, lacked the necessary compulsory powers for uniform application and those analysts appointed after 1875 still found the legislation difficult to operate.[10]

The Rôle of Public Analysts

Public analysts began work in a climate they perceived as hostile to their very existence. Poor remuneration for analysing and certifying samples of food was the basis of their sense of insecurity but analysts felt themselves to be distrusted even by the local authorities who employed them. The formation of a professional society was seen as one way of raising their status though, as their numbers depended on the number of local authority appointments available, this could be disadvantageous

---

5   Accum, 1820. Also an anonymous writer who adopted the phrase 'there is death in the pot' (II. Kings, 4, 40) for his title: *Deadly Adulteration and Slow Poisoning Unmasked, or Disease and Death in the Pot and the Bottle, 1830..*

6   Assisted by Dr Henry Letheby.

7   See Hassall, 1855.

8   *Select Committee on Adulteration of Food, Drink and Drugs,* 1856.

9   The Metropolitan Management Act, 1855, had made the appointment of Medical Officers of Health compulsory in all metropolitan districts, but only 15 Vestries and 11 District Boards (in addition to the City of London) had appointed public analysts by 1873. See *The Anti-Adulteration Review (AAR)*, August 1873, 8. By 1891 the number of public analysts in London had risen to 41. See *Twenty-First Annual Report of the Local Government Board* cited in *Food, Drugs and Drink*, I, 13, 5 November 1892, 8. The appointment of public analysts was not compulsory prior to the 1899 Act unless specifically required by the Local Government Board.

10   Courts applied the 1875 Act only to shops. The *AAR*, September 1879, 7, reported the failure of a prosecution in Lambeth against a man selling milk in the street. From 1879 'strict liability' applied, i.e. traders were forced to accept that ignorance of adulteration was no defence. See Paulus, 1974, 38.

for their society's influence.[11] However, the practising chemists who attended the inaugural meeting in 1874 were dissatisfied members of the Chemical Society who had been running a campaign since 1867 against its lax admission rules and the lack of qualifications amongst many of its members.[12] They were aware that Dr Augustus Voelcker, the Royal Agricultural Society's chemical adviser, had said in evidence to the parliamentary Select Committee examining the Sale of Food and Drugs Bill in 1872: 'there are not a dozen competent analysts in the kingdom'.[13] The initial meeting on 7 August 1874 therefore consisted of some 77 practising chemists invited in order to refute 'unjust imputations', to repudiate any proposals for interference with their professional independence and to establish mutual cooperation among public analysts.[14] Although a number of them held academic posts in London University and the London teaching hospitals, the founders chose to focus on the problems created by the legislation against adulteration and called their association, the Society of Public Analysts (SPA).

Their sense of injustice was intensified by the inclusion of an appeal system in the 1875 Sale of Food and Drugs Act. This required that when any dispute arose over the quality of foods analysed, a third sample should be tested by the Board of Inland Revenue's Laboratory (known as 'Somerset House' from its location), which thus became a 'court of reference'. As processes of chemical analysis were not yet standardized, the public analysts realized that their results might become open to contradiction in the courts by the 'government chemists' in Somerset House. Even before the 1875 Act was passed, public analysts had been concerned that appeals would lead to legal disputes which could undermine their rôle in issuing certificates of adulteration. When the appeals system began to operate there was friction between the public analysts and the Inland Revenue Laboratory which lasted until 1899.[15] Further disagreements arose between analysts and the Medical Officers of Health

---

11 By 1891, the Local Government Board reported that 235 public analysts were in post in England and Wales. Numbers remained stable at this level until 1920. See Paulus, 1974, 105. The consolidation of local government areas meant that there were only 74 public analysts in 1938, plus 25 qualified assistants. *Twentieth Annual Report of the Ministry of Health, 1938–39*, 45.

12 The following outline of the Society of Public Analysts is taken largely from Chirnside and Hamence, 1974, 7–8, though for much of the public analysts' early history these authors drew on Dyer, 1932. A brief summary of the SPA's development appeared in Horrocks, 1994.

13 Chirnside and Hamence, 1974, 9.

14 The *AAR*, September 1874, 4, reported that only 24 analysts attended.

15 Problems centred on the lack of food standards in the 1875 Act and the professional lack of agreement on analytical methods. The Inland Revenue Laboratory exacerbated the latter problem by not publishing its methods, thus giving rise to the suspicion that it was applying variable standards. The dispute was at its most acrimonious in the evidence given before the Select Committee on Food Products Adulteration, 1894–5. However, between 1875 and 1894, only 678 disputed samples were referred to the Inland Revenue Laboratory for adjudication. Of these, only 188 cases resulted in disagreement with the public analysts' certificates. See Hammond and Egan, 1992, 92–3, 156–7, 399. From 1895, the Laboratory was known as the Laboratory of the Government Chemist.

when the Public Health Act, 1875, came into force. Public analysts, coming as they did from the ranks of practical and academic analytical chemists, saw Medical Officers of Health as less competent and less experienced in chemical analysis than themselves.

By 1881, the SPA had formalized its objectives: first, to establish a degree of competency amongst analytical chemists;[16] secondly, to chart the composition of foods and to define and detect adulteration and, thirdly, to work out analytical techniques and processes. During the 1890s, parliamentary inquiries gave the Society an opportunity to influence legislative proposals. Two investigations, the Select Committee on Adulteration between 1894 and 1895 and the Departmental Committee on Preservatives and Colourings in Food of 1899, gave the SPA major platforms from which to express their views on food contamination and led the Select Committee to recommend that a central scientific expert bureau be formed to examine food thought to be adulterated.[17] However, the government's token response, which merged the laboratories of the Board of Inland Revenue and the Board of Customs into a Government Chemist's Department, left the public analysts dissatisfied as long as the appeals procedure still operated under the 1875 Act. Furthermore, the issue of preservatives in food was unresolved. The status of public analysts remained in doubt yet, as the twentieth century progressed, they were required to undertake new analytical work in biochemistry following the discovery of vitamins. They also faced the increasing task of testing foods under the Food and Drugs (Adulteration) Act, 1928, and the codifying Sale of Food and Drugs Act, 1938.

The Growing Pressure for Reform

London's food supply problems and the ineffectiveness of the anti-adulteration legislation meant debate about food quality and the need for further legislative reform continued after the early Acts were passed. Although groups like the Food Reform Society (formed 1880) and the Vegetarian Society (1847) actively arranged meetings and lectures, their militant anti-meat agenda restricted their membership and their influence. Some of their members, like Dr T.R. Allinson, and Miss May Yates of the Bread Reform League had particular objectives regarding food which were too specific for food quality legislation. A more important body was the Anti-Adulteration Association (1871–1886) which claimed to have its own laboratory for testing products. Its *Anti-Adulteration Review* carried endorsements of hotels, restaurants and lists of vendors of 'pure' products, including milk, teas, coffees, butter and cheese. After the 1879 Amendment Act was passed, food reform agitation died down and the Anti-Adulteration Association ceased to be active. When the *AAR* ceased publication in 1886, the SPA's *Analyst* was the only periodical systematically

---

16 Even after the Institute of Chemistry was founded in 1877, the status and knowledge required to be a professional chemist remained a matter of dispute between the chemists and both the Privy Council and the Board of Trade.

17 This recommendation was repeated by the Royal Commission on Arsenical Poisoning in 1903.

reporting food adulteration.[18] A new journal, *Food, Drugs and Drink* (later entitled *Food and Sanitation*), continued an anti-adulteration campaign from 1892, but with a different agenda and one that changed over time. Initially favourable to public analysts, by late 1893 it advocated 'the enforcement of the Food and Drugs' Acts, not in the interests of Public Analysts, or of any class or profession, but of the vendors of unadulterated articles, and of the consuming public'.[19] In only its third issue it proposed, like the Anti-Adulteration Association, 'to institute a Food, Drugs and Drink Analytical Commission', though little was heard of this project beyond 1893, and the journal ceased publication in August 1900.[20]

Faced with allegations that food was of poor quality and frequently adulterated, various branches of the food industry responded by organizing trade shows in London to demonstrate the high quality of their produce. The first Metropolitan Dairy Show, held in October 1876, became an annual event thereafter.[21] An annual Brewers' Exhibition commenced in 1879 and there were International Food Exhibitions annually between 1880 and 1882. The Fisheries Exhibition followed in 1883, a Health Exhibition in 1884 and a first specialist grocery exhibition in May 1896.[22] Public concern over food adulteration became less vociferous during the 1880s, though the international trade in adulterated foods was discussed by the series of International Congresses on Hygiene and Demography, the seventh of which was held in London in 1891, hosted jointly by the Society of Medical Officers of Health and the British Sanitary Institute.[23]

One voice advocating pure food and an end to the use of food additives was that of Charles E. Cassal (1858–1921), an active member of the SPA, initially as public analyst for High Wycombe, and later for Kensington. His practice as an analytical chemist expanded; he was able to add responsibilities for St George's Hanover Square (1886), St Mary's Battersea (1888), Kesteven and Holland (1890) before becoming public analyst for the City of Westminster (1901–21). A man of wide interests, Cassal was prominent in the SPA's attempts to enhance the status of public analysts.[24] He co-ordinated a conference of Metropolitan Local Authorities at St George's, Hanover Square, in May 1894, which sought to standardize procedures in London. The meeting passed resolutions to sample foods at railway stations and to

---

18 For official statistics based on quarterly returns by public analysts, see the annual reports of the Local Government Board, 1877–1913.

19 *Food, Drugs and Drink*, III, 71, 16 December 1893, 387.

20 *Food, Drugs and Drink* I, 3, 27 August 1892, 6.

21 *The Grocer's Journal*, 27 October 1876, 1136.

22 Ibid., 30 May 1896, 9–10.

23 Professor Brouardel of Paris first proposed this topic at a Congress held in Geneva in 1882. See *Lancet Reports, 1891*, 8. For the full list of Congresses (with a revised enumeration which made London the ninth, not seventh, in the series), see *Transactions of the 15th International Congress, 1912*.

24 Cassal was a Freemason and also a part-time soldier in the Volunteer Movement. He was commissioned Lieutenant in the Royal Engineers (1st London Volunteer Battalion) on 7 November 1885, promoted Captain on 17 September 1887 and Major on 22 January 1896. He was Lieutenant-Colonel in command of the 1st London Volunteer Battalion from 2 December 1902 to 4 December 1905. See the *Army List*, HMSO (annual series).

prosecute wholesalers and manufacturers alongside the retailers who were charged under the Sale of Food and Drugs Act.[25] Cassal's report was cited in the 1895 hearings of the Select Committee on Food Products Adulteration.[26] By 1899, as Vice-President of the SPA, he was becoming one of the public voices of the profession. In 1900, the Departmental Committee on Regulations for Milk and Cream[27] called Cassal to give evidence on behalf of the Kensington Vestry; and the parallel departmental inquiry by the Local Government Board into the use of preservatives and colouring matter in food gave him a further opportunity to speak forcibly against the use of additives in any form.[28] However, the latter inquiry's recommendations, that some preservatives should be allowed and that a Court of Reference be established, meant public analysts had failed to establish a case for pure food in the face of opposition from both retailers and food processors.

This sense of lost opportunity led Cassal, together with his mentor, Professor W.H. Corfield (1843–1903)[29] and others, to publish *The British Food Journal and Analytical Review* (*BFJ*) in direct competition with the SPA's own journal, *The Analyst*. Although the *BFJ*, which Cassal himself edited from 1899 to 1914, focussed on issues central to the work of public analysts, its overriding premise was that the existing system of certifying food samples as adulterated was negative and ineffectual, especially at a time when international congresses on hygiene had been discussing ways to impose 'permanent analytical control' on food products. As the courts applied the Sale of Food and Drugs Act, 1875, only to retailers, the *BFJ* sought to develop a comprehensive, industry-backed system of quality control which would endorse wholesome food products through a self-regulating agency, much as the Anti-Adulteration Association had advocated in the 1870s. The principal backers of the *BFJ* undoubtedly had clear ideas of their own about food standards but, for those who were public analysts or Medical Officers of Health, their official status meant that they could not appear to favour particular companies or products openly. Instead, the *BFJ* became a surrogate for evaluating standards of food products through an intermediary agency called The British Analytical Control. The intention, set out in the first issue of the *BFJ* in 1899, was that this body rather than individual analysts would endorse products meeting approved conditions.[30]

---

25 *Select Committee on Food Products Adulteration*, (1895), Q.7187 and Q.7190, to R.A. Robinson, Vestry of the Parish of St Mary Abbott's, Kensington.

26 *SC on Food Products Adulteration*, 1895, QQ.7235–7243 to R.A. Robinson. Robinson's evidence (Q.7225) included a proposal for a board of reference to set standards which was clearly inspired by Cassal's views.

27 *Departmental Committee on Regulations for Milk and Cream*, (1901) QQ. 9011–9114.

28 *Departmental Committee into the Use of Preservatives and Colouring Matter in Food*, (1902); Evidence of Major C.E. Cassal, QQ.3783–3815 and Appendix XXV.

29 Professor W.H. Corfield, was Professor of Hygiene and Public Health at University College, London, where Cassal began as his demonstrator. Corfield was public analyst for St George's Hanover Square, continuing as St George's Medical Officer of Health after Cassal took over as its public analyst.

30 See 'The prevention of adulteration by a permanent analytical control; The British Analytical Control', *The British Food Journal and Hygienic Review*, 1899, vol. 1, no.1, 6–7.

Despite the general decline in crude adulteration, the twentieth century opened with two major food scandals. Arsenic poisoning from beer led to 70 deaths in 1900 and resulted in a Royal Commission to investigate the causes, though a pure beer bill before parliament in 1906, promoted by Captain Courthope M.P., failed in the face of opposition from the brewers.[31] In the same year, public alarm following the publication of Upton Sinclair's novel, *The Jungle*, revived metropolitan food reform agitation for 'pure' food.[32] In the absence of any further legislation, other than the Margarine Act, 1907, The National Pure Food Association was formed in 1909. It faced strong opposition from the food retailers.[33] From 1910 to 1914, *The Grocer* highlighted differences between public analysts and the food reformers, cited the 'essential' nature of chemical additives to manufacturing methods, blamed poor quality on the cheap food policies of the multiple retailers and the Cooperative Societies, and excused manufacturers' unwillingness to disclose food ingredients on grounds of commercial sensitivity. The National Pure Food Association was succeeded by the Pure Food and Health Society of Great Britain.[34] In essence, this was a parliamentary pressure group seeking to establish the 'Court or Board of Reference' recommended by the Departmental Committee into Preservatives and Colouring Matter in Food in 1902[35] and secure the enactment of the existing laws against adulteration. From 1913, the *BFJ* became its 'official organ' until 1914. The *BFJ* had earlier added a sub-title in 1904, claiming to be the 'Official Voice of the International Commission on Adulteration'.[36] Neither endorsement changed the *BFJ*'s agenda: its major interests continued to be British food legislation and its applications, the composition of foods and preservation techniques, particularly the canning process. Despite Cassal's death in 1921, the *BFJ* became an established reference guide for public analysts.[37] By the end of the 1920s, its interrelationship with the British Analytical Control was clarified for readers:

---

31 Burnett, 1989, 235; Oddy, 2003, 31.

32 Sinclair, 1906, exposed the unsatisfactory hygiene in United States' meat-canning factories.

33 The politics of food reform are outlined in French, and Phillips, 2003, 448–62. See also French and Phillips, 2000, 30, 39, 55.

34 It was incorporated in 1913. See National Archives, Public Record Office, BT31/32163/130895, Company No.130895.

35 It had a Peer and six MPs on its Central Executive Committee.

36 Cassal claimed to be one of the joint-secretaries of the 'International Commission on Adulteration' but, apart from references to it in the pages of the *BFJ*, this organization is unidentifiable. Despite the many international congresses between 1890 and 1914 on a wide range of subjects, the Société Universelle de la Croix-Blanche de Genève was the only organization that bore any resemblance to an 'International Commission on Adulteration'. It held conferences in 1908 (Geneva) and 1909 (Paris). In 1908 'M. le colonel Charles E. Cassal' was listed as a member of the 'Délégation Anglaise', but a footnote explained that when he was called to take his place, he was 'Retenu au dernier moment loin de Genève'. See Société Universelle de la Croix-Blanche, 1909, 61. The *BFJ*'s endorsement of the 'International Commission on Adulteration' on its title page was removed in July 1914 (like that of the Pure Food and Health Society of Great Britain).

37 See Liverseege, 1932, which cites the *British Food Journal* equally with *The Analyst*.

The British Analytical Control, which constitutes the Analytical Department of the *British Food Journal*, exists to protect those manufacturers and importers of food and other products who produce or sell superior or good articles against the unfair competition arising from the sale of imitations and inferior and adulterated articles, and to protect the health and the interests of the public by directing attention to products which are pure, genuine and of good quality.[38]

The *BFJ*'s attempt to create an independent agency for the control of food quality was the only one of its kind which had any success. It came into existence as the rôle of the state was expanding and food quality was becoming the responsibility of local government public health inspectors,[39] medical officers of health and, increasingly, factory inspectors who assessed conditions in the large food producers' establishments.[40] The idea that the British Analytical Control should endorse food quality arose while environmental control was incomplete and, though its 'seals of approval' continued to be awarded until the 1970s, the system could not accommodate the widely differing scale of food production operations from the farm gate to manufacturers' pre-packed branded goods which developed during the twentieth century.

The Quality of Food, 1890–1938

Public analysts found two factors affecting food sold in the shops and on the streets of London that were beyond their control. The first of these was environmental. Poor-quality housing, overcrowding and the presence of many small industries was a hazard to the processing and storage of food. The slowness with which effective sewage treatment, refuse collection and piped-water supplies became available meant problems persisted into the twentieth century. In 1903, it was reported that sewage effluent in the river Thames was affecting mollusc beds at the mouth of the river, though cockles from contaminated areas were being sold in London. Three years later the Medical Officer of Health for Wimbledon found watercress beds in the river Wandle which were contaminated by effluent discharged from sewage farms, including raw sewage.[41] Secondly, the ever-widening area from which London's food was supplied meant that much food processing took place beyond the jurisdiction of London's public health inspection system. Thus while rail traffic extended the range of London's food supplies, longer travelling time meant that some foods, notably milk and fish, might be already stale when unloaded at railway stations in the metropolis.

---

38 *BFJ*, December 1929, p.124. In the USA, *Good Housekeeping Magazine* also issued seals of approval upon its advertisements from 1912 to 1927. See Goodwin, 1999, 281. The process was administered by Dr Harvey W. Wilby (1844–1930) who worked for the journal from 1912 after resigning as Chief of the Bureau of Chemistry in the US Department of Agriculture.

39 See Paulus, 1974, 114. A food inspectorate responsible to Medical Officers of Health was established by the Public Health (Regulations as to Food) Act, 1907.

40 In London, small basement bakehouses were the subject of a report by Dr Lakeman in 1882. See also Horrocks, 1994.

41 *BFJ*, April 1906, 66.

During the 1890s, numerous complaints were made against the use of boracic acid as an additive to preserve foods and extend their retail life.[42] Milk was frequently treated in this way as were the large quantities of liquid eggs imported from China. Besides the extensive network of docks and wharves on the river Thames, foodstuffs entering Britain via Glasgow, Liverpool and Bristol were frequently intended for London and were carried to the capital by rail. Thus meat, dairy produce, eggs, fruit and even some vegetables were increasingly likely to be imported foods and, when their shelf life neared its end, to be sold in street markets or by costermongers.

In 1912, London's public analysts made 24,964 examinations of food samples of which 2,329 (9.33 per cent) were adulterated.[43] Examples of adulteration early in the twentieth century included a grocer in Bow, East London, being fined for the sale of cocoa comprised of 50 per cent arrowroot, 30 per cent sugar and only 20 per cent cocoa, and a baker fined for using bad eggs for pastries.[44] Newspaper reports of rotten fruit for jam-making being seized in Bermondsey aroused concern about the questionable quality of cheap prepared foods of all kinds.[45] In November 1905, the Civil Service Cooperative Society was successfully prosecuted in Westminster for selling tins of spinach containing copper sulphate to retain the green colour of the spinach.[46] In one part of London, samples of 'Irish butter' taken from 14 shops in 1911 turned out to be largely margarine.[47] In 1919, coffee sampled in St Marylebone proved to be 59 per cent chicory and in Camberwell 37 per cent chicory; in St Pancras ten out of 36 samples of vinegar were adulterated.[48]

The small scale nature of much food production was a contributory hazard until the interwar years. In the London County Council area there were over 100 cowsheds, about 150 slaughterhouses, over 2,000 ice-cream premises and a great number of 'other food places' – more than 6,000 of which were in Westminster alone.[49] As a comprehensive inspection system developed, evidence of gross adulteration disappeared: bread, tea, coffee, butter, lard, pepper, mustard, and pickles, all of which had been subject to adulteration in the nineteenth century were largely free from it by the interwar years.[50] The production of bread in large scale factory bakeries and the sale of most of the remaining items in standard quantities, pre-packed by the food processor or retailer, were significant factors in this change in quality[51] though some examples of adulteration were still to be found, such as beer, spirits

---

42 For the food manufacturers' defence of this practice, see French, and Phillips, 2000, 100.

43 Board of Agriculture, *Reports from Commissioners, Inspectors and Others*, 1912–13, 204.

44 *BFJ*, December 1901, 392.

45 *BFJ*, September 1903, 197.

46 *BFJ*, November 1905, 228–9.

47 *Reports from Commissioners, Inspectors and Others*, (1912–13), 177. Of 138 samples analysed, 107 were margarine.

48 Ministry of Health, *Annual Report of the Chief Medical Officer for 1918–20*, 1920.

49 London County Council (LCC), *Annual Report of the Council, 1920, vol. III, Public Health*.

50 Filby, 1934, 195–210.

51 See Oddy, 2003, ch. 5.

or vinegar, to which water could easily be added. By 1925, when new regulations covering milk, meat, imported foods and the use of preservatives and colouring matter came into force, adulteration in London and the 40 largest provincial towns was down to 5.5 per cent of items sampled.[52] Even so, outbreaks of food poisoning in London in the late 1930s, caused mainly by meat (94), fish (53) and tinned fish and paste (32), indicated that the system of inspection was not perfect.[53] Milk also remained a problem. Samples arriving by rail or road in 1919 and 1920 revealed that approximately 6 per cent came from cows infected with bovine tuberculosis. The proportion infected rose to 9.1 per cent in 1930, and was still 7 per cent in 1937 and 1938.[54]

Conclusion

The continuance of adulteration long after it was made illegal by act of parliament was due to the fragmentary structure of local government in England and Wales and the inadequate provisions of the legislation. Adulteration was profitable for many retailers in the food, drink and tobacco trades while demand was outstripping supply; the risk that a small money fine might be incurred was worth taking. In consequence, food adulteration was practised initially to increase supply and later to extend shelf-life. Public analysts found their rôle undermined by the restricted nature of the Acts, and the low fees for their work. Moreover, as the grosser forms of adulteration disappeared, public concern diminished. By the late 1880s, the reports of *The Lancet*'s Analytical Sanitary Commission had become less frequent and less influential,[55] so that the attempts by public analysts and others to develop laboratories, journals reporting adulteration, and to create an independent system of food certification, had only limited success. Nevertheless, public analysts performed an important function by establishing the composition of the foods they tested[56] which led to standards being incorporated in later food legislation. From the late nineteenth-century onwards, interest in the purity of foods eaten was as much a reaction to the spread of industrialism as the arts and crafts movement or the *art nouveau* style of decoration. Nor was it confined to Britain: in the United States, the widely based reform proposal for 'pure foods' which developed from the 1880s onwards, achieved the passing of the 1906 Pure Food, Drink, and Drugs Act.[57] In Britain, the revival of pure food reform between 1910 and 1914 was less successful.

---

52 In the rest of England and Wales it was 7.7 per cent. *Seventh Annual Report of the Ministry of Health, 1925–26*, 1926, 33.

53 LCC, *Report of the County Medical Officer of Health for the Year 1938*, 7 listed 458 notified cases in 1937 and 270 in 1938.

54 LCC, *Annual Reports of the County Medical Officer of Health*, 1920, 1930, 1938. There is a more detailed study of milk by Atkins, 2000.

55 *Lancet* 1887, I, 1241: 'the more noxious kind of adulteration…has to a great part been suppressed'.

56 Analyses of foods which are comparable with modern food tables were being published as early as the 1880s. For examples, see Cheyne et al., 1884, 79–85.

57 See Goodwin, 1999.

Its objectives were often unclear and it faced concerted opposition from pressure groups such as the Federation of Grocers' Associations, the retail trade journal *The Grocer*, and the food manufacturers, which successfully prevented any extension of the food legislation.

Adulteration continued until analytical techniques were improved and sampling and inspection of food by public health inspectors was extended. During the interwar years it still attracted comment.[58] As long as the level of fines remained low, there were retailers prepared to take a chance by selling food of poor quality or not fit for human consumption. This encouraged manufacturers to rely on their own quality control methods to substantiate their advertising claims, rather than external validation.[59] As food advertising became more general, shopkeepers increasingly stocked manufactured and ready-prepared foods, the quality of which was determined by factory inspectors and food manufacturers' own warranties.[60] These changes in retailing meant that food in London was cleaner, more conveniently packaged and more standardized in quality.

References

Accum, F.C. *A Treatise on Adulterations of Food, and Culinary Poisons, Exhibiting the Fraudulent Sophistications of Bread, Beer, Wine ... and Other Articles Employed in Domestic Economy and Methods of Detecting them*, London, 1820.

Anon. *Deadly Adulteration and Slow Poisoning Unmasked, or Disease and Death in the Pot and the Bottle*, London, 1830.

Atkins, P.J. 'Milk Consumption and Tuberculosis in Britain, 1850–1950', in ICREFH V, 2000, 83–95.

Atkins, P.J. and Stanziani, A. 'From Laboratory Expertise to Litigation: The Municipal Laboratory of Paris and the Inland Revenue Laboratory in London, 1870–1914: A Comparative Analysis', in Van Damme, S. and Rabier, C. (eds) *Fields of Expertise: Experts, Knowledge and Powers in European Modern History* Cambridge, 2007.

Burnett, J. *Plenty and Want*, Third edition, London, 1989.

Cheyne, W.W. Corfield, W.H. and Cassal, C.E. *Public Health Laboratory Work*, (International Health Exhibition Handbook, 1884) London, 1884.

Chirnside, R. and Hamence, J.H. *The 'Practising Chemists': A History of the Society for Analytical Chemistry 1874–1974*, London, 1974.

Dyer, B. *The Society of Public Analysts and other Analytical Chemists. Some Reminiscences of its First Fifty Years and a Review of its Activities* (by C. Ainsworth Mitchell), Cambridge, 1932.

---

58 See, for example, Helena Normanton, 'The Adulteration of Food', *Good Housekeeping*, 1924.

59 By the interwar years, some firms in the food industry were carrying out more analyses than public authorities. See Atkins and Stanziani, 2007.

60 See Horrocks, 1994. For scientists' impact upon production and marketing of foods, see Horrocks, 1995. For the impact on retailers, see ICREFH VIII, 245–6 or, in more detail, Oddy, 2003, 100–105.

Central Statistical Office, *Annual Abstract of Statistics*, 97, London, 1960.

Filby, F.A. *A History of Food Adulteration and Analysis*, London, 1934.

French, M. and Phillips, J. *Cheated not Poisoned? Food Regulation in the United Kingdom, 1875–1938*, Manchester, 2000.

French, M. and Phillips, J. 'Sophisticates or Dupes? Attitudes toward Food Consumers in Edwardian Britain', *Enterprise and Society* 4, 3, 2003, 442–70.

Goodwin, L.S. *The Pure Food, Drink, and Drug Crusaders, 1879–1914*, Jefferson NC, 1999.

Hammond, P.W. and Egan, H. *Weighed in the Balance: A History of the Laboratory of the Government Chemist*, London, 1992.

Hassall, A.H. *Food and its Adulterations: Comprising the Reports of the Analytical Sanitary Commission of The Lancet for the Years 1851 to 1854 Inclusive Revised and Extended*, London, 1855.

Horrocks, S.M. 'Quality Control and Research: The Role of Scientists in the British Food Industry, 1870–1939' in ICREFH II, 1994, 130–145.

Horrocks, S.M. 'Nutritional Science and the Food Industry in Britain, 1920–1990' in ICREFH III, 1995, 7–18.

Lancet Reports of the International Congresses of Hygiene and Demography held from 1876 to 1889, London, 1891.

Liverseege, J.F. *Adulteration and Analysis of Food and Drugs*, London, 1932.

Oddy, D.J. *From Plain Fare to Fusion Food: British Diet from the 1890s to the 1990s*, Woodbridge, 2003.

Paulus, I. *The Search for Pure Food: A Sociology of Legislation in Britain*, London, 1974.

Schmiechen, J. and Carls, K. *The British Market Hall A Social and Architectural History*, New Haven, 1999.

Sinclair, U.B. *The Jungle*, New York, 1906.

Société Universelle de la Croix-Blanche de Genève, *Premier Congrès International pour la Répression des Fraudes Alimentaires et Pharmceutiques* [First International Congress for the Repression of Food and Chemical Frauds], Geneva, 1909.

Tames, R. *Feeding London A Taste of History*, London, 2003.

Transactions of the Fifteenth International Congress on Hygiene and Demography, Washington, 1912, Washington, D.C., 1913.

Official Publications

Board of Agriculture, *Report from the Departmental Committee on Regulations for Milk and Cream*, British Parliamentary Papers (BPP) 1901 (Cd.491) xxx.

Board of Agriculture, *Reports from Commissioners, Inspectors and Others, 1912–13*, BPP 1912–13 (Cd 6194) x.

House of Commons, *Report of the Select Committee on Adulteration of Food, Drink and Drugs, 1856*, BPP 1856, viii.

House of Commons, *Report of the Select Committee on Food Products Adulteration*, BPP 1895, x; 1896, ix.

Local Government Board, *Report of the Departmental Committee into the Use of Preservatives and Colouring Matter in Food,* BPP 1902 (Cd.833) xxxiv.

London County Council, *Annual Report of the Council, 1920, vol. III, Public Health.*

London County Council, *Annual Reports of the County Medical Officer of Health,* 1920–38.

Ministry of Health, *Annual Report of the Chief Medical Officer for 1918–20,* BPP, 1920, xvii.

Ministry of Health, *Seventh Annual Report of the Ministry of Health, 1925–26,* BPP 1926, xi.

Ministry of Health, *Twentieth Annual Report of the Ministry of Health, 1938–39,* BPP 1938–39 (Cmd. 6089) xi.

Chapter 9

Municipal Laboratories and the Analysis of Foodstuffs in France under the Third Republic: A Case Study of the Paris Municipal Laboratory, 1878–1907

Alessandro Stanziani

During the last quarter of the nineteenth century, the creation of municipal laboratories for the analysis of foodstuffs and beverages can be included in a more general tendency of the first years of the Third Republic, where municipalities were given management control of sanitation in food markets. I will look in particular at the Paris laboratory, the first and, most controversial, and I will ask two questions. First, was it designed to serve the interests of traders, or consumers, or local authorities? This question then leads to a second one, about the aim for which the laboratory was created. Was it supposed to protect public health or to regulate competition?

In order to find a satisfactory answer to these questions, it is necessary not only to take into account the founding principles of the laboratory, but also its practices. Food expertise raised several problems – to start with the designation of the experts and their methods. On the one hand, traders insisted that their skills, knowledge and experience were required to judge product quality, including organoleptic analysis. On the other hand, municipal authorities and some public opinion, favoured the 'objective' methods of science, such as organic chemical analysis.

More generally, traders emphasized that foodstuffs were not standardized products, and that it was impossible to conclude about adulteration only on the grounds of chemical analysis. For example, how could one demonstrate that an excess of water in wine (or in butter) was the responsibility of the producer rather than of 'nature'? For their part, scientists advocated listing the main components and their acceptable values for every product. This supposed the possibility of establishing a correspondence between products and expertise; unfortunately this was much more a project than a reality.

This conflict between economic actors and scientists on the form of expertise added to a tension between the central state and the municipalities on the distribution of regulatory power in food and beverage markets. In fact, different municipal laboratories used different methods of analysis, and the question arose of how to overcome the paradox that meat refused in Lille might be accepted in Paris. The only solution consisted in establishing an official scale of the methods of analysis valid for all the municipal laboratories; but this could be done only if these laboratories were submitted to state rather than municipal rules. This is to say, the creation of a national market is inseparable from that of national regulatory institutions.

In the following pages I will detail the history of these confrontations and their issues. First I recall the main economic theories on quality; then these arguments are tested on the historical experience of food adulteration in nineteenth-century France. This will lead me to explain the need for 'third party' expertise – municipal laboratories. I will focus on the Paris laboratory: after recalling its origin and original aims, the debates will be recalled about its methods of expertise, their significance and issues on the eve of World War I. The conclusion tries to explain different related issues: organoleptic versus chemical expertise, municipal versus national laboratories, judicial versus administrative rules on foodstuffs and beverages.

The Institutional Organization of Expertise

The first question concerns identifying the rationale for municipal expertise in food products, in other words the rationale for an institutional understanding of quality in food and drink. Traditional neo-classical economics does not grant good quality particular attention because, in a perfect information world, with perfect competition, there is no justification for a minimum quality standard.[1] Since the 1970s, following Akerlof and Stiglitz, economic theory has usually focused on good quality when speaking of information asymmetries. A better circulation of information, provided either by firms themselves (the reputation mechanism) or by the state (quality and information regulation) can overcome these problems.

According to some authors, in this situation, certification set up by the pool of producers will be more efficient than public certification.[2] Self-regulatory agencies command a greater degree of expertise and technical knowledge of practices and innovatory possibilities than the legislator or a public agency. Monitoring and enforcement costs are also supposed to be reduced.[3] Supporters of this solution equally note that the administrative costs of the regime are internalized in the activity, which is subject to regulation, while in the case of public agencies they are borne by taxpayers (unless they are funded by a tax on producers).[4]

However, self-regulation is not efficient when the costs of monitoring and controlling quality as organized by producers themselves are high. In large communities with 'anonymous individuals', self-regulation may encounter the problem of free-riding and enforcement. In such a case, self-certification may be devised more to confer utility on suppliers than to meet consumer preferences. The imposed quality may exceed that which will meet consumers' preferences while not being justified by externalities; the excessive cost will be born by consumers.[5]

In between pure self-regulation and state intervention, several forms of organizations are conceivable. For example, the state can either fix and monitor

---

1   Shapiro, 1982.
2   Raynaud and Valceschini, 1997.
3   Linnemer and Perrot, 2000.
4   Ogus, 2000.
5   Trebilcock, 1983.

the rules or delegate to local agencies. The solution can be derived from principal-agent theory, by reference to the costs of information upon which the rule-making decisions are to be based and those of monitoring compliance and enforcing the rules. Another mixed solution is when officials representing the public interest participate in the local committees of certification. The aim is to realize many benefits of self-regulation but control the costs which result from private agencies' rent-seeking.

Several aspects of both these arguments (neo-institutionalist and neo-classical) have been criticized, starting with the exclusive use of efficiency as a criterion to evaluate market and institutional performance. Individual economic actors can pursue non-optimal strategies, according to their beliefs, cultural traditions and economic environmental constraints. All the same, the raising as well as the functioning of institutions can hardly be explained by efficiency optimizing aims; political and social concerns seems to be prior in these choices.[6]

In order to test these opposing theoretical statements, in the following pages I will consider a given historical context, that is the food market in nineteenth century Paris and the activity of the municipal laboratory. In particular, at first the problems of food quality and adulteration will be evoked in order to answer the question of the quality identification of a product (via market, rules and/or institutions). I shall argue that different criteria of testing food (organoleptic or chemical) testify to the fact that 'tastes' are not simply 'psychological' or social/cultural variables but that they are institutionally embedded and vice versa, food exchange and consumption practices largely contribute to legal and institutional issues.

I shall also argue that neither the origin nor the functioning of the Paris laboratory responded to efficiency issues, but, rather, to an historical shaping of what food quality, exchange and market institutions were. In this, lobby pressure and the symbolic value of food in the social order played a key role. Finally, the institutional setting of centres of expertise responded to a broader political problem, that is the equilibrium, under the Third Republic, between the central state and the municipalities.

The economic context: Food and drink quality and adulteration

As I have demonstrated elsewhere,[7] an analysis of the adulteration of food and drink in this period lays bare the interconnections between market rules and institutions in the emergence of understandings and definitions of product 'quality'. The adulteration itself was achieved by many different processes: manipulation of organic chemistry, dilution, counterfeiting, and commercial fraud. For example, with wine, watering (*mouillage*) was widespread in large cities, encouraged by a municipal form of taxation (in volume), the *octroi*. Wines high in alcohol were transported and, once in town, diluted. According to the statistics of the Parisian *octroi*, in the early 1880s, watering accounted for at least one-sixth of the million hectolitres consumed annually in Paris.

---

6   Among others: Fligstein, 2001; Salais and Storper, 1993.
7   Stanziani, 2005.

Adding plaster to wine (plastering) was a traditional practice in the Midi, Spain and Italy to prevent spoilage on long trips due to changes in temperature. It affected Midi wines, between 25 and 40 per cent of French production, from 1875 to the 1910s.[8] In addition, the sugaring of wines was widespread from the 1870s, mostly in Burgundy and in the central-northern areas of France. Here sweetened water was added to the *marc* (grape pulp) or to the first vintage if it was not very alcoholic. This practice was legal until 1897 but a declaration had to be made to the tax department.

These trends in the wine market had differential impacts upon winegrowers and traders, according to their mutual relationships and the technical characteristics of wine making in particular areas. For example, plastering was not only supported by winegrowers and traders in the Midi, but also by their main buyers, the Paris *négociants*, and, more surprisingly, by some Bordeaux traders who blended local wines with those from the Midi or with Spanish (equally plastered) wines.[9] Rather, plastering was attacked by the hygienist movement which later (early 1890s) won the support of those Bordeaux winegrowers who were aiming to stop the development of the Midi as a rival district.

The government initially tolerated sugared wines because of the joint pressure of sugar-beet producers of the North and the increasing interests of Centre and West France producers, whose wines had been weakened by phylloxera. For obvious reasons, sugared wines were criticized in the Midi. At first in 1886 and again in 1897, the addition of sugar was submitted to an increasing tax, which became almost prohibitive at the turn of the century. Together with the reconstruction of vineyards and the increasing availability of Algerian wines, this explains the fall in sugared wine production from the mid-1890s.

A similar issue can be observed in the butter market. Here export prices showed a considerable rise, about 91 per cent, between 1850 and 1880; but, when the price of butter dropped by approximately 20–22 per cent in Normandy in next two decades, producers blamed 'fraud' and margarine.[10] Until the end of the 1860s, 'falsifications' of butter were limited to attempts to blend it with starch, lard or melted grease; 'however, these processes were so coarse that the public were not fooled.'[11] From the 1870s, adulteration was in two principal categories: leaving an abnormal quantity of the components of milk in the butter; and incorporating different fats and non-fatty material.[12] However, a major rupture came with the improved manufacture of margarine and its mixing with butter. This often took place in the Paris area, where there were ten margarine factories, of which the most important, the Société Anonyme d'Alimentation, was based in Aubervilliers.[13] Butter lobbies thus sought to pressure the government to adopt rules (the laws of 1887 and 1897) forbidding any mixture of butter with margarine.

---

8   Lachiver, 1988.
9   AN F 12 6873, 6874.
10   Ibid, 228, 366.
11   Vérin, 1905, 31.
12   Ibid., 30.
13   Girard and de Brevans, 1889.

Last but not least, there was widespread milk adulteration. The market for this product was increasing throughout the nineteenth century, especially during the last quarter of the century.[14] The installation of an efficient system of collection, pasteurization and transport by refrigerated vans made the fortune of dealers and dairy farmers in the zones near to cities. French dairying includes two zones, one to the west of a line joining Charentes to the Ardennes, and the other stretching from the Massif Central to the Jura and Savoy. In 1912, these zones had 67 per cent of the nation's livestock and produced 79 per cent of its milk.[15]

In the second half of the nineteenth century, the market for milk increased because of a new phenomenon: working mothers nursed less and started to buy milk. As a result, hygienists, always ready to link health and social policy, focused on the adulteration of milk. France followed the attention already given to this in England from the 1850s. If we accept the assertions of the hygienists and the English statistics, then milk was the most adulterated of all products.[16] However, despite media interest and the political role of milk adulteration (and probably because of this) no national rules on this product were adopted until 1935. The problem was that, unlike wine and butter, where the hygienist movement had almost unanimously condemned wine plastering and artificial colouration as well as butter frauds, in the case of milk they were more divided. This was so above all because of the major symbolic importance assigned to milk in the hygienist debate of that time; what is more, this attention took place in a context of a scientific uncertainty concerning milk diseases and the nutritional effects of skimming.[17]

To sum up, in France during the second half of the nineteenth century, the process of urbanization, the increasing complexity of commercial networks, and the rise of organic chemistry, meant that the question of product adulteration was at the very core of public debate. The new administrative and legal rules that followed were shaped by conflicts among economic lobbies that resulted from, first, their use of varied quality conventions and, second, information asymmetries. On the supply side, economic actors sought to exclude some of their competitors from the market through leverage in its legal-institutional organization. In addition, under the Third Republic, the influence of the scientists increased in the National Assembly and respect for the hygiene issue spread across the whole political spectrum.

For hygienists, the need to control food adulteration was one element in a broader movement for social reform. They condemned the greed of traders and railed against a legal system that failed to condemn them.[18] An important debating point was whether the rules were inadequate and needed changing, or whether their enforcement was weak. Either way, the institutions in charge were under scrutiny, along with their expertise in food and their methods of analysis.[19]

---

14 *Annuaire Statistique de la France* 1894, 333 ; 1899, 137.
15 Girard and de Brevans, 422.
16 Burnett, 1999, 38, 40.
17 See chapter 11 by Adel den Hartog.
18 Brouardel, 1881.
19 Vidal, 1882.

Municipal or State Organization of Expertise

The nineteenth century saw manoeuvring between the central and local states as to who would regulate food and drink. A government Consultative Committee for Hygiene was founded in 1849 and *département* councils were created under the authority of the respective prefects.[20] But significant direction from above was delayed until 1889 when the High Council for Public Health was launched under the aegis of the Ministry of the Interior.

Early on the municipalities were more active on food, after acquiring powers in laws of 1855 and 1867, and a decree of 1859. Their inspectors were empowered to sample the wares of pharmacists, grocers and food retailers and, if necessary, make seizures. Hygienists were in their element in cities because of the many environmental issues raised by rapid urbanization. There was a trend in the early years of the Third Republic to grant municipalities increasing powers, and the movement for the municipal laboratories found fertile soil. The International Congress of Hygiene held in Brussels in 1876 highlighted the role that the municipal laboratory played there,[21] and the following Paris congress (1878) stressed the need to organize similar laboratories in the main French towns. By 1885 this had been achieved in Paris, Le Havre, Reims, Rouen, Saint-Etienne, Amiens and Pau.[22] At first these laboratories were staffed by generalists because the hygienists believed in holistic preventative measures that included food habits, vaccination, housing, and public awareness.[23]

This broad approach was attacked during the trichinosis epidemic (1878–91).[24] There were calls for more detailed inspections using specialist scientific skills. Legislation was proposed in the Chamber of Deputies that sought the establishment of a special food inspection service at the Ministry of Agriculture and Trade. The controversial element of this was the legal and administrative status that the food inspectors and analysts would have. Should they be granted both powers of seizure and prosecution? Under French law this was problematic because of the clear distinction between administrative and judicial powers.[25] The Council of Hygiene advised the government to draw up interim regulations on this topic whilst awaiting a more general law, and it also requested the establishment of laboratories at the *département* level.[26] These suggestions met with resistance in Parliament from business interests on the grounds that trade would be affected and that inspectors were anyway not competent to judge the quality of food and drink.

Paris decided to press ahead under its existing powers. A municipal laboratory was first proposed in 1876, for the detection of artificially coloured wines. However, it was thought of as a way of controlling the market and not as a service open to the public. When the laboratory opened in 1878, it immediately faced protests from both traders and consumers, and it was not until two years later that it became a public

---

20 AN F 8170, Law of 18 December 1848 and Decree of 15 February 1849.
21 See chapter 7 by Peter Scholliers.
22 Du Mesnil, 1886.
23 Ibid.
24 Stanziani, 2003.
25 Hogg, 1881.
26 Ibid.

service. After this, the laboratory was used by the police and the prefecture, and also by private actors, many of whom were from the food industry seeking a neutral scientific view to settle a contractual problem.

The laboratory's budget quickly increased during the 1880s, from 129,800 francs in 1881, to 206,890 in 1883.[27] This was partly due to increasing public (municipal

Table 9.1   Paris laboratory tariff in 1886 (francs)

Charge	Products
Free	• Out-of-date food products
	• Watered down wine
5	• wine: proportions of alcohol and extracts; proportions of dry extracts
	• kitchen salt: proportioning of sodium chloride
10	• wine: artificial colouring;
	• milk: density, colour, proportion of butterfat;
	• potable water: analysis by hydrometric method;
	• chicory: proportion of ashes; search for foreign matter
	• meats, vegetables and preserves: microscopic examination, search for metals
	• sugar: prohibited dyes
	• sweeteners, glucose, honey: microscopic examination and proportioning with polarimeter
20	• wine: tasting, proportion of alcohol, extracts, ashes, tartar, sulphates
	• beer or cider: density of alcohol, ashes, acidity
	• flour, breads, paté and pastry: proportion of water, ash, gluten, foreign substances
	• Syrups and jams: proportion of sugar and glucose; dyes
	• Butter: water content, mixing with margarine and other greases
	• Coffee and cocoa: constituents, foreign substances
50	pharmaceutical products, beef extracts
100	drinking water
1,000	mineral water

Source: Laboratoire Municipal de Chimie de la Ville de Paris, 1886.

and state) subsidies, and partly due to charges on samples submitted by the public (Table 9.1). In 1881, for instance, the laboratory conducted 3,958 free analyses and 378 paid for by private customers; to this, one has to add 2,181 analyses of samples taken by municipal inspectors. Wine was the most analysed product, representing about half of the samples in 1883. Most of these came from the public and were dealt with free of charge because they were the subject of allegations of watering. By comparison, the second most analysed product, milk, was largely brought in by inspectors. In other words, wine adulteration was in part a public order question and in part a contractual matter between traders and retailers; whereas milk adulteration

---

27 Laboratoire Municipal de Chimie de la Ville de Paris, 1886.

mostly concerned the authorities, and the frequent tensions between producers, traders and retailers were solved informally. This is because the wine and milk markets were organized differently: while milk producers and dealers were under wholesale control, in the wine market there were regional differences coupled with increasing conflicts between wine growers, traders and retailers.

Despite a rapid increase in analysis, food inspection was still inadequate in Paris. In 1882, inspectors managed only 40,000 visits, including 5,260 visits to markets, 17,626 to restaurants, dairies and wine merchants, and 6,317 to grocers.[28] 20 inspectors sampled the wine in bistros, 43 dealt with butchers, and there were 20 for grocers and restaurants. So, the chance of a particular outlet being visited was very slight and there was a minimal deterrent effect, particularly for small dealers without a reputation to worry about.

Despite the system of inspection and analysis being relatively weak in its early stages in the 1880s, the food industry was nevertheless determined to oppose it vigorously. One debating point was the methods of analysis employed. Wine merchants and food traders were especially critical of the challenge that organic chemistry represented to their own organoleptic expertise. They argued that the science was inadequate and that it was capable, for instance, of confusing a bad vintage with an adulterated wine. The use of upper and lower limits for certain components of wine, beyond which adulteration was presumed, was particularly disliked.[29] As far as they were concerned, 'natural' products cannot be standardized.

In a report to the Prefect, the director of the laboratory, C. Girard, countered questions about methodology by pointing out that tasting (*dégustation*) *was* used, particularly for the top rank wines. He also argued that he had dual responsibilities, for both food safety and adulteration, and he was in favour of disclosing detailed information about both.[30] This proved to be a flash point between the municipal laboratory and commerce. The food industry was willing to appease hygienist and public opinion by accepting bans on products that were dangerous for health, but they felt that the laboratory was going too far in its insistence on disclosing information on quality, beyond what was necessary. In a sense they were right because the Prefect, in his report to the Ministry of Commerce, had to admit that the laboratory was just a simple source of information and that its analyses constituted only indices of presumption, not clear evidence for legal judgements.[31] As a result, the laboratory was forced on to the back foot, and in the 1890s judges even raised doubts as to whether its analyses were admissible as evidence.[32] This was because organic chemistry was open to question on the accuracy and stability of its observations.

In 1896 the Ministry of Finance set up a special Commission to identify standard criteria for analysing wines. This was composed entirely of scientists, in order to minimize arguments and to promote coordination among the various

---

28 Girard, 1887.

29 AN F 12 7417, Feuilles d'Analyse du Laboratoire de Paris [Analytical records of the Paris Laboratory], January 1884.

30 AN F 12 7417, Ch. Girard to Paris Prefect, 18 June 1884.

31 AN F 12 7417, Prefecture of police to Ministry of Commerce, 9 mars 1883.

32 AN BB 18 6025, letter from Paris Prefect to Ministry of the Interior, 18/3/1895.

laboratories.[33] Appropriate methods of analysis were agreed but, more importantly, the Commission also concluded that evidence in a judicial trial about adulteration must include other forms of corroboration, such as letters, business accounts, or verbal testimony. Tensions between municipalities and the central state were such, however, that rules were not formulated until the general law on food adulteration of 1905 was followed in July 1906 by a Ministerial Decree confirming the creation of a new Service for the Repression of Frauds at the Ministry of Agriculture. Under this new regime, Municipal laboratories were only allowed to survive by agreement, under ministerial control.[34] The balance of power had now shifted from the municipalities towards the central government. The Paris laboratory of Paris tried to hold out against this loss of independence by refusing to submit to the Service of Repression of Fraud. It even contested the value of the methods of analysis selected for use by the new Service. As a result, the Ministry refused the Paris laboratory official status and the courts refused to take its analyses into consideration.[35]

Conclusion

The process of urbanization paralleled the rise of a national market and an increase in the number of intermediaries between food producer and consumer. This phenomenon, together with the entry of chemistry into the realm of agro-food industry, raised serious information asymmetry problems. There was a new instability concerning common understandings of quality exacerbated by the common adulteration of some foodstuffs in the second half on the nineteenth century. Sometimes existing definitions of product quality broke down and their renegotiation proved problematic. This situation of generalized uncertainty gave rise to the attempts made by economic lobbies to conquer market share by turning legal rules and market institutions to their own advantage. This was mostly done by influencing official definitions of quality and adulteration of a given product which, in turn, made it possible to exclude some competitors from the market.

It was in this context that the question of expertise about products arose. In the absence of a prior agreement on quality between the parties to an exchange, recourse to an external referee was required. However, different interests of economic association, as well as the lack of coordination between central state administrations, encouraged municipalities to offer their own services for food inspection and analysis. This issue equally fitted with the broader tendency during the first years of the Third Republic to decentralize powers to the municipalities.

Municipal laboratories were set up in order to supply this service to both public officials and private contractors. However, both the appeal to public institutions and the methods used to evaluate products were not outside, but within, the political

---

33 AN F 12 6873, Decree of the President of the Republic on the Formation of an Expert Commission of the Ministry of Finance.

34 AN BB 18 6055, Internal note, Ministry of Justice, no date.

35 Décrets du 19/3/1907 (JO du 7/4/1907) et du 13/6/1907 (JO du 20/6/1907); AN BB 18 6031, Report of the Procurator General of the Appeal Court of the Ministry of Justice, 27/4/1909.

economy of food security. As such, public expertise was submitted to the same tensions as private expertise; in particular, organoleptic expertise was opposed to chemical analysis.

From this point of view, chemistry intervened to promote the standardization of public expertise, which, in turn, constituted a form of legitimating laboratories and public administrations vis-à-vis the public, while facilitating coordination between scattered units of public administration. Unfortunately, this form of expertise was unable to take into consideration non-standardized products, that is, the great majority of agro-food and drink products at that time.

By comparison, organoleptic expertise was able and willing to take into account product individualities and this kept safe a role for traders and economic professionals in product-quality development. However, this was done at the expense of the possibility of mobilizing this expertise in a formal legal framework. To sum up, the opposition between chemical and organoleptic expertise was between two criteria of product evaluation, two notions of the law (one close to administrative-police rules the second to judicial law) and two different forms of intersection between law and economics. Scientific analysis led to macro forms of regulation while organoleptic expertise was much more anchored to micro contractual arrangements.

In France, unlike other countries (for example Great Britain or Germany) these confrontations were solved in that standardized business expertise was organoleptic, while the state took over the power of municipalities on food control. This accompanied a shift of food security and food quality rules from a civil and/or penal status to administrative penal rules. It also mirrored a broader transformation in the middle years of the Third Republic towards more centralized forms of power.

Generally in western European countries, discussions and conflicts about food quality and security and the forms of the expertise in the period 1870–1914 confirmed that the process of product quality definition was not the result of simple psychological choices (neoclassical arguments) nor institutional constraints (neo-institutionalist approach). On the contrary, markets and institutions, consumption, and the emergence of 'quality' were all part of a definite historical legal and cognitive framework. In the short run, rules and actors' perceptions strongly influenced economic action (albeit not in a strongly deterministic path, but rather by fixing a set of possibilities). In the middle and long term, these same actions and perceptions contributed to the evolution of both the cognitive and the institutional framework. This is why product standardization and centralization of powers in market controls are so closely connected in twentieth-century history.

References

Annuaire Statistique de la France, various years.
Brouardel, A. 'Discussion Suivant le Rapport de J.-A. Pabst' [Discussion of the Report by J.-A. Pabst], *Revue d'Hygiène et de Police Sanitaire* 1881, 1035–43.
Burnett, J. *Liquid Pleasures*, London, 1999.

Du Mesnil, O. *Bureaux Municipaux d'Hygiène. Rapport sur leur Mode d'Organisation et de Fonctionnement* [Municipal Health Bureaux: Report on its Organization and Operation], Paris, 1886.

Fligstein, N. *The Architecture of Markets*, Princeton, 2001.

Girard, C. *Documents sur les Falsifications des Matières alimentaires et sur les Travaux du Laboratoire Municipal* [Papers on Food Adulteration], 2nd report, Paris, 1887.

Girard, C. and Brevans, M. de, *La Margarine et le Beurre Artificiel* [Margarine and Artificial Butter], Paris, 1889.

Hogg D. 'De l'Organisation de l'Inspection des Substances Alimentaires' [On the Organization of the Inspection of Foodstuffs], *Revue d'Hygiène et de Police Sanitaire* 1881, 431–50.

Laboratoire Municipal de Chimie de la Ville de Paris, 'Tarifs', *Revue d'Hygiène et de Police Sanitaire* 1886, 714–6.

Lachiver, M. *Vins, Vignes et Vignerons* [Wines, Vines and Wine-Makers], Paris, 1988.

Linnemer, L. and Perrot, A. 'Une Analyse Economique des Signes de Qualité' [An Economic Analysis of Quality Indicators], *Revue Économique* 51, 2000, 1397–418.

Murard, L. and Zylberman, P. *L'Hygiène dans la République* [Hygiene in the Republic], 1996.

Ogus, A. 'Self-regulation', in Bouckaert, B. and De Geest, G. (eds), *Encyclopedia of Law and Economics*, Cheltenham, vol. 5, 2000, 587–602.

Raynaud, E. and Valceschini, E. 'Controlling Quality and Competition Policy. An Official Label as an Example: The "Label Rouge" in Poultry Industry', in Schiefer, G. and Helbig, R. (eds) *Quality Management and Process Improvement for Competitive Advantage in Agriculture and Food*, Bonn, 1997, 265–80.

Salais, R. and Storper, M. *Les Mondes de Production* [Worlds of Production], Paris, 1993.

Shapiro, C. 'Consumer Information, Product Quality, and Seller Reputation', *Bell Journal of Economics* 13, 1982, 20–35.

Stanziani, A. 'Food Safety and Expertise: The Trichinosis Epidemic in France, 1878–1891', *Food and Foodways* 10, 2003, 209–37.

Stanziani, A. *Histoire de la Qualité Alimentaire, 1870–1914* [History of Food Quality], Paris, 2005.

Trebilcock, M. 'Regulating Service Quality in Professional Markets', in Dewees, D. (ed.), *The Regulation of Quality: Products, Services, Workplaces and the Environment*, London, 1983.

Vérin, L. *La Répression des Fraudes dans le Commerce du Beurre et la Fabrication de la Margarine (Loi du 16/4/87)* [Repression of Fraud in the Butter Trade], Unpublished Doctoral Thesis, Lille, 1905.

Vidal, E. 'La Nécessité de Nouvelles Mesures Légales pour Réprimer la Falsification des Substances Alimentaires' [The Need for New Legal Measures to Curb the Adulteration of Foodstuffs], *Revue d'Hygiène et de Police Sanitaire* 1882, 32–6.

Chapter 10

The 'War Against Food Adulteration': Municipal Food Monitoring and Citizen Self-Help Associations in Germany, 1870s–1880s

Vera Hierholzer

'In a number of cities the people have used self-help', the Imperial Health Department stated in 1878 in a survey about organization of food monitoring in the German Reich.[1] This statement is a surprise; historians have made state and municipal institutions the self-evident object of research on the establishment of modern food control in the nineteenth century.[2] The efforts of private organizations to regulate the production and sale of food have not been examined in Germany.[3] The thesis of this paper is that civil society was, at least during the early years of the German Reich, involved in food monitoring and that its efforts complemented state measures, especially at the local level.

Until the end of the 1870s, the legal basis for food monitoring in Germany was a patchwork of state and city borders, bye-laws, and administrative and police decrees. The Penal Code of 1871 did contain individual provisions on food traffic, but a unified system of norms, which could have been the basis of comprehensive preventive food monitoring, was still missing. Between the regulations of the individual territories, even among the local authorities of the same state, various differences existed. The only commonality was their mostly reactive character and the fact that they were often still connected to pre-modern decrees, as well as to specific local traditions. Systematic monitoring was achieved in very few territories; in most the actual controls were left to the cities, which were apparently overwhelmed and simply conducted sporadic checks. In general, they also lacked trained personnel.[4]

At the end of the 1870s, however, in several cities private associations were formed, the so-called 'associations against adulteration of food', which plugged this gap, at least temporarily, by developing their own food controls. This chapter will examine their origin and structure. It will analyse their strategies for the regulation of food quality and link them to the food monitoring activities of the cities.

---

1 *Stenographische Berichte*, 1368–82.
2 Ellerbrock, 1987; Grüne, 1994; Pappe, 1975; Reusch, 1986.
3 For associations in the United Kingdom see chapter 8.
4 Schmauderer, 1976, 159.

Establishment and Membership Structure of the Associations

Parallel to the advance of industrialization and urbanization, food control measures attracted more and more public criticism. A flood of publications complained about the lack of punitive measures for the increasingly clever frauds. The existing legal regulations seemed to be archaic in the context of a rapidly changing society and economy.[5] Decisive impulses in the official debate about food quality were given by an increasingly influential science, especially the nascent food chemistry, and the dissemination of research results caused a new public sensitivity about food quality.[6] In connection with an increasing dependency on a food system that was becoming more and more anonymous and differentiated, there was an increasing feeling of insecurity amongst the public.[7] Food seemed to be less and less familiar and the independent control of food quality to be impossible. After long and difficult negotiations in parliament, a unified food law was eventually enacted in 1879, which combined preventative and restrictive methods. But this gave only guidelines on the organization of food monitoring and it was not until World War I that food monitoring agencies and regular controls were established in all German states and municipalities.[8]

The founding of the Association Against the Adulteration of Food [*Verein gegen die Verfälschung der Lebensmittel*] happened at the height of the general debate, shortly after the government's plans to prepare a food law had manifested themselves. The initiative to set up such an association started in Leipzig with Ernst Leistner, who, unlike most others in the debate, was not a scientist but a writer.[9] In 1877, Leistner mobilized the population of Leipzig through a newspaper advertisement calling on them to organize self-help against food adulteration.[10] The initiators represented the establishment of the association as a reaction to the generally widening 'outcry against food adulteration', which, according to them, proved clearly that local authority control methods hitherto had been insufficient. The association aimed to mediate in the controversy. It wanted find a solid basis for discussion in order to avoid hysteria.[11] It presented itself as a collective movement, not pursuing a biased policy, but claiming to protect the consumer from fraud as well as protecting the industry from unjustified reproaches.

There was lively interest in other cities and the Leipzig association was immediately seen as a kind of a mother organization for local clubs across Germany.

---

5 E.g. Gewerbsmäßige Giftmischerei, *National-Zeitung*, 14 August, 1877; Die Verfälschung der Lebensmittel, *Donau-Zeitung*, 15 November, 1876; Löbner, 1878; Vogel, 1873.

6 Teuteberg, 1994. For similar developments in other European countries, see the contributions of Oddy and Scholliers, chapters 7 and 8.

7 For the conversion of food provision and culinary culture in connection with urbanization and industrialization, cf. Teuteberg and Wiegelmann, 1972. See also Teuteberg, chapter 2.

8 Gesetz, Betreffend den Verkehr mit Nahrungsmitteln, Genußmitteln und Gebrauchsgegenständen, *Reichsgesetzblatt*, 1879, 145.

9 He wrote comedies, anthologies, nationalistic songs, narratives and adventure stories.

10 *Zeitschrift des Vereins*, 1878, 141–2.

11 Ibid.

By the beginning of 1878, about 20 associations were in existence. Another 80 were in the process of establishment, but many of these never made it through the planning stages because they could not mobilize enough members.[12] Membership varied greatly: the association in Hamburg had 900 members and in 1879 was by far the largest. In the same year Leipzig had 500 members, and the association in Chemnitz 400. The Frankfurt and Rheydt associations, each with over 200 members, ranked fourth.[13] However, close collaboration under an umbrella organization led by Leipzig, as provided for in the statutes of most associations, was never attained.[14] Instead, there was a loose union of self-sufficient local associations held together by a newspaper.

The intention of the associations was to address all classes of the population and especially to represent the interests of the less well-off. Therefore, the membership dues in the Leipzig association were kept low.[15] The initiators of these associations were, however, almost exclusively upper-middle class as were the local boards of directors. Pharmacists dominated, followed by chemists and directors of chemical laboratories. A strong representation of teachers is notable, even exceeding the number of physicians. Other large groups of members were industrialists and businessmen as well as politicians, journalists, and lawyers.[16] The fact that the upper middle class dominated the movement was typical for the culture of German associations in the nineteenth century. The nature of the ordinary membership cannot be evaluated as no comprehensive lists survive, but the direction of the associations' policies was definitely decided by the professional elite.

Critics claimed that the movement was supported by unemployed physicians and pharmacists, as well as journalists who had no readers. The associations themselves rejected this by pointing to the selflessness, even the readiness to make sacrifices, among their members.[17] Indeed the critics had no real basis for their claims, as most association directors were, in fact, in secure jobs. However, the rebuttals did not mention motives that were not immediately monetary and which undoubtedly were important for some members. It seems that some businessmen, for instance, used their membership to enhance the public image of their businesses. Also, the frequently mentioned intention to prevent hysteria among the population, and to debunk unjust accusations, played into the hands of commerce. In these associations, entrepreneurs could promote their own interests without fear of being regarded as lobbyists by the public. The representation of the associations as self-help organizations of the

---

12 Ibid., 148–50. The newsletter listed associations in Bamberg, Bayreuth, Belzig, Berlin, Bremen, Bromberg, Karlsruhe, Köln, Chemnitz, Dresden, Eisleben, Frankfurt am Main, Gera, Hamburg, Hannover, Leipzig, Meiningen, Metz, München, Oschatz, Rheydt, Rosenberg, Rostock, Stuttgart and Tilsit. Ibid., 1879, 152. It reported also on similar associations in other European cities. Ibid., 1878, 148–150.

13 Ibid., 1879, 177–80.

14 Statuten-Entwurf, berathen am 19 September 1877, Stadtarchiv Leipzig, Cap. 35 No. 56, fol. 4–10.

15 § 13 Statuten des Allgemeinen Vereins gegen Verfälschung der Lebensmittel, Rheinisch westfälisches Wirtschaftsarchiv, 208, Nr. 189, Fasz. 3.

16 *Zeitschrift des Vereins*, 1877, 7, 14; ibid., 1878, 150–151.

17 Ibid., 1878, 148–150.

consumers lifted them above reproach. Pharmacists and laboratory owners could use their membership as a form of advertisement as well, and some gained regular and lucrative contracts to investigate food samples. The trust that the associations placed in these laboratories conveyed and attested reliability, objectivity, and competence.

Enlightenment and Dissemination of Knowledge: The Activities of the Associations

The constitution of the Leipzig association, which was copied in part by other local associations, stated as their cause support for the government in the fight against falsified or unhealthy food and other consumer goods. The ultimate goal was said to be the protection of the population from fraud and health risks.[18] As a reason for these actions they noted the inactivity of government agencies, especially at a local level. Attempts by the city government to work out effective defensive strategies had mostly faltered in the early stages. At the same time there were warnings against exaggerated public expectations and statements that ultimately it was the consumers' responsibility to protect themselves from attacks on their wealth and health. It was proclaimed that reforms of the law did not preclude self-responsibility of the consumer. The consumers, it was argued, were certainly partly to blame for their own situation.[19] They were told to buy fewer but more expensive food items rather than large quantities of almost certainly falsified food at unrealistically low prices. Like many physicians and food scientists, the association movement argued against irrational consumer habits.[20]

There is here a particular understanding of consumer citizenship. Even though the associations were critical of the incompetence of the existing monitoring system, they did question the then general assumption that responsibility for effective consumer protection should be on the shoulders of the state and the communes. They regarded the authorities' guidance alone as insufficient, and rather insisted on a lasting and active role for the consumer. The association movement constructed a citizenship that was at least partly constituted by a responsibility for one's own health and property and stood against the complacent attitude of expecting state protection.

The private citizen should, as much as the industrialist, act responsibly, and furthermore had 'moral responsibility' to act in the interests of the public good as well as in the interests of following generations.[21] Members, upon entering, vowed not knowingly to buy or sell any goods that were considered falsified by either the association or the authorities. Any purchase or sale of said products discovered afterwards necessitated notification of the association's board of directors.[22] The initiative of members was central, for in no way did the associations want to relieve them from their concern for qualitatively good foods. Instead, the goal was to give

18 § 3 Statuten.
19 *Zeitschrift des Vereins*, 1878, 157–158; ibid., 233–234.
20 Frevert, 1985; Tanner, 1999; Spiekermann, 2001.
21 *Zeitschrift des Vereins*, 1879, 108–9.
22 § 12 Statuten.

the members the basis for self-responsible actions in the future – the motto was assistance for self-help.

Due to this goal, the associations informed the public in lectures about possible food adulterations and their potential effects. During regular meetings, guidelines for shopping and for the treatment of food were explained. Experts demonstrated methods for the identification of food adulterations and answered members' questions.[23] The associations offered their members chemical tools and devices along with user manuals 'for use at home'. They also organized exhibitions which presented falsified and pure food for comparative purposes.[24]

Another tool for consumer enlightenment was the association movement's newsletter, which was edited by the board of directors of the Leipzig association. This not only included larger studies in specific fields and advice for readers but also discussed important new regulations governing food traffic. Acting as multipliers of knowledge, the associations wanted to facilitate its transfer to the broader population. This knowledge had previously been restricted to scientific circles. In regard to the growing information gap between food producers and consumers, the associations systematically disseminated information with the goal of avoiding the risk of fraud; they thought of themselves as 'guardians of trust', so to speak.[25]

Along with dissemination of knowledge and enlightenment of consumers, a second element surfaced in the activities of the associations: the active detection of food adulterations. Members, for one, could bring in food for examination but, secondly, the associations initiated controls in companies and markets. According to their newsletter, the special virtue of the associations was that, especially in smaller cities, they took it upon themselves as private persons to proceed against food fraud and so preserved closely knit local relationships.[26] Individual companies voluntarily placed themselves under the regular control of the associations as a means of building the trust of their consumers.[27] The associations established chemical-technical laboratories under the leadership of experts in order to complete these analyses, or they entered into contracts with already existing private laboratories.[28]

The extent and type of the analyses cannot be systematically established; only a few individual records remain. As in the state and municipal inspection stations, these laboratories mostly inspected basic nutrients and especially foods with a high risk of adulteration, such as chocolate, coffee, spices, and alcohol. But these establishments were more active than many local authority laboratories.[29] The results of the analyses were documented in a regularly updated publication available to members. On top of that, the associations published black lists of retailers and producers who, according to association inspections, sold falsified food – thus marking these fraudsters

---

23 E.g. *Zeitschrift des Vereins*, 1878, 149, 158, 198, 222–3, 398.
24 Friedrich, 1885, 13.
25 Cf. Berghoff, 2004, 62–3.
26 *Zeitschrift des Vereins*, 1878, 302–3.
27 Friedrich, 1885, 14.
28 E.g. Elsner, 1878, 3–5.
29 *Zeitschrift des Vereins*, 1879, 170–72; ibid., 1879, 244, 317.

publicly and so hoping to reduce the incentive for adulteration.[30] In addition, the results of inspections were regularly passed on to the local authorities for further investigation.[31]

Cooperation with Urban Food Monitoring Agencies

The level of actual cooperation of the associations with the local authorities varied from city to city. Apparently it did not always happen as envisioned at the establishment of the association. Often a city's agencies were uncooperative and somewhat uninterested in the actions of their local association.[32] Punitive investigation on the basis of the associations' inspections did happen frequently, but sometimes took a while to get started.[33] Other associations, however, reported that they were supported by the authorities 'in many ways'.[34] Especially in those cities without local authority inspection facilities, the associations took over the role of official contact for questions in regard to food quality, at least for a period of time.

In these cities, the authorities gradually began using the associations' laboratories for their own purposes and gave them regular inspection duties. This was the result of growing public pressure for a change in the monitoring of foods. The associations were in the right place at the right time. They possessed functional laboratories and chemical experts, and they were already experienced in the process of taking samples and performing analyses. Before the maturing of food chemistry and the creation of uniform standards for food research, the associations offered their know-how to the communes in the role of 'expert systems'.[35]

In contrast to private laboratories, which were also consulted as substitutes for city inspection stations, the associations, as unions made up of ordinary citizens, were less suspected of following partisan interests. A number of local authorities secured contracts with the associations regarding regular inspections for a fixed tariff and ordered their police departments to cooperate.[36] Thus, for a time, police and associations divided the labour of inspection between them. The police completed simple investigations themselves and more complex inspections were left to association laboratories.[37] Regular information in city newsletters kept the population informed about the activities of the associations and the possibility of their conducting food inspections.[38]

---

30 Cf. Tietzel and Weber, 1999.

31 § 10 Statuten.

32 Letter from Leistner, Leipzig, 27 August, 1877 and reply of the magistrate, Stadtarchiv Leipzig, Cap 35 Nr. 56.

33 *Zeitschrift des Vereins*, 1878, 166–167; ibid., 1879, 199–200.

34 Ibid., 1878, 345–347.

35 Giddens, 1997, 40–43, 107–13.

36 Kuttenkeuler, 1915, 510.

37 Letter of the magistrate of Frankfurt am Main to the magistrate of Erfurt, 11 November, 1889, Stadtarchiv Frankfurt, MA R 1505.

38 Notice of the magistrate, Frankfurt am Main, 2 November, 1880, Stadtarchiv Frankfurt, MA R 1505.

In several cities this arrangement was kept even after the passing of the food law in 1879. The law only provided indirectly for the establishment of municipal control stations by granting them the fines paid by the adulterators.[39] However, in the following years there were repeated decrees which demanded that state governments establish inspection stations, and the individual states usually then passed this responsibility on to the communes.[40] Eventually the communes were obliged to act, and fights broke out over whose jurisdiction the inspection stations should be under. Many cities simply lacked the funds to establish their own laboratories and employ full-time chemists. They took advantage of the existence of the associations in order to circumvent their responsibility to establish their own agencies. They pointed to the existing associations and tried to argue that the establishment of local authority laboratories was superfluous.[41] On the other hand, in different cities – Hanover, for instance – the food law was used as a catalyst to take the associations' laboratories into municipal ownership and place them under the administration of the city.[42] Apart from the acceptance of city contracts, the associations also tried to influence local decrees regarding food traffic. They criticized the existing norms and institutions, pointed out gaps, and several times offered additional or alternative proposals. The Chemnitz association, for instance, proposed a solution to its city government for the monitoring of milk traffic.[43]

Parliamentary debates on the food law were also followed and discussed critically. In 1879, a conference of delegates was called in order to work out an alternative proposal.[44] At its centre were basic rules for the organization of the local food-monitoring process. In cities with more than 50,000 inhabitants, inspection agencies were to be mandatory, with establishment costs to be provided by the communes. The organization of these agencies was to be the duty of the highest state authority in the individual state, and that authority was to be free to establish new stations if necessary or to buy into existing private organizations and associations. The agencies were expected to accept assignments, not only from the police, but also from private citizens at the lowest possible tariffs.[45] Additionally, a request was drafted that demanded the swearing in of the chemists employed by the associations, and of the members of the board, as state experts.[46]

---

39 § 17 Gesetz Betreffend den Verkehr mit Nahrungsmitteln.

40 E.g. letter from the Chancellor to the Prussian ministry of the interior, Berlin, 14 June 1887, Geheimes Staatsarchiv Preußischer Kulturbesitz, I. HA, Rep. 84 A, Nr. 2438.

41 Letter of the Sanitary Board to the Magistrate of Frankfurt, Frankfurt am Main, 20 October 1880, Stadtarchiv Frankfurt, MA R 1505.

42 *Hannoversche Monatsschrift*, 1879, 153–9.

43 *Zeitschrift des Vereins*, 1879, 4; Friedrich, 1885, 11.

44 *Zeitschrift des Vereins*, 1879, 145–147; ibid., 169–70.

45 Ibid., 1879, 177–80.

46 Gemeinsame Schritte der Vereine, *Zeitschrift des Vereins*, 1879, 194–6.

The Dissolution of the Movement

The association movement itself only existed for a few years. References to activities of the associations decline steadily from the early 1880s. The slow dissolution of the movement may have happened for several causes. One reason evidently was that the working relationships among the associations were not without problems, even within individual associations. The individual associations differed strongly in their main goals, especially because of their differing identification with commercial interests. Therefore, the actions against traders who were found to be distributing adulterated food varied significantly. Whereas some associations immediately made a report, others first gave warnings and prosecuted only repeat offences.[47] It was partially because of these opposing positions that it was impossible to unite the associations into one powerful movement. External problems accompanied the internal conflicts: several interested circles criticized the movement. Traders were especially afraid that publications and events put on by the associations elicited continuous anxiety among the population and thus impeded even honest business.[48] Several law suits were filed against associations or individual board members.[49]

Significantly more important was the fact that the associations were unable to generate lasting interest in their clientele: the consumers. Many associations came to that disappointing conclusion after only one year. They had found little or no support from the consumers, who hardly used the opportunity for food inspection.[50] The participation in meetings also seemed inconsistent and differed significantly among local associations. Whereas several associations reported a large following,[51] most noted decreasing numbers of visitors after the initial interest subsided.[52] The associations blamed 'indifference' and 'apathy' within the population, which, they claimed, had paralysing effects on their activities.[53] In short, the associations could not solve the issue of free-riding – a typical problem of self-regulation.[54]

As a consequence, the associations were dissolved after a short time. The activity of the mother association lasted apparently only for two years. By the end of 1879, the associations ceased to exist and no further reports of activities are recorded. The Leipzig association was mentioned in the directory of the city for the last time in 1881, although the association's laboratory remained in existence until 1884.[55] In other cities – Chemnitz and Frankfurt, for example – the associations remained active independently of the mother association until the end of the 1880s.[56]

---

47 *Zeitschrift des Vereins*, 1879, 257–9.

48 Ibid., 1879, 238–40.

49 E.g. *Zeitschrift des Vereins*, 1878, 185–6; ibid., 1879, 145.

50 Ibid., 1879, 257–9. Municipal laboratories of European cities had the same problems; cf. the article by Scholliers about Brussels.

51 E.g. *Zeitschrift des Vereins*, 1879, 151, 176.

52 Ibid., 1879, 148–149; 1877, 39–40.

53 Ibid, 1879, 238–240.

54 Cf. Stanziani, chapter 9.

55 Leipziger Adreß-Buch, 1878–84.

56 Friedrich, 1885. Letter of the magistrate of Frankfurt am Main to the magistrate of Erfurt, 11 November, 1889, Stadtarchiv Frankfurt, MA R 1505.

It must be noted at this point that the associations did not find much recognition within the population – not only the newsletter of the mother association as the movement's official organ ceased, but the increasing number of professional organizations of food chemists pushed the associations out of the limelight. What followed was a professionalization of the debate about food quality which required a sharper identification of scientific experts. At the same time, the establishment of the state and municipal food inspection stations progressed rapidly in response to increasing pressure from the central and state governments, as well as from the scientific associations. Food inspection stations were set up in major cities, servicing surrounding smaller communities as well, which were financed by the fines levied.[57] The laboratories of the private associations lost their importance. The associations could not maintain their stand against professional competitors in the field of food analysis – in the face of advancing scientific methods, constant changes in production techniques and legal complexities, they were at times overwhelmed by difficult investigations. The Frankfurt association, for instance, refused to inspect wine due to the costs and intricacy of the analysis, and likewise the examination of poisonous food dyes.[58] Their short-run cooperation with the municipal governments thus proved to be just an interlude.

Conclusion

The processes shaping industrialization in Germany in the nineteenth century caused an increasing awareness of problems with food quality. As a reaction to the serious official debates, private unions were formed in several cities, the so-called 'associations against the adulteration of food'. They saw themselves as an addition to the often criticized food control of the authorities and tried to rectify the problems within the food market with a number of different strategies.

Along with an extensive programme to enlighten consumers via lectures, public experiments, exhibits and newsletters, they built their own laboratories or entered into contracts with existing laboratories in order to facilitate the inspection of suspicious products for their members. The associations, thus, acted as multipliers of knowledge and decreased the asymmetry of information concerning the food market, which was often considered to be the reason for widespread frauds. Additionally, they conducted systematic visitations of businesses, took food samples and tested them for adulteration.

By publishing the results of these controls, they exposed fraudulent traders and thus acted as guardians of local food markets. They connected the indirect protection of the consumer, by teaching self-help, with means of direct protection, by exposing adulterations of food. The associations bridged a gap in the cities' food control that was becoming more and more pronounced with the advance of industrialization. The local authorities were not always cooperative but oftentimes accepted the private initiative of the associations gratefully. They used it to circumvent the expensive

---

57 Ellerbrock, 1987.

58 Letter of the chief of police to the magistrate, Frankfurt am Main, 27 December, 1884, Stadtarchiv Frankfurt, MA R 1505.

responsibility of establishing inspection stations and integrated the association-owned laboratories into the existing system, creating a system of job-sharing between police and associations. Eventually, the associations' laboratories partly became publicly owned. These arrangements are in accordance with the generally observed tendency that, in fields closely associated with industrialization, private unions became increasingly active.[59] Many times standardization on the part of the authorities lagged behind actual developments; only private engagement provoked innovation. The associations were, in a sense, an interim solution for problems of urban food control. In the long run, they contributed to their own dissolution by petitioning for the systematic establishment of a network of city and state inspection stations. The implementation of this scheme rendered them obsolete. Parallel to the increasing establishment of scientific societies and the professionalization of the food control industry, they lost importance and slowly disappeared.

References

Berghoff, H. 'Vertrauen als Ökonomische Schlüsselvariable. Zur Theorie des Vertrauens und der Geschichte seiner Privatwirtschaftlichen Produktion' [Confidence as a Key Economic Variable], in Ellerbrock, K-P. and Wischermann, C. (eds), *Die Wirtschaftsgeschichte vor den Herausforderungen durch die New Institutional Economics* [Economic History before the Challenge of the New Institutional Economics], Dortmund, 2004, 55–68.

Donau-Zeitung, 15 November, 1876.

Ellerbrock, K-P. 'Lebensmittelqualität vor dem Ersten Weltkrieg: Industrielle Produktion und Staatliche Gesundheitspolitik' [Food Quality before the First World War], in Teuteberg, H.J. (ed.), *Durchbruch zum modernen Massenkonsum. Lebensmittelmärkte und Lebensmittelqualität im Städtewachstum des Industriezeitalters* [Breakthrough to Mass Consumption], Münster, 1987, 127–88.

Elsner, F. *Untersuchungen von Lebensmitteln und Verbrauchsgegenständen, zugleich als Beitrag zur Frage der Lebensmittelverfälschungen ausgeführt im Laboratorium des Vereins gegen Verfälschung der Lebensmittel* [Investigations of Food and Consumer Goods], Berlin, 1878.

Frevert, U. 'Fürsorgliche Belagerung: Hygienebewegung und Arbeiterfrauen im 19. und frühen 20. Jahrhundert' [Hygiene Movement and Women Workers], *Geschichte und Gesellschaft* 11, 1985, 420–46.

Friedrich, L. *Bericht des Vereins gegen Verfälschung der Lebensmittel und zur Hebung der Hauswirtschaft in Chemnitz über die Thätigkeit desselben* [Report of the Association against Adulteration of Food], Chemnitz, 1885.

Giddens, A. *Konsequenzen der Moderne* [The Consequences of Modernity], Frankfurt am Main, 1997.

Geheimes Staatsarchiv Preußischer Kulturbesitz [Prussian Public Records], I. HA, Rep. 84 A, Nr. 2438.

---

59 Cf. Vec, 2006 on this topic.

Grüne, J. *Anfänge staatlicher Lebensmittelüberwachung in Deutschland. Der 'Vater der Lebensmittelchemie' Joseph König (1843–1930)* [The Origins of National Food Monitoring in Germany], Stuttgart, 1994.

Hannoversche Monatsschrift. 'Wider die Nahrungsfälscher!' Organ des Untersuchungsamts für Lebensmittel etc. in Hannover 1 (1878) – 2 (1879) [Against Food Counterfeiters!].

Kuttenkeuler, H. 'Entwicklung der Nahrungsmittelchemie' [Development of Food Chemistry], *Die Naturwissenschaften* 40, 1915, 510.

Leipziger Adreß-Buch [Leipzig Directory], Leipzig 1877–84.

Löbner, A. *Die Gesetzgebung des alten und des neuen Reiches wider die Verfälschung der Nahrungs- und Genußmittel* [Legislation by the Old and New Regimes against the Falsification of Food and Luxuries], Berlin, 1878.

National-Zeitung, 14 August, 1877.

Pappe, O. *Zur Geschichte der Lebensmittelüberwachung im Königreich Bayern (1806–1918)* [History of Food Monitoring in Bavaria], Marburg 1975.

Reusch, H.K. *Zur Geschichte der Lebensmittelüberwachung im Großherzogtum Baden und seinen Nachfolgeterritorien (1806–1954). Unter Berücksichtigung der Lebensmittelgesetzgebung und Nahrungsmittelchemikerausbildung im Deutschen Reich* [History of Food Monitoring in Baden], Karlsruhe, 1986.

Reichsgesetzblatt, Abteilung I, Berlin, 1879, 145.

Rheinisch Westfälisches Wirtschaftsarchiv [Rhenish-Westphalian Economic Archive], 208, Nr. 189, Fasz. 3.

Schmauderer, E. 'Die Beziehungen zwischen Lebensmittelwissenschaft, Lebensmittelrecht und Lebensmittelversorgung im 19. Jahrhundert, problemgeschichtlich betrachtet' [Relations between Food Science, Food Law and Food Supply in the Nineteenth Century], in Heischkel-Artelt, E. (ed.), *Ernährung und Ernährungslehre im 19. Jahrhundert* [Nutrition and Nutrition Education], Göttingen, 1976, 131–97.

Spiekermann, U. 'Historischer Wandel der Ernährungsziele in Deutschland. Ein Überblick' [Historical Change in Nutrition Goals in Germany], in Oltersdorf, U. and Gedrich, K. (eds), *Ernährungsziele unserer Gesellschaft. Die Beiträge der Ernährungsverhaltenswissenschaft, 22. Wissenschaftliche Jahrestagung der allgemeinen Gesellschaft für Ernährung e.V.* [Nutrition Goals of Our Society], Karlsruhe, 2001, 97–112.

Stadtarchiv Frankfurt [Municipal Archive of Frankfurt], MA R 1505.

Stadtarchiv Leipzig [Municipal Archive of Leipzig], Cap. 35 No. 56.

Stenographische Berichte über die Verhandlungen des Deutschen Reichstages [Stenographic Reports on the Debates of the German Parliament] 3. Legion, 2. Session, vol. 4, Anlagen, Nr. 206, Berlin 1878, 1349–70.

Tanner, J. Fabrikmahlzeit. *Ernährungswissenschaft, Industriearbeit und Volksernährung in der Schweiz 1890–1950* [Factory Meals in Switzerland], Zürich, 1999.

Teuteberg, H.J. and Wiegelmann, G. *Nahrungsgewohnheiten in der Industrialisierung* [Food Habits during Industrialization], 2nd ed., Münster, 2005.

Teuteberg, H.J. 'Food Adulteration and the Beginnings of Uniform Food Legislation in late Nineteenth-Century Germany', in ICREFH II, 1994, 146–60.

Tietzel, M. and Weber, M. *Von Betrügern, Blendern und Opportunisten. Eine Ökonomische Analyse* [Of Cheats, Dazzlers and Opportunists], Duisburg, 1990.

Vec, M. *Recht und Normierung in der Industriellen Revolution. Neue Strukturen der Normsetzung in Völkerrecht, staatlicher Gesetzgebung und gesellschaftlicher Selbstnormierung* [Law and Standardization in the Industrial Revolution], Frankfurt/ Main, 2006.

Vogel, H. *Die Verfälschung und Verschlechterung der Nahrungsmittel. Ein Beitrag zur diätetischen und socialen Reform* [The Adulteration and Degradation of Food], 2nd ed., Schwelm, 1873.

Zeitschrift des Allgemeinen Vereins gegen die Verfälschung der Lebensmittel [Magazine of the General Association against the Adulteration of Food], 1 (1878) − 2 (1879) (after 1879: *Zeitschrift gegen die Verfälschung der Lebensmittel*).

Part C
Food Innovations – The Product Perspective

Chapter 11

The Discovery of Vitamins and its Impact on the Food Industry: The Issue of Tinned Sweetened Condensed Skim Milk 1890–1940

Adel P. den Hartog

General

This study is centred on the question of how the food industry has applied new scientific evidence in marketing. The study covers the period 1890–1940, reflecting the age of the discovery of vitamins, which gave a new understanding of the relationship between food and health. Sweetened condensed milk in tins is chosen as a case study to illustrate how industry dealt with nutritional evidence. In the Netherlands, condensed milk was mainly an export commodity, for urban consumers who had no access to fresh milk. The cheaper and low-quality version of condensed milk was sweetened skim milk in tins, with all of the milk fat removed and consequently low in the fat-soluble vitamins A and D. As a by-product of butter making, fresh machine-skimmed milk (in Dutch *taptemelk* or *ondermelk*) was widely utilised in the Netherlands for animal feeding, in particular for pigs, and in milk condensing. It was also sold by the milkman in towns and cities for human consumption, but viewed by the general public as a poor man's food.[1] In Britain condensed skim milk was consumed by poor urban households, often for infant feeding. As a result of competition for this market in Britain, a bitter argument arose between the exporting Dutch condensed milk industry and the local producers of fresh milk.

The main sources of this study are two Dutch professional dairy journals and their British counterpart the *Milk Industry*. The Dutch dairy journals were well informed on what was happening in the UK. Relevant English articles were translated and published.

Milk Condensing

Based on the method of food preservation in glass by Nicolas Appert (1810), the American Gail Borden succeeded in preserving milk in unbreakable tins by adding

---

1   Van Hamel, 1928, 18; Rutte, 2000, 19–20.

sugar before condensing.[2] The sugar was necessary because a high concentration inhibits bacterial growth. In Europe, the US consul in Switzerland, Charles A. Pages, a former Civil War correspondent, established a small condensery with his two brothers in 1866. The Anglo Swiss Condensed Milk Company grew rapidly and in the 1870s it had factories in England, Norway and Germany. In 1905 the company amalgamated with the Société Farine Lactée Henri Nestlé, to become a giant in the food industry.[3]

Meanwhile, the Dutch dairy industry took an early interest in milk condensing. The firm N.V. Hollandia (1882) can be considered as the start of large-scale industrial milk condensing in the Netherlands, and other firms followed. In 1896 the margarine firm van den Bergh (Unilever) started producing condensed skim milk in Rotterdam, as a by-product of margarine, and other condensed milk factories followed suit, such as Lijempf in 1912.[4] A large part of the production of skim milk in tins was sold to British and German industrial cities, to poor neighbourhoods that had no milkman. In the Netherlands the need for condensed milk was limited because of an age-old system of fresh milk supply to the towns, in particular in the western part of the country. Condensed milk had advantages because it was free from pathogenic bacteria and hence positively received in a period dominated by the hygienists. Physicians warned against unbridled use for babies, but in their view it could be used as a complementary feed. The firm Hollandia went further by stating at the end of the nineteenth century that condensed sweetened milk could replace mother's milk. From around 1900 sweetened condensed milk was used even in better-off households.[5]

Dramatic changes occurred when in the 1870s cheap cereals from North America flooded the European market. In the Netherlands wheat farming was at stake, but the government maintained its liberal trade policy and agriculture adapted by developing niches in which there was less international competition. The already well-established sectors of horticulture and dairying modernized and expanded with a view to both the local urban market and export to the relatively close urban areas of England and Germany.[6] At this time private industry had a lead in milk condensing but dairy farmers soon began to realize that cooperative industrial production of only butter and cheese was too small a basis for the sector. In 1916 the Cooperative Milk Condensery Friesland produced its first condensed milk and became in the course of time a leader in the dairy food industry, both nationally and internationally.[7] Condensed milk, both full-cream and skimmed, was exported to European countries, in particular the UK and the tropics. Also Nestlé discovered the market for skim milk and for that reason the firm acquired a substantial interest in the Dutch Galak Condensed Milk Company in Rotterdam. According to Nestlé, its main policy was to produce full-cream sweetened condensed milk, but they also manufactured the

2   Lief, 1965, 6–7.
3   Heer, 1991, 42–80.
4   Wilson, 1970, vol. 2, 73–4; Lijempf, 1937.
5   de Knecht-van Eekelen, 1984, 253–8.
6   Mather, 2002.
7   Tjepkema, 1961, 58–9, 76.

cheaper skim milk products under foreign labels.[8] The growing urban population in the UK (Table 11.1) became a major outlet for Dutch condensed milk products.

Table 11.1   Population (millions) in the UK living in conurbations, 1871–1951

Date	Greater London	South-east Lancashire	West Midlands	West Yorkshire	Merseyside	Tyneside	Central Clydeside*	Total
1871	3.890	1.386	0.969	1.064	0.690	0.346	0.568	8.913
1881	4.770	1.685	1.134	1.269	0.824	0.426	0.673	10.781
1891	5.638	1.894	1.269	1.410	0.908	0.551	0.766	12.436
1901	6.586	2.117	1.483	1.524	1.030	0.678	1.343	14.761
1911	7.266	2.328	1.634	1.590	1.157	0.761	1.461	16.187
1921	7.488	2.361	1.773	1.614	1.263	0.816	1.638	16.953
1931	8.216	2.427	1.933	1.655	1.347	0.827	1.690	18.095
1951	8.348	2.423	2.237	1.693	1.382	0.836	1.758	18.677

*Central Clydeside figures for 1871–1891 are for Glasgow only.
Source: Mitchell and Deane, 1962.

A Revolution in Nutrition: The Coming of Vitamins and the Role of Milk Fat

In the nineteenth century the classical theory of dietetics faded away and a new science of nutrition emerged. Milk produced under hygienic conditions was perceived to be healthy because of its proteins and minerals such as calcium and phosphorus but the nutritional significance of milk fat was not yet known. The Netherlands has a longstanding tradition in nutrition research and its scientists, C. Eijkman and G. Grijns, along with F.G. Hopkins in the UK, played an important part in the discovery of those unknown indispensable substances in food, vitamins, which came to dominate nutritional and health thinking in the 1920s and 1930s.[9] The nutritional significance of milk fat was better understood with the discovery of the so-called fat-soluble vitamins. In 1917 C.E. Bloch described cases of serious eye diseases among Danish infants under one year of age. The diet of the orphans consisted of skim milk, which was practically free of milk fat. Bloch concluded that the absence of fat was the main cause of this serious form of malnutrition.[10] Nutrition research carried out in various countries revealed that milk fat was an important source of vitamin A and D, indispensable for infant and child feeding. In particular, the absence of vitamin A could lead to xerophthalmia and in the long run to blindness. In 1913 E.V. McCollum and M. Davis discovered something in butterfat and egg-yolk necessary for growth and bone development, later identified and named as vitamin D.[11]

---

8   Heer, 1966, 101.
9   Luyken, 1990.
10 McCollum, 1957, 231–2.
11 Ibid., 266–90.

Export of Condensed Milk to the UK and the Skim Milk Issue

In the 1890s the Dutch managed to get a strong foothold in the British market with the export of condensed milk and milk powder, although regulations were tightened at this time. Thus the Sale of Food and Drugs Act 1899 stated that tins of condensed, separated and skim milk must have a label with the correct contents. By 1900, 65 per cent of the imported condensed milk and milk powder in the UK came from the Netherlands.[12] In the UK the working classes could only afford the cheaper tinned skim milk, fresh cow's milk being too expensive. Besides, fresh milk in the period before the First World War was not always obtainable in towns.[13] After the First World War the UK continued as the major outlet for products from the Netherlands, although other markets were also opening up for full cream condensed milk (Tables 11.2 and 11.3).

Table 11.2   Export destination of Dutch tinned sweetened condensed milk (full cream) in metric tonnes, 1920–1939

Country	1920/24	1925/29	1930/34	1935/39
UK	9.3	10	7.8	3.9
Rest of Europe	5.3	3.1	2.7	8.8
Netherlands Indies	1.9	3.2	1.9	3.5
America, Asia, Africa	2.9	11	18.6	38.4
Total	19.4	27.3	31	54.6

Source: Netherlands Central Bureau of Statistics.

Table 11.3   Export destination of Dutch tinned sweetened condensed skim milk in metric tonnes, 1920–1939

Country	1920/24	1925/29	1930/34	1935/39
UK	55.2	95.5	82.2	60.4
Rest of Europe	2.8	1.5	6.5	1.7
Netherlands Indies	—	0.9	2.3	5.7
America, Asia, Africa	1.3	8.3	7.3	5.8
Total	59.3	106.2	98.3	73.6

Source: Netherlands Central Bureau of Statistics.

The British dairy industry considered milk consumption too low and tried to encourage it through intensive publicity campaigns, in particular in urban areas. They were well aware that condensed milk could be used instead of fresh milk and

12 Bos, 1978, 252, 416.
13 Burnett, 1979, 144, 184.

any relative fall in the costs of these 'competitive' articles would tend to restrict the market for fresh milk.[14]

Why was condensed skim milk such a successful product? An answer to this question can be found in an article by the Dutch dairy consultant in London, Ir. B. Gerritzen. In the UK the price of fresh milk was relatively expensive. Converted into Dutch cents in 1929 the consumer had to pay 26.5 cents for one litre of fresh milk in summer and in winter the price could increase to 31 cents. The price of a tin of sweetened condensed milk was 15 cents, which was equal to about one litre of liquid skim milk. There was also the advantage of storage, in a crowded urban setting with hardly any facilities for keeping fresh food; the open tin could be kept for quite some time because of the preservative nature of the sugar. Even rural consumers used tinned milk where supplies of fresh milk were restricted. Most striking is his comment on the absence of vitamins A and D, milk fats and the excess of cane sugar: 'the skim milk product is not suitable for infants, but people are sufficiently warned not to use it for that purpose'.[15] The main outlet for condensed skim milk was the urban market and because of its low price it was popular among the urban poor.

The National Farmers' Union took action against the import of condensed milk by using both economic and nutritional arguments. The Minister of Health was forced to set up a Departmental Committee and, under pressure from parliament, he drafted the Public Health (Condensed Milk) Regulations of 1923, which insisted on labelling the milk equivalent, and for, skimmed condensed milk, a statement that it was 'unfit for babies'.[16]

The British regulations caused much alarm in the Dutch dairy world. The weekly journal of the Dutch private dairy industry published the full regulations in English.[17] In a furious commentary, the measure was seen as a heavy-handed 'gun policy' against a 'peaceful' export activity. It commented that the Dutch exporters gave preference to full-cream products rather than skim milk, but large groups of the British population were in need of cheap milk products. The commentary concluded that artificial import impediments made the British people unable to satisfy their needs.[18] The managers of the Dutch dairy cooperatives were less alarmed, probably because their share in the export of condensed milk was still limited. They were pleased to note that an earlier British proposal to insist on the labelling 'unfit for infants' had not been implemented. The use of 'babies' in 1923, which referred to very young children, was thought to be an improvement and would not harm the sale of skim milk too much.[19] The Dutch dairy industry did not respond to the nutritional arguments and felt wronged by the situation.

In Britain a report on condensed milk in 1923 concluded that all of the investigated samples contained living bacteria. This caused consternation and reinforced actions against condensed milk and the trade press stated with satisfaction that the report had

14   Forrester, 1927, viii.
15   Gerritzen, 1929, 22, 2; 1930, 36, 8.
16   *Milk Industry* 2, 1922, 53, 55; 12, 1923, 55–58.
17   *A.Z. Melk Hygiënisch Weekblad* 1923, 278–80.
18   Ibid., 277.
19   *Officieel Orgaan* 1923, 587.

dealt a very severe blow to the condensed milk manufacturers.[20] Unfortunately for the writers of the report, they did not declare that the bacteria found were harmless. Probably under pressure from the condensed milk manufacturers, the publisher HM Stationery Office temporarily suspended the report in order to provide it with an introductory note. The general manager of Nestlé and Anglo-Swiss Condensed Milk Co was one of those who challenged the outcome of the report.[21] The chairman of the Food investigation Board stated in the introductory note that the bacteria found were not pathogenic. Agitation against imports of condensed milk continued.[22] In 1927, under pressure of parliament and the National Farmers' Union, the Minister of Health, Neville Chamberlain, decided to send a commission of British dairy experts to the continent, to Denmark and the Netherlands. The findings of the mission were published in the form of a government white paper. One of the conclusions reached was that the average cleanliness and purity of milk produced in the Netherlands was as high as that produced in Britain.[23] The British dairy industry was at variance with the findings and members of parliament continued to demand that the government take steps against Dutch milk products. In their eyes the report was an unwarranted certificate of merit for the Dutch and Danes at the expense of British tax payers. These reactions were published in the Dutch professional press, which had been relieved with the outcome of the mission, but remained worried.[24] In the event, the only concrete action taken by the British government was to make an amendment to the condensed milk regulations. The Public Health (Condensed Milk) Regulations (1927) required the words 'unfit for babies' to be more prominent on the label of machine skimmed condensed milk.[25] The fears of the Dutch were not unfounded; in 1929 the professional press revealed an alarming article that had appeared in the British periodical *The Farmers' Express* asserting that 'imports of machine-skim milk grow like a cancer, destroying health and injuring the legitimate home trade'.[26] The Dutch cooperative dairy industry stated in 1937 that skim milk had found its own market in the UK, among poor people and industrial workers, for whom fresh milk was too expensive.[27]

Commercial Interests and Nutritional Evidence

On the issue of condensed skim milk, it is striking that the Dutch dairy industry systematically avoided questions related to the nutritional impact on the use of skim milk, in particular for infants and young children. Other sectors of the food industry were more receptive to the newly discovered vitamins. Margarine manufacturers were among the first to realize the importance of vitamins. Their aim was to make

---

20 *Milk Industry* 2, 1923, 71; 3, 43.

21 Ibid., 2, 71–2.

22 Ibid., 3, 44.

23 Ibid., 8, 1928, 93.

24 *A.Z. Melk Hygiënisch Weekblad* 1928, 47; *Officieel Orgaan* 1926, 471.

25 *Milk Industry* 3, 1927, 55.

26 *Officieel Orgaan* 1929, 356.

27 *Officieel Orgaan* 1937, 289–90.

margarine as equal as possible to butter, in taste, appearance and in nutritional quality. In 1927 Unilever managed to produce a margarine enriched with stable vitamins A and D, prepared from cod-liver oil and making it nutritionally equal to butter.[28] In 1931 the horticulture sector stated that unsuspected sources of information showed that vitamins in fruits and vegetables were indispensable for health.[29]

Undoubtedly the dairy industry must have been informed about the scientific developments in nutrition and related sciences. In 1920 a Dutch version of a Danish article under the title 'Vitamins in milk' appeared in the professional press. The article mentioned among others the fat-soluble vitamin A.[30] A short article in 1922 reported the presence of a new vitamin, D, in cod-liver oil as well as in milk fat, important for human use.[31] The stubborn behaviour of the condensed milk industry is well illustrated by the reaction to a paper on the nutritive value of condensed milk published in the British journal *Milk Industry* (1927). The paper was translated and reprinted in the Dutch dairy journal and provoked emotional reactions. The concerned paper was an extensive excerpt of an old report published in 1911, *Machine-Skimmed Condensed Milk and Infant Feeding*, prepared by Dr F.J.H. Coutts for the Local Government Board. Dr Coutts argued that a diet consisting largely of skim milk meant fat starvation and was likely to lead to injurious results in the growth and development of a child. The report mentioned that in various parts of the country shopkeepers had observed a large increase of condensed skim milk. According to the shopkeepers interviewed, skim milk was largely used among the poor for feeding babies and ordinary household purposes. As for reasons why parents gave their babies skim milk, despite a plainly printed label notifying 'machine-skimmed milk', the answer given was 'poverty and ignorance'. Some mothers knew that full-cream milk was superior but were forced by poverty to buy the cheaper product. For many mothers the presence of sugar and the viscosity of the condensed milk gave a fallacious appearance of richness.[32]

The comment of the Dutch dairy weekly was simply that one should follow these events, despite the 'absurdity' of the argument put forward by the British milk industry[33]. Another illustration of the lack of will to understand the nutritional dimensions of milk fat is an article placed in the same issue of the weekly. An agronomist argued that condensed skim milk in terms of energy had a worthy place among other foods, and that one tin of skim milk had the same nutritional value as about 14 eggs. 'The fact a commodity does not contain fat is not objectionable, judging the importance of foods such as beans, sugar, jam and potatoes'.[34] This point of view was further supported by the then well-known food chemist and owner of a private food laboratory, Dr P.F. van Hamel Roos, who stated that condensed skim

---

28 Wilson, 1970, vol. 1, 342–3; vol. 2, 379.
29 den Hartog, 2004, 96.
30 *Officieel Orgaan* 1920, 245.
31 *Officieel Orgaan* 1922, 169.
32 *Milk Industry* 1927, 47.
33 *A.Z. Melkhygiënisch Weekblad* 1927, 311.
34 *A.Z. Melkhygiënisch Weekblad* 1927, 438.

milk is a nutritious food rich in proteins and carbohydrates.[35] The importance of the vitamins A and D for infants and young children was completely ignored.

In 1922 in the United States, the nutritionist E.V. McCollum was involved in hearings about the Anti-Filled Milk Bill, which discussed the replacement of milk fats by vegetable fats.[36] He drew attention to the presence of Vitamin A and the newly discovered vitamin D in milk fat. The information was published in the Dutch journal of the dairy cooperatives, but not taken up as a point of concern in relation to skim milk. Most likely, the skim milk issue in the UK caused concern in other countries. In 1924 the *Milk Industry* published an extensive list of countries with regulations governing the import of skim milk. The regulations included total prohibition, excessive duty compared to that on the full-cream variety, and special care in avoiding its use for infants. The list however comprised mainly the dominions and territories of the British Empire. The *Milk Industry* quoted a report on *Canned Goods in Relation to Public Health* prepared in 1924 by Dr W.G. Savage. According to this, any printed notice that skim milk was unfit for babies was a totally inadequate protection. Cheapness appeared to be the chief advantage of skim milk and Great Britain was practically the only large consumer in the whole world.[37]

A Crumbling Market

So far the export of condensed skim milk to the UK had not been directly threatened by the nutritional arguments, although they caused much uneasiness, but the economic depression in the 1930s meant that the British market did change. The strength of Dutch condensed milk exports, and in particular of skim milk, was eroded (Table 11.3). The newly elected National government of 1931 issued a number of import quotas in successive years. As a consequence, import quotas of condensed milk were reduced by half at the end of 1936 from the situation in 1932. A further constraint was the maintenance of the gold standard (to 1936) making export products priced in guilders expensive. Another difficulty for the Dutch was the Ottawa Conference of 1932 when a system of preferences was established within the British Empire. Dutch milk products were not only put into an unfavourable position in the UK, but also in a great number of other countries overseas. The precarious marketing position of the Dutch caused conflicts between the private and cooperative condensed milk industry. The cooperative dairy industry requested the Minister of Agriculture to establish a Dutch agency for milk products in London, but the private industry, fearing a kind of a state monopoly, was against this.[38]

In 1937 private industry again blamed the cooperatives for having increased their share on the British market by unfair means, such as price dumping and low quality[39]. This was firmly denied by the cooperative dairy industry.[40] Already in 1930

---

35   van Hamel Roos, 1928, 18.
36   *Officieel Orgaan* 1922, 169.
37   *Milk Industry* 1924, 23–25.
38   *Officieel Orgaan* 32, 19, 1937, 287; *A.Z. Melkhygiënisch Weekblad* 53, 1936, 445.
39   *A.Z. Melkhygiënisch Weekblad* 53, 1936, 441.
40   *Officieel Orgaan* 32, 19, 1937, 289.

the dairy consultant Ir. Gerritzen warned the Dutch cooperative milk industry that the call for protection among British farmers was becoming louder because imports were increasingly acquiring the character of dumping.[41] At the same time, private dairy industrialists published excerpts of lamentations against Dutch skim milk found in English newspapers.[42] The question of skim milk export to the UK looked like a never ending story, but came abruptly to an end when on the 10 May 1940 the Netherlands were dragged into World War II. Export to the UK then came to a complete standstill.

Concluding Remarks

The British Public Health (Condensed Milk) Regulations of 1923 and 1927 can be considered as early examples of compulsory nutrition declarations on a food label for the benefit of the consumer, but what were the basic reasons for the general lack of will of the Dutch condensed milk industry to deal carefully with skim milk, low in fat-soluble vitamins A and D, as infant and child food?

In the first place there is the general attitude of any food industry to utilize favourable arguments and to ignore unfavourable ones in food promotion. This is clearly demonstrated in how the horticulture sector and margarine manufacturers utilized favourable nutritional evidence. In this phase of development of the modern food industry most manufacturers used nutritional arguments indiscriminately in marketing.[43] The margarine manufacturer Unilever is an interesting example of a firm using nutritional evidence at an early stage in product development. Already in 1914 Lever Brothers had started nutrition research in close contact with Cambridge University, where F.G. Hopkins was later awarded the Nobel prize for his research on fat-soluble substances needed for growth.[44] The condensed milk industry was rather selective, by ignoring inconvenient facts about the absence of vitamin A and D.

The assertion that milk was unquestionably healthy dominated the dairy industry in the years 1890–1940. Its major concerns were centred on hygiene, tuberculosis in milk, safe transport and distribution to the consumers, and it was slow in absorbing new scientific evidence on the nutritional value of milk in terms of vitamins A and D.[45] The dairy industry in that period was too fragmented to set up a common research unit.

The basic reason for the often strong and emotional Dutch reactions to the British milk industry has to be found in its own struggle for survival. In the case of tinned sweetened condensed skim milk, the dairy industry was inflexible in dealing with the serious nutritional issues of poor, mainly urban, consumers. This illustrates that ignoring unfavourable new nutritional evidence can in the long run be detrimental to a particular food industry.

---

41 Gerritzen, 1930, 9.

42 Wolmerstett 1930, 30, 296. The newspapers cited in 1930 were the *Yorkshire Herald*, *Nottingham Evening Post*, and the *Bristol Evening Post*.

43 den Hartog, 1995, 270–272.

44 Wilson, 1970, vol. 1, 342–343.

45 Atkins, 2000; Mol, 1980; Orland, 2003.

Acknowledgement

Many thanks are due to Professor Derek J. Oddy, Emeritus Professor at the University of Westminster, for his valuable suggestions on urban Britain.

References

Algemeen Zuivel en Melk Hygiënisch Weekblad, 1920–1940.
Atkins, P.J. 'Milk Consumption and Tuberculosis in Britain, 1850–1950', in ICREFH V, 2000, 83–95.
A.Z. Melk Hygiënisch Weekblad, 'Maatregelen tegen Gecondenseerde Melk. Een Waarschuwing', [Measures against Condensed Milk] 19, 23, 1923, 276–80.
A.Z. Melk Hygiënisch Weekblad, 'De Voedingswaarde van Afgeroomde Gecondenseerde Melk', [The Nutritional Value of Condensed Skim Milk] 23, 3, 1927, 311–13; 47, 437–8.
A.Z. Melk Hygiënisch Weekblad, 'Actie tegen Hollandse Melk in Engeland', [Action against Dutch Milk in England] 24, 6, 1928, 46–7.
A.Z. Melk Hygiënisch Weekblad, 'Regeling van den Uitvoer uit Nederland van Magere Gecondenseerde Melk naar Engeland', [Export Regulations on Condensed Skim Milk to England] 32, 53, 1936, 438–46.
Bos, R.W.J.M. *Brits-Nederlandse Handel en Scheepvaart, 1870–1914, een Analyse van Machtsafbrokkeling op een Markt*, [Anglo-Dutch Trade and Shipping] Wageningen, 1978.
Burnett, J. *Plenty and Want: A Social History of Diet in England from 1815 to Present Day*, London, 1979.
Forrester, R.B. *The Fluid Milk Market in England and Wales*, London, 1927.
Gerritzen, B. 'De Plaats, die Nederland als Leverancier van Melk- en Zuivelproducten, Benevens Bacon, op de Britse Markt Iinneemt', [The Position of the Netherlands as Supplier of Milk, Dairy and Bacon to the British Market] *Officiëel Orgaan* 24, 22, 1929, 1–8.
Gerritzen, B. 'De Export onzer Zuivel Producten naar Groot-Brittannië, Speciaal wat Betreft de Afzet van Gecondenseerde Melk', [Export of Dairy Products to Great Britain] *Officiëel Orgaan* 25, 36, 1930, 7–11.
Hartog, A.P. den 'The Role of Nutrition in Food Advertisements: The Case of the Netherlands,' in ICREFH III, 1995, 268–80.
Hartog, A.P. den 'The Changing Place of Vegetables in Dutch Food Culture: The Role of Marketing and Nutritional Sciences 1850–1990', *Food & History*, 2, 2, 2004, 87–103.
Hamel, R.P.F. van 'De Voedingswaarde van Gecondenseerde Suiker Houdende Afgeroomde Melk. Een Belangrijk Volksvoedsel', [Nutritional Value of Condensed Skim Milk] *A.Z. Melk Hygiënisch Weekblad*, 24, 3, 1928, 18.
Heer, J. *Nestlé 125 years 1866–1991*, Vevey, 1991.
Hollandia, *Hollandia, Hollandse Fabriek van Melkproducten en Voedingsmiddelen 1882–1932* [Hollandia, a Dutch Milk Factory], Vlaardingen, 1932.

Knecht-van Eekelen, A. de *Naar een Rationele Zuigelingen Voeding. Voedingsleer en Geneeskunde in Nederland 1840–1914* [Rational Infant Feeding, Nutritional Sciences and Medcine], Nijmegen, 1984.

Lief, A. *A Close-up of Closures, History and Progress*, New York, 1965.

Lijempf, *Lijempf NV 1912–1937. Gedenkboek Samengesteld ter Gelegenheid van het Vijfentwintigjarig Bestaan der Vennootschap* [The Annals of Twenty Five Years], Leeuwarden, 1937.

Luyken, R. *Polyneuritis in Chickens, or the Origin of Vitamin Research*, Hoffmann La Roche, 1990.

Mather, A.S. 'European Agriculture 1865–1950: Feeding an Urban Population, War and Rural Society', *Review of Scottish Culture* 15, 2002, 30–40.

McCollum, E.V. *A History of Nutrition: the Sequence of Ideas in Nutrition Investigations*, Boston, 1957.

Milk Industry, 'The Condensed Milk Standard', 3, 2, 1922, 53–5.

Milk Industry, 'The Condensed Milk Regulations', 1923, 4, 12, 1923, 55–8.

Milk Industry, 'The True Facts about Condensed Milk', 4, 2, 1923, 71–8.

Milk Industry, 'The True Facts about Condensed Milk', 4, 3, 1923, 43–4.

Milk Industry, 'Nutritive Value of Skimmed Condensed Milk', 8, 2, 1927, 45–8.

Milk Industry, 'Public Health (Condensed Milk) Amendment Regulations, 1927', 8, 3, 1927, 55.

Milk Industry, 'Where the Skimmed Condensed Milk Comes From', 8, 8, 1928, 93–5.

Mitchell, B.R. and Deane, P. *Abstracts of British Historical Statistics*, Cambridge, 1962.

Mol, J. 'Van Melkinrichting tot Levensmiddelenfabriek' [From Dairy to Food Factory], *Voeding*, 41, 1980, 166–72.

Officiëel Orgaan, 'Vitaminen in Melk' [Vitamins in Milk], 15, 758, 1920, 245.

Officiëel Orgaan, 'Een Nieuwe Vitamine D' [New Vitamin D], 17, 852, 1922, 169.

Officiëel Orgaan, 'Mededeeling' [Communication], 18, 897, 1923, 587.

Officiëel Orgaan, 'Een Actie Tegen den Invoer in Engeland van Gecondenseerde Ontroomde Melk' [Action against Imports of Condensed Skim Milk in England], 21, 36, 1926, 471.

Officiëel Orgaan, 'Bestrijding van den Invoer van Gecondenseerde Magere Melk in Engeland' [Struggle over Condensed Skim Milk Imports in England], 24, 23, 1929, 356.

Officiëel Orgaan, 'Regeling van den Export van Gecondenseerde Melk naar Engeland' [Export Regulation of Condensed Milk to England], 32, 19, 1929, 287–91.

Orland, B., 'Cow's Milk and Human Disease: Bovine Tuberculosis and the Difficulties Involved in Combating Animal Diseases', *Food & History* 1, 1, 2003, 179–202.

Rutte, G. *De Kracht van Melk en Ad Menken* [The Power of Milk], Baarn, 2000.

Tjepkema, K. *Dat is 't Kondensfabryk, een Halve Eeuw Coöperative Condesindustrie in Friesland* [Half a Century of Cooperative Milk Condensing], Leeuwarden, 1963.

Wolmerstett, C. ' Nota Betreffende den Handel in Gecondenseerde Melk op de Engelsche markt' [Report on the Condensed Milk Trade to the English Market], *A.Z. Melk Hygiënisch Weekblad*, 26, 30, 1930, 294–9.

Wilson, C. *Geschiedenis van Uniliver* [History of Unilever] 's Gravenhage, vols 1 and 2, 1970

Chapter 12

First-Class Restaurants and Luxury Food Stores: The Emergence of the Soviet Culture of Consumption in the 1930s

Jukka Gronow

The Great Turn of 1936

As many observers and historians of the Soviet Union, Leo Trotsky among them, have pointed out, a major shift in the cultural politics of the country took place in the mid–1930s, which marked the final consolidation of Stalin's power.[1] The former ideals of revolutionary and social egalitarianism gave way to the emergence of a more hedonistic way of life. With some reservations, one could claim that this was the beginning of Soviet consumerism in the sense that individuals' aspirations towards better life-styles were no longer condemned as dangerous petit-bourgeois and anti-socialist deviations but were encouraged by the authorities. The political aspects of this change have been comprehensively analysed but the way that this change also found its expression in the sphere of material culture is less well known.[2] As Julie Hessler put it: 'By 1936, the consumer economy had been purged of nearly every vestige of war communism save the ban on private shops.'[3] This change was expressed in the slogan, first coined in 1931, of 'cultured Soviet trade'. One of the peculiarities of this turn was that luxuries, not basic necessities, were to form the cornerstone of 'cultured Soviet trade'. The consumer goods and food industries, in particular, took their models either from the 'grand emporia of the capitalist West' or the luxury goods market of the tsarist, pre-revolutionary, Russia. A new system of 'commercial Soviet trade' with department stores, luxury food shops, restaurants and cafés was created. These new Soviet consumer flagships were found only in big urban centres and cities. In addition to Moscow, they were established in Minsk, Kharkov, Vladivostok, Sverdlovsk and Irkutsk. Even some strategically important industrial centres or factory towns enjoyed these privileges. The centralization of consumer institutions in the capital was partially due to the fact that higher party functionaries and civil servants lived in Moscow, but the main reason was that until the Second World War industrial production was heavily centralized in Moscow. The

---

1   Trotsky, 1972; Timasheff, 1946.
2   Fitzpatrick, 1999; Stites, 1992; Hessler, 2004. For a more general presentation of the topics of this article see Gronow, 2003.
3   Hessler, 2004, 197.

distribution system strongly favoured the industrial workers of big machine-building and metallurgical factories, the electrical industry and other strategically important fields of production. In Soviet ideology, the industrial proletariat, and its most advanced and skilled groups in particular, was in the vanguard of the Revolution and victorious Socialism and was entitled to these privileges of consumption. This system of distribution was gradually extended to the individual Soviet Republics and even to more remote parts of the Soviet Union. But later on the system was still extremely centralized and people living in the countryside and small towns could only enjoy its benefits by visiting big cities.

From the beginning of the Second Five-Year Plan in 1933, more individual and more luxurious life-styles were officially encouraged, since it was now claimed that the country was living in a state of abundance and well-being. This was just a couple of years after the great famine, caused mainly by the forced collectivization of agriculture. It happened almost simultaneously with the end of the rationing of basic foodstuffs in 1935. The year 1936 is, in many ways, the high-water mark of this pre-war decade in Soviet history. According to Stalin's slogan: 'life has become better, life has become more joyous, Comrades'. In the summer 1936, the new Soviet constitution was celebrated by carnivals and public feasts, previously unknown in the Soviet Union.[4] They were meant to promote and propagate the new era of material well-being and high cultural standards by giving its citizens a foretaste of the coming abundance. The new Soviet man and woman were supposed to look happy, to enjoy life and even to mark their social status as model citizens by external symbols of 'high culture' and material well-being. Especially important were the many delights offered for sale by the new organizations of Soviet trade and catering, ranging from new custom-made and fashionable suits, dresses and shoes to perfumes and champagne, caviar and wine, as well as dinners in the newly opened first-class dance restaurants. On the other hand, the years immediately after 1936 witnessed the outbreak of the most repressive political terror exercised by the Soviet state.

The whole of the Soviet Union's material culture and all its institutions of public catering were created in a highly conscious manner. Every decision was made at the highest levels of administration by the People's Commissars and the Central Committee of the Communist Party, and often confirmed by Stalin personally. Experts from trade and industry presented arguments and reasons in favour of, or against, some product or another. These discussions and plans were well documented and are preserved in the Soviet historical archives. They provide an opportunity to follow in detail the emergence of a peculiar and historically unique culture of consumption.

Soviet Luxuries

Soviet industry and trade aimed to offer its customers much more than was necessary for the satisfaction of basic human needs.[5] These were, in the Soviet parlance, luxuries. Why should one produce millions of bottles of champagne – a decision

---

4 Sartorti, 1990.
5 Sokolov, 1998, 162–229.

made in the summer 1936 – instead of plain vodka, or open first-class restaurants instead of factory canteens?[6] These were, in the minds of the authorities, luxuries, but luxuries that were needed by the common people. At times the arguments were almost paradoxical. The reference to luxuries could also be used with irony. For instance, at a meeting of the directors of the newly established department stores, they complained that they did not have for sale many basic household utensils, like bowls, brushes, scissors, shoe laces, or wooden hangers, which self-evidently belonged to the basic assortment of any Western store. These things were not produced in the Soviet Union. Despite their ordinariness they had a 'character of luxury'. They were extremely rare and hard to get.[7] In talking about luxuries, however, the authorities more often referred to the new emerging demands due to the general well-being of the Soviet population. Today's luxuries would become tomorrow's necessities, no longer necessary in the sense of satisfying basic needs, but necessary for the conduct of an ordinary decent and cultured life. All commodities that were still relatively rare and consumed only by a few would soon be available to the great majority of the population. This was built into Soviet propaganda. The new luxuries that were now offered on sale in the new shops and restaurants in Moscow and other big cities served as the first concrete proof that this promise would become true.

The New Department Stores – the Pride of Soviet Trade

The Central Department Store (TsUM) in Moscow was the main department store in the Soviet Union. It was founded in December 1933 by government decree. It was also first of a series of new department stores that shortly afterwards followed in other big cities. The People's Commissar of Domestic Trade opened eight such exemplary department stores at the beginning of 1935. In addition to TsUM, on Kuznetskij Most in the very centre of Moscow, there were stores in Leningrad, Kharkov, Vladivostok, Irkutsk, Sverdlovsk and Minsk.[8] According to a report by the Ministry of Trade, the total number had reached 20 by January 1936. Before the opening of these new shops, no real department stores operated in the Soviet Union. Some had existed in the pre-revolutionary Moscow and St Petersburg, as well as in some other major cities, but they had practically ceased operating in the 1920s at the latest. This was equally true of all 'ordinary' shops. During the Second Five-Year Plan, cooperative stores, often with a very restricted variety of goods, were practically the sole retail outlets in the Soviet Union. The major part of the urban population received their daily necessities from distribution outlets attached to their workplaces, factories or educational institutions. The rural population was expected to be largely self-supporting and get the few items they could not grow themselves, like salt, soap and kerosene, from their local rural cooperatives. The closed factory outlets worked under the Organization of Workers' Supply (ORS). Supplies in them were strictly rationed and restricted.[9] By contrast, the new department stores, as well

---

6   Gronow, 2003.
7   Ibid., 17–28.
8   Dikhtiar, 1961, 387.
9   Osokina, 1997, 89–113.

as other more luxurious state shops that opened in the 1930s, were 'commercial' stores. In the Soviet Union this meant that they were open to anyone who had money and wanted to buy their products. In principle, there were no limitations as to what and how much one could buy. In consequence, they traded in goods that were not in *defitsit*, that is, goods that were not in short supply. In general the state kept the right to regulate their prices even though department stores and other commercial shops had a limited right to make deals directly with industry and even establish their own small production units. For instance, department stores, as a rule, had a fashion atelier attached to them, sewing clothes and accessories to order. The First Moscow Department Store had also a special children's department and an adjoining production unit to service it.[10]

The Opening of Luxury Food Stores in Soviet Cities

In 1926–27, at the end of the New Economic Policy (NEP), private shops accounted for 37 per cent of the domestic trade of the Soviet Union. Cooperative shops were responsible for the biggest share, with half the sales. With only 13 per cent, the state-owned shops were by far the smallest operators. All private shops were closed down at the beginning of the First Five-Year Plan in 1928–29. Very few cooperative or state-owned shops were opened in their place. While 41,000 private shops were closed during these years, only 3,700 cooperative and 1,900 state shops opened during the same time.[11] Shortly afterwards, strict rationing of all basic foodstuffs was introduced, due to the rapidly deteriorating food supply caused by the collectivization of agriculture. The start of the Second Five-Year Plan in the early 1930s thus witnessed both a lack of goods to sell and shops in which to sell them. The relatively few existing state-owned shops and cooperatives sold very few products, mostly only against strictly rationed coupons. In 1932, the *kolkhoz* markets were legalized again after being closed a few years earlier. In them, peasants could sell the produce from their small private plots in excess of the state deliveries demanded from them. They had a very large share in many food categories like eggs, milk, and meat, throughout Soviet times.[12] To complete this picture of Soviet provisioning in the early 1930s, in addition to state shops, cooperatives and kolkhoz markets, the ORS should also be mentioned. It ran numerous food outlets and canteens in factories, other workplaces and educational institutions and supplied workers directly from centrally-distributed provisions. At the beginning of the 1930s, the whole system of food distribution was organized under the People's Commissariat of People's Supply, thus emphasizing its non-commercial nature. However, in 1934, following the newly adopted policy, it was divided into two ministries of Domestic Trade and Food Industry respectively. Throughout the 1930s, many workers continued to receive a major part of their food supplies from factory outlets and canteens rather than from the commercial state shops.

---

10 Gronow, 2003, 89.
11 Gronow, 2003, 98.
12 Osokina, 1997, 147–54.

Following the closing down of private shops in the late-1920s, cooperatives were expected to take their place as retailers but the policy was later changed in favour of state-owned shops. As Hessler pointed out:

> As of October 1931, consumer cooperatives were specifically barred from handling such sales in order to concentrate on basic provisionment. The new shops and retail chains that proliferated in connection with this order were necessarily expensive, a selection skewed in favour of luxury goods, and the rudiments of customer service, so utterly lacking in the distribution system as a whole. These positive attributes formed the core of 'cultured Soviet trade,' an ideal that came to define the Stalinist approach to retailing.[13]

State shops became the ideal representatives of 'cultured trade'. Consequently, in 1935, the Ministry of Trade decided that cooperative chains should in future service only the countryside and state-owned shops the towns. One of the best examples of the new ideas penetrating Soviet trade in the mid-1930s was the establishment of two chains of luxury food stores in the main cities and towns of the Soviet Union. These were called *Gastronom* and *Bakaleya*. The People's Commissar of the newly founded Ministry of Food Industry, Anastas Mikoyan, who was extremely active in these reforms, was proud of having personally invented the name *Gastronom*. In November 1934 there were 105 *Gastronom* shops, rising to 139 in April 1935.[14]

Table 12.1   The officially required minimum level of product variety of Gastronom and Bakaleya shops in 1933 and 1934

GASTRONOM	1933	1934	Moscow Gastronom no 1 (former Elisejevskij)
Sausage and ham	20	25	40
Meat	—	8	35
Fish	39	72	202
Cheese	10	14	62
Canned fish	22	25	42
Confectionery	62	96	493
Wine and mineral water	144	208	309
BAKALEYA			
Cheese hollandaise	1	8	
Canned fish	12	24	
Confectionery	16	51	
Tobacco	15	28	
Flour	—	10	
Macaroni	—	32	
Plus several other unspecified items			

Source: RGAE F.7971, Op.1,D.77,L.66-9 and Gronow 2003, 101.

---

13 Hessler, 2004, 99.

14 RGAE F 7971, Op.1, D.77, L.65.

Gastronom could be found in 72 cities and 40 regions. By July 1936, the number of *Gastronoms* had reached 259.[15] The *Bakaleya* chain grew more slowly but had a shop in 27 cities and 13 regions. Both *Gastronom* and *Bakaleyas* were meant to be high-quality shops, not at all resembling previous Soviet food stores, cooperatives and other outlets which were often small, dirty and ill-equipped. Above all, their product variety was much greater from the very start (see Table 12.1).[16] Standards of service were expected to be on an altogether different level; they boasted, for instance, of organizing home deliveries.[17] These new shops were mostly located in the centre of Soviet cities and bigger towns.

Gastronom and *Bakaleya* shops were privileged showcases of the new Soviet abundance. This becomes clear by comparison with minimum product variety rules required in 1939 from other food stores. All shops were divided according to their size and importance into three classes. The first and best class shops had to keep at least 67 products on sale, the second class 52 and the third only 39.[18] The technical standards of *Gastronoms* and *Bakaleyas* were also on a much higher level. An inspection report of the Odessa city Soviet reported many elementary shortcomings in its shops, like a total lack of glass for counters and displays, weak lighting, a total lack of packaging materials, or shortages of small weights and measures.[19] The Moscow *Gastronom* no. 2, on the contrary, had from the start three refrigerators, a goods lift, 40 sets of scales, an internal telephone network, an errand boy, and so on. It delivered lunch boxes to 150 workers at the nearby Bolshevik factory.[20]

The opening of *Gastronoms* and *Bakaleyas* in the mid-1930s was a typical Soviet gesture. Instead of guaranteeing the availability of basic necessities to the majority of its people, the Soviet Government invested in relatively few but expensive luxury shops which catered for the well-to-do part of the urban population, skilled industrial workers and educated specialists. These were not only propaganda gestures or showcases: they found customers who were both willing and could afford to shop in them.[21] Gradually their network increased and they became accessible to a greater number of people. But most of all these new food shops and department stores were supposed to act as examples or models of cultured trade and as concrete proof of material abundance for the rest of the country. In these model shops the roles of the buyer and the seller would ideally be reversed from what was common in the Soviet Union. They were supposed to be characterized by a cultivated intercourse with the customer. They could show a smart display of goods and engage in both investigating and cultivating their customers' taste. Such cultured relations between seller and buyer were hardly ever met in reality in Soviet retail trade, which was

---

15 Narkom Vnutorg SSSR, Sovetskaja torgovlja, Moskva, 1936, 19.

16 RGAE F.7971, Op.1, D.77, L.66–9. See Gronow, 2003, 101.

17 A mere three per cent of food stores practised home deliveries in 1935, but as Hessler, 2004, 206, has pointed out, this practice received an enormous amount of publicity.

18 RGAE 7971, Op.1, D.394.

19 Hessler, 2004, 207.

20 Narkom Vnutorg SSSR. Sovetskaja torgovlja, 21, 24.

21 See Hessler, 2004, 201–2.

more often than not characterized – until modern times – by long queues, serious shortages of the basic necessities, and rude behaviour.

First-Class Restaurants or Factory Canteens

The mid-1930s was an important time in the development of Soviet restaurants and the restaurant culture.[22] In 1935, a state committee was given the task of improving the standards of Soviet restaurants, cafés and canteens. The People's Commissar of Trade, I. Veitser, who actively promoted new commercial institutions, was also behind these measures. Under his ministry, a new Central Administration of Restaurants and Cafés (GURK) was established in January 1936. Most restaurants placed under GURK were in the bigger cities. All other restaurants, some 800 altogether, belonged to cooperatives and were located in smaller towns. According to the estimates made by this state committee, closed factory canteens and those in educational institutions served half the population of the Soviet Union daily, and up to 90–100 per cent of the workers in bigger factories and students. The situation changed after the elimination of bread coupons and the end of general food rationing in 1935. As the committee argued, a new demand for better service and meals had arisen. What was even more important, it suggested, was that restaurants and canteens should be opened to cater for all paying customers and not only for a restricted list. The need to regulate and control such open restaurants had become obvious since in many places they were already reported to operate in response to popular demand. Several factory canteens in various parts of the country had already opened their doors – semi-legally or illegally – to a broader clientèle.[23]

The main proposal of the state committee was to categorize all restaurants into three quality classes. The first, and lowest class, consisted of all the closed workplace canteens. Ordinary open canteens, cafés, tea rooms and bars belonged to the second class. This second class was expected to expand in the future mainly with such modern self-service restaurants like *amerikanki* (small canteens with high tables to stand by), buffets, and *zakusochnyje* (snack bars), as well as specialized vegetarian and dietetic canteens. In order to encourage the establishment and development of such places, all the restaurants in this class were allowed to raise their prices by 30 per cent.[24] The third category, in traditional terms the first-class restaurants, encompassed all proper restaurants. As the state committee characterized them, they had quality design, good service and fine tableware. They were to cook meals only to order and were not allowed to have any mass-produced ready-to-serve dishes on sale. They were also encouraged to organize home-delivery and party services. The improvement of the poor quality of their food was not the only issue of these reform plans. The first-class restaurants and cafés had an additional important task in cultivating table manners among workers, as the demand for tableware indicated. It was not at all uncommon that ordinary factory canteens totally lacked forks and

---

22 RGAE, F.7971, Op.1, D.210a, L.29–30.

23 RGAE, F.7971, Op.1, D.210a, L.29–30.

24 RGAE F.7971, Op. 1, D. 326, L.6–19.

knives, not to speak of tablecloths, salt and pepper dispensers, as well as other such basic eating utensils.

Despite enjoying the support of higher government, the new line of opening and promoting luxurious and fine restaurants and cafés instead of ordinary factory canteens was not welcomed and approved of by all those involved. The directors of the newly established GURK were arrested and denounced in 1937. They were denounced as people's enemies or 'fascist bandits' and were accused of leading the people's food supply and the whole system of nourishment into a totally wrong direction. Their main crime was the very policy which had been adopted and promoted with great publicity just a year or two earlier. They had opened first-class quality restaurants and neglected to take care of ordinary workers' canteens, so the accusations claimed. In the same year, the Minister of Trade, I. Veitser, who had promoted more commercial activities was also arrested and 'repressed'. By opening new, fine restaurants, so the accusation went, the leaders of GURK had aimed at fulfilling the annual plans through the sale of fewer but more expensive dishes instead of a greater number of cheaper, mass-produced dishes. The overall value of 'mass dishes with a fixed price' was reported to have diminished by over 50 per cent during the previous year due to these new experiments.[25] In a manner typical of the times, the political hunt for traitors and 'Trotskyists' in the restaurant administration rapidly spread wider than the Central Administration of Restaurants and Cafés in Moscow. At the end of 1937, the local directors of restaurants in Leningrad were also put on trial and liquidated shortly after the Moscow proceedings against the directors at GURK. Their crime was similar to that of the central administration at Moscow: they had opened luxury restaurants at the cost of a major closure of ordinary factory canteens. They had neglected the real needs of the workers in order to promote their criminal cause and to make 'easy money'. It was true that masses of canteens had been closed in 1936 and 1937. This was due to the rapidly worsening food-supply situation – in many places canteens simply did not have any food to make any dishes – rather than the new policy of opening luxury restaurants. In 1937, there were only 46 better-class (that is, third-highest category) restaurants and 68 cafés and buffets in the whole country.[26] These could hardly be responsible for the closing down of thousands of factory canteens.

The best example of the often mutually contradictory and irrational tendencies which prevailed in Soviet politics is the building the Hotel Moskva in the very end of the 1930s. Moskva was a real showpiece of Stalinist Luxury. This huge building project, which required millions of roubles in investment, started on Stalin's personal initiative almost at the same time as other much more modest projects were condemned as ideologically dangerous works of the class enemy and detrimental to the genuine socialist cause. Its building is a good example of how such huge projects could change the ordinary plans and projections of the whole catering industry. The role of the Hotel Moskva as the real show piece of Soviet abundance was obvious. It was meant to lodge thousands of official party, trade union, cultural, etc., delegations from all over the country invited or commanded to various conferences in the

25 RGAE F.7971, Op.3, D.15.L.25.
26 RGAE F.7971, Op.3.D.15, L.8.

Kremlin. Stalin personally followed the project closely. It therefore had the highest priority and could bypass all other proposals like the building of several hotels and restaurants initiated by the economic planning offices. This project consumed all the finances budgeted for the building and opening of cafés in Moscow and other cities: in 1939, no other cafés could be opened in the whole of the Soviet Union. When the Hotel Moskva opened in 1940, it could boast of one huge, first-class restaurant, one luxurious café and 13 snack bars and buffets.[27] A couple of years earlier Moscow had seen the opening of another showpiece of Soviet abundance, the Café Lux. Compared to Hotel Moskva, it was quite modest project costing 'only' one million roubles.[28]

Socialist Realism in the Field of Material Culture

New department stores, luxury food stores and first-class restaurants were all visible symbols of the spirit of the 1930s in Stalin's Russia. They can be compared with the most renowned building project of the times, the building of the Moscow metro, or subway. The Moscow metro, with its highly decorated underground stations, became an important part of Soviet popular mythology.[29] Its symbolic message was actively referred to in public propaganda. Kaganovich, the Moscow party leader, expressed this idea: 'When our worker takes the subway, he should be cheerful and joyous feeling as if in "a palace shining with the light of advancing, all victorious socialism".'[30] Kaganovich saw the new Moscow metro refuting the false image propagated by the enemies of the Soviet Union that socialism was a barracks, peopled by look-alikes.

Similarly, the new department and food stores as well as cafés and restaurants were palaces for the people. Like the former palaces of the Tsar and the Russian nobility, which had been turned into museums, sanatoria or culture clubs, these new 'palaces' of the Moscow metro, as well as the new 'shrines' of the Soviet consumer culture, were open to the common people. But they were to become even more a part of the new joyous and abundant everyday life of the workers of the first Socialist country in the world. In this process, Moscow, as capital of the Soviet Union, gained the task of representing in a condensed form the whole bright future of socialism. It was the leading city in the Soviet *nomenklatura* of cities and towns.[31] The new showcases were open to every worker of the Socialist capital on their way to work or on their daily errands. And even less fortunate comrades, who lived in some far away corner of the Soviet Union, could enjoy a foretaste of the coming Socialist abundance and well-being on their visits to the capital. As official propaganda promised, this was the glorious future that would soon reach even their own, more backward, towns and villages. All these Soviet retail outlets, as well as the consumer goods and food products of better quality and greater variety, like perfumes, champagne, sausages

---

27 CMAM F.453,Op.1.D.35, L.1. and RGAE F 7971, Op.3, D.74, L.108.
28 RGAE F.7971, Op.3, D.74,L.110.
29 See Morozov, 1995.
30 *Pravda*, 20 May 1935, 3, cited in Colton, 1995, 327.
31 Papernyi, 1985.

and chocolates, which were put into production in the 1930s, can be seen 'shining with the light of the advancing, all victorious socialism'. They incorporated the spirit of socialist realism. As Sheila Fitzpatrick has pointed out, 'socialist realism was a Stalinist mentality, not just an artistic style. Ordinary citizens also developed the ability to see things as they were becoming and ought to be, rather than as they were.'[32] This socialist realist ideology had, however, a potential seed of discontent built in to it: what if the Party and the Soviet Government could not deliver what they promised? What if all the new goods and services were not within the reach of every citizen during or at the end of the on-going Five-Year Plan, as promised by the Party? Why should the workers of Moscow enjoy these new delights and pleasures whereas in other towns people were queuing all night through for a can of milk or plain black bread? The authorities lived under a continuous pressure to perform better and to fulfil their own promises. More often than not they could only answer to this pressure by finding scapegoats, people's enemies of various sorts, and by making ever new promises without any real resources.

During the 1930s, the Soviet authorities made many concessions to popular taste and adopted a more permissive attitude to material consumption, even allowing small expressions of individual taste. With some reservations, one could claim that this was the beginning of Soviet consumerism, legitimated by the Communist Party and Stalin personally. One could also claim that these changes left more permanent marks in the Soviet society and popular mentality than the earlier attempts of the 1920s, and the Soviet Cultural Revolution in particular, to mould the new Soviet man and woman. In any case, many urban institutions of public catering and food distribution, as well as popular eating and drinking habits and practices, saw daylight for the first time in the mid-1930s. The Soviet Union, which came to an end in 1991, was as much, if not more, a product of Stalin's 1930s as of the Revolution of 1917.

References

Archives

Rossiskii gosudarstvennyi arkhiv ekonomiki, [The Russian State Economic Archive] (RGAE), Moscow
Tsentralnyi munitsipal'nyi arkhiv goroda Moskvy, [The Central Municipal Archive of Moscow] (CMAM) Moscow.

Books and articles

Colton, T. *Moscow: Governing a Socialist Metropolis*, Cambridge, MA, 1995.
Dikhtiar, G.A. *Sovetskaja Torgovlja v Periode Postrojeniia Sotsializma*, [Soviet Trade during the Period of Building Socialism] Moscow, 1961.
Fitzpatrick, S. *Everyday Stalinism. Ordinary Life in Extraordinary Times. Soviet Russia in the 1930s*, New York, 1999.

---

32 Fitzpatrick, 1999, 9.

Gronow, J. *Caviar with Champagne. Common Luxury and the Ideals of the Good Life in Stalin's Russia*, Oxford, 2003.

Hessler, J. *A Social History of Soviet Trade: Trade Policy, Retail Practices, and Consumption, 1917–1954*, Princeton, N.J, 2004.

Landsman, M. *Dictatorship and Demand. The Politics of Consumerism in East Germany*, Cambridge, MA, 2005.

Morozov, A.I. *Konets Utopii. Iz Istorii Iskusstva v SSSR 19-kh Godov*, [The End of Utopia] Moscow, 1995.

Osokina, Ye. *Za Fasadom Stalinskogo Izobilija. Paspredelenie i Rynok v Snabzhenie Naselenija v Gody Industrializatsii, 1927–1941*, [Behind the Facade of Stalinist Abundance] Moscow, 1997.

Papernyi, V. *Kultura 'Dva'*, [The Culture 'Two'] Ann Arbor, 1985.

Sartorti, R. 'Stalinism and Carnival. Organization and Aesthetics of Political Kolidays,' in Günther, H. (ed.), *The Culture of Stalin's Period*, London, 1990.

Sokolov, A.K. (ed.), *Obshcheshtvo i Vlast'. 1930–gody. Povestvovanije v Dokumentakh*, [Society and Power in the 1930s] Moscow, 1998.

Sombart, W. *Liebe, Luxus und Kapitalismus. Über die Entstehung der modernen Welt aus dem Geist der Verschwendung,* [Love, Luxury and Capitalism] Berlin, 1986 (1st ed. 1913).

Stites, R. *Russian Popular Culture. Entertainment and Society since 1900*, Cambridge, 1992.

Timasheff, N.S. *The Great Retreat. The Growth and Decline of Communism in Russia*, New York, 1946.

Trotsky, L. *The Revolution Betrayed.* New York, 1972 (1st ed. 1937).

Chapter 13

A Shop Window of the Regime: The Position of Prague as the Capital in the Preferential Supply System of Selected Czechoslovakian Cities, 1950–1970

Martin Franc

In the Czech milieu, Prague has always held a special position as the natural and undisputed metropolis. In 1950, there were 931,525 inhabitants living there. Twenty years later, the population surpassed one million. Supplying Prague with food was always an issue of particular importance for the functioning of the entire country. In 1955, Prague represented 10.7 per cent of total food sales in the Czechoslovakia, and more so for some commodities: for instance more than 25 per cent of coffee, nearly 30 per cent of poultry, and 19 per cent of total sales of fruit. Generally speaking, the overall average was exceeded in sales of foods whose production was next to impossible in a city (e.g. eggs, poultry) or those representing a certain degree of luxury (coffee, chocolate, wine). On the other hand, the consumption of bread and spirits remained below the average of other regions.[1] These trends remained unchanged in the 1960s as well.[2] Plans from 1963 projected an average per capita expenditure of 3,700 crowns in the food shop network nationally in 1970, whereas the respective figures for Prague, as the regional hub and the most important tourist business centre, were more than one thousand crowns higher.[3]

---

1   Bread: 5.4 per cent of total consumption; Liquor: 5.4 per cent; Sugar: 6.5 per cent. Domestic Trade Ministry (DTM), 1956 Annual report on domestic trade. Nat. Archives, f. Kancelář Antonína Novotného, box 172. Prague's share of the turnover in public consumption of foodstuffs in 1955 was around 11 per cent. Its share of the grocery turnover of small enterprises reached 52.7 per cent in 1955, which was the second-lowest regional share.
2   Vavříková, 174–175.
3   'Analysa současného stavu a generel rozvoje maloobchodní sítě a sítě veřejného stravování na území hlavního města Prahy do r. 1970' [Analysis of Present State and General Development of Retail Trade Network…] Prague City Archives (PCA), f. Odbor obchodu [Commerce Dpt.]

Structure of Supplies

Before considering the role of Prague in the supply process, some facts must be mentioned regarding the shopping network. The 1948 February coup, together with economic changes that preceded and followed this event, significantly altered retailing and public catering in Prague. Their structure was substantially changed and reorganized. There were more than 15,000 private retail units in 1948 and just 397 'socialist cooperative stores'. These proportions had changed by 1951. Only 3,215 privately owned outlets survived, while the 'socialist sector' controlled 6,969 shops and 1,863 pubs and restaurants. These figures show that many shops were closed following the retail transition into state hands.[4] The decrease was justified by the necessity to transfer labour into production. Moreover, with a sole proprietor, many small shops were regarded as superfluous.[5] Efforts to liquidate 'retail capitalism' continued further. In 1957, all of Prague contained a mere 915 private shops and pubs. Sixty-six shops sold food products, as well as another 149 private pubs. By the end of 1960, only 50 private units survived in Prague, most of them small tobacco shops owned by disabled persons.[6]

Analagous to the state of affairs in East Germany, the state took over shops in cities at the beginning of the 1950s, while consumer cooperatives dominated distribution nationwide.[7] They were completely subservient to the regime. Local administrative bodies also had a significant influence, as they ran most public catering units and, for some time, factory canteens. The disbanding of private outlets in practice enabled a broad reconstruction of the whole retail network, which was administered by local councils in cooperation with the Ministry of Internal Trade. Plans for a new location pattern emphasized the city centre and its liveliest business arteries – in particular a cluster of retail units within the so-called Golden Cross, the liveliest business district in Prague.[8] Paris Street, 'the sole Prague Boulevard', was to become another centre of socialist shopping, topped symbolically from 1954 by the monumental Stalin Memorial on the Letná Hill.[9] As to the suburbs, their composition of population was of key importance. Workers' quarters in particular were supported.

Centrally-located outlets followed the Soviet-inspired trend of creating so-called trade centres that stocked a broad selection of goods and had long business hours. A central shopping centre was established within the Golden Cross, on Na Příkopě street.[10] The augmentation of selected units, in particular those in the suburbs, was officially presented as desirable progress in comparison with tiny private outlets

---

4   The decrease in number of shops began already shortly after World War II. See Anon, 1967.

5   PCA, Rada ÚNV [CNC Council], Jan. 27, 1952.

6   Kádár, 1961.

7   From 1964/65 consumer cooperatives were entitled to set up their outlets as an amendment to the existing state trade shop network. Cf. PCA, f. Odbor obchodu.

8   Agenda for All-State Conference on Domestic Trade and Nutrition. PCA, f. Odbor obchodu.

9   Anonymous, 1954.

10 Anonymous, 1952, 200.

lacking hygiene.[11] But it caused problems downtown because retail units there had no room to expand, and the concentration of shops only on major thoroughfares was criticized for overloading the small numbers remaining and reducing convenience for customers.[12] Public catering enterprises were fused together organizationally as well.

The preference given to the working class, as mentioned earlier, at one point was linked with efforts to create a representative image for important trading streets, in particular during the early years of this era. An example is the efforts to establish so-called 'gastronomies': enormous delicatessen stores with a wide selection, on the Soviet model. Three gastronomies were proposed for Prague. The first one was at the Golden Cross, while the other two were supposed to be located in the workers' quarters. The notion that socialist catering should serve the working class was demonstrated by efforts to establish catering units for workers at the most exclusive locations.

The so-called class view was perhaps most distinctly demonstrated with the establishment of a network of so-called free shops. These were shops where, during the period of rationing, people could buy products without rations for significantly higher prices. The free market was thus supposed to be complementary to the regulated one in the sale of surpluses remaining after the rations had been distributed. However, certain social strata were completely dependent on the free market, among them in particular the tradesmen and private entrepreneurs, who did not 'join the working process'. In the establishment of free shops, neighbourhoods with a majority working-class population were given priority.[13] The propaganda claimed that it was the new elite who were supposed to do their shopping in these new shops.

During the period of rationing in the early 1950s, efforts were made at state enterprises to discriminate in favour of canteens administered by unions, and also school cafeterias.[14] In factories, some otherwise unavailable goods were distributed by unions. This practice waned after the abolition of rationing. However, in a time of distribution crisis, the supply of the network of smaller shops was curtailed to a greater extent than was the case in larger shops and industrial canteens received preferential treatment in order to ensure that workers in critical branches of industry and transport were provided for. Also at such times, it was assumed that workplace canteens would receive preferential treatment in the supply network.[15] But workplace canteens and school kitchens became the object of significant criticism in the 1960s due to the low quality of meals served.[16] In workplaces, the number of consumers

---

11 E.g. Špalková, 1954.

12 National Archives, f. Kancelář Antonína Novotného, box. 172.

13 PCA, Rada ÚNV, July 17, 1951.

14 In 1952, Prague had 560 workplace cafeterias and canteens. By 1955, this number had declined to 481. In 1956, Prague's share in the overall turnover in workplace and school was 10.9 per cent. DTM, 1956 Annual report on domestic trade, Nat. Archives, f. Kancelář Antonína Novotného, box. 172.

15 Ibid., box 172. In 1961 workplace cafeterias served 1.3 million meals, which signifies that 28 per cent of employees took their meals at such facilities.

16 MSÚ-A AV ČR, f. Ivan Málek, box 220.

actually declined. At the same time, school kitchens had to cope with stringent limits on resources per pupil.

The period 1954–56 saw the peak in emphasis on the interests and needs of 'working people'. After Stalin's death, the regime aimed more to satisfy the basic needs of the population as a whole. Later, it was argued that a 'social centre' was needed away from downtown Prague for the benefit of the average worker-consumer, and the downtown centre was now to concentrate on quality-catering units in higher categories.[17] In 1957, Jindřich Rež presented this shift in ideas concerning the composition of the shopping network. In his words, 'the downtown shopping centre should, in the future, include shops that are visited by last-minute buyers, or window-shoppers.'[18] The location of international hotels also influenced the pattern of shops.[19] From the second half of the 1960s, the importance of Paris Street rose again. At the outset, this was due to the concentration of tourist services there and, later, due to completion of the Hotel Intercontinental at the end of Paris Street.[20]

The rationalization plans for building or reconstruction of the retail network could not be realized without complications. The particular interests of enterprises and organizations often influenced the planners' ideas. Setting up warehouses and offices at attractive downtown addresses became a nuisance throughout the period under review, which the planners fought against. However, their efforts were often unsuccessful.[21] Even a full respect for rationality in location could not eliminate the basic issue. In the early 1950s, particularly, trade lagged behind insofar as economic priorities were concerned, with necessary investments completely lacking.[22]

Prague also played a key role in a parallel distribution network, which was inaccessible to the common consumer and served the highest functionaries.[23] So-called TUZEX shops were established in 1957 by government decree for the sale of foods, consumer goods and the rendering of services for foreign exchange, and they were a continuation of the earlier, more modest shop DAREX. TUZEX shops offered exclusive domestic, but mainly foreign, goods, which were unavailable in the general distribution network. Prices were set on the basis of average prices in selected western European countries. TUZEX's major aim was to gain as much foreign currency as possible. In the TUZEX shops, the predominant currency in use was the so-called TUZEX crown. Not only tourists from western countries, but also Czechoslovak citizens who possessed a TUZEX account (for instance due to their employment abroad), were entitled to shop there. These TUZEX crowns became very soon a subject of busy surreptitious trade. The importance of TUZEX rose sharply in the 1960s. This was connected with rapid development of the travel industry as well as with the rising number of Czechoslovak citizens working abroad,

---

17 Rež, 1957a.

18 Rež, 1957b.

19 A special enterprise was set up for hotels and restaurants designated for the travel business.

20 PCA, f. Odbor obchodu, Deputy Mayor Havlíček's letter dated Feb. 5, 1965.

21 E.g. PCA, Odbor obchodu.

22 E.g. Zhodnocení činnosti obchodních organizací na území hlavního města Prahy. [Evaluation of Commercial Organizations' Activities], PCA, Rada ÚNV, Jan. 29, 1952.

23 Doskočil and Žáček, 2004.

particularly in developing countries. The distribution of the TUZEX shop network depended on the number of potential customers. Therefore, most of these shops were located in Prague. TUZEX may be considered as one of the symbols of a kind of diversion from the system that preferred the 'workers'. An average worker, who did not have the opportunity to work abroad as an assembler, for example, had no legal opportunity to purchase such attractive and prestigious goods.[24]

New Forms of Food Retailing

Prague played a major part in the introduction of new forms of retail sales. This corresponded with the density of its shopping network, as well as with its role as a focus for consumers from other parts of the country.

The preference given to working-class neighbourhoods was most prominently manifested during the introduction of supermarkets, which appeared in Czechoslovakia in 1955. The first opened in the Prague proletarian quarter of Žižkov, on Hussite Street.[25] Supermarkets experienced an enormous boom and just three years later there were 58 of them in Prague alone, the overwhelming majority selling food.[26]

Shops selling ready-to-cook food were another advertised novelty. The development centre of this kind of production was installed not far from one of the most frequented department stores. Another special shop to introduce domestic food novelties, the House of Foods, was also opened on Wenceslas Square in 1957. This sold new Czech products and also foreign-made delicacies. In time it became the most exclusive centre of food sales in the country.

Numerous experiments in public catering flourished in Prague also. There were foreign-cuisine restaurants, including exotic ones, and also self-service restaurants that were intended to play a role similar to that of self-service shops in retail sales.[27] Despite their relative popularity, these never gained a dominant position, mainly due to problems in preparing food in such enormous quantities. Their impact was limited to certain types of customers, especially the workers.[28]

Allocations and Deliveries to Shops in Prague

Because the archives of the Ministry of Domestic Trade remain inaccessible even now, it is difficult to reconstruct the delivery system. I have had to rely on scattered evidence preserved in the papers of the Trade Department in the Central National Committee in Prague.

---

24 On TUZEX, see Zpráva o průběhu cestovního ruchu v roce 1966 [1966 Report on Travel Business], National Archives, f. Kancelář Antonína Novotného, box 173. This number rose 141.2 per cent between 1960 and 1966 from 90.4 million crowns to 218 million crowns.

25 Prague 6, a 'bourgeois district', was generally passed by when new self-services were opened. See Hach, 1957.

26 Větrovský, 1956, 11.

27 Cf. PCA, Rada ÚNV, Aug. 7, 1956.

28 The first self-service canteen was opened in the second half of the 1950s.

There seem to have been two distinct phases, similar to the formation of the sales network. During the first, priority was given to Prague as an industrial centre. The distribution plan of the Ministry of Domestic Trade, which was responsible for deliveries, divided cities, towns and municipalities up according to their number of workers and the government's directives insisted on the need to ensure continuous deliveries for this group as the most important objective.[29] In the rationing period, such structuring seemed logical, but it survived long after rationing was abolished. Later, other factors were taken into consideration, such as the volume of tourism, or the administrative character of the respective location. Ironically, what were efforts to rationalize the entire system, actually introduced inequities, for instance the volume of supply depended on the ranking of customers in the power hierarchy.

A gradual trend towards decentralization, and the mid-1960s abolition of compulsory purchasing from favoured suppliers, indicate some flexibility, but many rigidities of the 1950s system survived. For example, the complicated system of calculating directive plan data gave opportunities for the exercise of personal influence. Also events could undermine plans, as happened when the political developments in 1961 induced shopping hysteria and a delivery crisis, with the result that a Ministry of Domestic Trade directive called for the 'preferential feeding of towns and industrial locations, factory and school canteens, factory canteens in industrial works or in their immediate vicinity'.[30] Subsequent documents testify that agricultural areas were no longer discriminated against – perhaps the progress of agricultural collectivization enhanced their socialist credentials.[31]

The exact formula used for distribution is still unknown. Obviously, it must have been an extremely detailed document. Prague was included in the top-ranking group, along with other industrial centres and regional capitals.[32] It seems, however, that the metropolis occupied an even more influential rank than others in this group. Traces of unilateral preference can be found even at the beginning of our period. For example, the network of non-ration shops in Prague retained their priority status even during the 1961 crisis.[33] The responsible officials decreed that no restrictive measures should be applied to deliveries to the capital.[34]

Certain countryside districts and towns had, on the other hand, to cope permanently with their demands not being met. Let me quote a Report on the Investigation Results of an anonymous complaint concerning a lack of meat, meat products, eggs, and butter in the district of Prostějov, dated May 29, 1961 and preserved in Antonín Novotný's office papers in the Prague National Archives. The author of this report agrees that the complaints are entirely justified since

---

29 However, an anonymous report blames consumer cooperatives for preferring agricultural villages to industrial worker ones. National Archives, f. Kancelář Antonína Novotného, box 172.

30 Ibid.

31 Ibid.

32 Ibid.

33 PCA, Odbor obchodu, or Rada ÚNV, Apr. 23, 1957.

34 E.g. National Archives, A. Novotný's Ofice, box 172.

the Prostějov district ranks 4th, so far as the volume of delivered goods is concerned, among the South Moravian districts. This also corresponds to the rank of importance of the Prostějov district within the framework of this region. The quantities are, however, insufficient for [adequately] supplying the Prostějov district.

Higher deliveries of foodstuffs for Prague reflected from the very beginning the position of the city as an industrial centre, as well as its importance as a regional focus. But, on some occasions, if deliveries to the city were increased, the surrounding Prague region, that is to say its rural hinterland, suffered from shortages. And vice versa: Prague emptied during holiday periods. The regime therefore attempted to relocate parts of the Prague food allocation to well-known summer resorts in its surroundings.

Similar to the structure of the retail network, food allocations accentuated the positive image of the metropolis for those who lived there, in particular the workers.[35] As international tensions eased with Khrushchev's policies in the Soviet Union, the metropolis now aimed to show a friendly face to the outside, mainly to visitors from abroad. Foreign visitors streamed into the country in numbers previously unimaginable. Using 1956 as a starting point, their numbers increased 392 per cent in just three years, and 792 per cent to 1962. Whereas at the beginning of the 1950s, only tens of thousands crossed the borders every year, there were now 3.5 million foreign visitors to Czechoslovakia in 1966, of whom 750,000 came from capitalist countries. At this time, tourists visited Czechoslovakia more often than Poland or Hungary.[36] In the same year, earnings derived from foreign tourism reached 4.1 percent of the total small enterprise earnings. Prague, therefore, maintained its position as the most important tourist destination, despite the fact that the influx was constrained by a lack of hotel accommodation and efforts to encourage visitors to travel to other parts of the country.[37] By comparison with the previous period, the importance of Prague as the state capital was singled out more visibly. This might have been in connection with a certain revival of the emphasis on the Czechoslovak state.

The gradual transformation of image was reflected also in criticisms of abuses and deficiencies in supplies. The question 'what would people say abroad?' gained in importance. An early example is provided in the remark of a reader printed in journal of the Central National Committee (CNC) of the Capital *Nová Praha* [The New Prague] in the second half of 1956. The author criticized the quality of the breakfast in a well-known downtown restaurant, noting that among the group present was a foreigner.[38] The report on supplies for the second quarter of 1959 presented by

---

35 Even Christmas carp were allocated in a manner favourable to Prague citizens. See PCA, Rada ÚNV, Nov. 18, 1952. There were some opposite trends; see the list of institutions with preferential supplies, PCA, Odbor obchodu, Sep. 28, 1950.

36 Czechoslovakia's share of global tourism in 1965 stood at 2.5 per cent despite a worldwide decline. Hungary's share was only 1.1 per cent. NA, f. Kancelář Antonína Novotného, box 173.

37 Kašpar, 1969, a NA, f. Kancelář Antonína Novotného, k. 173. According to analysis from 1965, Prague received 80 per cent of foreign visitors. See Slovenský národný archív, f. Povereníctvo obchodu 1964-68, box 17, sign. 76.

38 Chyský, 1956.

the Commercial Department in the CNC Council stated that officials 'intervened directly, directing egg deliveries to the key shops and catering units of Restaurants and Canteens Prague, especially into those frequented by guests from abroad'.[39]

With regard to the position of Prague as by far the most important tourist destination in the country, this redefinition of representation could not signify anything other than the further strengthening of the hitherto privileged position of the city. The preferences in supply were primarily limited to the historical heart of the city and the customers from peripheral quarters were resentful of this situation. The position of centrally-located shops was strengthened in the later period by the distribution of goods in accordance with shop turnover. This benefited the city thanks to the purchasing power of the local population and also to the custom of shoppers from elsewhere.[40]

In 1962 the downtown district, Prague 1, had 7.7 per cent of the city's population but 22.8 per cent of foodstuff shop sales. The relevant report stated that 'Prague 1 will remain the all-city shopping centre in the future, too'. This discrepancy was even higher in public catering units: this same district having nearly 41 per cent of the city's turnover.[41] In connection with the gradual development of the international travel, a group of 345 foodstuff and industrial retail shops was earmarked and the authorities were ordered to take care of preferential supplies into this network. Among these 345 shops, 75 (22 per cent) were located in Prague, at the most frequented downtown locations, eventually around the international hotels, airport, etc.[42] Besides common goods, these shops were to display famous culinary specialties, such as Prague ham and top brands of Czech beer. Fifty catering units were given preferential supply status: most of them from the metropolis. However, despite this, the report on the travel trade for 1965 admits that the shop network, along with the quality of transportation, were the elements criticized most frequently by the foreign tourists in Czechoslovakia.

Representatives from the city of Prague were not particularly satisfied with the situation described and they requested further strengthening of preferential deliveries for the capital. The Ministry of Domestic Trade supported this at least partially.[43] Nevertheless, the city could not eliminate supply problems – perhaps because it was an issue that could not be solved without radical economic changes.

Even if the complaints of the Prague representatives are viewed as mere rhetoric, the metropolis can not be seen as an island of sufficiency. This is the Czechoslovak reality of the 1950s and 1960s. Prague, just like the whole country, suffered permanently from the chronic lack of certain goods. For instance, the Informative Report on Supplies, Second Quarter, 1959, states that 'serious disorders' were manifested in the city in deliveries of meat, meat products, eggs, potatoes and curds. Among other shortages listed were legumes, tinned milk, herrings, poppy, peanuts,

39 Informativní zpráva o zásobování za II. čtvrtletí 1959 [Information on supplies, 2/Q 1959], PCA, Odbor obchodu.

40 PCA, Rada ÚNV, June 24, 1958.

41 Analysa současného stavu... [Analysis of Present State...,] see footnote (3).

42 NA, f. Kancelář Antonína Novotného, box 173.

43 Anon., 1967.

canned olive oil, sterilized gherkins, the better sorts of stewed fruit, unsweetened tinned milk, cinnamon, chicken and meat soups, and potted shrimps.

The mismatch of supplies between the densely populated suburbs and the Prague downtown can be illustrated by the controversy over distribution to the ninth Prague district, that is to say the industrial quarter of Vysočany. The debate was held at a meeting of the CNC Council on June 24, 1958. The session commented that the downtown was better supplied only with fruits and vegetables. Other commodities, for instance fish products or honey, were in short supply throughout the whole city.

One special theme within the issue of the preferential supply of the capital which calls for individual elaboration but can be mentioned here only briefly, is the provisioning of social events. The regime paid special attention to these events, not merely by arranging sufficient supplies of goods and proper decorations, but also by introducing new products to the market. For example, the so-called Spartakiads, mass physical culture events, took place every fifth year from 1955 onwards.[44]

In conclusion, Prague enjoyed an extraordinary position in the food supply system in the 1950s and 1960s. In the first phase, starting in 1956, Prague was perceived as an industrial city with a high concentration of workers, good purchasing ability and high centralization, and later the city's image was key. Delivery preferences were justified by the position of Prague as the capital of the country and, at the same time, a major tourist destination. From the second half of the 1960s, emphasis was placed increasingly on the downtown area due to its importance, particularly with regard to foreign visitors. On the other hand, an important part of the common supply network was also concentrated in central Prague. The construction of shops in the suburbs, especially in the new housing estates, lagged behind.

Despite its preferential position, Prague could not avoid problems connected with the lack of certain kinds of foodstuffs. Although, over the course of time, the symbolic significance of higher order goods gained in importance, the capital never attained the level of East Berlin, which aspired to compete with its western part. Nevertheless, Prague did serve as a shop window of the regime, although in the course of time the question of who should be looking in that shop window underwent significant change.

References

Anon. 'Pracující Ženy Mohou Nakupovat Večer i v Neděli' [Working Women May do their Shopping in the Evenings or on Sundays], *Nová Praha* 12, 1952, 200.

Anon. 'Další Nákupní Střediska Otevřena' [New Shopping Centres Opened], *Nová Praha* 8, 1954, 134

Anon. 'Kolotoč Kolem Obchodu' [A Merry-go-round about Trade], *Nová Praha* 21, 1967, 6.

Chyský, J. 'Zásobovací Problém?' [Supply Problems?], *Nová Praha* 19, 1956, 18.

---

44 E.g. M. Munclinger's letter to Deputy Mayor B. Havlíček, dated Feb. 28, 1965. PCA, f. Odbor obchodu.

Doskočil, F. and Žáček, P. *Průlom. Agentem CIA Uvnitř Komunistické Nomenklatury* [CIA Agent inside the Communist Nomenclatura.], Prague, 2004.

Hach, A. 'Dejvice jsou Pozadu' [Dejvice is Lagging], *Nová Praha* 1, 1957, 27.

Kádár, Š. 'Od Hokynářů k Socialistickému Obchodu' [From Grocers to the Socialist Shop], *Nová Praha* 4, 1961, 16.

Kašpar, J. 'Praha ve Světle Cestovního Ruchu' [Prague in the Light of the Tourist Trade], *Nová Praha* 15, 1969, 10.

Rež, J. 'Od Brambor až po Spartaka' [From Potatoes to a Škoda Car], *Nová Praha* 6, 1957a, 10–11.

Rež, J. 'Jak Budeme Nakupovat ve Středu Města?' [How Shall we Do our Shopping Downtown?], *Nová Praha* 16, 1957b, 10–11.

Špalková, B. 'Moderní Prodejny Místo Zatuchlých Krámků' [Modern Outlets Instead of Smelly Shops], *Nová Praha* 4, 1954, 54.

Vavříková, J. 'Pražský Jídelníček Očima Lékaře' [The Prague Menu in Physicians' Eyes], in Janáček, J. (ed.), *Book of Prague 1965*, Prague, Orbis, 1965.

Větrovský, F. 'Samoobsluha-Pokroková Forma Prodejen' [Self-Service: A Progressive Form of Shopping], *Nová Praha* 2, 1956, 11.

Chapter 14

Born-in-the-City:
The Supermarket in Germany

Peter Lummel

'Shop as you please,
Pay as you leave!'[1]

After the founding of the Federal Republic of Germany in 1949, an explosion of innovative industrially-produced food occurred which was not surpassed until 1970.[2] The innovative dynamism was clearly connected with both the desire to consume and the consumption possibilities of that time. Both economic and mental backgrounds have often been examined.[3] The keywords were: 'consumption jam' after the post-war period; the Marshall Plan; the EEC; the so-called *Wirtschaftswunder* or 'West German Economic Miracle'; the political slogan 'Prosperity for Everyone'; as well as the real, and at the same time mental, urbanization of society. Therefore, it is the two decades until 1970, which is – within the theme of 'Food Innovation: the Product Perspective' – of special interest for understanding radical changes. However, food innovations can only be understood within the complete food chain context. This includes structural changes in farming, as well as changes within retailing, in kitchen equipment, and in citizens' consumption as well. Distributing foodstuffs proves to be an essential factor.[4]

Between 1949 and 1970, urban retailers transformed the German food market through the use of self-service and by product innovations. In accomplishing this, it is obvious not only that self-service gained acceptance (self-service may undoubtedly be described as the largest change in twentieth-century retailing), but also that supermarkets came into existence. At first, both of these retail changes occurred exclusively in cities and larger towns. Within a few years, supermarkets already reached sizes of up to 2,000 square metres and were rightly described as 'giants among grocery stores'.[5] As a premise, one might assume that during this period most retail innovations were to be found in the supermarket as new and ultra-modern distribution forms. Although the supermarket's general significance for retailing in

---

1   For a short definition of self-service and supermarkets, see Schulz-Klingauf, 1960, 15.
2   Lummel and Deak, 2005, 179–86.
3   Wild, 1994; Andersen, 1997; König, 2000.
4   For a broad overview of daily needs shopping in Germany, see Lummel and Deak, 2005.
5   *Selbstbedienung*, 10/1962, 6ff.

the early Federal Republic is undoubted, there are only a few studies about this topic. Besides some overviews about twentieth-century retailing exemplified by the work of Hans Jürgen Teuteberg and Uwe Spiekermann, there is also a recent article about the supermarket in Germany.[6] Furthermore, Derek Oddy analysed the development of UK supermarkets in an earlier publication following the ICREFH III Symposium.[7]

In this chapter, questions will be asked such as: why did supermarkets come into being in cities? Which customers preferred shopping in this type of retail outlet? What food and retail innovations started in the supermarket? What share did supermarkets have in the German food retail market as a whole? How far did the supermarket remain purely an urban retail type up to 1970? Did hypermarkets or shopping centres in the countryside present any competition in those days? The first section introduces typical food innovations of the years from 1949 to 1970. The second section deals with the birth of the supermarket, and the city as place for supermarkets will be specifically investigated in the third section. The fourth section will explore more thoroughly supermarket innovations up to 1970. In the last section, the question will be asked how far dynamic modernization in the supermarket influenced innovations in the food industry.

The main source material, which until now has not been evaluated, is the *Self-Service and Supermarket* (*Selbstbedienung und Supermarkt*) trade journal, published monthly by the Institute for Self-Service in Cologne from 1957 onwards. This medium was the official organ of progressive retailing in the Federal Republic. By publishing ground breaking studies, as well as exchanging experience, both domestically and internationally, the periodical was extremely influential in the implementation of both self-service and supermarkets.[8] For this chapter, *Self-Service and Supermarket* has been analysed from 1957 to 1971.

Food Innovations in the Early Federal Republic

To start with one example: around 1960, German coffee roasting companies began marketing their beans in vacuum-sealed packs and with a pre-printed price recommendation. With an attractive design, the packs were then delivered by the industry in standardized cartons which could be easily placed on to the self-service distributor's shelves. A few years earlier, distribution companies partially roasted raw coffee by themselves. Coffee beans had in turn to be weighed out, filled into paper bags and priced according to customers' quantity requirements during the sales procedure: a time-consuming and labour-intensive process. As this example clarifies, food innovations of the 1950s and 1960s were also innovations in packaging as well.[9] Before 1950, most merchandise was sold, among other things, from tin cans, glass

---

6   See Spiekermann, 1995, especially 211ff.; Spiekermann, 1997; Teuteberg, 2005; Lummel, 2005.

7   Oddy, 1995, 187–99.

8   The importance of this journal is described in ISB-Institut für Selbstbedienung, 1988.

9   Teuteberg, 2005, 34–7.

jars, barrels and storage containers. After 1950, new products were produced for sales via self-service. Packing facilitated transport and protected the foodstuffs from both contamination and destruction. In addition, to stabilize carton packing, the tin-plated can and synthetic materials gained wider acceptance. Industry increasingly produced brand-name products. The exterior appearance was attractively designed, easily recognizable and contained information about the merchandise.

Table 14.1   The most important food innovations in Germany, 1949–1970

1949	Pfanni: Potato dumplings as semi-finished food
1952	Bluna: Lemonade
1954	Thomy: tubed delicatessen mayonnaise
1956	Thomy: tomato ketchup
1959	Nesquik: readily soluble cocoa powder
1960	Alete: baby food/Kraft: "Miracoli" ready-to-serve pasta meal
1961	Mars: chocolate bar
1962	Iglo: fish finger, frozen food / Whiskas: cat food
1964	Sunkist: fruit juice beverage in tetrahedron packet
1965	Long-life milk in tetrahedron packet/Ferrero: "Nutella" chocolate spread
1966	Cappy: orange juice
1967	Non-returnable beer bottles
1968	Sprite: soft drink
1969	Natreen: artificial sweetener
1970	Dr Oetker: frozen pizza

An overview of the food-industry's most important innovations demonstrates how many food-items sold were convenience products (Table 15.1).[10] From 1949, it became possible to produce formerly time-costly potato dumplings both quickly and easily with the help of Pfanni's potato powder. In 1960, the Kraft Company launched a classic ready-to-serve meal on to the market. With the name 'Miracoli', it was an Italian pasta dish with sauce, herbs and Parmesan-style cheese. In only a few minutes, it promised by mixing together, a 'piece of Italy on a plate' without having to stir the pasta sauce for hours. With its Nesquik, the Nestlé group produced a cocoa powder from 1959 that was soluble even in cold milk. From then on, children could prepare their own cocoa easily.

The invention of long-life milk in tetrahedron packs was revolutionary in the 1960s. Since 1965, it was possible for households to buy larger quantities of milk and stock these, not needing refrigerator storage. The most successful frozen-food innovations were Iglo's fish fingers in 1962 and Dr Oetker's first frozen pizza in 1970. With these it was possible to prepare lunch in only a few minutes. Innovations in the confectionery sector were also numerous. Nutella chocolate spread made by the Ferrero company in 1965, was an important development which since then has

10 For the most important food and trade innovations between 1810 and 2005 in a graphical presentation, see Lummel and Deak, 2005, 179–86.

changed children's traditional breakfasts, while Mars' first chocolate bar in 1961 was a new kind of snack.

Novelties were not always completely new. Often only variations of available foodstuffs were introduced. This is observable upon looking at non-alcoholic drinks: Bluna in 1952, Sunkist fruit-juice beverage in 1964, Cappy orange juice in 1966, and Sprite soft drink in 1968, were arriving on the market. Hundreds of innovations were added every year. However, for real success in the food market, the merchandise had to be placed on retail shelves. Therefore, the question arises: what role has the supermarket played as distribution pioneer and how far was this an urban phenomenon? Before this question can be answered, however, the birth of the supermarket must be examined.

The Birth of the Supermarket

The supermarket had its origin – where else – in the USA.[11] There, initial experiments with self-service in shops with turnstiles, low shelves and exit controls in the form of checkout registers were found from 1912. From 1931 onwards, at the latest, there were large-area self-service shops that could rightly be called 'super markets'. Whereas the USA had 20,000 supermarkets in the middle of the 1950s, in West Germany there were almost 750 self-service shops with small selling spaces – often not larger than 100 square metres – that could hardly be called supermarkets. In 1955, Germany's food retailing was predominantly in 130,000 small counter-service shops.[12] Any idea of what a supermarket might be was not very clear, either within the population or also among retail experts. The question was rather discussed as a matter of principle, as to whether self-service would succeed in the Federal Republic. At that time, either filling a shopping cart or bagging by yourself was often regarded as 'inferior', 'American' and generally incompatible with the German mentality.[13]

Doubts seem legitimate: on the one hand, at that time, it was not yet foreseeable how consumption-oriented the Germans would change in the following years; on the other hand, a self-service shop required considerable investment capital due to necessary interior furnishings, including modern checkout areas, special shelves, refrigerators and new see-through entrances. There was also a considerable risk factor for such retailers, who opted only for small-sized self-service points-of-sale. Nevertheless, there were pioneers from 1954 onwards, who via their USA travels were convinced of the new possibilities of rationalizing retailing and they invested in large self-service stores. The first so-called 'large capacity shops' (Grossraumläden) arose with over 400 square metres of selling space. Such a shop was opened in Duisburg, in 1954, by the retailer Schätzlein; it may have been the earliest example but there were other nearly simultaneous openings by Stüssgen and Eklöh.[14] Soon

---

11 Bowlby, 1997.

12 *Selbstbedienung* 3/1958, 2; for counter-service shops, see Spiekermann, 1997.

13 Voswinkel, 2005, 213.

14 Hallier, 2001, 189; there was a similar development in other European countries. For early supermarkets in UK, see Oddy, 1995, 191. For supermarkets in Czechoslovakia, and especially in the capital Prague since 1955, see Franc, chapter 13.

these large shops bore the auspicious name 'supermarket'. In any case, this superlative was earned by Germany's first real 'supermarket' in Cologne's Rheinlandhalle. It was opened by Herbert Eklöh in September of 1957, with a selling area of 2,000 square metres and with parking for 200 cars. As such, Germany had by far the largest supermarket at that time in Europe.[15] Through this opening, the supermarket had definitely arrived in Germany.

Supermarkets and the City

But where exactly did the supermarket come into being? Undoubtedly the first supermarkets were opened in the cities of North Rhine-Westphalia, in Cologne on the Rhine or both in Duisburg and Essen in the Ruhr area. In 1962, the Cologne institute for self-service (*ISB*) published the first study regarding the current status of supermarkets in West Germany.[16] They recorded about 500, of which 190 were surveyed. Only two per cent were in towns with less than 20,000 inhabitants. By contrast, 76 per cent of all German supermarkets were in cities with more than 100,000 inhabitants and, of these, 34 per cent in cities with over 500,000 inhabitants. West Berlin was a good example of the attraction of starting supermarkets in big cities because, in 1962, 7 per cent of all supermarkets were to found there. But what was the reason for such a concentration of supermarkets in big cities? As opposed to the small traditional grocery store, supermarkets needed far more customers than the population from a small neighbourhood. One of the first research efforts about the chances of supermarkets written in 1960 stated that supermarkets needed a selling area with 12,000 to 15,000 people.[17] The most likely potential for this number of consumers existed in the city. Preferred locations were in major streets (75 per cent) or busy shopping streets (33 per cent). From customer interviews it was known, though, that on average they did not walk further than 500 metres for their grocery shopping.[18] Due to increasing individual motor traffic, the supermarket was also interesting for those who passed the shop on their way to work or who could reach the supermarket by car in adequate time. The facilities of generous parking areas were decisive for drivers. This was also the reason why supermarkets did not merely develop in city centres, but from the very beginning were also extremely successful on the outskirts of towns. Many customers lived in new suburbs and another consideration was that generous parking was available both next to large sales areas and to warehouses for possible new supermarkets.

However, it was not only the quantity of potential customers which let supermarkets come into being in cities, but also the specific qualities of urban-dwellers. According to customer interviews, in their early years, supermarkets appealed primarily to

---

15 ISB-Institut für Selbstbedienung, 1988, 10f., 38, 44–46. In 1938 the pioneer Eklöh opened the first self-service shop, in Osnabrück.

16 *Selbstbedienung* 10/1962, 6ff.

17 See *Selbstbedienung und Supermarkt*, 5/1960, 8f. also to information below.

18 *Selbstbedienung und Supermarkt*, 7/1964, 5–8.

younger city-dwellers of the age group between 18 and 44 years.[19] These people were 'modern' and that meant oriented towards the West. For them, both speed and pleasure resulting from the variety of merchandise, were decisive in choosing to shop in supermarkets. Amongst this group of modern-oriented people, the working woman was the most important customer. By 1970, 28 per cent of women had taken up employment. This group often had to organize the household and bring up children simultaneously beside their outside work. Working women also greatly appreciated that doing a large shop in a time-saving manner increased their 'leisure time'. An important advantage of supermarkets in the 1960s was the dimension whereby a greater selection of new foods was offered.

Simultaneously, especially among modern town-dwellers, a break-up of the once close relationships between merchant and customer began. The customer who had achieved a certain prosperity level, moreover, had increased demands and had no problem from day to day in deciding where to shop. However, the population's mobility and the availability of the car as standard transport, was the reason why hypermarkets and shopping centres could be established from the late 1960s. Their most suitable location was out of town in the so-called 'green belt' with even more food items and gigantic parking lots.[20] While supermarkets in 1965 had 15 per cent of the entire retail food sales, in 1970 this reached 26.8 per cent and in 1975, 31.5 per cent. Together the hypermarkets' and shopping centres' food departments had 0.1 per cent in 1965, 9.5 per cent in 1970 and 16 per cent in 1975.[21] Also the urban discount stores (Aldi, Lidl, etc.) had not yet taken a leading position in the food retail market.[22]

This statistical evidence shows that the city population's needs for more and more food innovations were satisfied in these years by urban supermarkets. Moreover, establishing both hypermarkets and shopping centres outside the city during the 1960s did not contradict the importance of cities as innovation centres. By 1970, a change to grocery shopping had taken place which was oriented toward urban customers. Due to society's general mobility, customers were ready to organize their large purchases outside the city. Furthermore, it can be presumed that both hypermarkets and shopping centres on the green belt could accelerate by urbanizing rural customers' buying behaviour, as well. The first indications of that can be found

---

19 On supermarket customers in the 1950s and 1960s, see Prinz, 2003, 329ff.; *Selbstbedienung* 1/1957, 5–10, 8/1959, 7, 2/1960, 34, 3/1960 13, 9/1960 30, 4/1962, 20; *Selbstbedienung und Supermarkt*, 7/1964, 5–8.

20 80 per cent of hypermarkets were located in rural areas in 1975. See Weller, 1978, 13f.; for similar trends in the UK, see Oddy, 1995, 191.

21 EHI-EuroHandelsinstitut (eds), 2004, 120f., 235. Shopping centres with American dimensions started in Europe in the early 1960s. The first one in Germany was the Main-Taunus-centre outside of Frankfurt/Main, which opened in 1964. The first boom of shopping centres in Germany was between 1970 and 1975; see EHI-EuroHandelsinstitut (eds), 1995. For the first hypermarkets in the south west of France, see Téchoueyres, chapter 20.

22 No authentic statistics about discounters exist before 1970. Today discount shops control about 40 per cent of the market. See also Deak, 2005.

in 1965.[23] In 1960 – as customer interviews demonstrated – the more conservative rural population still predominantly rejected supermarkets and self-service. Only 16 per cent had grown accustomed to self-service in rural regions at this time.[24] Putting items into the shopping basket on one's own was more like theft than customer freedom! Obviously, superabundance on the supermarket shelves was not compatible with the widely held and taken-for-granted principle of consuming sparingly and the ubiquitous preference either to produce or process food occasionally on one's own.[25]

Innovations in the Supermarket

The introduction of self-service provided a basis for further innovative possibilities. Self-service was at first tested in smaller shops beginning in 1949; however, it could only develop all its possibilities of rationalization in supermarkets with more than 400 square metres of selling space. Primarily, labour costs could be reduced, an important consideration due to the high pay increases of those years.[26] Nonetheless, innovations, which were developed in supermarkets by 1970, were more labour-saving. The variety of merchandise was new, in accordance with the 'everything-under-one-roof' slogan, and with a central checkout area. Consequently, the first internationally valid definition was: 'a supermarket must have a sales area of at least 400 square metres. It must also sell fresh fruits and vegetables, meats, and other items necessary to meet one's daily nutritional requirements'.[27]

The supermarket offered much more merchandise that previously could be obtained in different shops. Fruits and vegetables were traditionally bought at the market, on the street, or else in speciality shops. There were both fresh meat and sausages at the butcher's, cheese and dairy produce in dairies, and delicacies in delicatessens. But the supermarket not only integrated all of these foodstuffs: it was also the place where completely new categories of goods could be bought for the first time by a broad mass of consumers and in a wide and affordable selection; frozen foods and canned goods of most diverse types, for example, including baby or animal food. The ever-increasing extension into non-food products was another consequence of the supermarket's comprehensive self-image. Both technological and logistical

---

23 There is no tension between our thesis of the particular importance of the city for the development of supermarkets and the urban buying behaviour established there with the shopping possibilities outside the city in the form of shopping centres or hypermarkets. In 1965 we hear for the first time that urban tastes were to be found more and more in rural areas, especially because many city dwellers moved out. See *Selbstbedienung und Supermarkt* 9/1965. 18–26.

24 *Selbstbedienung* 9/1960, 30.

25 Dardemann, 2005; a 1964 survey of the 'Allensbach institute' showed that the rural population spent about half as much on food as urban consumers (52.83 DM vs. 91.35 DM). See *Selbstbedienung und Supermarkt* 6/1964, 12.

26 The trend of increasing wages and salaries was one of the most discussed aspects of retailing in the years around 1960. See S*elbstbedienung und Supermarkt*, 5/1961, 3.

27 Schulz-Klingauf, 1961, 281.

innovation was a central characteristic in addition to the gigantic assortment. At first, considerable investments were required for this in sales areas. Supermarkets needed modern self-service shelves, gondolas, refrigerators, deep-freezes as well as both meat and sausage counters. It was new to standardize shop fittings independently of individual floor plans. Due to this, equipment for merchandise became fundamentally more effective and thereby more cost-efficient.[28]

Both checkout areas and their further developments proved to be a major challenge for supermarkets. Especially during rush hours on both Fridays and Saturdays, they became the so-called 'eye of a needle' for streams of customers. Since even increasing staff did not help, supermarkets were interested in technical optimization.[29] Beginning in the 1950s, they invested in modern electronic cash registers, which were equipped with both storage memory and could also print out both slips and receipts. At checkout counters, numerous cashiers worked, often supported by additional staff who helped customers with packing, not only as a service, but also to accelerate the check-out procedure. Only a few supermarkets already followed the American example and extended their checkout-counter by using a conveyor belt.[30] This system lasted until the 1970s, when operator convenience and higher check-out speed could again be achieved via computer-assisted, electronic registers and scanners.

Packaging in supermarkets now took place behind the scenes. Previously, the first supermarkets had tried to avoid both time-consuming and expensive wrapping behind the counter if at all possible. From the beginning, they invested in packing machinery especially for fruit, vegetables and cheese, which was concentrated within an area outside the sales floor. In the late 1950s, distribution companies began either setting up packing centres or outsourced wrapping to a packaging company.[31] Warehouses were centralized as well. With the goal of having more sales space, the large supermarket chains particularly set up central storage units which were equipped with the most modern technology and from where vehicles with cold storage could deliver foodstuffs both quickly and as needed.[32] All these details confirm that in the 1950s and 1960s, the supermarket was not only the most successful, but also the most modern type of business in the German food retail market.[33]

---

28 Voswinkel, 2005, 213; Teuteberg, 2005, 30ff.

29 For the whole context, see Rennert, 1976; ISB-Institut für Selbstbedienung, 1988, 194ff.

30 The first one was the supermarket chain Otto Reichelt, Berlin in 1958.

31 It is no accident that the first trade fair specializing in packaging came into being in Germany in 1957.

32 Innovations in logistics can only be touched on as a subject. It would be useful to research the whole context of the retail trade up to the structural changes through the global market and the creation of the European common market.

33 Before reunification in 1990 the supermarket remained the most successful distribution form in German food retailing.

Supermarkets and the Food Industry

The rise of the supermarket and the many retailing innovations were responsible for bombarding German society with ever more new food-industry products. The success of both would not have been possible without the respective innovation dynamics of each other. There were a number of developments which primarily took place due to necessity and pressure from the other. From the retail perspective, the industry had to take over work that in the past had been part of the traditional counter-service shop's tasks. In the middle of the 1950s, many foodstuffs still had to be weighed out, cut up or handed out in shops, before they could either be filled up or bottled. By the mid-1960s, however, 98 to 99 per cent of merchandise reached the modern supermarket pre-packed.[34] Also, the standardization of packaging had an advantageous impact particularly in supermarkets. In 1961, there still were for instance more than 400 different round-can formats.[35] Soon, all foodstuffs already came into the shop standardized, stackable and on pallets of European standards. In this way they could be effortlessly brought to the shelves via modern technology.

Retailing changes did not always take place voluntarily. Modern food commerce exerted enormous pressure on the food industry. Retail chains demanded that industry produce only such foodstuffs as were standardized in size and with sufficient information to make a customer advisory service unnecessary. In the meantime, the powerful self-service retailers recognized that their wishes could become matters of life and death for the food industry, resulting from the retail chains' downward price pressure on the food industry, which exists up to today.[36] In turn, industry increasingly exerted pressure on retailers to list merchandise. It was the supermarkets' contribution both to integrate the flood of novelties on to shelves and to be able to present these effectively. If, in 1958, there were still on average 998 food items on sale in self-service stores and supermarkets, ten years later, there were 2,927 items.[37] In particular, the brand-named merchandise grew fastest (1956: 40 per cent; 1967: 60 per cent). Retailers soon recognized that the quantity of products was not essential for sales results, but rather the turnover speed of individual items. Nevertheless, considerable pressure existed not least due to the industry's advertising campaigns offering all the merchandise possibly demanded by customers.

Conclusion

For a broad mass of consumers it was the urban supermarket where the flood of food novelties in the 1950s and 1960s was to be found for the first time. There, the urban customers – very often young working women – were looking not only for products known from commercials. Due to their increasing desire for both change and enjoyment, they were also open-minded towards unknown foodstuffs. Whole categories, like frozen food, ready-to-serve meals, baby food and confectionery items

---

34 *Selbstbedienung und Supermarkt* 9/1964, 42–51.
35 *Selbstbedienung* 2/1961, 3–6
36 *Selbstbedienung* 10/1959, 1ff.; see also Oddy, 1995, 192.
37 *Selbstbedienung und Supermarkt* 3/1968, 5–10

for children first gained acceptance in urban self-service stores and supermarkets. Supermarkets were dependent according to their credo of 'everything-under-one-roof' to acquire novelties and constantly add more items to their product range to increase their attractiveness. Many technological and logistical innovations demonstrated that the supermarket was the most modern distribution form in German food retailing. And supermarkets were successful. With 26.8 per cent of entire food retail sales, no other type of business had better results. Up to 1970, both discounters in towns and hypermarkets and shopping centres outside the city did not play a decisive role. Simultaneously, the rural population began mimicking both urban demands and fashions in these years.

Looking back at the supermarkets' dynamic years until 1970, this success also had its negative aspects, the most significant being the rapid decline of small counter-service shops, which had traditionally characterized the retail landscape of Germany. The victory of supermarkets was at the same time the victory of big multiple chains, which left hardly any space for small-scale businesses. But the retail network's dramatic thinning out, with so-called 'food deserts' in rural areas, could have become dangerous, particularly for both elderly and the ill. To some extent, Germany maintained a network of purchasing possibilities by comparison with other European countries. Gaps in the network could partially be closed by mobile shops and supermarkets[38] on the one hand and especially in the New Länder in the East via small discounters.

In retrospect, during the time between the years 1949 to 1970, the very large food retail innovations can be summarized as the supermarket becoming the central catalyst for innovations within the food industry and for transforming food habits, as well as both modernizing and urbanizing West German society.

References

Andersen, A. *Der Traum vom guten Leben: Alltags- und Konsumgeschichte vom Wirtschaftswunder bis heute* [Dream of the Good Life], Frankfurt/Main u.a., 1997.

Bowlby, R. 'Supermarket Futures', in Campbell, 1997, 92–110.

Campbell, C. (ed.) *The Shopping Experience,* London, 1997.

Dardemann, K. 'Zwischen Selbstversorgung und Selbstbedienung' [Between Self-Sufficiency and Self-Service], in Lummel and Deak, 2005, 61–7.

Deak, A. 'Discount aus Deutschland – Über Aldi informiert' [Discounts from Germany], in Lummel and Deak, 2005, 117–23.

EHI-EuroHandelsinstitut (eds), *Shopping-Center-Report. Innenstadt – Stadtteil – Grüne Wiese*, Köln, 1995.

EHI-EuroHandelsinstitut (eds), *Handel aktuell. Strukturen, Kennzahlen und Profile des deutschen und internationalen Handels* [Trade Update], Köln, 2004.

---

38 In Europe, mobile supermarkets were first found in France. See *Selbstbedienung und Supermarkt* 5, 1960, 38.

Erhard, L. *Wohlstand für Alle* [Prosperity for Everyone], Langer, W. (ed.), Düsseldorf, 1957.

Gross, G. *An All-Consuming Century: Why Commercialism Won in Modern America,* New York, 2000.

Hallier, B. (ed.) *Praxisorientierte Handelsforschung – 50 Jahre EHI-EuroHandelsinstitut* [50 years of EHI-EuroHandelsinstitut], Köln 2001.

ISB-Institut für Selbstbedienung (eds), *50 Jahre Selbstbedienung. Sonderausgabe Dynamik im Handel* [50 Years of Self-Service], Köln, 1988.

ISB-Institut für Selbstbedienung (eds), *Selbstbedienung* [Self-Service], 1/1957–12/1961.

ISB-Institut für Selbstbedienung (eds); *Selbstbedienung und Supermarkt* [Self-Service and Supermarket], 1/1962–12/1971.

König, W. *Geschichte der Konsumgesellschaft* [History of Consumption Society], Stuttgart, 2000.

Lummel, P. and Deak, A. (eds), *Einkaufen: Eine Geschichte des täglichen Bedarfs* [Shopping for Groceries], Berlin, 2005.

Lummel, P. 'Der Supermarkt' [The Supermarket], in Lummel and Deak, 2005, 105–116

Oddy, D.J. 'From Corner Shop to Supermarket: The Revolution in Food Retailing in Britain, 1932–1992', in ICREFH III, 1995, 187–99.

Prinz, M. (ed.), *Der lange Weg in den Überfluß: Anfänge und Entwicklung der Konsumgesellschaft seit der Vormoderne* [The Long Way to Abundance], Paderborn u.a., 2003.

Rennert, H. *Datenkassen. Kosten, Leistungen moderner Kassiersysteme im Handel. Rationalisierungs-Gemeinschaft des Handels beim RKW e.V.* [Power of Modern Checkout Counter Systems], Köln, 1976.

Schulz-Klingauf, H.V, *Selbstbedienung: Der neue Weg zum Kunden* [Self-Service: the New Way to Customers], Düsseldorf, 1960.

Spiekermann, U. 'Rationalization as a Permanent Task. The German Food Retail Trade in the Twentieth Century', in ICREFH III, 1995, 200–20

Spiekermann, U. 'Rationalisierung als Daueraufgabe. Der deutsche Lebensmitteleinzelhandel im 20. Jahrhundert' [Rationalization as a Permanent Task], *Scripta Mercaturae* 31, 1997, 69–129.

Teuteberg, H.J, 'Vom alten Wochenmarkt zum Online Shopping' [From Old Farmers' Market to Online Shopping], in Lummel and Deak. 2005, 19–46.

Trentmann, F. *Beyond Consumerism: New Perspectives on Consumption*, London, 2002.

Voswinkel, S. 'Kompetenz und Ratlosigkeit. Der sich selbst bedienende Kunde' [Authority and Perplexity], in Lummel and Deak, 2005, 213.

Weller, T. *Das SB-Warenhaus: Vom Markt verlangt – vom Markt begrenzt* [The Self-Service Department Store], Düsseldorf, 1978.

Wildt, M. *Am Beginn der 'Konsumgesellschaft'. Mangelerfahrung, Lebenshaltung, Wohlstandshoffnung in Westdeutschland in den fünfziger Jahren* [At the Beginning of Consumption Society], Hamburg, 1994.

Chapter 15

The Changing Position of Exotic Foods in Post-War Amsterdam

Anneke H. van Otterloo

Amsterdam is today a cosmopolitan city with a strongly multicultural character. Residents and visitors alike are able to find almost any 'exotic' food their hearts and stomachs desire. Markets, shops, catering businesses and restaurants are (semi)public places for the demand and supply of a variety of new foods and foodways, among which many are of foreign origin.[1] Exotic vegetables, fruits, fish and condiments are to be found at the daily street markets, such as the Albert Cuyp and the Ten Kate markets. Although Amsterdam has comparatively fewer inhabitants (739,104 in May 2005) than other big European cities, the Dutch capital certainly rivals these others with respect to its global spirit.

The abundant availability of foods from all continents was never so great as it is today. For example, while there were no Chinese-Indonesian restaurants in the city in 1930, the numbers grew from two in 1945 to 44 in 1960, and to around 95 in 2005.[2] Yet what has happened in Amsterdam – and indeed the Netherlands as a whole – to explain such a change of taste for the exotic? Throughout the past few decades, Chinese-Indonesian restaurants have also spread from the big cities in the west of the country to all provinces, even to the smallest of villages. The embedding and appropriation of exotic foods 'out' and 'at home' is part of the most important post-war food innovation in the Netherlands, which originated in Amsterdam. When, how and why did this happen and in which order of cuisines and meal components?

The order of appropriation of foreign meals and specific meal components is dependent on the specific structure of the indigenous meal pattern.[3] Moreover, the adoption order of exotic cuisines is related to former colonial relationships. Further to this, I would like to call attention to two broad and complex concepts that may

---

1   The adjective 'exotic' is opposite to 'indigenous'; exotic is a relative concept, because over time it may turn into indigenous through naturalizing (people) and embedding (foods). Exotic, moreover, may have the connotations 'strange' and 'far away', that is lacking in 'foreign' (opposite to 'native'). Exotic here roughly stands for people and foods of Asian, African, South-American, or Mediterranean origin, while foreign also includes North-American and Western-European origin.

2   Van Otterloo, 1987; Iens Independent Index, 2005.

3   See Mestdag, 2002, 141–4, on the reception of Italian food in the Belgian meal. By analogy, the order of adoption of exotic foods and dishes in the Dutch meal pattern may pass from the less structured meals or meal-components (lunch, side-dishes, snacks, breakfast), to the most structured meals (hot meal, evening dinner).

serve as frames of interpretation. Firstly, structural changes in the food chain and, secondly, Arjun Appadurai's dimensions of globalization, or expanding cultural flows.[4]

From the perspective of food and cookery, at least three dimensions are relevant to the question of diffusion of new exotic foods in Amsterdam, namely: flows of exotic foods (ingredients and food products), flows of exotic cookery knowledge, and flows of exotic people. The city may be seen as the dynamic economic and socio-cultural junction of these flows. Naturally, Amsterdam is not the only European city where such flows are manifest.[5] Economic and cultural capital is distributed hierarchically throughout differentiated city populations, which has potential consequences for the dynamics of exotic foods innovation, both on the supply and the demand side.[6] Locations of intersection of supply and demand in the urban food chain, in the field of eating 'out' as well as 'at home', are markets, shops, catering businesses and restaurants. The specific focus of this chapter is on such locations in the food chain, rather than on meal patterns. Materials and sources are based on research and recent data.[7]

The Establishment of Exotic Foods in Amsterdam (1945–1975)

Throughout the 1940s and 1950s, the number of locations for the distribution and preparation of exotic foods in Amsterdam increased considerably. An early demand for and supply of Chinese foods had already developed during the interwar period, but after 1945 the exotic culinary culture expanded. Initially this was limited to small groups of residents and visitors and was inconsistent with Dutch foodways. These were simple and traditional, and even the process of industrialization from the 1850s onwards, that encouraged national integration of meal patterns, was only completed around 1960.[8] Until this time, only a few exotic foods, such as spices, beverages, rice and pasta (used in desserts), had found their way on to Dutch dinner plates. Needless to say, these once exotic elements had been reworked and 'indigenized' into Dutch dishes and meals.[9]

Food innovation through buying exotic ingredients and snacks at markets or shops to cook and eat at home, or eating out in (exotic) restaurants was rare, although a cautious start had been made. The existing Dutch tradition was to eat meals at home with the family. Even lunches were taken from home to work: sandwiches were brought to the canteens and coffee houses near to work, to be washed down with

---

4   Van Otterloo, 2000, 238–40; Appadurai, 1990, cited in Warde, 2000; Appadurai, 1996.

5   As a concept 'flows' is rather vague, but useful enough to our purpose; for examples, see Warde, 2000; Warde and Martens, 2000, 69–91; Leung, 2002; Pang, 2002.

6   Bourdieu, 1986; see Mintz, 1986, for the diffusion and embedding of sugar in the global food chain.

7   Van Otterloo, 1987, 2002; Berendsen, 1997; Rijksschroeff, 1998; Hogeboom and Van der Molen, 2004; Wynia, 2005.

8   Jobse-van Putten, 1995, 499–506.

9   Ibid., 96–153, 349.

coffee or milk. Eating out was simply 'not done' by residents of Amsterdam at that time, although eating a croquette from the Kwekkeboom shop on the Damstraat, an ice cream from Venice in the Reguliersbreestraat, or a filled bun from Heck's cafeteria at the Rembrandtplein, was a popular custom.[10] Those who belonged to the restaurant clientele and looked down on these places, were most likely wealthy gastronomes who frequented the stylish Dikker and Thijs establishment at the Leidsestraat, or were foreigners, businessmen or perhaps visitors. Even as late as 1960, 85 per cent of the Dutch population reported that they never ate out in restaurants.[11]

Yet, during the same period between 1945 and 1960, the broader diffusion and appropriation of new exotic foods in the city of Amsterdam made its definitive start. Apart from developments in city life, this was related to the sudden shift in power relationships between the Netherlands and its colonies in the East Indies; the declaration of independence was formally signed in 1949.[12] In the decades leading up to and after this event, various heterogeneous groups of repatriates and people from mixed Dutch-Indonesian descent arrived intermittently. This amounted to 180,000 people, not including around 100,000 military personnel who returned from service.[13]

These repatriates and 'immigrants' had a taste for Indonesian food. This food was itself of a hybrid character, while ingredients, dishes and cookery style, such as the *rijsttafel,* were of a combined Indonesian, Chinese and Dutch origin. Although these people spread all over the country, they generated a demand for exotic foods, dishes and ingredients. In this part of Asia, foodways had been different to those of the Dutch; the value attributed to the meal was much greater. The practice of producing snacks and dishes, like *sateh* and *loempia*, and meals like *nasi* and *bami* migrated to the Netherlands along with the people.

In those early years, badly-off repatriated women hired themselves out as cooks (*kokkis*) to provide the Dutch with exotic relishes, dishes and meals. In Amsterdam, Aunt Mia at the Oudezijds Achterburgwal was one of the first to establish an eatery in her living room, where her clientele could take potluck for a few coins.[14] These developments stimulated the revival of the few previously existing Chinese restaurants in the Amsterdam harbour area by encouraging them to capitalize on this new demand. The owners hired Indonesian *kokkis* in their kitchens, expanded their menus with new dishes, and promoted their restaurants as being Chinese-Indonesian.

Most repatriated Dutch-Indonesian people relied for their home cooking on ingredients imported in small quantities by travellers or bought from *tokos* (shops and stalls), which sprang up in the Hague, Rotterdam and Amsterdam. Interestingly, the early clientele of the first few exotic shops and eateries in Amsterdam were not those possessing much economic capital or used to visiting 'high standard' restaurants.

---

10 Albert de la Bruheze and van Otterloo, 2003, 322–5.

11 Montijn, 1991, 103–105.

12 In August 2005, the Dutch government, in hindsight, changed its position and recognized the earlier Indonesian declaration of independence of 17th August 1945.

13 Van Otterloo, 1987, 128; Rijkschroeff, 1998, 64–7.

14 Montijn, 1991,105; Rijkschroeff, 1998.

Rather they belonged to the cultural elite of the city, consisting of Bohemians, students and others who had little money but a curious palate. Between 1945 and 1960, the number of Indonesian restaurants in Amsterdam had risen from zero to nine, and Chinese-Indonesian from two to 44.[15]

From the 1960s to the 1980s, the Chinese-Indonesian restaurants flourished. The entrepreneurs, mainly from Chinese origin, recruited their kitchen personnel via chain-migration from family and neighbours in their native villages. People from mainland China also came to try their luck in the new exotic markets of the West. Although the number of restaurants in the Randstad area, including Amsterdam, declined after 1980, it remained buoyant in the big cities.

Eating in Chinese-Indonesian restaurants became fashionable in Amsterdam among people without any relationship with Indonesia. Although the dishes were adapted to the Dutch taste and, at the time, lacked sophistication, the clientele experienced the exotic atmosphere and taste as being something very special.[16] To many daring eaters, 'going Chinese' was their first experience of eating out. Indonesian recipes were experimented with in the kitchen at home, as recommended and adapted in the newspapers and women's magazines. *Margriet* urged its readers to have a change and try something new. Soon the big food industry, such as Conimex, also tried to get a share in the new exotic foods market, developing 'eastern products'; advertisements for tinned *nasi* and *bami* could already be seen before the war and again in 1950.[17] Small native entrepreneurs running snack bars in Amsterdam expanded their assortment with Asian flavours by 'inventing' new snacks like *nasi* balls, *sateh* and *loempias*.

From the 1960s onwards, the demand for Mediterranean ingredients, dishes and prepared meals in shops and restaurants also increased. Along the Singel, there was a Yugoslavian restaurant, where students came to eat *djuveç*. Middle-European dishes were also available at the Wienerwald Grill in the Kalverstraat.[18] French dishes were well-established at home and in the classic and expensive restaurants, but now French *bistros* also emerged. Italian, Greek, Spanish and other Mediterranean ingredients and dishes started to appear.

Shops and stalls seized upon the new demand. Green and red peppers, courgettes, aubergines, garlic and other hitherto sparsely used or unknown vegetables, fruits and herbs went on sale at the Albert Cuyp market, side by side with Asian spices and specialities.[19] This new supply was also related to the arrival of many guest-workers from Mediterranean countries.[20]

---

15 Van Otterloo, 1987, 129–31; Rijkschroeff, 1998, 67–73.

16 Exotic foods are reworked in the food-chain (van Otterloo, 2000, 238–40), and may be indigenized or adapted in the meal pattern at home. Sometimes or by some, they may be rejected permanently. Other possibilities are *restyling* (adding foreign flavourings to local foods and *authentication* (seeking 'authentic' replication of foreign dishes (Warde, 2000, 312–3). See Cottaar, 2000; Gabaccia, 1998; and van Otterloo, 1987, for similar distinctions.

17 Salzman, 1985, 15–16.

18 Montijn, 1991, 104–106.

19 Van der Weg and Douwes, 2005, 124.

20 Immigration figures for Amsterdam are dealt with in the next section.

Among the indigenous Dutch population, the practice of taking foreign holidays in warmer and sunnier climates also increased. Back home they wanted to eat the foods they had first tasted and learned to appreciate in foreign climes. The supermarket chain Albert Heyn was the first to break into this new market of foreign and exotic products, which were associated with holiday memories, even introducing wine, not commonly drunk at the time. However, although some were keen to try new things, those with less cultural and economic capital, rejected these new foods, instead filling their caravans with potatoes and cans of meatballs and apple sauce to eat under the Spanish or Italian sun.[21]

Expansion and Differentiation of Exotic Foods in Amsterdam (1975–2005)

From the 1960s and 1970s onwards, the size and composition of the Amsterdam population began to change significantly. The native residents now wanted to live in single-family dwellings in the suburbs. About the same time, new flows of immigrants began to enter the city and alter the ethnic composition of its population. New population increases occurred when Turks and Moroccans decided to not return home as had been anticipated. Instead, they aimed to re-unite with their families in Amsterdam, or bring brides from their homelands, and moved into the low-quality housing found in the nineteenth-century workers' districts located around the city centre, which had recently been vacated during the suburbanization process. Following the independence of Surinam in 1975, immigrants from here and the Netherlands Antilles also increasingly flocked to the city. Within a period of about twenty-five years (1959–1984), the demographic character of Amsterdam had completely changed. This process continued in the decades to come.

The changing number of foreign immigrants, as compared to native-born residents in Amsterdam, from the 1990s onwards, is shown in Table 15.1. Today, the various categories of immigrants make up nearly half of the population, while – *mutatis mutandis* – the natives will occupy a minority position in the future. Differences in household composition between the ethnic groups parallel these developments in the city from the eighties. Children or other relatives are most often present in Turkish and Moroccan households, while households without children and (young) one-person households are most numerous among the native residents.[22] Given that household composition is a well-known factor influencing eating habits, one may assume that the radical demographic changes described, have had an important impact on the structure of food demand and supply in Amsterdam. The abundant presence of exotic vegetables, fruits and other foods at markets and shops reflects this fundamental change, as is discussed below.

The migration of foreign foods and cookery knowledge followed the migrating people into the city once more but, again, not at the same pace.[23] For instance, it was initially difficult for Turkish housewives to get the proper ingredients to cook their own dishes; the first migrant generation returned from holidays back home with bags

---

21 Van Otterloo, 1987, 131; Jobse-van Putten, 1995, 341–2.
22 De Feijter et al. (z.j.), 34.
23 Van Otterloo, 1987, 126–7; Cabaccia, 1998; Cottaar, 2000, 261–5.

Table 15.1   Relative size (per cent of total) and origin of population groups in Amsterdam

Population groups	1992	1995	2001	2010 (predicted)
Non-western non-indigenous	29.1	32.2	36.7	43.4
Surinamese	8.7	9.6	9.8	9.7
Antillean/Aruban	1.5	1.5	1.6	2.0
Turkish	4.0	4.3	4.8	5.5
Moroccan	5.8	6.5	7.8	9.4
South European	2.0	2.3	2.4	2.5
Other non-industrialized countries	7.0	8.0	10.4	14.3
Industrialized countries	9.8	9.7	9.6	9.7
Total non-indigenous	38.9	41.9	46.3	53.1
Indigenous Dutch	61.1	58.1	53.7	46.9

Source: Adapted from Dagevos and Odé, 2002, 12.

and suitcases full of (dried) products like bulghur wheat, lentils, chickpeas, beans, vine-leaves, tomato and sweet pepper purees, herbs, dried vegetables and *suçuk* (sausage). Over time, increasingly more ingredients became available in the markets or from Turkish shops in the city.[24] The Albert Cuyp market stallholders modified their wares along with the changing groups that made up the city population. From the end of the 1970s onwards, many small shops and stalls were set up to supply the migrants from Surinam, the Antilles and Africa. Vegetables like cowpeas, fruits (papaya), herbs, salted meat and other products from these countries began to be traded, even by Dutch market vendors.[25] Later on, indigenous Dutch people also came to these shops, albeit mainly for Turkish bread, cheeses and olives only. Surinam is renowned for its originally multi-ethnic population and diverse cuisine, including many Asian elements. In 1978, the first Javanese-Surinamese *warung* (food-shop annex eatery), named *Warung Spang Makandra* opened in De Pijp district, close to the Albert Cuyp market. Nowadays, the prominent Amsterdam food writer Johannes van Dam has identified nineteen of these small restaurants (with catering service) in Amsterdam, half of which are concentrated in the Albert Cuyp district. The dishes and meals are inexpensive and the clientele tends to be of a mixed native and multi-ethnic background.[26]

A relatively new site for the exchange of exotic foods is the Islamic butcher. From the 1970s onwards, the demand of Islamic households in the old city districts encouraged the sale of *halal* products. Between 1975 and 2005, these butchers, mainly from a Turkish or Moroccan background, increased in number from four to 109.[27]

24 Wynia, 2005, 95–7.
25 Van der Weg and Douwes, 2005, 122.
26 <http://www.spangmakandra.nl/> (accessed 29 November 2006).
27 <http://www.os.amsterdam.nl/pdf/2004_factsheets_2.pdf>(accessed 21 August 2004).

Their clientele, it appears, varies according to ethnic composition of the districts in which they are situated: more than half of the customers in Bos en Lommer (66 per cent foreign families) are immigrants, while in Oud-West (39 per cent foreign families), 70 per cent are native Dutch people. Interestingly, the latter frequent these shops because of their proximity and the fact that Turkish and Moroccan products, like certain yoghurts, are not available in regular supermarkets.[28]

Many other types of exotic food stalls and shops have also appeared in the city centre and the surrounding districts in recent years. These small businesses provide dried, fresh or prepared relishes, snacks and dishes from all corners of the world, such as *shoarma* and *falafel* from the Middle-East, usually eaten in a pitta bread. From the 1980s onwards, the popularity of prepared, ready-made and fast foods grew enormously. McDonald's got a firm foothold in the city. Kebab houses, 'Argentine' grills, African eateries, Thai and Japanese restaurants and doughnuts followed suit. The position of the Dutch snack bars of old began to be threatened, as did that of the long-established Chinese-Indonesian restaurants.[29] However, tokos and stalls continued to maintain an important place in the city's network of exotic food provision. These small businesses, selling Asian spices and dried products, also often ran catering services. Take-away Asian (Indonesian and Chinese) dishes have become a firmly established part of the trend for quick and easy foods since the 1960s. Another aspect of this is the profusion of pizzerias, spread all over the city, which offer take-away and delivery services. The Dutch version of this originally Italian dish has been adapted into the most popular prepared fast food ordered by Amsterdam households.[30] Exotic and foreign foods have thus permeated the various Amsterdam food chain locations of supply and demand.

Foreign foods have also pervaded the broad field of culinary knowledge and appreciation in the city through experience, books and magazines. Food writers discuss couscous and coriander, striving for 'restyling' and 'authentication'.[31] Many foreign foods have been introduced to the shelves of supermarket giant Albert Heyn, the preparation of which is explained in *Allerhande*, the supermarket's monthly free recipe magazine. The dishes can be cooked at home, with sauces, oils and ready-made flavourings provided by Honig and Conimex, a company mentioned earlier. These big Dutch food companies sell, respectively, more or less 'indigenized' Chinese-Indonesian and Italian foods, educating cooking customers on how to use these delicacies.

In the same vein, cookery knowledge has been reworked and adapted by small ethnic entrepreneurs from different backgrounds when preparing or retailing exotic foods from another tradition than their own for commercial purposes. These activities are part of the ongoing process of the 'commodification' of cultural resources.[32]

---

28 Hogeboom and van der Molen, 2004, 34–43.

29 'Horeca in Amsterdam', *Fact Sheets no.2,* March 2005, www.os.amsterdam.nl

30 In August 2005, we counted over 210 places in Amsterdam to go to or to call, mentioned by *Pizzabel*, <http://www.pizzabel.nl/amsterdam> (accessed 29 November 2006).

31 Van Dam, 2005, 154, 315; see note 16 for the four options of reworking and appreciation of foreign and exotic foods and cookery knowledge in the food chain.

32 Rath, 2002.

Turkish immigrants thus transformed themselves into sellers of Greek or Italian foods. The flows of foreign foods and cookery knowledge also clearly influenced the Dutch meal pattern at home. Between 1978 and 1994 the kilo of pasta consumed annually per capita quadrupled. The production of accompanying ready-made sauces and dry mixes started in 1973; ready-made kits for a 'world cuisine' dinner appeared on the market circa 2000. Young people, working couples and one-parent families in the city had unmistakably exchanged potatoes for pasta.[33]

The exotic trend became even stronger in the field of eating out. An unprecedented growth in number and range of foreign restaurants of various qualities has taken place since the very first Chinese eateries appeared in the city in the 1930s and 1940s. Recent municipal statistics reveal that Amsterdam now has the largest nightlife centre in the Netherlands. The number of cafés and Dutch snack bars has declined, being overtaken by restaurants, many of which serve exotic cuisines (Figure 15.1).

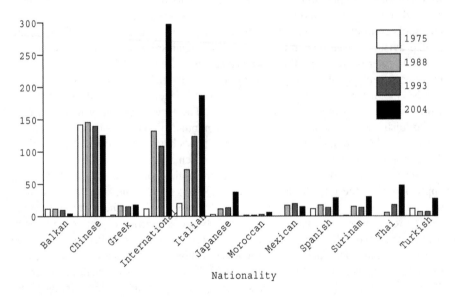

Figure 15.1   Number of restaurants by type of cuisine in Amsterdam, 1975–2004

Chinese restaurants appear to have been relegated to third place, with 'international' or 'fusion' kitchens at the top of the rankings. Japanese and Thai food has also become popular. The city of Amsterdam, we may conclude, has become a breeding ground for wide-scale foreign and exotic food innovation, resulting from a dynamic and entangled mixture of migrating foods, cookery knowledge, and people. Food is one of the possible indicators, which may shed light on the global character of a city. The locations of intersection of supply and demand in Amsterdam are conspicuous places to observe this development. The small and cheap places

---

33 Berendsen, 1997, 24–7. World cuisine kits more often than not rest on sheer producer fantasy.

providing Surinamese and Turkish food bear witness to this, no less than the famous Japanese Okura Hotel and the new bagel cafés scattered throughout the city.

Conclusion

Post-war Amsterdam has developed into a global city, offering a cosmopolitan range of foreign and exotic foods to inhabitants and visitors alike. This was a gradual development over a long period of time. This chapter has presented some concepts and data, which rather may answer the question of when, how and why this took place.

Arjun Appadurai's notion of cultural flows making up globalization is useful in broadly analysing what has happened to the city of Amsterdam to explain this change. Flows of people, cookery knowledge and foods migrated to the city, and were picked up both on the demand and supply sides of the local food chain, resulting in the diffusion, embedding, and appropriation of foreign foods, with new food habits generally (though not always) dispersing from the city to the country.

The VOC (United East-Indies Company) trade from 1602 onwards was crucial in the initial processes of the diffusion of exotic, foods.[34] Spices and beverages, coffee, tea and chocolate were followed by exotic dishes, snacks, complete meals and the knowledge of how to prepare them. The diffusion process accelerated after 1900, especially after the Second World War. Decolonization, labour migration and the Dutch refugee policy brought new flows of foreign and exotic people, foods and knowledge to the city again and again. With the rise of affluence and mobility, and the radical socio-cultural changes from the 1960s onwards, the process speeded up once again.

But what has happened more specifically at the city level? The metaphor of the pressure cooker may illustrate the quick dynamic socio-economic and socio-cultural processes at the junction of these flows. The influx of immigrants has led, as we saw, to sweeping demographic changes. About half of the Amsterdam population is now of foreign origin, though not all of exotic descent. These people have brought about an extended demand for exotic foods, while also spreading these foods to the indigenous population, mainly via the supply side. Exotic foods have now been diffused everywhere in the food chain, from big companies to small family enterprises. Apparent locations of intersection and interaction of demand and supply in Amsterdam are (super)markets, shops, catering businesses (also on the Internet), kebab or falafel eateries, and the extremely varied range of restaurants throughout the city. As recent figures suggest, the small and specialized exotic shops in Amsterdam, like Islamic butchers, have survived the threatening rise of the supermarkets longer than the regular butchers. Interesting processes of commodification and borrowing of cookery knowledge take place at the locations of supply. Immigrant entrepreneurs from, for example, Turkey, appear to be significantly represented in the small food trade and catering business, also selling Greek or Mediterranean tastes. Furthermore, the Amsterdam nightlife attracts tourists and offers more chances to the small

---

34 See note 1 for the definition of foreign and exotic.

immigrant entrepreneurs in the food catering business than elsewhere. The city thus combines the cultural conditions with a mix of people on the demand side, favouring an increase in supply (trade and catering) of exotic foods.

New foods often, though not always, diffuse from the higher to the lower strata, being, according to Pierre Bourdieu, an important means of generating social distinctions in taste. This chapter demonstrates that there are some indications that the dynamics of taste and distinction among the inhabitants and visitors in the city has been influential in the general process of diffusion and appropriation of exotic foods. The extent of cultural and economic capital among the city population affects the demand for 'something new' to be served up at the table. In Amsterdam, young people, students, artists, tourists, yuppies and the like are always well represented, having a willingness to experiment with new exotic dishes. They try first and, in the long run, the rest of the population follows; at least this has applied to certain cuisines until now.

In the Netherlands, this has certainly been the case for the originally foreign French (trickled down from high to middle over centuries), the Italian, and the Chinese-Indonesian cuisines. Respectively, these developments took place for reasons of cultural supremacy in Europe, foreign travel, colonial history and sheer taste. Over time, the Dutch have developed the four positions towards these cuisines, which Alan Warde has proposed as a model of diffusion of foreign and exotic foods: rejection, indigenization, restyling, and authentication.[35] 'Out' and 'at home' they have been appropriated into the Dutch meal system in the long run, from the less structured lunch dishes and snacks to the most structured dinner meals.[36]

The Italian kitchen 'out' in Amsterdam consists of a huge pizza catering sector and quite a few restaurants (111 in 2004), all varying in quality and price, but not different from any other global or even local cities. The presence of the Chinese-Indonesian cuisine 'out' and 'at home' is specifically Dutch. The restaurants were cheap from the beginning, which attracted public interest, giving the exotic entrepreneurs a chance to establish themselves. The Dutch preference for cheapness and large portions is catered for. Global Amsterdam has retained and increased its taste for 'the East'. In the booming Asian sector far-reaching expansion and differentiation has taken place, as the separation of Chinese and Indonesian restaurants shows. Attempts at authentication are mainly to be found up-market, for instance the famous Japanese chef Akira Oshima at the Okura Hotel. Differentiation also took place in the exotic restaurants, representing other continents, while the category 'international' points to the opposite trend of mingling and integration.

References

Albert de la Bruhèze, A. and Otterloo, A.H. van 'Snacks and Snack Culture in the Rise of Eating out in the Netherlands in the Twentieth Century', in ICREFH VII, 317–337.

---

35 See note 16.
36 See notes 1 and 3.

Appadurai, A. 'Disjuncture and Difference in the Global Cultural Economy', *Theory, Culture and Society* 7 (1990), 295–310.

Appadurai, A. *Modernity at Large: Cultural Dimensions of Globalization,* Minneapolis, 1996.

Berendsen, M. *Worden Aardappeleters Pasta-eters? Opkomst en Acceptatie van Macaroni, Spaghetti en Andere Pasta in het Nederlandse Voedingspatroon in de Loop van de Twintigste Eeuw* [Rise and Acceptance of Pasta in the Dutch Diet], Unpublished Masters Thesis, Erasmus University, Rotterdam, Faculty of Society and History, 1997.

Bourdieu, P. *Distinction: A Social Critique of the Judgement of Taste* London, 1986.

Cottaar, A. 'Een Oosterse Stad in het Westen. Etnisch-Culinaire Pioniers in Den Haag' [An Oriental City in the West], *Tijdschrift voor Sociale Geschiedenis* 27, 2000, 261–280.

Dagevos, J. and Odé, A. *Minderheden in Amsterdam. Contacten, Concentratie en Integratie* [Minorities in Amsterdam], Amsterdam, 2003.

Dam, J. van *Lekker Amsterdam. Gastronomische Gids* [Amsterdam: Gastronomic Guide], Amsterdam, 2001.

Dam, J. van *Dedikkevandam. Van aardappel tot zwezerik* [From Potatoes to Zwezerik], Amsterdam, 2005.

Feijter, H. de et al., *Nieuw Amsterdams Peil. Wonen, Werken, Leven in een Multiculturele Metropool* [Amsterdam: Living and Working in a Multicultural Metropolis], Amsterdam, 2001.

Gabaccia, D.R. *We are What we Eat: Ethnic Food and the Making of Americans,* Cambridge, MA, 1998.

Hogeboom, L. and Van der Molen, J. *Islamitische Slagerijen in Amsterdam. Een Multicultureel Tafereel* [Islamic Butchers in Amsterdam], University of Amsterdam, Department of Sociology and Anthropology, 2004.

Iens Independent Index, *Restaurants van Amsterdam en Omstreken* [Restaurants in Amsterdam], Amsterdam, 2004 and 2005.

Jobse-van Putten, J., *Eenvoudig, Maar Voedzaam. Cultuurgeschiedenis van de Dagelijkse Maaltijd in Nederland* [Cultural History of the Daily Meal in the Netherlands], Nijmegen, 1995.

Leung, M.W.H. 'From Four-course Peking Duck to Take-Away Singapore Rice: An Inquiry into the Dynamics of the Ethnic Chinese Catering Business in Germany', *International Journal of Entrepreneurial Behaviour and Research* 8, 1–2, 2002, 134–147.

Mestdag, I. 'Italiaans op Mijn Bord? Een Onderzoek naar de Receptie van de Italiaanse Keuken in België aan de Hand van het Maaltijdpatroon' [A Study of the Reception of Italian Cooking in Belgium], *Tijdschrift voor Sociologie* 23, 2, 2002, 139–162.

Mintz, S. *Sweetness and Power: The Place of Sugar in Modern History,* Harmondsworth, 1986.

Montijn, I. *Aan Tafel. Vijftig Jaar Eten in Nederland* [Fifty Years of Eating in the Netherlands], Utrecht/Antwerpen, 1991.

Oshima, A. et al. *De Katsekikeuken,* Amsterdam, 2003.

Otterloo, A.H. van 'Foreign Immigrants and the Dutch at Table, 1945–1985. Bridging or Widening the Gap?' *The Netherlands Journal of Sociology* 23, 1987, 126–144.

Otterloo, A.H. van 'Chinese and Indonesian Restaurants and the Taste for Exotic Food: A Global-Local Trend', in Cwiertka, K. and Walraven, B. (eds), *Asian Food: The Global and the Local*, Richmond, 2002, 153–167.

Otterloo, A.H. van ' Voeding in Verandering' [Changes in Eating], in Schot, J.W., Lintsen, H.W. Rip, A. and Albert de la Bruhèze, A.A. (eds) *Techniek in Nederland in de Twintigste Eeuw* [Technology in the Netherlands in the Twentieth Century], vol. 3, Zutphen, 2000, 236–247.

Pang, C.L. 'Business Opportunity or Food Pornography? Chinese Restaurant Ventures in Antwerp', *International Journal of Entrepreneurial Behaviour and Research* 8, 1–2, 2002, 148–161.

Rath, J. *Immigrants and the Tourist Industry: The Commodification of Cultural Resources*, Paper Presented to the XVth World Congress of Sociology, Brisbane, Australia, July 7–13, 2002.

Rijkschroeff, B.R. *Etnisch Ondernemerschap. De Chinese Horecasector in Nederland en in de Verenigde Staten van Amerika* [Ethnic Entrepreneurship], Capelle a/d IJssel, 1998.

Salzman, C. 'Margriet's Advies aan de Nederlandse Huisvrouw Continuiteit en Verandering in de Culinaire Geschiedenis van Nederland 1045–1975' [Continuity and Change in the Culinary History of the Netherlands], *Volkskundig Bulletin* 11, 1985, 1–27.

Warde, A. 'Eating Globally: Cultural Flows and the Spread of Ethnic Restaurants', in Kalb, D., Land, M. van der, Staring, R., Steenbergen, B. van and Wilterdink, N. (eds), *The Ends of Globalization: Bringing Society Back in*, New York, 2000, 299–317.

Warde, A. and Martens, L. *Eating Out: Social Differentiation, Consumption and Pleasure*, Cambridge, 2004.

Weg, M. van der and Douwes, M. *100 Jaar Albert Cuypmarkt* [100 Years of the Albert Cuypmarkt], Amsterdam, 2005.

Wynia, M. *Jullie Eten is Wit, ons Eten is Rood. Eetcultuur, Identiteit en Integratie* [Eating Culture, Identity and Integration], Unpublished Masters Thesis, Department of Sociology and Anthropology, University of Amsterdam, 2005.

Chapter 16

The Immigrant Impact upon London's Food since c.1850

Panikos Panayi

Introduction

Although its historiography has roots in the nineteenth century, the impact of immigration upon the British diet has only recently begun to receive serious attention from scholars. Academic writing on migration has tended to ignore its impact and has, instead, usually focused either upon the relationship between migrants and more established populations or, more recently, aspects of identity.[1] At the same time, British scholars working upon the history of food have not focused upon the importance of immigrants in the evolution of dietary patterns in English homes and restaurants.[2] Those researchers who have recognized the importance of immigration, have usually examined its influence after 1945.[3]

In recent years, however, a series of publications have appeared upon the importance of immigration upon dietary patterns in both Britain and beyond. To take the example of America, major studies have been published by Hasia R. Diner and Donna Gabaccia. The first of these focused upon the ways in which the food of migrants changed during the migration process,[4] while Gabaccia concentrated on the ways in which immigration transformed food in America.[5] Similarly, Anneke van Otterloo has devoted much attention to the impact and significance of foreign foods in the Netherlands.[6] In Britain the recently published collection of essays edited by Anne Kerhsen will prove seminal for those interested in the impact of and relationship between food and immigration.[7]

Using the example of London, the major focus of immigration to the UK, this essay will argue that migrants played a major role in the evolution of the dietary patterns of Londoners, in particular, but the British population as a whole since 1850. The article progresses chronologically, examining two periods: 1850–1945 and 1945–2005. While the most dramatic impact occurred after 1945, significant changes, initiated by migrants, began in the century before 1945. The essay concentrates upon

---

1 Panayi, 1999, 1–31.
2 See, for example, Drummond, 1958; Burnett, 1989.
3 Tames, 2003.
4 Diner, 2001.
5 Gabaccia, 1998.
6 See chapter 15.
7 Kershen, 2002.

the importance of migrant 'personnel' in the development of London's food and the introduction of new products by newcomers.

But why concentrate upon London? Most importantly this is because of its importance as both a migrant and culinary centre over the past 150 years. Each stream of newcomers which has moved to Britain, from the Irish, Jews, Germans and Italians in the nineteenth century, to the arrivals from the Empire and Commonwealth after 1945, as well as more recent immigrants, was drawn by the pull of the capital.[8] Similarly, many of the most significant developments in British diet since 1850 have their origins in the capital.[9] But is London representative of the rest of the UK, or is it a cosmopolitan metropolis, which has more in common with other continental capital cities? In terms of immigration, and more especially its impact upon food, there were distinct characteristics in the period before 1945 because many provincial cities had little experience of migrants. On the other hand, migration has affected the entire country since 1945.[10] A focus upon 'haute cuisine' would reveal the uniqueness of London, both before and after 1945, because of its ability to attract many of the continent's leading chefs. The narrative assesses the typicality of the capital of the former British Empire.

Street Sellers, Retailers, Waiters and Chefs: 1850–1945

Foreigners played two main roles in the food supply of Londoners from c.1850–c.1945. First, they found employment in the retailing and catering sector from top to bottom. Second, migrants helped the spread of new foods, the best example being ice cream. Thus Mayhew recognized Jews 'as an integral, but distinct and peculiar part of street-life', especially the 100 Jewish street sellers who dealt in fruit and cakes. Jews also recycled tea leaves and controlled the import and sale of 'fruits, especially green fruits, such as oranges, lemons, grapes, walnuts, cocoa-nuts &c., and dates among dried fruits'.[11] Mayhew also detailed 'How the street-Irish displanted the street-Jews in the orange trade'.[12] Twenty years after Mayhew published his work, ice-cream vendors had become 'a common feature in London – and they were, virtually to a man, Italian'.[13]

Victorian and Edwardian London also counted many immigrant shopkeepers, as we can see by looking at Germans and Jews. The former developed a rich ethnicity revolving around religion and politics and helped by geographical concentration, especially in the East End and West End of London.[14] One aspect of this ethnicity consisted of the supply of German food. London German newspapers before 1914 contain adverts for all manner of products. For instance, we find evidence of the 'Damm'sche Braun- und Schwarzbrot-Bäckerei' in Fitzroy Square, the heart of

8   Merriman, 1993; Kershen, 1997.
9   Tames, 2003; Ehrman et al., 1999.
10 Panayi, 1999, 9–10.
11 Mayhew, 1968 (originally 1861), vol. 2, 115, 116, 122, 132–5.
12 Ibid., vol. 1, 106–7.
13 Sponza, 2002, 18.
14 Panayi, 1995.

the German West End, which sold its products via thirty retail outlets throughout the capital, most of them owned by Germans.[15] The largest German delicatessen in London before 1914, H. Appenrodt, had branches throughout the West End, suggesting that non-Germans also sampled the products of this firm. It made its own sausages, and also advertised a variety of hams, together with 'Pommeranian goose breast'.[16] Germans also became important as bakers and butchers in London at the end of the nineteenth century and played a significant role in the supply of bread and pork to the capital's population.[17]

As diet forms a central role in the maintenance of Jewish ethnicity, shops and restaurants for this community sprang up throughout the East End of London, where the overwhelming majority of the expanding east European community lived by 1914.[18] Three organizations developed to control the production and sale of food according to Jewish dietary laws in the form of the Kashrus Commission, the Schechita Board and the Beth Din.[19] The London *Jewish Chronicle* contained countless adverts for Kosher retailers. Jewish restaurants also developed in the capital, the most famous including Bloom's and Stern's in the East End,[20] although others developed elsewhere as the Jewish population dispersed towards the suburbs.[21] As the twentieth century progressed, Jews became important in the provision of food throughout the country, as two of the most famous British grocery and catering firms, J.S. Lyons[22] and Tesco,[23] were established by members of this community.

Migrants also became important in catering. In the first place, they included many waiters. By 1911 ten per cent of people involved in this occupation in London were Germans.[24] Swiss waiters also became important, so that the London branch of the Union Helvetia counted 400 members in 1900.[25] As a consequence of the War and the disappearance of Germans due to xenophobic hysteria,[26] the nationalities of London waiters changed, with Italians becoming increasingly important, until, as a result of the internment of this group in 1940, Greek Cypriots began to take their place.[27] Migrants also became chefs and managers in catering establishments in London, both before and after the First World War. Such individuals had often served in hotels and restaurants throughout the continent. Gustave Fourault, for example, born in France in 1858, served an apprenticeship in the Café Anglais in Paris, and

---

15 *Londoner General-Anzeiger*, 1 May 1904.

16 Ibid., 3 January 1914.

17 Panayi, 1995, 130–1.

18 Green, 1991.

19 *Really Jewish Food Guide*, 1991.

20 Jewish Museum London (henceforth JML), 1983/370, 'Bloom with Good Food'; JML 1986/136/11/1, 'Sam Stern's, Kosher Caterer'.

21 Black, 1994, 70–3.

22 Bird, 2000.

23 Corina, 1971; Powell, 1991.

24 Panayi, 1995, 125.

25 *Rütli*, 6 October, 1900.

26 Panayi, 1991.

27 Colpi, 1991, 80; Oakley, 1987.

then moved 'to take control of the kitchen of the Hotel Bristol, London', after which he became manager of the Princess Restaurant in London.[28]

Foreign restaurants sprang up in London before 1945. A guide to eating out from 1901 listed 119 establishments of all types, including 23 serving French food, 14 Italian restaurants, three German and one Jewish.[29] We can best divide foreign restaurants into three. First, French and Italian, which emerged in the 1860s and 1870s, initially 'patronised by the 8,000 or so French immigrants lodging in Soho, but their novel cuisines soon appealed to "Bohemian" English artists, actors and authors'. The most famous establishments included Pinoli's, Romano's, Oddenino's, Frascati's and Kettner's.[30]

We can also identify restaurants with origins in other European countries, including German and Jewish ones. Meanwhile, the Dutch Tea House opened in Leicester Square in 1907.[31] Several Viennese style establishments, including the Vienna Café, Rumpelmayer's and the Grand Vienna Café, also surfaced before the First World War, although none would survive the conflict.[32] By the 1920s the Spanish restaurant, Martinez, had opened in Swallow Street, between Piccadilly and Regent Street.[33] One diner particularly enjoyed the 'succulent juicy Spanish olives' with 'a glass of perfect sherry'.[34] By this time the Salonika Greek restaurant had also opened in central London.[35]

Catering influences also arrived from beyond Europe, particularly India and China. The fascination with curry represents one aspect of the influence of the Raj manifesting itself in the capital of the British Empire.[36] Cook books appeared in London, often written by individuals who had lived in India, from the middle of the nineteenth century.[37] A handful of Indian restaurants had also opened in London before 1945.[38] The longest lasting is Veerasawmy's, established in 1926 by E.P. Veerasawmy and still in existence today. The owner had previously opened a firm with his name in 1896 'for the purpose of introducing to the British public the food products of India'.[39] Chinese restaurants in London before 1945 had more to do with serving the communities of immigrants from China in the capital than they did with appealing to the curiosity of English tastes. Before 1914 the main area of concentration was in Limehouse in the East End of London, where around thirty businesses developed, including catering establishments.[40] After 1914 the Chinese

28 *Caterer*, 15 October, 1902.
29 Davis, 1901, pp.xxi–iv.
30 Burnett, 2004, 95–6.
31 *Caterer*, 15 March, 1907.
32 Boniface, 1981.
33 Hooton-Smith, 1928, 102.
34 Foster, 1924, 84.
35 *Caterer*, 15 July, 1920.
36 Chaudhuri, 1992, 238–42.
37 Dawe, 1888; Hervey, 1895.
38 See, for instance, *Caterer*, 15 April, 1904; Chapman, 1996, 10.
39 *Caterer*, 15 January, 1898; Veerasawmy, 1936, 11.
40 *Caterer*, 15 July, 1908; Roberts, 2002, 157.

community of London moved towards Soho, so that by 1945 a few English people had begun to eat in restaurants of this type.[41]

Foreigners also played a significant role in the development of dining out at the top end of London society. The Savoy took off at the end of the nineteenth century under the influence of the Swiss migrant César Ritz, who became manager in 1889 and brought over perhaps the most famous French chef, August Escoffier. Ritz also founded the London hotel which bears his name in 1905. Ritz and Escoffier were just the elite employed at such high-class establishments, as the staffs included migrants from top to bottom. Celebrity foreign chefs also worked elsewhere in the capital. In addition to Escoffier, they included Charles Elmé Francatelli and Alexis Soyer. Collectively, these three produced some of the most important cookery books in Britain before 1914, which helped to introduce wealthier English households to French style 'haute cuisine'.[42]

Migrants also influenced the consumption patterns of the working classes before 1945, including fish and chips. John K. Walton believes that the idea of Soho 'as the birthplace of the fried fish trade and London's Jewish community as its originators' is an idea that 'needs to be taken seriously'.[43] Other authorities have pointed to the importance of fried fish in Jewish diet, while some speculation exists about whether fried potatoes originated in France.[44] Furthermore, many Jews owned fish and chip shops in London in the early part of the twentieth century.[45] Italians played a central role in the spread of ice cream consumption in the capital from the late nineteenth century. However, the variety of this product sold by the Italian penny ice-men in Victorian London, would, over time, transform itself into the British smooth whip, developed by the migrants themselves, as well as the ice cream bricks, in whose spread the originally Jewish firm of Lyons played a leading role.[46]

The Multiculturalization of London's Food after 1945

Despite the importance of migrant influences upon the eating patterns of Londoners before 1945, the domestic diet of most sections of the capital's population would have mirrored the national picture, dominated by 'English' food habits. Surveys of consumption during the 1930s indicate the popularity of fried breakfast, for instance.[47] Since 1945 dramatic changes have occurred in the food consumption patterns of London, in which migrants have played a major role, reflecting their overall influence on the capital. Not only has the Empire come home from South

---

41 Roberts, 2002, 157–9; Tames, 2003, 121–2.

42 Currah, 1973; Morris, 1938; Montgomery-Massingberd and Watkin, 1989; Mackenzie, 1953.

43 Walton, 1992, 24.

44 Priestland, 1972, 27–31; Walton, 1992, 23–5.

45 Further work needs to be carried out on this subject, but Jessica Gould, a Jewish woman whom I interviewed on 13 April 2004, pointed out that her father and all of her uncles owned fish and chip shops in east London after the First World War.

46 Sponza, 2002; Crowhurst, 2000; Bird, 2000, 142–7.

47 Crawford and Broadley, 1938.

Asian and the Caribbean, migrants have also arrived from other parts of Europe, especially Ireland, Italy and Poland.[48] Newcomers play a large role in London's economy, especially as manual labourers and shopkeepers and have also influenced the demography, geography, dress and language of the capital.[49]

The impact of newcomers upon London's food since 1945 needs consideration against this background, pointing to the fact that migrants have had a more profound influence since 1945 than previously. We can begin with catering and retailing and, more specifically, with fish and chips, which, in the post-war period, has developed into an important signifier of British identity so that even *The Times* could describe it as that 'traditionally British dish'.[50] However, much evidence points to the ownership of fish and chip shops by Chinese and Greek Cypriots after 1945, both in London and in the provinces.[51] Fish and chips simply represent the most ironic aspect of the presence of migrants in food retailing and catering in London. Turkish Cypriots, for instance, owned many of the Wimpy Bars, essentially hamburger restaurants, present in high streets throughout Britain and beyond before the arrival of McDonalds during the 1970s.[52]

If Germans played a role as bakers and butchers before 1914, migrants after 1945 have acted as small-scale grocers, supplying both their own ethnic communities and London's population as a whole. The ubiquitous Asian corner shop reached its highpoint in the 1980s, before the extension of Sunday trading hours. First generation migrants have generally owned such establishments, as their offspring move into more rewarding work, a pattern which applies not simply to South Asians, but groups such as Greek Cypriots. More recently arrived migrants from other parts of the world move in to carry out such work in their place, so that Turks, for example, now own many of the shops working long hours in the capital.[53]

Ethnic food communities have also developed in the capital. While many immigrant retailers have an ethnically mixed clientele, others open in areas which have a predominance of one particular group. Post-war London has developed a series of geographically concentrated ethnic minorities.[54] In many cases food represents a fundamental signifier of difference especially for Jews and South Asians, who have rich food economies in the capital.

Anglo-Jewry has actually witnessed a period of decline since 1945 because of a lack of new immigration and increasing exogamy and social mobility, reflected in the decline of Kosher food.[55] A survey of the capital's Jews from 2003 revealed that nearly half of all respondents frequently ate non-kosher food outside of their home.[56] Similarly, the Kosher School-Meals Service, which, in the middle of the 1950s,

48 Panayi, 2003.
49 Panayi, 1999.
50 *The Times*, 24 September, 1971.
51 Walton, 1992, 2.
52 London Metropolitan Archives (henceforth LMA) Acc3527/384, *Wimpy Times*, Spring, 1971.
53 Jones and Ram, 2003; Anthias, 1991, 55–60.
54 Panayi, 2003, 69.
55 Endelman, 2002, 242–8.
56 Graham, 2003, 14.

provided 2,500 meals per day, or half a million per year,[57] had reached a crisis point by the 1970s.[58] Furthermore, many Jewish catering establishments closed, including Stern's in Stepney in 1952.[59] But the provision of Jewish food in London has also changed, both geographically, in terms of the move from the East End to the suburbs of the north west, and in terms of the providers, who have increasingly consisted of larger suppliers, most notably Rakusen's, as well as supermarkets, which have kosher sections in areas of Jewish settlement. Foreign influences, especially Israeli and American, have also had an impact upon the consumption patterns of London Jewry.[60]

The development of Indian food in London is seemingly irreversible. Asians counted about ten per cent of London's population by the end of the twentieth century, with concentrations in particular areas, according to religion. While the centre of Sikh London lies in Southall, Wembley serves the same role for Hindu Gujaratis and the East End has become the headquarters of Bangladeshi London. These areas contain numerous food shops catering primarily for these communities. But South Asians reside throughout the capital, so that Indian grocery shops have become widespread. This contrasts with the early post-war period when only a handful of such stores existed in London.[61] The size of the South Asian population of London and the UK as a whole has also led to the development of large companies which trade in Indian products, many of them based in London. By the middle of the 1980s the largest of these included Bestaways, NATCO, Sutewalla and Pathaks. Raj foods in Park Royal in west London has produced ready-made frozen meals since the 1980s. Tilda rice, meanwhile, began in Harrow in 1970.[62] Companies founded by South Asians have not simply grown because of the size of the ethnic minority market, but also because the ethnic majority have acquired a taste for Indian cuisine, by eating at their local 'Indian' restaurant.

This takes us to perhaps the major way in which post-war migrants have impacted upon the eating patterns of Londoners, i.e. by opening up thousands of restaurants which sell food aimed at all sections of the capital's population, reflecting not just the national picture, but also the situation elsewhere in Europe,[63] as well as north America.[64] The numerous European restaurants which existed in the capital before 1945 provided a basis for the ethnic minority food explosion which has taken place since then. Whereas the early establishments catered for a primarily middle class clientele, virtually all Londoners have at least sampled a 'foreign' cuisine since 1945.

---

57 LMA/Acc/2805/6/1/115, 'A Message from the Chief Rabbi to the Jewish Community of London', March, 1953.

58 *Jewish Chronicle*, 2 June, 1972.

59 *Scotsman*, 2 January, 1952.

60 Zeff, 1986, 58–75; *Kashrut directory*, 1972, 10–13; JML, 1991.105.771, 'Rakusen's Pure Food: Price List, March, 1968'.

61 Panayi, 2003; Desai, 1963, 56–67.

62 Panayi, 2002, 54–5; Tames, 2003, 120; *Asian Business*, 20 July, 1990.

63 Van Otterloo, chapter 15.

64 Gabaccia, 1998.

Londoners now have a bewildering variety of choice, as the capital has received recognition as a global culinary centre.[65]

We can briefly examine the three most widespread types of foreign cuisine. First, there is Italian food, with roots in the pre-1945 restaurants. By the 1960s Italians had established coffee bars serving cappuccino and espresso throughout Britain, but especially in London, where *trattoria* had also become widespread. Italians also opened numerous sandwich bars, which did not serve primarily Italian food. Growth continued into the 1970s, although by the 1980s chains such as Pizza Hut had popularized 'Italian' food to a greater extent than individual restaurants could do.[66]

Chinese restaurants also began to take off in London from the early post-war decades, mirroring the national picture. Again, they built upon the handful of establishments existing before 1945. Much of the expansion occurred because this ethnic group found a niche product which appealed to a mass market, a process reflected throughout the West. A large percentage of the Chinese in Britain simply migrated from Hong Kong to staff the ever increasing number of restaurants. By 1961 the number of Chinese eateries in London totalled around 250, many of them situated in Soho, although by this time, suburban areas also had similar establishments. Chinese takeaways also took off so that by the beginning of the twenty-first century, about 8,000 establishments of all sorts existed in Britain as a whole.[67]

While we might see Chinese and Italian in London food as part of a global phenomenon, the same does not apply to 'Indian' restaurants, which have emerged in Britain as a result of migration from South Asia. Those restaurants which existed in the capital before 1945, aimed at a generally higher class of clientele, have little to do with the establishments which developed after 1945. These new restaurants reflect a type of ethnic clustering in employment, mirroring the Chinese picture. Bangladeshi sailors, who had served as cooks on British ships, opened many of the early establishments.[68] While this particular occupational origin may have become less important over time, the percentage of Bangladeshis amongst 'Indian' restaurateurs has remained high so that they owned 7,000 of the 8,000 that existed in the UK as a whole in 1995, a picture reflected in London.[69] Nevertheless, the capital contains a wider variety of institutions for two main reasons. First, areas such as Southall and Wembley have restaurants owned by Sikhs and Hindus respectively. These sometimes serve meals different from those found on the Bangladeshi menu, although others simply mirror them, especially if they aim at a non-Asian clientele, for whom familiarity can prove an important attraction. Just as importantly, the status of London as an international metropolis, in which choice of food represents one aspect of its global position, means a readiness of the international and English bourgeoisie to sample unusual products.[70]

---

65 *Independent*, 17 April, 2005; Phillips, 2004.

66 Colpi, 1991, 138–43.

67 Roberts, 2002, 161–203; Shang, 1984, 11–28; Ng, 1968, 29–31; *The Times*, 2 October, 1961.

68 Panayi, 2002a, 54.

69 Chapman, 1996, 14.

70 Chapman, 1999, 137–8, 141–2.

Italian, Chinese and Indian food represent the most popular dishes available to Londoners. But all manner of other cuisines from throughout the globe now exist in the capital, including Thai food, a cuisine which has recently taken off. Restaurants established by migrants represent just one aspect of the increasing multiculturalization of food in London, as the capital's population can eat the food which it samples in restaurants and takeaways at home. While some Londoners may not venture into shops established by immigrants, they would certainly use supermarkets, which now contain a wide range of international foods, whether tinned, chilled or frozen. For the most adventurous, supermarkets sell the ingredients required to cook Thai, Indian, Italian, Greek or many other dishes from scratch.[71]

Conclusion

Migrants have therefore had a significant impact upon the dietary habits of Londoners since 1850. This appears more obvious after 1945, connected with larger scale immigration, particularly from the British Empire and Commonwealth. But migrants played a significant role in determining the diet of Londoners before 1945, whether through the establishment of J.S. Lyons, by the selling of ice cream or oranges in London's streets, or by staffing many London restaurants and hotels from top to bottom. At the same time, larger groups such as Jews, with distinct dietary patterns, established their own food communities in the areas where they concentrated. Developments in the post-war period have emphasized the patterns established in the years before 1945. Because of the larger scale of immigration, and its internationalization, a greater variety of groups now live in London in larger numbers, who have consequently had a more significant impact upon the dietary patterns of the capital's population.

Is London unique? How does it compare with other parts of Britain? Clear similarities certainly exist between the capital and the provinces. Ice-cream sellers, for instance, traded in many parts of the country by 1914. Jewish communities, on the other hand, were concentrated in the major British cities before 1945. Foreign restaurants remained largely, although not completely, absent from the provinces. The status of London as an international culinary capital distinguishes it from other British cities and means it has more in common with continental capitals, a situation which continued after 1945. On the other hand the increasing multiculturalization of food in London after 1945 reflects the national picture. Most provincial cities now have a share of Italian, Chinese and Indian restaurants, if not other cuisines.

References

Anthias, F. *Ethnicity, Class, Gender and Migration: Greek Cypriots in Britain*, Aldershot, 1992.

Bird, P. *The First Food Empire: A History of J. Lyons & Co.*, Chichester, 2000.

Black, G. *Living up West: Jewish Life in London's West End*, London, 1994.

---

71 Panayi, 2002b, 194–201.

Boniface, P. *Hotels and Restaurants: 1830 to the Present Day*, London, 1981.

Burnett, J. *Plenty and Want: A Social History of Food in England from 1815 to the Present Day*, 3rd ed., London, 1989.

Burnett, J., *England Eats Out: A Social History of Eating out in England from 1830 to the Present Day*, Harlow, 2004.

Chaudhuri, N. 'Shauls, Jewellery, Curry and Rice in Victorian Britain', in Chaudhuri, N. and Strobel, M. (eds), *Western Women and Imperialism: Complicity and Resistance*, Bloomington, IN, 1992, 231–44.

Chapman, P. *Curry Club Bangladeshi Restaurant Curries*, London, 1996.

Colpi, T. *The Italian Factor: The Italian Community in Great Britain*, Edinburgh, 1991.

Corina, M. *Pile it High, Sell it Cheap: The Authorized Biography of Sir John Cohen, Founder of Tesco*, London, 1971.

Crowhurst, B. *A History of the British Ice Cream Industry*, Westerham, 2000.

Crawford, W. and Broadley, H. *The People's Food*, London, 1938.

Currah, A. (ed.), *Chef to Queen Victoria: The Recipes of Charles Elmé Francatelli*, London, 1973.

Davis, N.N. *Dinners and Diners: Where and How to Dine in London*, 2nd ed., London, 1901.

Dawe, W.H. *The Wife's Help to Indian Cooking: Being a Practical Manual for Housekeepers*, London, 1888.

Desai, R. *Indian Immigrants in Britain*, London, 1963.

Diner, H.R. *Hungering for America: Italian, Irish and Jewish Foodways in the Age of Migration*, Cambridge, MA, 2001.

Drummond, J.C. *The Englishman's Food: A History of Five Centuries of English Diet*, London, 1958.

Ehrmann, E., Forsyth, H., Peltz, L. and Ross, C. *London Eats Out: 500 years of Capital Dining*, London, 1999.

Endelman, T.M. *The Jews of Britain, 1656 to 2000*, Berkeley, CA, 2002.

Foster, A.E.M. *London Restaurants,* London, 1924.

Gabaccia, D. *We are What We Eat: Ethnic Food and the Making of America*, Cambridge, MA, 1998.

Graham, D. *Secular or Religious: The Outlook for London's Jews*, London, 2003.

Green, J. *A Social History of the Jewish East End in London, 1914–1939*, Lampeter, 1991.

Hervey, H.A. *Anglo-Indian Cookery at Home: A Short Treatise by the Wife of a Returned Indian Officer*, London, 1895.

Hooton-Smith, E. *The Restaurants of London*, London, 1928.

Jones, T. and Ram, M. 'South Asian Business in Retreat? The Case of the UK', *Journal of Ethnic and Migration Studies* 29, 2003, 485–500.

Kashrut Directory and Religious Services Guide, London, 1972.

Kershen, A.J. (ed.), *London: The Promised Land? The Migrant Experience in a Capital City*, Aldershot, 1997.

Kershen, A.J. (ed.), *Food in the Migrant Experience*, Aldershot, 2002.

Mackenzie, C. *The Savoy of London*, London, 1953.

Mayhew, H. *London Labour and the London Poor*, London, 1968 (originally 1861).

Merriman, N. (ed.), *The Peopling of London: 15,000 Years of Settlement from Overseas*, London, 1993.

Montgomery-Massingberd, H. and Watkin, D. *The London Ritz*, London, 1980.

Morris, H. *Portrait of a Chef: The Life of Alexis Soyer*, Cambridge, 1938.

Ng, K.C. *The Chinese in London*, London, 1968.

Oakley, R. *Changing Patterns of Distribution of Cypriot Settlement*, Coventry, 1987.

Panayi, P. *The Enemy in our Midst: Germans in Britain During the First World War*, Oxford, 1991.

Panayi, P. *German Immigrants in Britain During the Nineteenth Century, 1815–1914*, Oxford, 1995.

Panayi, P. *The Impact of Immigration: A Documentary History of the Effects and Experiences of Immigrants and Refugees in Britain since 1945*, Manchester, 1999.

Panayi, P. 'The Spicing up of English Provincial Life: The History of Curry in Leicester', in Kershen, A.J. (ed.), *Food in the Migrant Experience*, Aldershot, 2002, 42–76.

Panayi, P. 'The Impact of Immigrant Food Upon England', in Oltmer, J. (ed.), *Migrationsforschung und Interkulturelle Studien: Zehn Jahre IMIS* [Migration Research and Intercultural Studies], Osnabrück, 2002, 179–202.

Panayi, P. 'Cosmopolis: London's Ethnic Minorities', in Gibson, A. and Kerr, J. (eds), *London from Punk to Blair*, London, 2003, 67–71.

Phillips, C. *Time Out London Eating and Drinking Guide*, London, 2004.

Powell, D. *Counter Revolution: The Tesco story*, London, 1991.

Priestland, G. *Frying Tonight: The Saga of Fish and Chips*, London, 1972.

Really Jewish Food Guide 1991, London, 1991.

Roberts, J.A.G. *China to Chinatown: Chinese Fast Food in the West*, London, 2002.

Sponza, L. 'Italian "Penny Ice-men" in Victorian London', in Kershen, A.J. (ed.), *Food in the Migrant Experience*, Aldershot, 2002, 17–41.

Tames, R., *Feeding London: A Taste of History*, London, 2003.

Veerasawmy, E.P. *Indian Cooking: For Use in all Countries*, London, 1936.

Walton, J.K. *Fish and Chips and the British Working Classes, 1870–1940*, Leicester, 1992.

Zeff, L. *Jewish London*, London, 1986.

Part D
Eating Fashions – The Consumer Perspective

Chapter 17

Scientists at the Table: The Cultural Significance of Scientists' Festive Meals in Berlin, 1830–1940

Ulrike Thoms

Berlin has never been a metropolis like Paris, London or New York, but from around 1800 it was such a lively centre of culture and science, that the term 'Classical Berlin' (*Berliner Klassik*) has become common recently.[1] Clubs and scientific associations brought together scientists and made them visible within city life. The first of these clubs, the 'Monday club' (*Montagsclub*) was formally constituted in 1749 in order to finance the members' meals at their meetings, and other table fraternities (*Tischgesellschaften*) followed.[2] They took up the tradition of the famous literary salons, thus following an ideal of bourgeois conviviality, but based on intellectual stimulation and social networking rather than the cuisine and the joy of eating. Many scientists pleaded for a specific relationship with regard to bodily needs and pleasures: mind and body stood at two opposite poles; the stomach's position was inferior compared with the mind's search for truth.[3] Remarkably this position was left virtually unquestioned during the nineteenth century. The number of festive meals that scientists ate increased, their content and structure changed and they were publicized proudly. The following account will investigate this development and ask what these findings tell us about the relationship between science and the city. Cities have almost always been the place for academic life: universities were located in cities because cities housed the government and the court, and were centres for travel, the exchange of information, and the location for the publishing houses that spread scientific information.

Berlin was considered to be the German cultural metropolis, dominating all other German cities in terms of science and the arts.[4] Scientists helped to establish this impression by making themselves and their science visible as an important aspect of social, political and economic life. In doing so, they stressed their indispensable role in the coming of the knowledge society, not only for their social status, but also for

---

1   An excellent overview on the cultural and scientific history of Berlin around 1800 is offered by <http://www.berliner-klassik.de> (accessed 29 November 2006).

2   For its history see also <http://www.gesetzlose-gesellschaft.de/index.phtml> (accessed 29 November 2006).

3   Bundesarchiv Koblenz, R 73, Nr. 19, 2.

4   Briesen, 1990.

financial reward. During this process, scientists' public meals became the means of communication between the city and science. For the scientists this was so important that they were willing to forego traditional views about the role of the body, its needs and pleasures.

The Professional Scientist and His Body

There was a duality in scientists' thinking: a scientist should search for truth and improve himself by study; bodily aspects and needs should be disregarded, particularly finance, which should be ignored altogether.[5] Eating was a necessity and modesty was the ideal to which researchers should strive. Their biographers described them as disinterested in bodily needs and pleasures, and only interested in science.[6] Of course, this was part of the scientist's self-portrayal, and was deeply influenced by ancient dietetics: being able to regulate the satisfaction of bodily needs meant being strong-willed and self-disciplined. Sobriety and modesty were thought of as noble properties and eating a time-consuming, bothersome affair.[7] In line with this approach, when scientific meetings were reported, the idea of intellectual exchange and companionship of gentlemanly scientists dominated.[8] If scientists' meals were ever reported, no details were given about quality. Autobiographies of intellectuals and scientists almost never mention the food they had or liked. Instead, they restrict themselves to describing their scientific and professional development as a logical, targeted process of developing personal skills.

The Foundation of Scientific Associations and their Regular Meetings

Scientists and learned men of the eighteenth and early nineteenth centuries communicated mainly by vast amounts of letters. Due to their growing numbers, personal communication was insufficient to keep up with developments as science became more specialized, or as a means of getting to know people and maintain growing numbers of contacts. This was especially felt by Lorenz Oken, who founded the Society of German Researchers in Natural Sciences and Physicians (*Deutsche Gesellschaft der Naturforscher und Ärzte,* hereafter *DGNÄ*) in 1821. From 1822, this society met every year in a different city. Personal encounters, face-to-face discussion and enjoyment were cultivated during these meetings more than formal lectures. With this in mind, according to Oken's founding manifesto, it was important to sit 'down at a table at least in the evenings ... so that the friendships become more numerous and intimate'.[9] Unfortunately, we know nothing about the menus of the meals which, during the early years, were financed by the citizens of the towns

---

5   Shapin, 1998; Daston, 1995.

6   See the example in Shapin, 1998.

7   Letter from Wilhelm Humboldt to his wife 10 August 1814, in Heckmann, 1981, 360.

8   Shapin and Schaffer, 1985.

9   Oken, 1821/1997.

in which the meetings took place.[10] Later, when the number of participants grew from some 20 to over 100, it became difficult to organize lodging and catering.[11] Moreover, the organizers felt that such big meetings were perceived as a burden by the smaller towns. The Society therefore decided to organize and pay for everything themselves, so 'that the smaller towns have more advantages than disadvantages, as it cannot be comfortable for these places to have so many guests in their midst for eight or more days, without being properly provided for.'[12] Although the Society saw its meetings as having economic and social benefits for the respective towns, nevertheless, the towns paid tribute to science as well by honouring the *DGNÄ* with a reception. For example, when the Society met in Berlin in 1828, the town arranged an impressive dinner: 20 tables – each for 24 persons – were laid out and beautifully decorated in a large hall. There would be '*Liedertafeln*' [choirs] placed in the centre, with 72 singers from the musical associations and theatres entertaining members during the meal.[13] While the table arrangements were described in detail, the reports say nothing about the quality of the food. This shows how the educated bourgeois, the '*Bildungsbürger*', considered meals: appearance was very important, as it showed the attention and love with which the meal had been prepared. By contrast, the quality of the food itself was not so important. As the number of public meals grew, the practice was heavily criticized. When the Academy of Science (*Akademie der Wissenschaften*) gave a dinner in remembrance of the fortieth anniversary of Alexander von Humboldt's return to Europe, a journal complained bitterly: 'Our highest scientific corporation is not backward in feasting itself, with its so-called special dinners (*Zweckessen*).'[14] Satirical magazines mocked these 'special dinners' and the appearance of the 'special dinner men', whose bellies and faces clearly showed pleasure and luxury to be their sole interest.[15]

By 1850, the natural sciences had become an indispensable factor of production whose enormous power was impressively demonstrated at the Crystal Palace Exhibition in London in 1851.[16] Around the same time, regular exchanges between scientists at an international level began with scientific congresses. The term 'congress', in common use today, was adopted from the political world and meant a meeting of statesmen.[17] Using this term for scientific meetings was a claim to participation and power in political, economic and social life. Interestingly, congress reports began to show a 'material' interest in what was eaten: increasingly they commented on the meals, though still clinging to ascetic ideals rhetorically and stressing scientific exchange as the meeting's main purpose.[18]

---

10 See the report from the third meeting in Würzburg in 1824, in Pfannenstiel, 1958, 43.

11 Sixth assembly in Munich, 1827, ibid., 48.

12 Ibid.

13 Seventh assembly in Berlin 1828, ibid., 50.

14 *Allgemeine medicinische Central-Zeitung* 13, 1844, 544.

15 Marggraff, Hermann: Die Zweckesser, in Heckmann, 1981, 396.

16 Brain, 2003; Rydell, 1993.

17 *Das große Conversations-Lexicon*, 1851, 806.

18 15. Stiftungsfest der Gesellschaft für wissenschaftliche Medicin am 13 Dezember 1856, in *Medicinisches Centralblatt*, 1856.

Changes in Science and Scientific Representation in Public

These developments took place within a world in which eating out was becoming fashionable and restaurants were being established in almost every large city during the last decades of the nineteenth century.[19] A number of medical doctors occur among the authors of gastrosophic handbooks arguing for the possibility of educating the body's lower senses. In doing so, the taste of food was lifted from a mere physiological category to that of an art, so that the gastrosophical discourse could be attached to the bourgeois discourse about education.[20] Even the educated bourgeoisie slowly realised that eating was not only a physiological need, but also something that demonstrated connoisseurship. Displaying sophisticated connoisseurship instead of splendour became an accepted means of distancing oneself from the old elite, who had demonstrated their influence by conspicious consumption. Sophistication was important, especially for the educated classes of bureaucracy. Most of their members were not rich at all but their social position forced them to participate in the culture of being seen at such events. This included dinner invitations, which often meant a burden upon household expenditure.[21] The financial disruption was reduced by an emphasis upon sophistication. Demonstrating connoisseurship was not the same as serving dishes from expensive ingredients but rather by preparing and serving meals perfectly. This made it easier for scientists to participate. As the need of society for scientifically educated people grew, the social position and incomes of scientists rose significantly.[22] Around 1800, holding a chair had been an honour, but a professor received only a couple of hundred Thalers a year. In order to survive, he needed to have another income, either from an inheritance or from another job. A hundred years later being a professor meant having a full-time occupation and being paid between 6,000 to 40,000 Marks a year.[23]

Reality and ideals differed sharply: Max Weber, though leading a comfortable life on his mother's money, and later his wife's, still required new students to lead an ascetic life.[24] He was no exception. Biographies show that ascetism was still important for understanding science. The biographers of Rudolf Virchow, the famous German bacteriologist, emphasized his ascetiscm,[25] even though Virchow spent his yearly income of 40,000 Marks on a lavish lifestyle.[26] When attacked for being greedy, he stated that one could not expect a professor to participate in a hard and stressful struggle simply because of a promise of glory. Instead, a professor should have the possibility and choice of earning respectable sums of money. In this way, Virchow stood for a new type of professional scientist who calculated his market value in money and demonstrated it through his lifestyle. His attitude also

---

19 Jacobs and Scholliers, 2003.
20 Anthus, Antonius (i.e. Gustav Blumröder): Der Eßkünstler, cited in Heckmann, 1981.
21 Meyer, 1982.
22 From 1870 to 1910 the number of university Professors grew from 1183 to 2537.
23 Ringer, 1987, 43.
24 Kaesler, 2001.
25 Goschler, 2002.
26 Ibid., 95.

influenced his way of presenting science to the public. When the Anthropological Society held a congress in 1887 Virchow was its president and organized the meeting according to his personal preferences. So the congress dinners differed from the simple meals the scientists had shared some ten years before: the grand banquet on August 8th, with decorative printed menu, comprised seven courses.[27] Some years later, Virchow was involved in the organization of the Tenth International Congress of Hygiene in Berlin. The official report of some 450 pages is very interesting, as it listed not only the participants, but also gave the programme. Most remarkable is the fact that nearly a quarter of the pages went on the arrangements and organization of the meeting: on the feast the city of Berlin organized for the 5,526 participants, about the 17 dinners of the different disciplinary sections in Berlin hotels, the balls, the garden party in the New Palais at Potsdam, the farewell party of the Berlin medical association and, finally, the reception of the participants by the Empress.[28] All these happenings were arranged in highly formal ceremonies, in which everyone had to play his specific role. In fact, the meetings celebrated the modern natural sciences. This becomes very clear through the description of the assembly hall, which was compared with a 'temple, similar to the temple of Zeus at Olympia or to the Parthenon at Athens'. The speakers 'seemed like the priests of Aeskulap, standing at the bottom of the statue while pronouncing their great truths'.[29] Most striking is the degree of formalization which changed the congress into a kind of service to science. All such meetings followed a schedule which is basically still in use today. They resembled the Emperor's reception during his official visits to towns.[30] An opening ceremony takes place with speeches from the president and local officials on the first day, or a part of it, after which a dinner and/or reception occurs. The following two or three days are filled with scientific sessions, perhaps interrupted by excursions, until the last day, which is then closed by a general discussion and a farewell ceremony.

One might think that social emulation – widespread in the German bourgeoisie to which the scientists belonged – led to this formalization of scientific meetings.[31] But there are some ways in which scientific dinners differed: firstly, they were not based on a regular exchange of invitations, like bourgeois dinners. Secondly, women had been almost excluded, whereas a bourgeois dinner was organized around them as the social centre of the meal. Finally, the meals did not serve to prove the housewife's qualification and were not private at all. Instead they were public affairs, being organized, cooked and served by professionals. Moreover, the organizers tried to give them a distinct visual appearance, which reflected the respective science: on the occasion of the congress of anthropologists in 1887, for example, the menu tried to evoke the middle ages, by using seemingly medieval names for the dishes.[32] Other menus adopted the visual appearance of scientific writings by giving sources

---

27 Tischkalendarium, in Stutzenbacher, 1895, 167.
28 Verhandlungen, 1891, 223ff.
29 Ibid., 227–9.
30 See Elsner, 1991, 295–315.
31 Vondung, 1976.
32 Tischkalendarium, 1895, in Stutzenbacher, 1909.

for the pictures in footnotes and by using scientific jargon.[33] Apart from amusing their guests, scientists were jokingly expressing their claims to play a major part in shaping the future of society. During the nineteenth century the impact of science had changed dramatically. It had become significant in the economy and an important element in the nation's struggle for power.[34] Remarkably, the gastronomic discourse perceived these changes and responded to them. Previously, gastronomic handbooks had only referred to aristocratic meals as fashionable, but later they offered menus from the dinners of scientific associations as outstanding examples of gastronomic events.[35] The organized dinner was definitively linked to a highly professionalized gastronomy, and thus to the development of the urban hotel and restaurant trade, which had discovered conferences to be interesting business ventures. Once established, conference business gained special importance, especially as congress centres and halls were founded around 1930 and the newly established tourist organizations began to cater for these special clients.[36]

Public Meals as Advertisement for Science and the Nation: The Example of the Kaiser-Wilhelm-Gesellschaft

The growing importance of scientists' conference meals is very well documented by those of the *Max-Planck-Gesellschaft*. Its forerunner, the *Kaiser-Wilhelm-Gesellschaft* (*KWG*) was founded in 1911 to further German science, especially fundamental research into the natural sciences.[37] Within the life of the society, meals played an important role and different types of meals existed for different occasions: meals were held for the celebration of certain events such as the inauguration of new institutes or important centenaries.[38] The so-called president's dinners were combined with lectures by famous scientists. Then there were the regular monthly stag parties and finally the 'breakfasts', being lunches which followed every meeting of the administrative bodies, comprising scientists as well as state notables and sponsors from industry and society.[39]

The opening of the society's first institute in 1911 was celebrated in an extensive ceremony, to which journalists, sponsors, state representatives, the society's administrative and scientific staff and the Prussian King had been invited. It started at 11 a.m in the institute and finished with a sumptuous dinner at the *Kaiserhof*, which was the first grand hotel in Berlin.[40] The organization took place in close collaboration between the administration of the *KWG* and the Kaiserhof. The hotel

---

33 See Würtz, 1995, 43.
34 See Jessen and Vogel, 2002.
35 Compare Universal-Lexikon, 1909; Stutzenbacher, 1901.
36 See Winkler, 1990.
37 Kaufmann, 2000.
38 See Archive of the History of the Max-Planck Society (hereafter AMPG), AMPG, Rep. 1A, Nr. 842–56, 2526–31.
39 It is worth noting, that the participants themselves had to pay the 3 Marks, see AMPG, Rep. 1A, Nr. 842.
40 Das Grand Hotel, 1987.

suggested two menus, both comprising eight courses for a price of 20 Marks, including wine, whereas coffee, liqueur and tobacco cost extra. This was not at all cheap, but not too expensive, as a three-course meal in a Berlin restaurant amounted to at least 10 Marks.[41] The *KWG* compiled a guest list, worked out the seating arrangement, printed the entrance tickets, received confirmations or cancellations and selected the following menu, which was printed for everyone.

Dinner of the *KWG* and the Chemical Institution Association on 23 October 1912

Cream of Artichoke Soup
Sole Fillet 'Walewska'
English Roast Mutton with a Variety of Vegetables
Goose-Liver Truffle in a Pastry Crust
Brussels Turkey on the Spit, with Salad
Iced pears with Curaçao
Warm cheese dishes
Fruit[42]

This dinner is representative of the nineteenth-century German hotel industry and restaurant cuisine at its best, though exceeding the normal number of courses by two.[43] Choosing this hotel and menu showed the scientists' claim to a right to luxury. It is significant that the *KWG* tried to stick to lavish meals even in troubled times: after the outbreak of the First World War, prices rose remarkably. Nevertheless the menus stuck to the old model at least until October 1916.[44] Six months later, problems had increased: the *Kaiserhof* refused to make suggestions 14 days in advance, as it was unsure what food would be available.[45] The number of courses was cut down to four. Accordingly, the price was reduced to 12 Marks but the menu, consisting of Chicken soup, Rhine salmon, Veal with vegetables and cheese, still differed clearly from the wartime food normal people could afford. As ration problems increased, the *KWG* stuck to the four-course model, even though its price had risen to 28 Marks.[46]

Menu for the General Assembly of the *KWG* on 10 October 1917

Potato Soup
Grilled Rhine Salmon with a Herb Sauce
Mushrooms Gratiné, Polish Asparagus with Potatoes
Apples in a White Wine.

---

41 Drummer, 1993, 139.
42 AMPG, 1. HA, Rep 1A, Nr. 843, 127.
43 Drummer, 1993.
44 AMPG, 1. HA, Rep. 1A, Nr. 847.
45 AMPG, 1. HA, Rep. 1A, Nr. 848, 19.
46 AMPG, 1. HA; Rep 1A, Nr. 849, 99.

The relative opulence of this dinner illustrates the importance of science and the willpower of the sponsors to support it even in difficult times. To take part in such a lavish meal, to leave the laboratory and library, was not a problem for the scientists who were no longer criticized when enjoying corporeal pleasures and demonstrating a high-class lifestyle. On the contrary, it was expected that they would participate in dinners. On several occasions, the president of the *KWG* requested directors to take part in order to keep in contact with the administration, the public authorities and industry. Thus the meals functioned as a means of communication with the outside world. When times got bad during the world economic crisis, the society ran out of money and could no longer afford a high-class cuisine service. It tried to retain its tradition of society dinners by organizing beer evenings (*Bierabende*) with sandwiches. Between 1920 and 1925 the *KWG* held their meals in the clubrooms of another society, the '1914 Society', in order to save money. On other occasions, it organized everything itself, as in November 1925, when an event was planned to take place in one of its institutes. The secretary of the society borrowed the necessary chairs and tables, cutlery, glasses, dishes and so on.[47] Instead of preparing an exhaustive and highly formalized meal, salads and sandwiches were ordered from the famous *traiteur* Borchardt.[48] However, as soon as possible, it returned to the custom of festive meals: in December 1925 the society again held a festive meal in the *Kaiserhof* at which a three-course meal for 10 Marks per person was served. The menu, consisting of Soup, Roast Veal, Kidneys and Vegetables, and Cheese and Butter mirrored the constraint of what was available and the general trend of a simplified cuisine.[49] Even in Nobel Prize banquets, one can find the number of courses being reduced.[50] At times when the society had no money, presentation played an even more important role, as the society had to be advertised to the world.[51] As the number of invitations to members of the Reichstag and journalists, and the arrangement of public lectures show, the society tried to make itself better known to the general public.[52] In consequence, the *KWG* received unsolicited offers from other hotels which had already hosted other scientific organizations, such as the German Research Association. Even spas wrote letters to advertise their facilities for the society's meetings.[53]

Adolf Harnack, the president of the society, was fully aware of the importance of exchanges between science, society and the economy. He therefore tried to create a permanent meeting place for the society. It was conceived as a kind of clubhouse, in which foreign guests could also be accommodated. It was hoped that this would help to alleviate the international isolation which World War I had brought to German science. On 7 May 1929, the 'Harnack House' was opened. It contained large conference rooms and catering facilities for up to 500 people. Every day it offered

---

47 See AMPG, 1. HA, Rep. 1A, Nr. 851.

48 AMPG, 1. HA, Rep. 1A, Nr. 851, 16, and his offer, ibid. 19.

49 See AMPG, 1. 'HA; Rep. 1A, Nr. 851, 29.

50 Söderlind, 2003.

51 AMPG, 1. HA, Rep. 1A, Nr. 851, 4.

52 AMPG, 1. HA, Rep. 1A, 851, 84.

53 AMPG, 1. HA, Rep. 1A, 851, 56, 65.

a cheap lunch for the scientists working in the surrounding institutes.[54] During the 1930s it developed into a kind of convention centre for Berlin, as it was also open to other clubs and organizations. A number of them used it regularly.[55] The Harnack House was not an isolated place for science. Its public lectures informed people about new scientific topics and attracted press comment. At times the society felt it must respond, as an example from 1930 illustrates. When State Secretary August Müller criticized the high expenditure for a dinner as tactless, the society's representatives notified all participants.[56] The society urged the author of the article to publish a counter-statement in order to correct the impression that money was being wasted on the amusement of a few people. Nevertheless, Müller's counter-statement warned members to familiarize themselves with the life of normal people, instead of leading a life of splendour.[57]

After 1933 the situation became even more difficult, as the National Socialist doctrine rejected theoretical science, especially fundamental research. Scientists were urged to demonstrate their use to society and the power of science.[58] Festive official receptions were a means to do so, especially by demonstrating Germany's scientific power and influence to German and foreign politicians. Directly after the takeover by the National Socialists, a lecture by Albert Defant (1884–1974), the founder of physical oceanography with a highly regarded international reputation, was organized in the Harnack House at the request of the State Minister.[59] Invitations to 194 people included Hitler and all the Reich ministers, members of the *KWG* and notable members of industry and society.[60] A meal consisting of Meat Broth, Haunch of Venison à la forestière and Crème Madeira followed, which was not too opulent, but still representative enough to make clear the society's importance and place in the National Socialist state. This tactic was successful, as the society was generously funded by the Nazi regime in the hope that science would help fulfil armament supplies and the achievement of industrial and agricultural independence. In consequence, during the late 1930s even the society meals regained some of their former glamour. Menus from 1936 and 1937 had five courses again with dishes from bourgeois German cuisine.[61] The regime saw events like these as important for the cultural and tourist programme in Berlin. To avoid scheduling conflicts and to maximize the advertising effects, an 'Events Exchange Bureau' (*Vermittlungsstelle für Veranstaltungen aller Art*) was founded in order to coordinate events in the capital in the most effective way for tourism; it even registered events in the Harnack House as an aspect of Berlin's cultural attraction for tourism.[62]

---

54 AMPG, 1. HA; Rep. 1A, Nr. 2527, 42.

55 AMPG, 1. HA; Rep. 1A, Nr. 2528, 97–99 and ibid., Nr. 2531, 1–3.

56 Müller, 1930, 1.

57 Bundesarchiv Koblenz, R 73/19.

58 See the report on a reception of the president in *Neue Rundschau* 14. Nov. 1937, in AMPG, 1. Abt., Rep. 1A, Nr. 2528, 177.

59 Bundesarchiv Koblenz, R73/27, 3.

60 See the guest list Bundesarchiv Koblenz, R73/27.

61 See for example: AMPG, 1. Abt., Rep. 1A, Nr. 2528, 121, 172.

62 AMPG, 1. Abt., Rep. 1A, Nr. 2529, 14.

Summary

From the beginning of the nineteenth century onwards, science had to advertise itself to become a 'real' profession. Public dinners were one opportunity to communicate with the public in order to stress the important role of science. Science was perceived as a source of national power and was displayed to the public by glamorous feasts and meals. In doing so, these meals became not only an economic factor for gastronomy, but could be used in the city's representation of itself as a place of innovation, with a vibrant economy, culture and lifestyle.

References

Brain, R. 'Exhibitions', in Heilbron, J.L. (ed.), *The Oxford Companion to the History of Science*, Oxford, 2003, 283–6.

Briesen, D. *Berlin – Die überschätzte Metropole. Über das System deutscher Hauptstädte von 1850 bis 1940* [Berlin – The Overrated Metropole], unpublished dissertation, Essen Köln, 1990.

Das Grand Hotel, in Korff, G. and Rürup, R. (eds), *Berlin, Berlin. Die Ausstellung zur Geschichte der Stadt* [Berlin: Exhibition on its History], Berlin, 1987, 204–301.

Daston, L. 'The Moral Economy of Science', *Osiris* 10, 1995, 3–24.

'Der Präsident der Kaiser-Wilhelm-Gesellschaft empfängt', *Neue Rundschau* 14 Nov. 1937.

Drummer, C. *Ausbreitung und Wandel des außerhäuslichen Verzehrs im Zeitalter der modernen Urbanisierung. Die Entstehung des Restaurantwesens in ausgewählten deutschen Großstädten 1880–1930* [Eating out During Urbanization], unpublished manuscript, Münster, 1993.

Elsner, T. *Kaisertage. Die Hamburger und das wilhelminische Deutschland im Spiegel öffentlicher Festkultur* [The Burghers and Wilhelmine Germany Mirrored by their Feast Culture], Frankfurt a.M., 1991.

Goschler C. *Rudolf Virchow: Mediziner – Anthropologe – Politiker* [Rudolf Virchow: Physician – Anthropologist – Politician], Köln, 2002.

Heckmann, H. *Die Freud des Essens. Ein kulturgeschichtliches Lesebuch* [The Joy of Eating. A Lecturebook], Hamburg, 1981.

Jacobs, M. and Scholliers, P. (eds), ICREFH VII, 2003.

Jessen, R. and Vogel, J. (eds), *Wissenschaft und Nation in der europäischen Geschichte* [Science and Nation in European History], Frankfurt u.a., 2002.

Kaesler, D. Max Weber: Ein Forscherleben zwischen Geld und Geist' [Max Weber: A Scientist's Life between Money and Intellect], in Dörries, M., Daston, L. and Hagner, M. (eds), *Wissenschaft zwischen Geld und Geist*, Berlin, 2001, 29–45.

Kaufmann, D. (ed.), *Geschichte der Kaiser-Wilhelm-Gesellschaft im Nationalsozialismus. Bestandsaufnahme und Perspektiven der Forschung* [History of the Emperor William Society under National Socialism], Göttingen, 2000.

Meyer, J. (ed.) *Das große Conversations-Lexicon für die gebildeten Stände* [The Big Encyclopaedia for the Educated], vol. 18, Hildburghausen, 1851.

Meyer, S. *Das Theater mit der Hausarbeit. Bürgerliche Repräsentation in der Familie der wilhelminischen Zeit* [The Hassle of Household Work], Frankfurt a.Main, 1982.

Müller, A. 'Preisabbau durch Arbeitsgemeinschaften' [Price Reduction by Working Groups], in *General-Anzeiger der Stadt Frankfurt,* 20 June 1930, 1.

Oken, L. 'Erster Aufruf zur Versammlung der deutschen Naturforscher (1821)' [First Call for the Assembly of German Natural Scientists], in Engelhardt, D. von (ed.), *Forschung und Fortschritt. Festschrift zum 175 jährigen Jubiläum der Gesellschaft Deutscher Naturforscher und Ärzte* [Research and progress. Festschrift on the occasion of 175 years of the Society of German Natural Scientists and Physicians], Stuttgart, 1997, 17–19.

Pfannenstiel, M. *Kleines Quellenbuch zur Geschichte der Gesellschaft Deutscher Naturforscher und Ärzte. Gedächtnisschrift für die hundertste Tagung der Gesellschaft. Im Auftrag des Vorstandes der Gesellschaft verfasst* [Small Source Book on the History of the Society of German Natural Scientists and Physicians], Berlin, 1958.

Redactions-Comité (ed.), *Verhandlungen des X. Internationalen Medicinischen Congresses, Berlin, 4–9 August 1890* [Proceedings of the 10th International Medical Congress], Berlin, 1891.

Ringer, F. *Die Gelehrten. Der Niedergang der deutschen Mandarine 1890–1933,* [The Decline of the German Mandarins] München, 1987.

Rydell, R.W. *World of Fairs. The Century-of-Progress Expositions*, Chicago, 1993.

Shapin, S. and Schaffer, S. *Leviathan and the Air Pump. Hobbes, Boyle, and the Experimental Life*, Princeton, NJ, 1985.

Shapin, S. 'The Philosopher and the Chicken', in Lawrence, C. and Shapin, S. (eds) *Science incarnate*, Chicago, 1998, 21–50.

Söderling, U. 'The Nobel Banquets – a Century of Culinary History', 2003. See http://nobelprize.org/award_ceremonies/banquet/menus/soderlind/ (accessed 29 November 2006).

Stutzenbacher, *Das Diner. Practische Anleitung zu dessen Service und Arrangement* [Dinner: Practical Advice for its Service and Arrangement], Berlin, 1st ed. 1893, 2nd ed. 1895, 3rd ed. [1901].

Titze, H. 'Das Hochschulstudium in Preußen und Deutschland [University Studies in Prussia and Germany]', *Datenhandbuch zur Deutschen Bildungsgeschichte* [Data Handbook on the History of Education] Bd. 1: Hochschulen, Teil 1), Göttingen.

Universal-Lexikon der Kochkunst [Encyclopaedia on the Art of Cooking], 2 vols, 8th rev. ed., Leipzig, 1909.

Vondung, K. (ed.), *Das Wilhelminische Bildungsbürgertum. Zur Sozialgeschichte seiner Ideen* [The Wilhelmine Educated Bourgeois], Göttingen, 1976.

Weber, M. 'Wissenschaft als Beruf' [Science as Profession], in Weber, M. (ed.) *Gesammelte Aufsätze zur Wissenschaftslehre* [Collected Papers on the History of Science], 3rd ed, Berlin, 1968, 582–613.

Winkler, K.A. 'Kongresse und Tagungen in multifunktionalen Einrichtungen' [Congresses and conferences in multifunctional institutions], in Institut für

Tourismus (eds), *Arbeitskreis Freizeit- und Fremdenverkehrsgeographie,* Berichte und Materialien 8, Berlin, 1990, 7–19.

Würtz, H. (ed.), *Mahlzeit. Aus der Speisekartensammlung der Wiener Stadt- und Landesbibliothek, 230. Wechselausstelung im Wiener Rathaus Juli–Oktober 1995* [Appetite. From the Menu Collection of the Town and County Library in Vienna], Wien, 1995.

Chapter 18

Reforming Diet at the End of the Nineteenth Century in Europe

Alain Drouard

Introduction

A movement for dietary reform developed in Europe during the second half of the nineteenth century, towards the end of the processes of industrialization and urbanization. Doctors and hygienists condemned the 'modern' diet. They did not merely denounce overeating and meat-based diets but suggested in their place a regime which they called by turns 'naturist', 'simple', 'natural', 'rational', or 'vegetarian'. More or less synonyms, all of these adjectives characterized reform which was not limited to diet but also aimed at both the individual and society. Indeed, reform, far from limiting itself to the issue of working-class diet, everywhere in Europe was inseparable in the minds of its advocates from a programme fighting against 'degeneracy' and the 'evils of society', namely alcoholism, syphilis and tuberculosis. In this way, dietary reform was intertwined with the flow of ideas and movements, such as hygiene, eugenics and nudism.

Developments in chemistry and organic chemistry led to the emergence of the science of nutrition. Once food was defined by its chemical composition and its calories, formulating a diet came down to setting nutrient requirements corresponding to the needs of different categories of the population. Diet reform attacked modern diets and also the food values given by nutrition science. In most European countries reformers presented naturism and vegetarianism as the best, or the only possible, alternative to the 'modern' diet, but the suggested reforms differed greatly from one country to another. Was this diversity the consequence of economic and social development? Were the most urbanized and industrialized countries – Britain and Germany – more involved than others – like France – in dietary reform? Even though historical context explains national differences to some extent, the reform movements would never have existed without the action and work of pioneers such as Paul Carton, Rudolf Steiner, or Bircher Benner. Besides the influence they had over their contemporaries, their diets – mixing tradition and innovation – pre-empted the emergence of contemporary organic agriculture and foodstuffs.

The Historical Context of Diet Reform

In numerous European cities, the end of the nineteenth century coincided with the disappearance of the traditional diet based on cereals and starches. Gradually it was replaced by more diverse foodstuffs, including an increased consumption of animal proteins, sugar and alcohol. While the new diet was developing in the twentieth century, the nature of work was changing: it was becoming less manual, more technical and administrative.

The research of Lavoisier, Chevreul and Liebig changed the understanding of food. Although talk about food's vegetable or animal origins continued, two different categories began to be distinguished: nitrogenous foods or 'albuminoids', used to regenerate body tissues and organs, and non-nitrogenous foods termed 'combustibles' or 'respiratory', in which combustion generates heat due to the oxygen absorbed by the lungs. Since 'the nutritive value of food, of our diverse solid or liquid foods, results quite exactly from their chemical composition and their digestibility',[1] there was hope of finding a 'rational' diet. To reach that goal, one had to establish recommended allowances, i.e. the food quantities to be given daily to man in order to keep him healthy. Like the body's needs, these daily nutrient allowances depended on age, sex, and physical activity. After the work of Carl von Voit (1831–1900) and Wilbur O. Atwater (1844–1907) the balance method and the theory of calories developed. Atwater used energy balances to establish calorific conversion coefficients and nutritional standards which are still used today. In France, the advocates of a rational diet created the *Société Scientifique d'Hygiène Alimentaire* in 1904. The Society had a two-fold mission of research and teaching into 'the study and the popularization of the best scientific and economic diet for man in all life conditions and at every age, as well as into the establishment of the rules of food hygiene which need to be pursued by social enforcement.'[2]

The 'modern' diet has been criticized by doctors and hygienists since its inception. It was presented by its opponents as a sum of errors even more harmful because they were perceived to be at the root of diseases:

> Dietary mistakes are at the root of all diseases. Yet the recommended diet followed nowadays represents a challenge to common sense and is a scientific heresy. Indeed, a very hearty, meaty, concentrated meal that everybody is looking for by prejudice or prescription is the most important source of arthritic and infectious diseases for overeating and over-strong foods weaken the vital forces by over-stimulating them without moderation, burn the alimentary canal and the bowels through the excessive combustion they necessitate, and finally poison the body with the large amount of normal or badly processed toxic waste that they generate.[3]

Similar arguments were used by other critics of the modern diet. In Britain, animal proteins were accused of producing toxic waste – purines – which create diseases

1   Alquier, 1906, 1.
2   Lettre du Président de la Société Scientifique d'Hygiène Alimentaire au Président du Conseil, 5 juin 1906 (dossier Fondation–Archives SSHA).
3   Carton, 1932, 13.

as they accumulate in the body. Alexander Haig, a London consultant physician, argued that an excess of uric acid in the bloodstream was at the root of all disorders and he urged people to adopt a diet that minimized the production of the substance. He claimed (1908) the ideal diet was that of the 'strong, hearty and healthy' British peasantry a century earlier: restricted to bread, cheese, milk, vegetables and small amounts of home-grown fresh fruit in season.[4] In Germany and Denmark, followers of Haig recommended abstinence from meat. In 1912 the Danish physiologist, Mikkel Hindhede, noting that the uric acid was not precipitated in the urine test of subjects on a potato diet, suggested eating three or four pounds of boiled potatoes moistened with melted butter, fruit, milk and the water in which the potatoes were boiled.[5]

The Diet Reformers

By the end of the nineteenth century and in the first decades of the twentieth century, dietary reform was part of the programme of numerous movements and groups inspired by naturism and vegetarianism. Beyond their different opinions, these groups had in common that they linked dietary reform to the reforms of the way of life and of society. They belonged to what Christian Topalov called a 'reforming nebula', i.e. groups with only one thing in common: the will to reform society.[6] Among them were bourgeois as well as figures of the intellectual elite, even anarchists and working-class militants.[7] Many of them thought that dietary reform would affect many generations and limit, or even put an end to, the 'degeneracy' which threatened modern society. At the risk of simplification, two main groups among the advocates of dietary reform can be distinguished: naturists and vegetarians. Naturism and vegetarianism are not synonymous. Indeed, a large number of naturist doctors remained advocates of a varied and eclectic diet. Considering man as omnivorous, they left vegetarianism for certain pathological cases or used it only intermittently. While being advocates of a predominantly vegetarian diet, they did not prohibit meat as long as it was in small portions.[8] Naturism was not only concerned with vegetative or animal functions; it aimed at reconciling the individual with himself,

---

4   Haig, 1908, 561.

5   Hindhede, 1914, 163–7.

6   Topalov, 1999, 13, wrote: 'The metaphor of the nebula ... exempts the offering of a definition of "reform" as if it were a concept, an established ideology or a movement recognizable by the ideas it professes. On the other hand, it allows the adoption of a simple convention: every person linked to the institutions, associations and circles that constitute "the reform's places, circles and network" were considered as 'reformers'.'

7   As Ouédraogo, 1998, 74, put it: 'Between 1917 and at least 1930, anarchists were among the most well-known supporters of Cartonism. They then linked that Cartonian naturist diet with their demands of natural treatments, pacifism, etc, and made it an integral part of their gospel for a healthy social regeneration'.

8   Monteuuis, 1907, 10; His diet was 'fruitarian' in the morning, half carnivorous at lunch and vegetarian at night.

offering the possibility of reform and regeneration. This regenerative aim explains the convergence with vegetarianism.

The vegetarian programme did not restrict itself to abstinence from meat but aimed at regenerating bodies and souls through a return to a simple and healthy life in harmony with the laws of nature. The refusal to eat meat rested on moral as well as scientific reflections. On top of their compassion for animal suffering, vegetarians believed that meat consumption partially explained men's violence and brutality. They believed men are neither omnivorous nor carnivorous. Because of his teeth structure and digestive system, man is fructivorous. A meat-based diet weakens him and also produces toxins which accumulate, weakening the body and creating 'clogging' diseases. The dysfunction of the digestive system was one of the main causes of diseases. Elie Metchnikoff's theories (1845–1916) on curdled milk as a plus in the body's battle against pathogens and as a factor in the extension of the life span, received a particularly positive feedback in the vegetarian circles in the first decades of the twentieth century. Vegetarians and naturists favoured the weakening of the body as an explanatory factor in disease. While both denounced modern therapy and overeating, they did not agree on the remedies necessary to restore the defensive capacity of the body. Vegans were more radical than vegetarians for they banned all products of animal origin such as milk, cheese and eggs.[9] In their quest for individual and collective regeneration, some vegetarians and naturists also became followers of nudism.[10]

Case Studies

In spite of common tendencies wherever diet reform appeared, the debates it stirred up did not follow the same path.

Britain

Britain's place in the diet-reform movement at the end of the nineteenth century was the result of an early establishment of vegetarianism. Indeed, the first vegetarian society in the world was created on 30 September 1847, at Ramsgate, Kent, under the initiative of Joseph Brotherton, a Member of Parliament, already known as a

---

9　Amid the anarchist movement in France, Georges Butaud (1868–1926) launched an intensive propaganda at the end of World War I in favour of veganism, a condition necessary according to them for the regeneration of social order. With Sophie Zaïkowska he founded a vegan colony in Bascon near Château-Thierry, a vegan club in Paris and Georges Butaud launched a review *Le Végétalien*. Among the supporters of veganism, it is also necessary to mention the name of Arthur Merrheim. called Mono (see Merrheim, n.d.), Drs Fougerat de David de Lastours and E. Tardif. In Britain, the term 'vegan' was not used before 1944 when the UK Vegan Society was founded.

10　Even though it developed less in Germany, nudism surged in France in the 1920s. The naturist doctors Gaston and André Durville then founded the first naturist society in France, as well as the naturist island in Villennes sur Seine, the first naturist city in the world (Physiopolis) and a little later the naturist centre of the Ile du Levant.

defender of the humanitarian cause and an opponent of the death penalty. Brotherton questioned man's right to slaughter animals for food and added that human beings, when uncorrupted, were opposed to the acts of slaughtering and eating animals. According to Brotherton's Christian faith, these feelings were given to man by God. Another idea expressed during this meeting was the idea that man had not been omnivorous in Eden; something several writers had already pointed out. Vegetarianism was connected to other reforms and meat eating to other evils. In fact, it was hoped that the adoption of the vegetarian principles would lead to 'true civilization, to universal brotherhood and to the general increase of human happiness' and that vegetarianism 'tended to the abolition of war, and the many other evils originating in a departure from the principles of humanity'. The following year, at the society's first annual meeting, there were 478 members present. In 1849, London's vegetarians decided to organize the spread of vegetarianism. They formed The London Vegetarian Society with its own publication *The Vegetarian*. While religious doctrines were influential within the Vegetarian Society at its inception and in the decades that followed, the radicals and poets of the romantic period, especially Shelley, made more converts.

One of the most significant and renowned advocates of vegetarianism in the late nineteenth century was the playwright and critic, George Bernard Shaw (1856–1950), who acknowledged Shelley's influence on him. Another significant member of the British vegetarian movement at that time was Henry Salt (1851–1939) who wrote *A Plea for Vegetarianism* which converted Gandhi in 1888. A more specific Christian vegetarian society, The Order of the Cross, was founded in 1907 by Reverend John Todd Ferrier (1855–1943). Its faith was based on the idea that the original teachings of Christ included vegetarianism before it was obscured by the Pauline message.[11]

One is struck by the extent of the debates over the diet issue at the turn of the twentieth century. As Margaret Barnett observed:

> Many caught up in the crazes did not consider themselves faddists at all but contributors to a genuine food reform movement which the scientific advances had launched. For most, of course, faddism would be no more than a passing fancy or topic of conversation: few among the working classes could afford the luxury of dietetic eccentricity in the years before the First World War. Even those who could not or would not take the fads seriously, however, must have found them hard to ignore. Their fame was spread by hundreds of books and articles, cartoons, jokes and jingles, catchy advertisements and even plays and novels. For the general public, there were lectures, food reform societies and sports fixtures where cultists vied with 'normal' eaters to demonstrate the physical rewards of a particular regimen. Sanitoria and spas, meanwhile, overflowed with wealthy hypochondriacs availing themselves of fashionable new dietary cures ...[12]

---

11 In his book *On Behalf of the Creatures* whose first title was *On Human Carnivorism* published in 1903, John Todd Ferrier mentioned many early advocates of vegetarianism including Swedenborg who influenced the largest early Christian vegetarian community, The Bible Christians. He quoted also Pope, Shelley, Rousseau and the utilitarians.

12 Barnett, 1995, 155–6.

This outburst of faddism differed from previous experience not only in promising to be exceptionally long-lasting but in attracting a large number of participants. Sporting events with vegetarians competing against meat-eating athletes helped to publicize vegetarianism. In 1903, both winner and runner-up of a Berlin to Vienna walk were vegetarians. George Allen, sprinter and record-holder for long-distance walking in 1904 was a fruitarian. Successful vegetarian sportsmen included cyclist James Parsley in 1896 and Eustace Miles, British amateur tennis champion, in 1899. The movement thus made more and more converts, so much so that at the approach of World War I, vegetarian meals were served in upper-class British society.

Germany

In reaction to the traditional diet as well as the food industry, several initiatives, theoretical and practical, came into existence for the promotion of alternative forms of diet in German cities between 1880 and 1930. Generally called *Lebensreformbewegung*, the movement was directly linked to the movement for natural health (*Naturheilbewegung*), which had already gathered all the advocates of natural methods. The advocates of natural methods and reform were neither marginal nor sectarian. They were recruited in Germany among the urban middle class, i.e. among people with high levels of education and qualifications. The first vegetarian society – *Deutscher Verein für natürliche Lebensweise* – was founded in Leipzig in 1867 by the theologian Eduard Baltzer. Later, more vegetarian societies were founded in German cities. Many naturist associations existed: for example, there were 84 Kneipp Societies and the German Union for life and healing in harmony with nature gathered more than 100,000 members spread over more than 750 local associations.[13] The *Lebensreform* movement was not limited to Germany. It could be found in other German-speaking countries like Austria or Switzerland. A first international congress of vegetarian societies was held in Dresden in 1908.[14]

Spreading reform was done through the creation of dietary stores (*Reformhäuser*) – the first one opening in Berlin in 1887 – and through the production of foods and other goods (*Reformwaren*). The reformers also created rural communities (*Landkommune*). The first one was founded in 1887 by the vegetarian painter Diefenbach. The longest lasting one was probably the Eden village, created in the 1890s close to Orianenburg, to the north of Berlin. Fruit and vegetable agriculture was its main activity, with community members producing jams and fruit juices, along with a meat substitute called 'Healthy Strength'. In 1907, among the 149 women and 138 men in the village, 16 were craftsmen, eight storekeepers and employees, four painters and designers, eight persons of independent means, five teachers, artists and musicians, 17 gardeners, ten other representatives of industrial jobs and six unemployed. From the 1900s, the vegetarian colony of Monte Verita on the heights of Ascona, in the Tessin region, gathered intellectuals and artists – anarchists, theosophists, socialists – who wanted to break their ties with society. Its members lived communally in wooden houses and cabins. In addition to the production of

---

13 See Kneipp, 1938.
14 Initiated by the vegetarian society of Manchester.

fruits and vegetables, people practised natural medicine (*Naturheilkunde*) and a sanatorium was established. Vegetarianism combined with nudism: the members of the community engaged in outdoor physical exercise and dancing. Anarchists such as Kropotkin, or social democrats such as Karl Kautsky, or August Bebel and Otto Braun, Rudolf Steiner and Isadora Duncan, spent time there, while Hermann Hesse described it as 'a group of German, Dutch and Austrian idealists – plant eaters – yearning for a sort of vegetarian Zionism'.[15]

Rudolf Steiner (1861–1925) was the father of anthroposophy and the precursor of biodynamic agriculture. He advocated a vegetarian diet based on human nutrition theory. In 1924, he stated that in order to live, man needs proteins, fats, carbohydrates and minerals. Plants, which contain proteins, gather them from the ground and the air. Men need plants like plants need men. Indeed, we breathe in oxygen and breathe out carbon dioxide. And carbon dioxide is absorbed by plants which discard oxygen thanks to photosynthesis. He concluded that human beings need to eat plants. Even though Steiner's diet was mainly vegetarian, it did not prohibit the consumption of animal proteins and especially a little portion of meat every week for those who could not digest vegetable proteins. Nevertheless, excessive consumption of animal proteins was dangerous because it could generate arteriosclerosis. To be beneficial, cereals, vegetables and fruits had to be grown according to methods excluding the use of chemical fertilizers.[16] It entailed the formation of a network of producers and distributors and in 1928 the Demeter brand was created to guarantee the origin of the productions of biodynamic agriculture. As early as 1923, Rudolf Steiner imagined the devastating consequences of a change in cattle diet, talking about animals which would become mad if they were to undergo a meat-based diet.[17]

Switzerland

Dr Bircher Benner (1867–1939) was the main representative of the diet reform movement. Unable to be cured of his chronic insomnia by traditional means, he began outdoor exercise and hydrotherapy according to the techniques of Vincent Priessnitz (1799–1851) and Sebastian Kneipp (1821–1897), and he successfully followed a vegetarian diet. This success led him to create a clinic in 1897. Starting from a physio-energetic theory that made solar rays the primary source of energy for man, he concluded that plants most aptly stocked this energy and subsequently recommended a diet based on fruits, vegetables and cereals. As a primary element of his lacto-vegetarian diet, he suggested his famous 'muesli' made of oats, apples, hazelnuts and milk. This diet became famous for providing the sick with essential vitamins and minerals not available in food that had been altered by cooking.

---

15 Hess's quotation in Merta, 2003, 91.

16 Rudolf Steiner explained his methods in a cycle of conferences on *Alimentation biodynamique*, 1924.

17 In a conference on 13 January 1923 on *Santé et Maladie*.

France

Created in 1882, the French vegetarian society succeeded an ephemeral Parisian Vegetarian Society founded by Dr Hureau from Villeneuve, in 1880, with the purpose of discovering the best diet for the human species. After a difficult start, its members became more numerous by 1900 and the Society's review – *La Réforme alimentaire* – was re-published under the title *Organe des sociétés végétariennes de France et de Belgique*. In 1909, the Society claimed 1,175 members, among whom were numerous doctors like Fougerat de David de Lastours, Eugène Tardif, the Durville brothers, and Albert Monteuuis. Among the doctors inspired by naturism and vegetarianism, Paul Carton did not only denounce the dangers of overeating and of meat-based diets. He wanted to recreate a 'strong and healthy race' and suggested solutions to vanquish the 'social evils' of his time: tuberculosis, alcoholism and venereal diseases.[18] Carton was an original. Even though he was in line with traditional Hippocratic medicine, he did not reject the bringing-in of modern science. Indeed, his diet included elements of different origins, some from nutrition science, and others from a conception of health mixing neo-hippocratism, occultism and Christianity. Even though Paul Carton was ignored by the medical experts of his time, his followers have kept his message alive until today.[19] Carton was born in Meaux, in 1875, in a catholic, middle-class family. After attending secondary school at the Saint Etienne Institute, he started medical school. After employment in several hospitals, he worked at the Pasteur Institute with Emile Roux and Elie Metchnikoff. He then practised medicine in Paris, initially assisting Dr René Marie, the senior consultant of the Brévannes hospital, Seine et Oise, finally taking over his role and keeping it until his death in 1947. As a tubercular patient condemned by doctors at the age of 26, Carton had turned to vegetarianism and recovered. In 1911, he attacked over-eating in the treatment of tuberculosis and held it responsible for more deaths than healing. The following year, he published his second book on 'killer' foods and discovered Georges Hébert's natural exercise method based on physical exercises practised outdoor in the nude, in the air and in the sun. Carton adopted it and put it into practice at Brévannes.

As the starting point of his analysis, Paul Carton drew up a report upon the failures of modern society, which he saw as heading the wrong way because it did not rest on a true knowledge of man and did not respect the 'laws of nature':

> If our race had been healthier, stronger and more prolific, if it had kept up its natural immunities through a simpler life, a more rustic type of food, a stricter obedience to the laws of nature, it would have been spared the defects of degeneracy and the attacks of the

---

18 Paul Carton, 1917, 1. See also Danjou, 1908. Among the few naturist and vegetarian writers who attached importance to the theme of degeneracy, Danjou was more interested in eugenic solutions and looked into the issue of the conditions of procreation. Danjou's eugenic concern translated into a call for individual responsibility in a mode similar to that of prescriptions in terms of healthy diet rather than a demand for coercive or collective measures.

19 Among his main followers were Drs. André Schlemmer and Jacques Chauveau who both wrote on Carton and his method. Carton's name is often quoted in the media inspired by ecology.

enemy. The mistakes have been enormous, the punishments stormed down with a terrific force.[20]

Everything is linked together in the universe. The individual, as well as the society, is governed by some natural and supernatural laws which everyone must respect. Every violation is punished by disease. Paul Carton criticized both industrialization, for taking man away from nature, and modern science, which contributed to a misconception of health by severing the ties between man and his environment:

> Nowadays, science has artificially separated human beings from their natural environment. It has studied them as if they had an independent existence, as if they were the only masters of their destiny, as if they were free to disrupt their preliminary physiology with impunity and live fearing neither God nor man. It ensued in radically false notions on what health really was, on the origin of diseases, on the process of real and lasting recovery and finally on the means of regenerating individuals.[21]

Diet was incorporated in a body of prescriptions and laws to form a synthesis that Carton called 'the health decalogue'. Beyond the 'natural-artificial' opposition, he insisted on synthesis, i.e. the laws, the behaviour of the body, and vitality of the spirit which presided over the practice of naturist medicine. This synthesis aimed first and foremost at reconciling a Hippocratic tradition and modern medicine. Paul Carton did not reject the medicine of his time. Even though he acknowledged its merits in the battle against infectious diseases, he still stressed that it was heading the wrong way in view of the increase in chronic and degenerative diseases, which he considered as diseases of civilization. A traditional diet must replace the modern diet of 'intoxicating foods' (alcohol, fermented drinks, meat, fish), 'industrial foods' drained of their vitamins (with excessive added sugars, canned foods) and also harmful culinary preparations (containing excess fats, spices, stimulants, coffee, tea, cooked or sterilized foods).

> There is only one healthy diet in the world, it is the traditional diet of the strong race of peasants in the past, i.e. a simple, modest diet as less meat-based as possible. It is indeed rational to eat simple and natural delicacies, harvested in their immediate environment, to prepare them without any culinary refinement, to see meat as a condiment more that food and to leave the table yearning for a little more.[22]

Even if Carton considered diet the main reason for good health and the key to curing diseases, he recognized that it could only insure health and happiness if it was used in conjunction with the 'natural, vital and spiritual laws' ruling human life and constituting the health decalogue whose goal was to reach a complete reform of the individual, as his Law X concluded: 'Tend towards becoming one's own doctor by reforming one's own self and by fearing beyond everything all the symptomatic and pharmaceutical treatments'.

---

20 Carton, 1932, 14.

21 Ibid., 2.

22 Carton, 1932, 14.

Conclusion

In most European countries, as World War I loomed, the decline in fertility, social class conflicts and international tensions led diet reformers to blame modernity. In spite of their different orientations, all considered that their mission was not only to save the individual but also a western society threatened by 'degeneracy' and decline. The recommended solution was to respect the laws of nature and live in harmony with them. Beyond individual health, the diets inspired by vegetarianism and naturism claimed to have the power to reduce violence and aggressiveness enhanced by the consumption of meat. Finally, vegetarianism appeared as a global project of reforming conditions of existence, based on the quest for a 'natural' way of life unfolding not only in a diet but also in health and medicine. As for naturism, it seemed to crystallize the anguish of declining, falling, parting from original harmony, generated by the speed of progress, urbanization and industrialization. There still remained an ambiguity: while it objected to modern existence in the name of a puritan ethic, it expressed the middle classes' aspirations and hopes, in terms of the attention paid to treatments and body hygiene. Blaming the industrialization of agriculture and its harmful effects, the diet reformers anticipated the concerns of modern diet and ecology. They were the most numerous and influential in the most industrialized and urbanized countries, i.e. Britain and Germany. Their number and influence remained more limited in France which was still very much a rural society. On the other hand, they suggested a reform of the individual before that of society and they all placed food at the centre of this reform.

References

Alquier, J. *Les Aliments de l'Homme* [The Foods of Man], Paris, 1906.
Barnett, L.M. 'Every Man his own Physician: Dietetic Fads, 1890–1914', *Clio Medica* 32, 1995.
Carton, P. *La Tuberculose par Arthritisme. Etude Clinique. Traitement Rationnel et Pratique*, [Tuberculosis by Arthritis], Paris, 1911.
Carton, P. *Les Trois Aliments Meurtriers. La Viande, l'Alcool, le Sucre* [The Three Killer Foodstuffs: Meat, Alcohol and Sugar], Paris, 1912.
Carton, P. *La Cure de Soleil et d'Exercices Chez les Enfants* [The Cure for Children by Sunlight and Exercise], Paris, 1917.
Carton, P. *Le Décalogue de la Santé* [The Health Decalogue], Paris, 1932 (1st ed. 1922).
Danjou, G. 'Quatre Grandes Réformes' [Four Important Reforms], *La Réforme Alimentaire* 15 October 1908.
Haig, A. 'Some Mistakes which may Prevent the Best Results of the Uric-Acid-Free Diet', *Medical Record* 74, 1908.
Hindhede, M. *What to Eat and Why. Including the Famous Hindhede Cookery Recipes: A Complete Change to a Healthy, Simple, and Cheap Mode of Living*, (English adaptation by C. A. Bang), London, 1914.

Kneipp, S. *So sollt ihr leben: Winke und Ratschläge für Gesunde und Kranke zu einer einfachen, vernünftigen Lebensweise und einer naturgenässen Heilmethode* [Live Thus: Signs and Advice for the Healthy and the Ill], (1st ed. 1889), München, 1938.

Merrheim, A. *Discours d'un Empirique sur l'Alimentation* [An Empirist's Discourse on Food], Paris, n.d.

Merta, S. *Wege und Irrwege zum modernen Schlankheitskult. Diätkost und Körperkultur als Suche nach neuen Lebensstilformen 1880–1930* [Food and Physical Culture in the Search for New Lifestyles], Stuttgart, 2003.

Monteuuis, A. *L'Alimentation et la Cuisine Naturelles dans le Monde* [Natural Foods and Cuisine Around the World], Paris, 1907.

Ouédraogo, A.P. 'Assainir la Société: Les Enjeux du Végétarisme' [Cleaning up Society: The Stakes of Vegetarianism], in *Un Corps Pur*, Paris, 1998.

Schlemmer, A. *La Méthode Naturelle en Médecine* [Natural Methods in Medicine], Paris, 1969.

Steiner, R. *Nutrition and Health*, Conferences of 31 July and 2 August, 1924.

Topalov, C. (ed.), *Laboratoires du Nouveau Siècle. La Nébuleuse Réformatrice et ses Réseaux en France, 1880–1914* [Laboratories of the New Century : The Reforming Nebula and its Networks in France], Paris, 1999.

Todd Ferrier, J. *On Behalf of the Creatures: A Plea Historical, Scientific, Economic, Dynamic, Humane, Religious*, London, 1930.

Wirtz , A. *Die Moral auf dem Teller* [The Moral on the Plate], Zurich, 1993.

Chapter 19

Turtle Soup and Water Porridge: Some Social and Cultural Perspectives on Food Habits in the City of Oslo, 1860–2000

Virginie Amilien

Social and cultural factors are central to food habits in cities. Several authors have pointed, for instance, to the differences between the upper classes eating meat and white bread and the lower-class diet of cereals and black bread that emerged in European cities.[1] Food markets in cities played a role in these patterns, influencing the choice of foods available. The emergence of differences between upper and lower classes in cities throughout Europe also fits the Norwegian map of food habits in nineteenth century. Democratization has gradually changed this map with, for instance, the more common use of meat. In 1999, about 90 per cent of the population ate bread three times a day and had meat or fish or sausages with boiled potatoes for dinner.[2] However, recent sociological studies have continued to emphasize a social distinction in urban food habits for the urban middle class, particularly expressed through the purchase of special foodstuffs, food-snobbery and membership of a cultural elite, often combined with body size control.[3]

The aim of this chapter is to observe the evolution of food habits in the 'city' in the upper and lower social classes over the last century, and to examine the impact of social class on food and consumption changes in Oslo. Particular attention will be given to the last generation of the capital's inhabitants and contemporary urban food, not only from socio-cultural perspectives but also by using concrete examples to underline the fact that economic interests, as well as political choices, are strong factors in change. After reflecting on the concept of social class and how it can be useful for such a study, this chapter will concentrate on the description and change of urban food habits. Historical references and ethnographic material about food habits in Oslo between 1860 and 1980 provide contrasting ways of thinking about food culture, with the urban elite on the one hand and the working class on the other hand. Concrete examples from cookery books, coffee consumption, mushroom

---

1   Flandrin and Montanari 1979. For instance, chapters by Montanari or Grieco.

2   Fagerli, 1999, 79–80.

3   See for example in Bugge, 2005, or <http://www.sifo.no/files/file58301_stabburet. pdf> (accessed 29 November 2006).

picking and kitchen design will be given. These diverse illustrations offer a better understanding of whether or not the cultural elite played a role in influencing Norwegian food habits. Placing today's situation in an historical context will enable a better understanding of how different the impact of the elite culture was.

Class and Distinction

This chapter will draw upon the works of the Norwegian ethnologist Edvard Bull, who studied the Norwegian 'under class' of smallholders, cottagers, servants and the working class.[4] He defined the working class as those who do not possess the means of production, although he criticizes the conception of a class as one singular group because 'Classes are rather aggregations of persons round a number of central nuclei.'[5] The idea of possession is central in the concept of class as emphasized by Bourdieu through the concept of 'capital'. Property and money compose economic capital, but there are many other forms of capital that affect social class. Bourdieu introduced the concept of *social field* based on relationships within the social space and the way cultural, social, economic, ethnic and symbolic capital is distributed.[6] In a liberal economy, theoretically leading to a 'democratization of the market', mass production and consumption might erase class divergences. However, social differences persist due to knowledge capacity, information, distribution channels and buying power.[7]

The Norwegian working class emerged about 150 years ago and did not get any legal meaning or social power before the 1920s or 1930s. Oslo's upper class represented the opposite part of an established social hierarchy. By 1850, some merchant families in Oslo had gained economic power and thus constituted a rising middle class. However, this chapter will focus on the two class extremes and their food habits in a diachronic perspective, in the expectation that mechanisms of change that we observe in urban food culture in Oslo nowadays may be better understand.

Food and the City of Oslo – Two Opposite Classes

Located in the southern part of the country on a fjord, Oslo (Christiania), the capital of Norway, was for several centuries a place of strategic importance for the Danish aristocracy.[8] Around 1860, the upper class of Oslo was still strongly influenced

---

4   A concept that does not really appear before 1840–1860 , as discussed in Bull, 1972, 335.

5   Bull, 1972, 2–13. Quotation from Cole, G.D.H., *Studies in Class Structure*, London, 1935.

6   Bourdieu, 1979.

7   Bourdieu, 1993, 601, but also in Norway (Bugge, 2005). The concept of distinction is often used nowadays in research on Norwegian food habits, particularly when describing the identity of the urban middle class.

8   Bergen, which was also capital of Norway for a time, played a central role in the Hanseatic exchanges and was the largest harbour city where foreign foodstuffs were imported.

Figure 19.1 **Menu from a dinner given in honour of the great explorer Fridjof Nansen, 1896**

by Denmark. Powerful storekeepers and high-ranking civil servants read Danish, German and French, travelled to foreign countries and hosted foreign people, they had 'European' eating habits and enough money to import exotic and rare foodstuffs.[9] Bull refers to the visit of an English professor from Cambridge at the beginning of the nineteenth century, who was surprised by the contrast between the

---

9   Before the establishment of the first hotels and restaurants, foreign travellers were hosted at the finest houses.

Figure 19.2   Menu from a dinner at the 150th anniversary of the Norwegian military academy

amount of food the rich people had, and the number of hungry beggars in the city.[10] In a book written in 1820, discussing the currency situation and the need to restrict the import of foreign goods, he noted that 'the consumption of unnecessary foreign goods like cacao, vanilla or capers by an elite of about 10 per cent of the population cannot justify Norway's need to import those products.'[11] Other texts underlined a real fascination for continental food and expressions, sometimes by denigrating the Norwegian.[12] Older books from the end of eighteenth century describe the upper class diet as based on a mixture of dairy products and bread combined with 'fresh meat', 'fish' or 'vegetables'.[13] The food was quite varied – including different types of

---

10 Bull, 1972, 34–5.

11 Helseth, 1820.

12 'Everything which is real Norwegian and simple, doesn't have any interest'.

13 For example Lindström, 1846, or other references in Notaker's own portal about cookery books: < http://www.notaker.com/old_bibl.htm > (accessed 29 November 2006).

vegetables and exotic fruits and spices coming from abroad. Menus for feasts differ from the everyday, showing a strong foreign influence, particularly from Germany and France. Turtle soup, 'potage chasseur à la Bohémienne' or 'Jambon de Bayonne à la gelée' are some expressions which perfectly reflect the type of vocabulary and foodstuffs of the urban upper class. Menus were consequently written in French,[14] the accepted language of cooking[15] as well as the mother tongue of the king, Karl Johan of Sweden, who ruled both countries from 1814. Even following independence and the coming of a new Royal family, in 1905, many French expressions could be found in Norwegian cookery books and restaurant menus or for feasts (see Figures 19.1 and 19.2).

If Oslo was the heart of the country where many rich people lived, the capital also had the highest concentration of poor people.[16] Sundt emphasized that 'those who moved from rural areas to the city were really poor, and it was their poverty that influenced them to leave the village for the unknown' in the city.[17] At the end of the nineteenth century, the worst problem was not food but housing, with an average of five people, plus livestock, in one small room, often located in the suburbs.[18] Even

Table 19.1   Menu from a tavern in Christiania in the 1860s

Meal	Food	Spirits	Beer
Breakfast	Bread or a sandwich.		
Noon	Soup with meat or peas. Meat, potatoes, bread. Fish soup once a week.		
Afternoon	Bread or sandwich.		
Evening	Stew and bread.		
Price (in shillings)	11s.	14s.	4s.

Total: c.30 shilling, with a daily salary of 30–60s. (maximum 60s. on the best days)
Source: Sundt, 1870, 113.

if lack of space was worse than lack of food, the diet was extremely poor. The daily diet was based on black coffee and bread,[19] especially unleavened bread of oats or barley, porridge and dairy products made from skimmed milk. Vegetables were generally absent and fruits rare. Salted or dried fish and meat could sometimes form part of a Sunday dinner. Festive dishes were based on more butter, soup, some pork

---

14 Notaker, 1991.
15 Amilien, 2001.
16 A famous Norwegian ethnographer, Sundt, 1870, 10 and 71–2.
17 Sundt, 1858, 63.
18 Idem, 20.
19 'En bid tørt børd og til variasjon mangengang bedærvet sild og poteter.' or 'Middagsmat fikk vi nok ikke hver dag. Det gikk mye på brød og kaffe, mest svart sikorikaffe.' Idem, 163.

products and rice porridge.[20] And for this special occasion the bread was wheaten. 'Nevertheless, there was often not enough food for dinner, even for father. I remember once I went to the factory to give him food, it was bread in one hand and coffee in the other.'[21] The type and amount of food varied from day to day, depending on the money earned: dry bread on 'bad days' and hot meals on the 'good days.'[22]

Cooking was anyway restricted by the fact that working days were long and few people had their own kitchen, sharing rather with two to six other families. People who lived alone or could not eat at home, used taverns or public houses, where the diet depended on their disposable income. Sundt gives an example of the daily menu and the money clients paid in one of those public houses. (Table 19.1)

While porridge and dairy products were common to the whole Norwegian population, the difference between fresh, salted and dried meat and fish, and the frequency with which these products were eaten, reinforced the daily distinction between social classes. Also, occasional access to banquet food emphasized two different attitudes in relation to food; with thrift, simplicity and austerity on the one hand, and money, complexity and gastronomy on the other hand. The 1860s also marked an economic and political break with corporations losing power in a climate of growing liberalism. Despite a rigorous toll system, new commercial structures transformed the urban food market and increased the availability of foodstuffs. Differences at the end of the nineteenth century between city and countryside in terms of the distribution system were accentuated by divergences between imported luxurious foodstuffs on the one hand and Norwegian basic milk and bread products on the other hand.

In the twentieth century the meal structure changed after 1920 from two hot and two cold meals a day, to one hot and three cold meals a day. The consumption of oven bread, as a replacement for unleavened or 'flat' bread and the growth of the rice-paper packed lunch or 'matpakke' – inspired by the 'Oslo breakfast' – extended to the whole urban population.[23] The food industry, food policy and modern food distribution have also directly affected urban food habits, for instance through margarine or milk consumption.[24] In addition, the teaching of home economics in schools has been influential.[25]

The population of the city of Oslo doubled between 1900 and 1960[26] and oil wealth has radically transformed the Norwegian economy from a previously thrifty culture into a wealthy and less parsimonious one. The spread of television made possible the broadcasting of weekly food programmes by 'Norway's food mother', Ingerid

---

20 Idem.

21 Idem.

22 Idem.

23 More information in Lyngø, 2000, 155–70.

24 Kjærnes, 1993.

25 Home economics was obligatory at school from 1959. It was reintroduced again in 2005 because the government wished to compensate for the lack of knowledge about food in the country. The institutional matpakke is now also a part of political debate and the idea of a free hot lunch at school has been considered many times.

26 <http://www.ssb.no/emner/historisk_statistikk/aarbok/ht-020110-053.html> (accessed 20 September 2005).

Espelig Høvig, while the growth of immigrant food shops in cities progressively transformed fruit and vegetable consumption. A new era began from about 1980 in terms of urban food habits and class distinction. For these reasons, it is necessary to distinguish between two distinct periods, i.e. between 1860–1980 and after 1980.

Urban Food Habits, Changes and Influences in Oslo

Until the First World War there were very few changes in food habits and little mutual contact between different social classes. Flat bread, dairy products, different types of porridges, salted meats and dried or fermented fish remained basic foodstuffs, derived from traditional food. Porridge is especially interesting because of its dual value; as a part of daily food habits and as a main part of traditional events, with an intimate link between culture and cult:[27] water porridge for everyday use and sour-cream porridge for marriages and confirmations. Traditional recipes inspired by festive foods give a mixed picture of older food habits, common to both upper and lower classes,[28] and are well represented in present-day official descriptions of Norwegian food culture, both orally and in cookery books. Yet food culture was not an active part of the nationalist programme in Norway, and it took almost a century from the first cookery book until 'nation-building' books began presenting the wealth of Norwegian cuisine. For many years cookery books were literal translations of foreign texts and presented an adapted view of European cooking. Not until the 1930s did popular books appear reflecting popular kitchen culture. Cookery books came late to Norway: appearing first in Oslo,[29] they reflect the role played by the urban upper class in Norwegian food culture.

The first Norwegian cookery book appeared in 1831 and was directly aimed at the middle class.[30] Cookery books were not popular until the 1980s, and between 1831 and 1980 an average of only two or three publications came out each year. After an increase over the past fifty years, and a tenfold increase during the last ten years, they have become profitable for paperback publishers. But change in food habits is not guaranteed. Interviews with booksellers show that it is 'nice little women from west Oslo'[31] – an area with the highest concentration of people with high economic and cultural capital – who buy cookery books. In a project about

---

27 Particularly when porridge is eaten for birth or religious banquets, with many porridge names which refer to religious symbols. Grøn, 1984, 93–4.

28 This romantic description is quite understandable after Norway was given to Sweden. The country was able to make its own constitution but the new nation wanted to distance itself from its four hundred Danish years. Rural life was the most different to Danish city life and peasant culture became a national model.

29 In his book about cookery books in Norway, Henry Notaker notes that the 'capital city has always been a centre for book production in Norway', which also probably influenced the amount of intellectual life in the city, and the rise of the first restaurants.

30 As explained in Notaker, 2001, 31–2.

31 'Pene slanke damer fra Oslo vest kjøper kokebøker om norsk mat', from Amilien, 2002.

new kitchens,[32] the urban elite were found to have numerous cookery books in their kitchens; the middle-class have fewer, but a sprinkling of trendy foreign books (like Jamie Oliver); and lower-class have no books at all, other than some school home economics textbooks hidden in cupboards. Cookery books, as well as restaurants,[33] underline quite clearly the different views of the respective social groups.

Nonetheless, the upper class has attempted to influence urban food-ways. When frugality constituted a threat for Norwegian people, some members of the urban elite tried to intervene and inform the population about 'natural' food products that were available for everyone and easy to find. The best-known case was Dr Sopp (i.e. Dr Mushroom), a biologist who around 1900 undertook to introduce mushrooms into Norwegian food habits.[34] In spite of his efforts, and many campaigns about mushrooms and berries during the world wars, mushrooms were rarely picked. By contrast, in Finland mushrooms are well known, and newspapers print mushroom reports during the season. Shellfish are another example where popular prejudice is stronger than social emulation. Shellfish, already found in the upper-class menus of the 1800s, today remain an exclusive type of food, even though sea-snails and mussels can be collected in Oslo fjord.

The two social classes not only retain different economic and cultural capabilities but also different food mentalities. They reveal a way of thinking about food culture that reflects dissimilar views of the world.[35] The lower class values peasant culture, built on traditional Norwegian products which bears witness to a poor and frugal society, whilst the upper class uses foreign ingredients as well as unfamiliar words as a means of expression. An increasing part of the educated urban middle class is now joining the European culinary patterns. An obvious example is the daily consumption of wine, commonplace in southern Europe but very uncommon in Norway for economic, historic and moral reasons. Although wine consumption was not visible in national surveys until 1990, it is slowly increasing amongst the urban middle class of Oslo, and is a reminder of upper-class menus of the 1800s, where each course had its own wine.

Urban Society Between Rural Model and National Food Policies

In fact, two ways of understanding food have evolved in parallel over the past 200 years, without significantly impacting on one another. Although Grøn[36] assumed that there were mutual influences between social classes, in reality the Norwegian upper class had little impact, particularly by comparison with the rest of Europe, where the authority of the aristocracy was stronger. Until 1850, the Norwegian upper class was more inspired by French cuisine than by Norwegian, without any real contact between the two. Apart from foodstuffs first introduced by the upper class, such

---

32 This concerns only 20 families. See Amilien et al., 2004.

33 We could find similar arguments in the rise of restaurants. See ICREFH VII.

34 He managed anyway to promote pasta and his name is still used on labels on Norwegian pasta like macaroni.

35 Amilien, 2001.

36 Grøn, 1984, 14–20.

as sugar or coffee, which progressively became part of the lower class daily diet between 1830 and 1870, there was little direct impact. Around 1860, during the national romantic period, Norway established its own constitution and rural society became a model. The new national identity was built on rural manners, which hearkened back to traditional Norwegian culture, whilst urban life appeared over-influenced by Danish habits. While Flandrin and Montanari wrote of Europe in the middle ages that 'the cultural and social function of food was becoming more fixed, and the upper class developed a social table convention built on a "non-peasant" way of eating and of table manners',[37] it was almost the opposite for the Norwegian urban middle class from 1860. In *The Eternal Snow*, T. Bomann-Larsen[38] describes Oslo's middle class eating like peasants, with a knife stuck in the table, in spite of their important economic power. In Oslo, rural society was absorbed and transformed into an urban model.

Industrial expansion and the two World Wars did not change the frame of reference. Norwegian independence in 1905 created a revival of interest in traditional foodstuffs, and food culture began to emerge as part of a new national image. Inspired by the minister Hulda Garborg, who wanted to promote national dishes, the association for rural women (*Bonde kvinnelaget*) from around 1930 collected local recipes and notes on traditional products, thus creating a huge body of work that emphasized the role of rural and lower-class urban diet in the creation of a national image. The period around the Second World War led to radical change, with an agricultural policy based on the concept of autarky and bulk production. Local characteristics progressively disappeared for the benefit of one common product available to all. White, mild cheese, the most popular cheese consumed in Norway, is a wonderful example of this new politically acceptable food.[39] Differences between city and countryside were even more marked when urban consumers became totally dependent on bulk production and the distribution system. Different foodstuffs, such as canned food and pre-prepared foods were created specifically for the urban market.

Social Distinctions in Oslo, 2005

There are still distinct differences between social worlds in Oslo, reflecting the old divisions between food mentalities. Factors such as frequent travel, identification with a social group interested in dieting and body shape, or economic circumstances, could be reasonable explanations of these differences. On the one hand, Oslo is a 'growing' city, in which there is an open market and an incredible choice of foodstuffs. On the other hand, the choice of foodstuffs still depends on social field. The group constituting the upper class and the cultural elite is very complex and varied, with different degrees of economic and cultural capital. Sports stars, for

---

37 Flandrin et Montanari, 394.

38 Bomann-Larsen, 1996.

39 The consumption is still enormous and recent dairy report for the first semester 2005 shows that *Norvegia*, a cheese with a real local name, represents 50 per cent of the whole consumption of white mild cheese on a national scale. See <http://www.tine.no/page?id=24&key=5926> (accessed 29 November 2006).

instance, represent a visible part of this new urban upper class with high economic capital. Interviews with all the players of one of Oslo's famous football teams show that most of them consider tacos and pizza as the type of 'food they prefer'.[40] The urban intelligentsia, with high cultural and economic capital, constitute another extremely interesting group because they are so articulate. Far from tacos and pizza, they consume expensive European and exotic foodstuffs, yet they are also proud of local foods, such as organic farm produce or local cheese from their district of origin. The concept of social class is no longer as useful, but inside a social field we observe different powers (money, linguistic skills) and their respective distinctions.

New kitchens work as a showcase for urban social distinction, often in the small details, like oil bottles and spices. In the 20 kitchens visited, the 'upper' social group had many types of olive oils and fresh kitchen spices such as basil or fresh thyme decorating their kitchen, while the group with lower economic and cultural capital had soya oil in the fridge and a dried-spice rack on the kitchen wall. Another strong social marker came from observation of discourse and means of expression. Informants could speak about the same dishes or foodstuffs, about the same fitted kitchen they had dreamt of and purchased, but they did not use the same language. Words and expressions of the upper social group showed self-confidence in their own taste and choice, while the language and behaviour of the lower social group revealed insecurity and doubts. Although the basic tastes, mostly built on a mix of lightness and minimalism, were quite similar,[41] the cultural urban elite just knew they were right.

One of the most famous and effective improvements in modern Norwegian cuisine was the success of the National Cooking Team who won *Le Bocuse d'Or* not just once but several times. They succeeded by utilizing a common food philosophy based on a skilful combination of European food style and Norwegian natural resources. Often called 'nature cuisine', this food mentality provides an opportunity for upper class and lower class traditions to coincide in a new food culture. This world of food is nowadays led by the educated urban middle class, having both the cultural capital and the economic resources necessary to support its development. Restaurant experiences and recipes from cookery books have become a part of day-to-day food habits, particularly at the weekend when free time and pleasure take over. Yet consumption of natural products, that have their special segment of the market, requires good logistics. The urban food system is dependent on production and distribution, which have a very strong influence on urban, and rural, food habits.

Conclusion: Can Two Parallels Actually Meet?

For almost two centuries, the influence of the urban elite on lower class food habits was weak, if we compare Norway with other European countries. Social stratification

---

40 21 players were asked. Pasta came second. A few of them named beef and potatoes, while one liked 'French cuisine'. Foreign players said they preferred rice, which is easily understandable because most of them come from Africa, except a European player who liked sushi. From *Lyn Football Magazine*, May 2005, 25–9.

41 And so did the chosen kitchen model.

theory explains that new food products came first to the upper class but were then dependent on the democratization of the market to reach the lower classes. As Dass says in an ethnographic masterpiece of Norwegian poetry, 'my pocket will not allow me elaborate dishes from countries afar.'[42] Extreme poverty and the absence of an aristocracy partly explain that the two mentalities did not meet until recent times. On the one hand, changes in food habits have been complex. In her study about a rural community in the Northern part of Norway, Lien underlines the influence of cosmopolitan channels, like national newspapers and TV, a large choice of food, and economic freedom.[43] But, this is not enough. On the other hand, cultural habits evolve very slowly, as shown by shellfish and mushrooms, which are not eaten although they are locally available.

From mentalities to class distinctions, the complexities of urban food do not only illustrate a social 'cross-over' of habits and manners or a complex mixing of social worlds, but also underline the consequences of a determined choice in agriculture and consumption policies. The urban social world is not only the place for 'progressive differentiation,' as discerned by Bourdieu,[44] but also for progressive homogenization. Food mentalities meet through common threads determined by food policy. Built on genuine necessities due to world agricultural agreements, urban food politics seem to be based on the myth of 'consumer demand'. The promotion of local products on the urban market over the past ten years emphasizes the role of political decisions and marketing on urban food consumption and begs the question about the real origins of power and influence between social classes. During the last century, urban consumers became more dependent on state decisions and markets controlled by political and economic interests, than on the interplay of social distinctions. Once food products become democratized and commonly available, many factors like cultural habits, everyday routine, social identity, nostalgia or family usages, can influence consumer choices in a liberal society.

References

Amilien, V., Bergh,T., Helstad, S. K., *Tanker fra Nye Kjøkken* [Thoughts from New Kitchens] SIFO fagrapport No.1, Oslo, 2004. < http://www.sifo.no > (accessed 29 November 2006).

Amilien, V., 'Askeladden au Royaume de France, ou Dualité de la Cuisine Traditionnelle Norvégienne' [The Duality of Traditional Cuisine], in Auchet, M. (ed.), *Le Secret d'Odin: Mélanges Offerts à Régis Boyer*, Nancy, 2001.

Amilien, V., 'The Rise of Restaurants in Norway in the Twentieth Century' in Jacobs, M. and Scholliers, P., ICREFH VII, 2003.

Bomann-Larsen, T., *Den Evige Sne: En Skihistorie om Norge* [The Eternal Snow: A Ski Story about Norway], Oslo, 1996.

Bourdieu, P., *La Distinction – Critique Sociale du Jugement* [Distinction: A Social Critique of the Judgement of Taste], Paris, 1979.

---

42 Dass, 1954, lines 30–34.
43 Lien 1987, 194–6.
44 Bourdieu, 1979.

Bourdieu, P., (ed.) *La Misère du Monde* [The Weight of the World: Social Suffering in Contemporary Society], Paris, 1993.

Bugge, A., *Middag en Sosiologisk Analyse av den Norske Middagspraksis* [Dinner: A Sociological Analysis of Norwegian Dinner Practices] Doctoral thesis, University of Trondheim, 2005.

Bull, E. *Arbeidermiljø under det Industrielle Gjennombrudd* [The Working Class during the Industrial Revolution], Oslo, 1972.

Dass, P. *Norlands Trompet*. [The Trumpet of Nordland], English translation by Theodore Jorgenson, Northfield, Minesota, 1954.

Døving, R. *Rype med Lettøl: En Antropologi fra Norge* . [Food Anthropology from Norway] Oslo, 2003.

Fagerli, R. *Endringer i Nordmenns Matvaner på 80– og 90– Tallet* [Changes in Norwegian Eating Habits 80–90], Sifo Report 1-1999, Lysaker, 1999.

Flandrin, J.L. and Montanari, M., *Histoire de l'Alimentation* [Food History], Paris, 1997.

Grøn, F. *Om Kostholdet i Norge fra Omkring 1500– Tallet og opp til Vår Tid*. [About Norwegian Diet from 1500 to 1950] Oslo, 1984 (1st publication in 1942).

Helseth, H. 1820, in Notaker Matportal, <http://www.notaker.com/old_bibl.htm> (accessed 29 November 2006).

Kjærnes, U. 'A Sacred Cow – Case of Milk in Norwegian Nutrition Policy' in Kjærnes et al. (eds), *Regulating Markets – Regulating People*. Oslo, 1993.

Lien, M., Fra Boknafesk til Pizza [From Traditional Dish to Pizza], *Occasional Papers in Social Anthropology* 18, Oslo, 1987.

Lindström, C.W. 1846, see Notaker Matportal, <http://www.notaker.com/old_bibl. htm> (accessed 29 November 2006).

Lyn Football Magazine 1 [Journal of Oslo's Football Club], Interview with Football Players about their Food Habits, May 2005.

Lyngø, I.J. 'Symbols in the Rhetoric on Diet and Health – Norway 1930: The Relation between Science and the Performance of Daily chores', in ICREFH V, 2000, 155–69.

Notaker, H. *Den Norske Menyen*. [The Norwegian Menu] Oslo, Det Norske Samlaget, 1991.

Notaker, H. *Fra Kalvedans til Bankebiff. Norwegian Cookbooks up to 1951. History and Bibliography*, Gjøvik, 2001.

Sundt, E. *Om Piperviken og Ruseløkbakken* [About Two Areas in Oslo], Christiania, 1858.

Sundt, E. *Fattigforholdene i Christiania* [Poverty in Christiania], Christiania, 1870.

Chapter 20

Food Markets in the City of Bordeaux – From the 1960s until Today: Historical Evolution and Anthropological Aspects

Isabelle Téchoueyres

Today in the city of Bordeaux new open-air markets are sprouting up, along with many events exhibiting food products in public space. This is also true of other towns and villages in France, although it is a recent phenomenon. The paradox lies in the fact that this is occurring while at the same time 'traditional' shops and neighbourhood daily markets are closing down for want of customers, many of whom are travelling to suburban shopping centres, including hypermarkets.[1] This trend reveals deep transformations in food behaviour among consumers, and a shift in the functions and representations of food markets.

In order to examine this phenomenon, I will start by describing the evolution of significant food markets in Bordeaux over the past 40 years, underlining the links with municipal urban planning. I will then discuss the strategies that Bordeaux inhabitants adopt to acquire the food they want, showing the specific place that open-air markets occupy. I will then analyse the success of such commercial outlets and the way they fit in with contemporary social and food habit transformations.

Bordeaux Food Outlets

Contextual Overview

Bordeaux is the major city and administrative centre for the region of Aquitaine, which is characterised by a relatively high proportion of inhabitants involved in agriculture. The rural space, besides sylviculture along the Atlantic coast and vineyards around Bordeaux, is divided into a multitude of relatively small farms with a varied production. The city today has about 260,000 inhabitants, to which must be added the population of adjacent suburban settlements, amounting to a total of 700,000.

---

1 For the beginning of hypermarkets and shopping centres, see Lummel, chapter 14.

For centuries, the city food supply was ensured by numerous open-air markets. In 1854,[2] 68 markets took place daily in the département of the Gironde, compared with 119 today; yet most of them are now only seasonal or weekly. Bordeaux itself had 33 daily markets in 1854, while only four survive today, next to ten open-air weekly markets of various sizes (ranging from over a hundred to only four stalls). This quantitative evolution betrays restructuring and, more precisely, a shift in function and use.

Without aiming to be exhaustive, I will describe a few milestones in this evolution. 1969 saw the birth of the first hypermarket in the south west of France, in the suburbs of Bordeaux: Carrefour Mérignac. It was then a rare curiosity. Following this event the early 1970s were marked by the demolition of one of the busiest precincts of the city centre, Mériadeck, as part of a new urban scheme planned by the municipal authorities. The destruction of whole blocks of mainly derelict buildings gave space for a new administrative and office centre, necessitating the re-housing of low income families. New suburban development resulted in the creation of two hypermarkets, Carrefour Lormont (right bank of the river) and Auchan le Lac (left), just before 1980, at the same time that small grocery shops were disappearing from the city centre. Following the transformation of Mériadeck, the first commercial shopping centre with the only hypermarket in the city centre, Auchan Mériadeck, opened in 1980.

Food provisioning in Bordeaux underwent considerable changes. Our object here is not to present a thorough economic survey but rather a selection of features illustrating the subsequent evolution in consumer behaviour and urban social life. In particular, I will look at the metamorphosis of the most renowned municipal market, les Capucins.

Marché des Capucins

Les Capucins, long called 'the belly of Bordeaux', remains the major daily food market. It developed at the southern entrance of the city, which was then occupied by monasteries; hence its name. In the 1860s, with urban reorganization and the proximity of the new railway station, Gare St Jean, this market was the result of a municipal decision to move the cattle market a few hundred metres south, closer to the slaughterhouse, and build a metal and glass market hall on the Place des Capucins. This location gave respectability, especially when the Université des Sciences moved next door. At the beginning of the twentieth century the market still featured all types of trades (leather, textiles, crafts). In 1963, for practical reasons of expansion and accessibility, a brand new wholesale market was built at Brienne, further along the southern outskirts of the city, by the river and beyond the train station. Because of the diversity of transportation means available, the proximity of slaughterhouse installations and the building of new facilities, Brienne became very competitive and many wholesale traders moved there, thus decreasing the attractiveness of Les Capucins. The latter did nevertheless manage to keep some

---

2   *Bordeaux* 1994.

wholesale trade until 1999. Then, with the transfer of all wholesale business, Brienne turned into a 'Marché d'Intérêt National' and its activity took off.[3]

In order to facilitate the continuation of bordelaise habits, the imposition of European Union (EU) norms on the Capucins building were postponed until 1996. However the hall was really aging and renovation was badly needed, while the City wanted to erase the image of poverty in this part of town. The area surrounding Les Capucins, in between the railway station and the St Michel district, has long been known as the immigrant part of the city, with people mostly from Spain and Portugal, then more recently from different regions of Africa. Prices on the market were always very attractive, especially for bulk goods. Up until the end of the mid-1990s, the whole area came to life for wholesale business as early as midnight and continued until five or six o'clock, then the retail business would take over until noon. Besides its essential economic function, this market has become a myth; it was famous partly because of the character of the tradesmen and women, their way of speaking, the way they addressed customers, and the way news was debated in public. This vibrant night and early morning life gave birth to numerous novels, plays and books as well as sociological studies.

The future of the market was at the centre of controversy in Municipal Meetings as early as the 1980s. Some stressed the necessity to preserve its image of 'conviviality', while others argued for a break away from its 'degraded space'. Finally the covered market was closed in 1996, completely renovated to the required standards, and reopened in 1999, now under the management of a private group, Géraud and Sons Ltd, who operate over 200 markets in France. The rents of stalls are now higher, making them less attractive to stall holders, and the opening hours are similar to other markets: 6am to 1pm, Tuesdays to Sundays inclusive. After bitter resistance to these changes, a dozen independent open-air stalls have started in the street Elie Gintrac. Les Capucins is still an attractive market, but the clientèle is significantly different, since renovation programmes in the old parts of Bordeaux have attracted a better-off population. The regeneration of the whole area is still a very sensitive topic. The nearby Place St Michel, around the 114 m high gothic belfry, accommodates twice a week its own centuries-old open-air market, and is also famous for its flea market. Colourful and picturesque, the St Michel market has become a stronghold of civil resistance to the municipal vision of 'cleanliness' and 'normality', the meeting place of modern 'social outcasts' defending their idea of neighbourhood solidarity and identity.[4]

Retail Markets

Only three other covered markets continue to operate on a daily basis, from 7am to 1pm. The Victor Hugo market in a busy section of the city is located in a modern style venue built in the 1950s, including several levels of parking space. Renovated

---

3   With 50,000 square metres of installations on 15 ha, it now serves the south west of France and five million inhabitants. It is the third largest nationally for fruit and vegetable distribution, as well as flowers and fish.

4   *CQFD*, 2004.

in the mid-1990s, it now stands next to a concert hall and only hosts eleven stalls. Les Grands Hommes, in a more residential area, chic and richer, was also a thriving market in a 1950s round concrete hall; it was demolished and rebuilt in 1990 as an up-market shopping centre, with the market in the basement. Now an architectural curiosity, this is one of the few places left in the city centre to buy groceries. A third market further north in the residential area of les Chartrons has almost died out (four stall holders), and is today more famous for its antique shops; its early twentieth century round stone hall serves as a cultural venue for exhibitions and shows. The gradual decline of traditional municipal covered markets in Bordeaux has run parallel to the development of supermarkets since the 1970s.

However, according to the person in charge of markets for the city authorities, although covered markets seem to be out of fashion today, open-air markets are in full bloom. While they all stem from demand by local associations or neighbourhood councillors, they are nevertheless part of specific urban planning schemes. Since the 1970s, many new weekly open-air markets have opened, especially in the last two decades. I will distinguish between different types. Some, like Le Grand Parc (1975), La Lumineuse or Arlac (1990s), followed the construction of new public housing estates and were set up in addition to modern shopping galleries, probably with the aim of giving an air of village life to areas of high rise blocks. Other markets, like organic markets or the new one on the waterfront, are set in attractive historic or scenic places.

The first organic market started in the early 1980s. Located in the regenerated eighteenth century precinct of Bordeaux, it came to be known as the Marché St Pierre. Every Thursday it had about twenty stallholders, mainly producers from the Dordogne and Lot et Garonne. It also offered a restaurant service with vegetarian menus, and went on until late in the afternoon. A victim of its own success, this market moved to the waterfront fifteen years later, after the transformation of the Bordeaux embankment. Finally, in July 2005, it settled further down the river on a spacious site specially designed for markets. It is shrinking a little, down to fifteen stalls, although after 25 years most of the same stall holders are still there, except for the caterer. The waterfront situation, a little out of the busy city centre, means that there is little custom in the immediate neighbourhood, and there is now competition from three other organic markets on the fringes of the city.

The day of the week matters a lot: markets at week ends attract a younger population with more purchasing power. In 1999 the now famous and very attractive Sunday Marché des Quais was created, also known as *le Colbert*, after an old warship moored there as a museum. It was set up as part of the great river side renovation project, following the disappearance of port traffic, in order to make the embankment more attractive after the demolition of numerous warehouses. The 5 km long waterfront has been landscaped and includes a bicycle-roller-blading trail and a walking area, with a couple of cafés-terraces and playgrounds for children. Seventy merchants and caterers display their goods. Oyster farmers, cheese and wine makers offer tasting opportunities, and many people go there all year round to have their lunch or brunch and spend a day out. Artists and second-hand book dealers are also there, encouraging people to linger.

Following the same logic of the transformation of the Bastide area across the river, the first evening market started in 2003, on Fridays from 5 pm to 10 pm. This is a long forsaken area, after the disappearance of the many industries that used to employ a great deal of the local labour up until the 1970s. The city is trying to inject new life just across the old stone bridge from the city centre. Designed public housing blocks, office buildings, cinemas and restaurants, even botanical gardens, line the large avenues leading to the waterfront. The trend of evening or night time markets is also spreading rapidly to many villages in Aquitaine during the summer season.

Besides these open-air venues, there are still a few costermongers in the city centre. They stand on street corners with a simple wooden cart laden with mountains of fruits and vegetables. Up until about twenty years ago, these *marchands des 4 saisons* were in fact market fruiterers and greengrocers from Les Capucins who went to sell their morning leftovers in the busy streets during the afternoon. This has since changed: only about five of them still exist today, setting up their stalls early in the morning. They are not selling leftovers from the market any longer, but rather up-market goods very well displayed in rush baskets, featuring seasonal local delicacies (like mushrooms or early cherries).

In the last two decades a number of food events have come into existence, the oldest one being the *Foire aux Jambons* (ham fair, including pig, duck and goose products), which takes place twice a year in the Place des Quinconces next to the *Foire à la Brocante* (antiques fair). Now also every year there is the *Bon Goût d'Aquitaine* (October), the *Marché de Noël* (Christmas) and *Les Régalades* (May), and also the *Fête du Vin* (June), the *Fête du Fleuve* (June–July), the *Printemps d'Albret* (April), and the Agricultural Show (May). These successful events give food producers and processors opportunities to sell their products directly to urban dwellers. Many of the events coexist next to a cultural attraction; they are combined into a 'package' for an outing, a pleasant walk, a festive event. Products displayed are either 'traditional' products bearing a regional identity, (such as *foie gras* and *confit*, pig products, regional cheeses, Basque, Corsican, Aveyron, Périgord specialties, etc.) or novelties and curiosities such as local ostrich meat preserves, unusual jams, new local beers, snails, candied nuts, etc..

Over the past 40 years, changes in form, if not so much in content, of contemporary markets reveal the new place they occupy in people's behaviour concerning food supply. Markets are not the only and necessary place to buy food: there is a wide choice for customers today, especially now that people are mobile and travel easily. Prices are generally higher than in most shops, while goods tend to represent up-market quality; this illustrates the distinction logic of Claude Grignon, where the upper classes always want to keep a distance from their inferiors. The transformation of the image of markets follows this pattern: from low prices and poor customers to high quality goods and richer consumers.[5]

---

5   Grignon and Grignon, 1981.

Food Provisioning Strategies by Bordeaux Inhabitants[6]

Food Classification and Place of Purchase

In detailed discussion about their shopping, people admit that they shop for most things in supermarkets at least once a week, but some products are bought elsewhere, very often directly from producers. Wine for instance often comes directly from chateaux or wine cooperatives, or else via personal contacts. Meat, which is the object of much care in the region's food habits, is preferably bought from a trustworthy butcher who is known to get his meat from reliable farmers. Some people even buy directly from slaughterhouses, then store the meat in their deepfreeze. Poultry and eggs are also usually bought either from farmers in the rural areas around Bordeaux or in open-air markets. Duck, especially fat duck with fat liver, is always bought from farmers, either directly or through contacts. Some fruits, like apples, an important food all year round, are also frequently bought directly from producers. People are willing regularly to drive long distances into the countryside to supply themselves with goods they value. Most people frequent their local open-air markets or travel to one further away where they know they will find the product they are looking for. Generally speaking, fruit and vegetables are always preferably bought in markets, where people like to think they are dealing with the producer – although they are not dupes – and the reasons they invoke for such preferences are mostly to do with freshness and taste.

From my surveys, it seems that many city families perpetuate the yearly ritual of home preserves. The most popular one is duck liver preparations, as well as *confit*; yet fish bought from river fishermen, such as the highly praised shad (*alose*), lamprey or eels, are also the subject of home treatment. It might come as a surprise, in the contemporary context of food modernity – described as 'destructuration' of the meal, individualization, and preference for ready-made foods – to witness the importance still given to such painstaking, home-made preparations intended to be handed out to relatives or, more likely, to be shared with friends.

It must be stressed that Bordeaux has long been the major commercial outlet of a rich hinterland and, as a harbour city, for imports (sugar, peanuts, rum, codfish). Bordeaux inhabitants know they live in a rich region where a great diversity of quality foods is at hand. Since the 1990s, with the support of the Chamber of Agriculture, farms are opening to welcome visitors. Specific events are organised and attract many city dwellers who love going to spend a Sunday on a farm, visiting, sharing a meal and buying a few products to take home. This is an illustration of Asher's concept of 'metapole', the new urban territory which includes its surrounding rural space; this implies that the population of such a territory share the same habits, particularly concerning food behaviour – I saw this confirmed when investigating rural families in Aquitaine.[7]

---

6   This research is based on ethnographic observation directly on the different sites, as well as on several investigations: interviews concerning food habits with families in Bordeaux and suburbs, and a survey among visitors of the Bordeaux 2005 Agriculture Show.

7   Ascher, 2005.

Choice and Reflexive Eaters

In the face of such a tremendous range of food, each person has the responsibility of choice. This acknowledgment leads me to refer to the concept of hypermodernity, which is founded on the reflexivity of actors.[8] While modernity was defined in terms of individualization, rationalization, social distinction and economization, hypermodernity finds its roots in reflexivity.[9] Food matters are a particularly rich terrain where reflexivity operates because of the dimensions involved in the ingestion of foods: from a biological necessity to the construction of our personality. Choosing what to eat, preparing and cooking food, sharing it in the form of a meal, all such elements follow patterns which define our belonging to a culture, a community.[10] Besides, one must be careful to preserve one's health, which involves taking into account all nutritional precepts paraded by the media. Relying on the anthropology and sociology of food, I would stress some of the characteristics of 'hyper modern eaters'. At once more individual and more sociable, being involved in various spheres of sociability (professional, leisure, family, associative); more autonomous yet aware of their own feelings, contemporary eaters have to manage diverse rationalities.[11] This seemingly contemporary freedom, leaving individuals free to choose their social relations or the goods they want, leads to self-reflection. All actions, even beliefs, are the result of one's personal responsibility, rather than just the heritage of a tradition. Food choices follow this pattern: they are different according to situations (time, place, company). This of course generates forms of anxiety which might explain why contemporary eaters, refusing to be reduced to passive consumers, need to multiply sources of supply in order to take control of their choices.

The Makings of Market Attractiveness

What is striking is that the money value exchanged at markets is trivial compared to expenditure in supermarkets. Yet buying in such places remains highly praised. Actually I should not say 'remains' but rather 'is now', since thirty years ago markets were often regarded as outdated places fit only for the needy. Their current attractiveness in Bordeaux is in fact part of a global trend in the Western world: a craving for an 'authentic' provenance of food products and personalised relations, along with home-made foods and cuisine.[12] What Zukin shows as being the privilege of the upper 'creative' classes as a distinctive action, can be found in Bordeaux, such as the organic markets or the Sunday Marché des Quais, while buying on markets in general remains fairly popular. For, in Bordeaux, easy availability of choice in foods,

---

8 Ibid..
9 Giddens, 1991.
10 See Poulain, 2003.
11 Ascher, 2005.
12 Cf. Zukin, 1995, and the current success of open-air markets in the United States although it was not a tradition there.

combined with the pleasure of cooking and sharing meals, is perceived as intrinsic to the regional way of life, gastronomy being valued as a cultural trait.

I have described the shifting function of markets as compared with 40 years ago. I mentioned that prices are generally higher than in supermarkets; one could also point out that purchasing in supermarkets is also more rational and time-saving (and time management is an important aspect in our society) because everything is in one place[13] – while purchasing on markets could be thought as more time consuming since you have to queue and pay at each stall. Yet rationality, functionality and economy are not sole motivations for contemporary consumers.

'Retailment' and Market Goods

People go to markets for specific products; the aim is therefore different from the mainly utilitarian supermarket shopping which involves buying ahead for a week or a month. It is obviously not necessary – in the utilitarian sense – for people to purchase there; it is rather a deliberate choice, involving pleasure. Ascher describes contemporary shopping by distinguishing between three types of purchases that every individual performs in turn: basic and repetitive ones; specialized and purposeful ones; and 'retailment' shopping, that is the combination of retail purchases and entertainment. De la Pradelle underlines the latter.[14] Food on markets is exhibited and we are allowed to handle and taste (to a certain extent of course); the consenting customer is seduced, free to wander from stall to stall. This playful aspect is an element of commercial efficiency: the stallholders are more actors than merchants, showing that their work is pleasant, masking profitability under the pleasure of offering. The busiest markets are at the week ends, during people's free time. Whereas going to the market was once a daily chore, now it is a weekly pleasurable leisure activity. As for retired people, it is at once a means to fill time and socialize. Actually, on the internet site of Bordeaux, markets are classified under the page *'cadre de vie'* [environment], next to historical curiosities, parks and promenades. Tourist brochures feature them as local curiosities, leisure activities and festivals while most Bordeaux food events take place during festive periods, as distinct from daily routines.

Although there is no such thing as a market product, it seems that goods are transfigured and more seducing on a market. The freshness of products is a quality widely granted to market goods, because they appear closer to their natural state: free of packaging, fruits and vegetables seem to arrive directly from the soil to the stall; the complex commercial process which takes the products through successive hands is denied. The typical market good must be local or home-grown, or home-made, and is opposed to standardised products. It embodies the spirit of a specific place or of a producer. Corresponding to a representation of the 'countryside', markets bring nature close at hand right into the city centre. Although the number of official quality signs and denominations of origin are multiplying throughout the E.U., such signs seem to have no relevance on the market; what make sense are local toponyms, geographical names of origin, even though most of the time they

13 For supermarkets, see Lummel, chapter 14.
14 De la Pradelle, 1996.

do not stand for a specific quality (Macau artichokes, Blayais asparagus, Périgord strawberries, Noirmoutiers potatoes, Nantes corn salad, Brittany cauliflower). Or else, as ingredients attached to old (therefore traditional) culinary specialties, or even to a person's name, perhaps the producer, they are necessarily trustworthy. One actually consumes something more than just the market product: food stands for a souvenir, an image, a memory of a short temporary verbal exchange, the pleasure of having found something unusual. Even restaurants use the special image that market products necessarily bear when they advertise the *menu du marché*.

A Special Place

When Augé develops the concept of *non-lieux*, he explains how modernity, which includes an excess of time and space combined to individuality, produces undifferentiated places.[15] These are designed out of utilitarianism, for the accelerated circulation of people and goods. Hypermarkets and large shopping centres, all following the same pattern in any city in France, are examples. In opposition to this are places which are significant, which bear the mark of history, where people can recompose their identity and sense of belonging, sharing collective values. Markets are definitely such places. I have already shown the festive aspect of markets. A festive event means gathering the community around a common theme, enabling people to get into contact with one another, thus to re-experience society as a social bond.

Although the city is not economically dependent on its markets nowadays, we have seen how they are part of urban development schemes, contributing to the regeneration of long deserted areas. They are a means to make citizens discover and enjoy a new urban space. Yet customers are not only visitors consuming a cultural activity, they also feel as actors in their own community. By their appropriation of the public space, inhabitants experience the sense of belonging to a place, to be at home. The market operates as a celebration of the past, like a tradition, a cultural heritage as well as an expression of solidarity. Shopping on the market is the perpetuation of tradition, a sign of adhesion to the spirit of the place. Cities and associations artificially recreate a sense of community by inventing common history, common roots. While globalization and homogenization prevail in daily life, and are particularly potent in supermarkets, markets and related food events emphasize differentiation.

As citizen rather than just a consumer, being in a market is being part of the public space, a place where sellers and customers are equals. Interactions are often picturesque, comedy-like, where each protagonist plays a role. On markets, being sociable is an easy thing and people tend to talk to neighbours they would not normally talk to: since everybody is there with a purpose, it is easy to drop the conversation and depart. Conversations play an important part, where each protagonist seems to deliver the most private and intimate information about any subject, yet both parties know that this implies no further engagement. It is what Simmel calls 'market friendship' where, under apparent familiarity and privacy,

---

15 Augé, 1992.

conventional themes are discussed; words make up as many ties, creating a hearty yet superficial and circumstantial friendship.[16] Small talk generates common ground and the temporary abolition of social barriers, along with an ephemeral experience of freedom. Sharing the same experience, the narration of minute local events makes one feel part of the local community. The market place can be compared to the *agora*, the meeting place of co-citizens. Supporting this assertion, I have shown in what ways purchasing there is different from being just a supermarket consumer, facing an anonymous powerful commercial company where one feels reduced to an elementary cog in the world economy. I want to draw attention to the expression 'citizen consumer', meaning a consumer who is aware of the collective dimension of his acts such as environmental issues, who takes care of his health by choosing the right foods, and who has in mind to keep our rural communities alive by buying 'local'. In a world dominated by individual values and the tyranny of the self, the market reactivates the virtues of the *agora* where everybody is an actor in his own city again.

Through the contemporary consensual attachment to markets, the observer might infer a craving for vestiges of the past. References to a vague traditional society rich in warm relationships, simplicity and conviviality which modern civilization has destroyed, are clear. Markets retain the illusion of sociability, the pleasure of urban life on a human scale, where the crowd is friendly, in what one might call the anti-modern city. However the very anachronism of the market logic is in fact inherent to hypermodernity: consuming anachronism and elements of the past are typical of contemporary society. The success of markets and particularly of the functions they perform for social groups, can be linked to the current development of rural tourism and farm markets; for eaters, it gives meaning to what is ingested.

References

Anthropology of Food 4, 2005, 'Local Foods', < http://www.aofood.org/ > (accessed 29 November 2006)

Ascher, F. *Le Mangeur Hypermoderne* [The Hypermodern Eater], Paris, 2005

Augé, M. *Non–Lieux, Introduction à une Anthropologie de la Surmodernité* [Introduction to an Anthropology of Supermodernity], Paris, 1992.

Bordeaux: Le Journal de la Ville, n° 253, juillet, 'des Marchés en Couleur' [Markets in Colour], 1994.

CQFD, 18, December 2004, <http://www.cequilfautdetruire.org> (accessed 20 November 2006)

Giddens, A. *Modernity and Self-identity*, Stanford, 1991.

Grignon C. and Grignon, C. 'Alimentation et Stratification Sociale' [Food and Social Stratification], *Cahiers de Nutrition et de Diététique* 16, 4, 1981, 207–217.

Poulain, J.P. *Manger Aujourd'hui: Attitudes, Normes, Pratiques* [Eating Today], Paris 2003.

---

16 Simmel, 1980.

De la Pradelle, M. *Les Vendredis de Carpentras* [Market Day in Carpentras], Paris, 1996.
Simmel, G. 'Sociologie de la Sociabilité' [Sociology of Sociability], *Urbi* 3, 1980, 112.
Zukin, S. *The Cultures of Cities*, Oxford, 1995.

Chapter 21

Conclusion

Peter J. Atkins and Derek J. Oddy

ICREFH's mission is to organize symposia and publications – this book is the ninth in the series – aimed at understanding European food in all of its aspects (cultural, social, economic, political), as it has changed over the last 250 years. Our approach is avowedly international and inter-disciplinary and we regard this as a strength, since it gives our deliberations 'hybrid vigour'.[1] The coordination of scholarship is essential in any such enterprise and we hope that the reader will have found a harmony of voices rather than a cacophony.

In this short final section we will not attempt to summarize the book's argument. Instead this is a good place to lay out a number of thoughts on the future of European food history in the short-term. The first is the somewhat dispiriting conclusion that there is still a need to argue the case for food history. Its neglect is due to the common observation that food lies in the realm of the everyday and therefore it is in danger of seeming too banal for serious academic analysis. This applies at every stage of the food chain, including the invisibility of the restocking of supermarkets at night time, the de-skilling of kitchen tasks as we prefer to heat up ready meals in the microwave, and the modern lack of attention to family meals and the convivial enjoyment of food. There is always something more important to do than spend time on food. ICREFH rejects the trivialization of this most fundamental aspect of life and we strongly assert the importance of research on food history. In recent years enthusiasm has been generated by food writers, cooks and popular food historians, and we welcome the impetus they have given. However, we have some doubts about the (understandable) elitism of their emphasis upon recipes from 'superior' cuisines. This sells magazines and cookery books, and makes good television, but the selection of material is eclectic and tends to ignore, firstly, the inconvenient complexity of variations across space and of change through time, and, secondly, it neglects the broader economic and social context in which historical analysis must be set. By contrast, ICREFH's investigations have always aimed for greater depth and fuller understanding of the nature of changing food habits in the wider, mainstream sense of affecting whole populations.

Second, while our studies here of individual cities have yielded many valuable insights, we are well aware of the need for comparative history in order to understand similarities and differences of experience. This may take the form of a commentary

---

1 It is understandable perhaps that not everyone shares our view. Critics of edited volumes of this sort usually complain of miscellany, but we have rather been accused of an alleged excess of 'unity of concerns, approaches and interpretations'. Spary, 2005, 768.

on a case study in its more general context, as with the paper by Nicolau-Nos and Pujol-Andreu where Barcelona is seen relative to Spanish and general European trends, or it may be a direct comparison of two cities, as in Atkins's study of London and Paris. Comparative history has its limits, though, as understood eighty years ago by Marc Bloch, but its recent incarnation as *histoire croisée* is highly promising. This relies upon pragmatic and reflexive induction and is well-suited to food history.[2]

Comparative history depends upon the time-scale of cultural change. Since 1989, ICREFH's symposia have shown how industrialization and urbanization are fundamental in changing the domestic environment and patterns of food consumption. Their effects on food-processing technology, on food distribution and retailing systems, have transformed products, outlets and places for (and times of) eating food. Many such changes are the result of marketing by international or multinational companies with the aim of expanding their global markets. In this respect, the initiation of change and its leadership has been external to Europe, since marketing dynamics originated principally in the United States of America. In Europe, a major theatre of war twice in the twentieth century, access to this 'western' food culture has depended upon political regimes, foreign influence, and even occupation, as well as national cultures. When artificial barriers to change have been removed, such as the demise of communist regimes in central and eastern Europe, there has been accelerated short-term catch-up to match western Europe. Large food processors and major retailers, such as British, French and German supermarket chains, are leaders in the introduction of 'fusion' foods and 'functional' foods to European consumers. By crossing cultural boundaries, or claiming special health-giving attributes, these foods are gaining a growing acceptance as part of the European diet in the twenty-first century. This is a compelling reason for studying food history now that policymakers across Europe are beginning to express concern at health problems.

Third, the depth and quality of archival materials varies between European states, partly due to the local history of bureaucracy and partly as a result of the destructive impact of war and weeding due to lack of storage space. In addition, one is left with the feeling that the unevenness of the general food history literature is a function of levels of interest in each nation, possibly culturally filtered. ICREFH has compiled a list of some 500 food historians, revealing real national differences: 116 of them are based in France and 102 in Germany, but only 42 in the United Kingdom. This raises the question of who will write the detailed histories of underrepresented regions, and there is a clear responsibility of international organizations such as ICREFH to encourage scholarly effort across the whole continent.

Finally, the methodological approaches and theoretical perspectives have varied in ICREFH symposia. We celebrate this variety, but we believe that further strength in European food history might be gained from working increasingly in teams, with sets of research questions that allow collaboration and comparison of results. In addition, there is a need for closer attention to definitions. This was clear, for instance, during the symposium session discussing 'eating fashions – the consumer

---

2   For more on comparative history and *histoire croisée*, see Sewell, 1967; Segal, 2001; Kocka, 2003; and Werner and Zimmermann, 2006.

perspective', where the question was raised as to the definition of a luxury product or a fancy food, and whether this should be on sociological, historical, legislative or financial grounds. Critical reflections upon such definitions and upon theoretical underpinnings are important tasks for the future.

ICREFH's immediate research agenda[3] concerns the twentieth century, during which nutritional problems have changed from under-consumption and poor physical development to over-consumption, with sedentary over-weight populations becoming widespread across Europe. During the second half of the century, the supply of food products became progressively more industrialized and the availability of ready-prepared foods grew spectacularly. With international travel and large population movements a feature of life in Europe, experience of foreign foods and cuisines has increased but cooking skills have declined. Industrialized foods have replaced home-cooked traditional or regional dishes, so that while consumers have benefited from the increased range of foods and ready meals in the shops, the reaction to this mainstream trend is already evident in health issues and the demand for organic foods. At the beginning of the twenty-first century: 'Food can not be enjoyed indiscriminately any more'.[4] Food history has much explaining to do.

References

Hartog, A. P. den 'The Diffusion of Nutritional Knowledge: Public Health, the Food Industry and Scientific Evidence in the Netherlands in the Nineteenth and Twentieth Centuries,' in ICREFH VIII, 2005, 282–94.
Kocka, J. 'Comparison and Beyond', *History and Theory* 42, 2003, 39–44.
Segal, R.A. 'In Defence of the Comparative Method', *Numen* 48, 2001, 339–73.
Sewell, W.H. 'Marc Bloch and the Logic of Comparative History', *History and Theory* 6, 1967, 208–18.
Spary, E.C. 'Ways with Food', *Journal of Contemporary History* 40, 2005, 763–71.
Werner, M. and Zimmermann, B. 'Beyond Comparison: Histoire Croisée and the Challenge of Reflexivity', *History and Theory* 45, 2006, 30–50.

3 For Oslo Symposium, 2007.
4 Hartog, 2005, 290.

Index